A Guide To Multimedia

Victoria Rosenborg

Barbara Green

Jeff Hester

Walt Knowles

Mike Wirsching

NRP
NEW RIDERS
PUBLISHING

New Riders Publishing,
Carmel, Indiana

A Guide To Multimedia

By Victoria Rosenborg

Published by:
New Riders Publishing
11711 N. College Ave., Suite 140
Carmel, IN 46032 USA

Printed in the United States of America   2 3 4 5 6 7 8 9 0

Library of Congress Cataloging-in-Publication Data

```
Technology Edge : guide to multimedia /
Barbara Green ... [et al.].
       p.      cm.
       Includes index.
       ISBN 1-56205-082-6 : $29.95
       1. Multimedia systems.    I. Green,
Barbara, 1956-
 QA76.575.T441993
 006.6—dc20 92-46579
       CIP
```

Publisher
David P. Ewing

Acquisitions Editor
Brad Koch
John Pont

Associate Publisher
Tim Huddleston

Managing Editor
Cheri Robinson

Product Line Director
Michael Groh

Developmental Editor
Peter Kuhns

Editors
Geneil Breeze
Alice Martina-Smith
Lisa Wilson
Rebecca Whitney

Technical Editors
Bob Dronski

Editorial Assistant
Karen Opal

Book Design
Amy Peppler Adams

Layout and Production
William Hartman,
Hartman Publishing

Proofreader
Rob Tidrow
Lisa D. Wagner
Nancy Sixsmith
Geneil Breeze

Indexed by
Sharon Hilgenberg
Sherry Massey

Composed in Utopia and MCP Digital by
Hartman Publishing

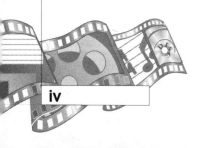

About the Authors

As Director of New Media, Victoria Rosenborg is responsible for managing the development of multimedia/new media products for HarperCollins Publishers. Before Harper, she founded R&R Development Corporation with the goal of developing multimedia software. Victoria designed and coded the Windows Information Manager (WIM), a monthly electronic journal featuring hypertext, graphics, animation, and sound. WIM was noted by Bill Gates in his keynote speech at the 1992 Annual Multimedia/CD-ROM Conference. In addition to product development, Victoria has authored articles and spoken at conferences, on the topic of multimedia. Before *A Guide to Multimedia*, Victoria authored the multimedia chapter for Jim Boyce's book Maximizing Windows 3.1, published in 1992 by New Riders Publishing. Before becoming infatuated with multimedia, Victoria was a Systems Consultant for American Express.

New Riders Publishing extends special thanks to the following contributors to this book:

Barbara Green, who contributed the *Guide to Multimedia Disk* and the chapter "Authoring a Multimedia Document" is a freelance writer and editor with a background in video production and artwork. She has contributed to training materials for Microsoft University, and for Interactive Generation, a multimedia specialist in Seattle.

Walt Knowles (the author of "Using Multimedia in the Corporate Environment) spent five years at Asymetrix Corp. in Bellevue, WA, where he participated in the development of the ToolBook development environment, and founded the applications and consulting group. In June of 1992, he started his own consulting business, Rainforest Software and now does most of his work in ToolBook and other multimedia systems applications. He has written an article on ToolBook application development for Dr. Dobbs Journal, and recently served as technical editor of a book on Windows rapid application development for Ziff-Davis Press. In addition to his consulting work he is a church organist and choir director and enjoys cross-country skiing.

Jeff Hester contributed "Making Multimedia Work with Your Hardware" and is an A/E CAD Coordinator for Fluor Daniel in Irvine, CA. He has ten years of architectural and structural design experience, and has used AutoCAD since 1985. Mr. Hester is a co-author of *AutoCAD 3D Design and Presentation* and *AutoCAD: The Professional Reference,* both published by New Riders Publishing. Mr. Hester juggles his time between developing PC-based 3D presentations and CAD management.

Michael Wirsching wrote "Multimedia from the End User's Perspective" and "Managing Different Types of Media." He has worked as an engineer designing ski boots and laboratory equipment for atmospheric physics and for soft-tissue biomechanics research. In addition Michael has worked as a television producer for commercial broadcast and PBS television. He has produced instructional materials on video, for classroom, and for computer-based training.

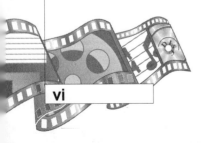

Dedication

This book is dedicated to my family. I love you all and want to thank you for always being behind me one hundred percent:

Rutger Rosenborg, Suzanne Rosenborg, Jennifer Fricke, Richard Rosenborg, Eric Rosenborg and Karina Rosenborg.

This book is also dedicated to Jeff D'Avanzo and Susan Poncher, my two Los Angeles connections to sanity.

Finally, this book is dedicated to Bill Gates and Microsoft. Without the man and his company, my life would be very different today.

Acknowledgments

More than most, this book was a collaborative effort, the result of many people all pulling together. New Riders and the authors are grateful to the following people:

Thanks to all of the authors who agreed to write chapters. Many thanks to Jeff Hester, Mike Wirsching, Barbara Green, and Walt Knowles.

To Nick Arnett and Nana Kuo, for providing tons of material, contacts, explanations and laughs whenever they were most needed.

To Kim Richardson and Marc Garza at HarperCollins, for listening whenever book and work deadlines collided.

To all the members of the CompuServe Multimedia Forum, for information, suggestions, ideas and "Notable Quotables".

To all of the companies whose products are mentioned in this book, and to all of the press contacts who answered questions and provided photographs.

To Tim Huddleston, for an enjoyable dinner at Comdex and for continuing to support this book when he might have given up on it.

To Brad Koch, for signing the book in the first place (I hope he doesn't regret it) and for supporting the idea of bundling the book with a disk.

To John Pont, for all of his patience, for finding other authors, and for his help in pulling the disc together.

To Geneil Breeze, for her help in getting the outline and deadlines coordinated.

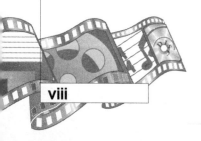

To Peter Kuhns for all his effort in editing the chapters, and for being at the office late at night.

To Karen Opal, for her help in managing the flow of materials of this book.

To all of the other people at New Riders Publishing who worked long and hard to complete this book.

Finally, thanks to those individuals and companies who also provided help, but who have been neglected here, purely by oversight.

Trademark Acknowledgments

New Riders Publishing has made every attempt to supply trademark information about company names, products, and services mentioned in this book. Trademarks indicated below were derived from various sources. New Riders Publishing cannot attest to the accuracy of this information.

> Microsoft Project is a registered trademark of Microsoft Corporation.
>
> Targa is a registered trademark of Truevision.

Trademarks of other products mentioned in this book are held by the companies producing them.

Warning and Disclaimer

This book is designed to provide information about multimedia. Every effort has been made to make this book as complete and accurate as possible, but no warranty or fitness is implied.

The information is provided on an "as is" basis. The authors and New Riders Publishing shall have neither liability nor responsibility to any person or entity with respect to any loss or damages arising from the information contained in this book or from the use of the disc or programs that may accompany it.

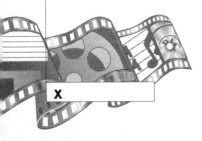

Concents as a Glance

Table of Contents

2 Using Multimedia Windows at Work 63

3 Making Multimedia Work with Your Hardware 117

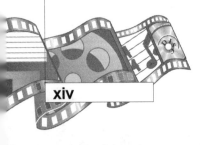

Part Two: Multimedia in the Business Environment

4 Using Multimedia in the Corporate Environment   187

5 Multimedia from an End-User's Perspective   235

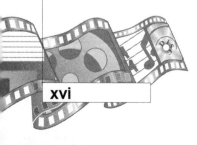

6 Multimedia from the Developer's Perspective   255

Part Three: Managing Multimedia

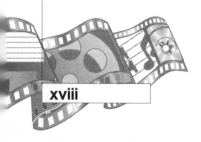

8 Avoiding "Muddymedia"   357

9 Managing Different Types of Media 393

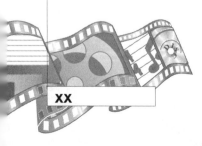

Part Four: Creating Multimedia Documents and Applications

10 Authoring a Multimedia Document   469

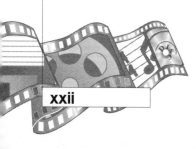

Epilogue: The Future of Multimedia 513

Introduction

Just what is multimedia? *Multimedia* is the incorporation of sound, animation, still images, hypertext, or video used in conjunction with computing technology. It's also been described as "something a group of technologists came up with just to impress each other." Multimedia certainly can be impressive—you can run video in a window on your desktop and have music coming out of your PC speakers—but you may find yourself wondering "Why bother?" How can adding sound, images, animation, and video make business applications more profitable and make end users more productive?

Before Windows 3.1 was released, multimedia was expensive to implement and impractical for most situations. Now, with Windows 3.1, multimedia is ready to make its entrance into mainstream computing. Although several types of multimedia standards (the Apple Macintosh and IBM's Ultimedia) already exist, Windows 3.1 has become the most popular and affordable route for multimedia. As a result, multimedia soon will be integrated into other programs, the same way word processing programs have begun to incorporate sophisticated desktop publishing (DTP) features.

The desktop publishing comparison is even more fitting because the acceptance of multimedia parallels the DTP revolution. When word processors began offering many fonts and style options, some users went overboard, incorporating many different elements into a single document. It took longer to write a memo than ever before. After a while everyone became accustomed to the power of these packages. The "Gee Whiz" factor went down and productivity levels went back to normal. One significant change did occur, however: you expect memos and other correspondence to have a certain crisp, typeset quality.

This book helps you get the most out of multimedia, without making the same "Gee Whiz" mistakes early desktop publishers made. You learn when multimedia should be incorporated into your company's computing environment, how you can make multimedia profitable, what types of applications make sense for in-house development, and when you should contract work to other companies.

Who Should Read this Book

A Guide to Multimedia is designed primarily for experienced (intermediate to advanced) computer users who have little or no exposure to multimedia. Another type of reader who can benefit from this book is one who already has experience with the multimedia, having invested in and used existing hardware and software. If you characterize yourself as either one of these readers, you probably also fit into one of the following groups:

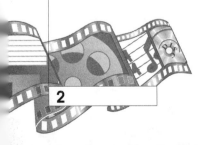

➤ **Are you a "curious" about multimedia?** If so, you probably are interested in multimedia in general and want an overview of the technology. You may be trying to determine whether you should invest in multimedia at all. *A Guide to Multimedia* can help you in each of these areas: Multimedia's numerous technologies are introduced in general early in the book—the first chapter alone discusses the benefits of text, video, imagery, sound, and other media. The price range of multimedia software and hardware may be all you're interested in if you are trying to determine whether the investment in new multimedia equipment is worth it.

➤ **Are you ready to buy multimedia equipment?** You already may believe multimedia provides opportunities that make it worth the investment. If you are ready to invest in this technology, *A Guide to Multimedia* provides "best-use" scenarios for the equipment you will be purchasing.

If you are shopping for a particular multimedia peripheral or software package, this book can help you with your purchasing decisions. Available hardware and software is compared and "best-use" studies of different multimedia components help you narrow your search.

➤ **Do you already own multimedia equipment and not know what to do with it?** If this is your first encounter with this hot technology, learn how to take advantage of its capabilities by reading about integrating multimedia into Windows and creating your own multimedia applications. Create a more persuasive business presentation, design an easy to use multimedia application, or just enhance a memo—*A Guide to Multimedia* helps you use multimedia effectively.

If you have used Windows but know little about computers, you also can benefit from this book by focusing on the terms and technologies that make up the multimedia industry.

Even if you are an experienced computer user, multimedia may seem confusing or complicated because it combines art, music, graphic design, programming, and even aesthetics. Learn from the experts about the best way to integrate these disciplines with your interests. Each chapter provides numerous tips and suggestions from experienced multimedia developers from all fields.

➤ **Are you interested in multimedia's future?** Are you an experienced multimedia user who wants to preview emerging developments in the field? If you look forward to trying new products and are willing to make the investment, stay ahead of the industry by reading about emerging multimedia technologies. The multimedia industry continues to grow and will affect every area of communications and electronics. Stay ahead by reading about new standards and emerging multimedia technologies.

What this Book Contains

This book explains what multimedia is, what you need to start using multimedia, the differences between competing multimedia standards, and how you use multimedia elements in everyday computing.

You also learn how to design multimedia applications for the corporate environment. Part of the development process is the proper management of all the media elements you want to include in your multimedia application. You read about choosing and organizing all the media you can use, including sound and video devices, so that they work properly within your Windows environment.

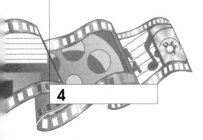

The book examines the future of multimedia and how today's research will be reflected in tomorrow's technology.

Chapter 1, "A Multimedia Overview," gives you a precise definition of what multimedia is and the elements that define the term. The chapter quickly examines multimedia's origins and then discusses media you currently can take advantage of in your work. You learn about the advantages and disadvantages of adding hypertext, sound, images, animation, and video to Windows documents and your own applications. The chapter introduces you to the multimedia PC (MPC) and the requirements necessary to take advantage of multimedia applications and documents. You also learn about some of the competing standards available in the marketplace.

Chapter 2, "Using Multimedia Windows at Work" shows you how features such as OLE and hypertext help take multimedia out of the realm of experts and put it into the hands of corporate America. If you already have Windows 3.1, you may not know that Windows contains a number of multimedia capabilities for use with applications. This chapter shows you how to use Windows' multimedia with OLE in case you need to present an idea to a large group of people or forward a document to another employee.

Chapter 3, "Making Multimedia Work with your Hardware," explains the different types of media devices that can be used with your multimedia PC. You learn about the compact disc (CD) formats for computing, different options for sound boards, the capabilities of each type of video technology, and other hardware you can use with your computer. The end of the chapter discusses the Windows applets—the MIDI Mapper and the Sound applet—that you can use with Windows documents and applications.

Different device drivers included with Windows 3.1 are discussed; you learn how to install them using Control Panel or by manually editing the Windows initialization files.

Chapter 4, "Using Multimedia in the Corporate Environment," examines different areas in business that can take advantage of multimedia. Communication using multimedia is much more effective than traditional types of correspondence; new uses can be found for email and databases with the inclusion of multimedia. Other network-related communication is examined—local area networks (LANs) and telephone network-based services are examined as they relate to multimedia.

This chapter shows you other ways to implement multimedia internally, such as in-house training, and shows you how to improve sales by including multimedia in presentations and other business-client communication.

If you are new to multimedia computing, Chapter 5, "Multimedia from an End-User's Perspective," was written for you. It describes how to explore a multimedia application and gives an overview of how to navigate quickly and easily through hypertext documents. You also learn about Windows behind the scenes.

Chapter 6, "Multimedia from the Developer's Perspective," was written for the end-user who is familiar with multimedia, and is ready to start developing a title. This chapter advises you on how to justify costs and development time to upper level management. It tells you how to manage the large learning curve that is part of your first development effort. You learn how to design an effective application by looking at examples from other platforms (such as the Mac's Hyper-Card) and tells you where to go for more information. It looks at the type of person who succeeds at multimedia development, the necessary skills, and how those skills may be

acquired through other disciplines. The chapter ends by describing the Windows MCI string interface, and how you use it during multimedia development.

Chapter 7, "Planning Your Multimedia Project," is a step-by-step overview of what's involved in creating a title. You see how to manage the process from start (project selection) to finish (distribution). You learn how to determine the cost of creating your title and how to pick the right authoring tool for the project. Finally, you examine the different means of distributing a multimedia application and pick the one that's right for your project.

Chapter 8, "Avoiding Muddymedia," helps you structure the content of your multimedia title. Structure is one element that can make or break a multimedia application. This chapter helps you determine whether your idea can benefit from multimedia, or if it should remain a paper-based document. You learn to judge your target audience and determine the best type of structure for your electronic document. The chapter also helps you decide which media to incorporate in your project, and what amount of media is overkill.

Chapter 9, "Managing Different Types of Media, " shows you what's involved in preparing media files for incorporating into your documents. You learn how to create and prepare these files in-house, or where to go if you need to obtain the media files from an outside source. The chapter helps you choose from the many different types of fonts, sounds, images, animation, and video. You also read about different file formats for each type of media, including waveform and MIDI files, and different text and graphic image formats.

Chapter 10, "Authoring a Multimedia Document," is used in conjunction with the *Guide to Multimedia Disk*. With this chapter and the sample multimedia document on the disk, the author leads you step-by-step through the design and development process. You learn to lay out and storyboard an idea, gather multimedia elements for it, and how to assemble your document. Run the sample document on the *Guide to Multimedia Disk,* to see visual examples of each part of the development process—the multimedia document displays pop-up dialog boxes that discuss the purpose and construction of each button, slider bar, hypertext link, and image.

The Epilogue, "The Future of Business Multimedia," is for the reader who wants to learn where this technology is going and how new multimedia improvements will be reflected in future software and hardware. You read how improvements in networks will enable users to exchange large media files in Wide Area Networks (WANs). You read about research being conducted in the areas of electronic newspapers, interactive video, and mini computing.

Appendix A, "Glossary," can help you with difficult terms and acronyms encountered in multimedia.

Appendix B, "Installing the *Guide to Multimedia Disk,*" provides instructions on how to use the disk that comes with this book and gives an overview of the applications contained on the disk.

What You Need To Get Started

To get started in multimedia, you need a personal computer with an 80386 processor (or higher), 640K of conventional memory plus 1024K of extended memory, a 30M hard disk drive (or larger), a SVGA graphics card and monitor, a two button mouse, a CD-ROM drive, an audio board with speak-

ers or headphones, and a MIDI I/O port. The hardware just described defines an MPC (a multimedia-ready PC). Chapter 1 describes the MPC specification.

To optimize the performance of your multimedia PC, you should upgrade to Version 5 of MS-DOS. You also need Microsoft Windows 3.1. (It is possible to use Windows 3.0 with the Multimedia Extensions 1.0, but you miss some of the added features offered in Windows 3.1).

NOTE
Even if you do not have the equipment required for multimedia, you still can use the multimedia document on this book's disk if your system has at least the following:

> ➤ 16MHz 80386SX or higher processor

> ➤ 2M RAM (4M recommended)

> ➤ A high-density drive (if you have only a 1.4M high-density drive, copy the sample disk to a 1.4M disk)

> ➤ A hard disk with 4M available disk space

> ➤ A VGA monitor and graphics card

> ➤ A Windows-compatible mouse or pointing device

> ➤ DOS 3.1 or higher

> ➤ Windows 3.0 or higher

In addition to the operating system software, you need multimedia applications. If you purchased your MPC (or you upgraded your standard PC with an MPC upgrade kit), the hardware manufacturer probably provided you with some sample applications.

NOTE If you want to get started in multimedia development, please see Chapter 3 for a description of the equipment needed for development.

Conventions Used in this Book

Throughout this book, certain conventions are used to help you distinguish the various elements of Windows, DOS, their system files, and sample data. Before you look ahead, you should spend a moment examining these conventions:

➤ Shortcut keys are normally found in the text where appropriate. In most applications, for example, Shift-Ins is the shortcut key for the Paste command.

➤ Key combinations appear in the following formats:

Key1-Key2: When you see a hyphen (-) between key names, you should hold down the first key while pressing the second key. Then release both keys.

Key1,Key2: When a comma (,) appears between key names, you should press and release the first key and then press and release the second key.

➤ On-screen, Windows underlines the letters of some menu names, file names, and option names. For example, the File menu is displayed on-screen as **F**ile. The underlined letter is the letter you can type to choose that command or option. In this book, such letters are displayed in bold, underlined type: **F**ile.

➤ Information you type is in **boldface**. This applies to individual letters and numbers, as well as text strings.

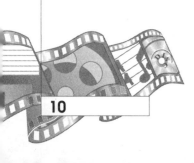

This convention, however, does not apply to special keys, such as Enter, Esc, or Ctrl.

➤ New terms appear in *italics.*

➤ Text that is displayed on-screen but which is not part of Windows or a Windows application—such as DOS prompts and messages—appears in a `special typeface`.

Special Text Used in this Book

Throughout this book, you will find examples of special text. These passages have been given special treatment so that you can instantly recognize their significance and so that you can easily find them for future reference.

A Guide to Multimedia features many special "sidebars," which are set apart from the normal text by icons. The book includes three distinct types of sidebars: "Notes," "Tips," and "Warnings."

NOTE

A note includes "extra" information that you should find useful, but which complements the discussion at hand instead of being a direct part of it. A note may describe special situations that can arise when you use Windows under certain circumstances, and tell you what steps to take when such situations arise. Notes also may tell you how to avoid problems with your software and hardware.

TIP

A tip provides you with quick instructions for getting the most from your Windows system as you follow the steps outlined in the general discussion. A tip might show you how to conserve memory in some setups, how to speed up a procedure, or how to perform one of many time-saving and system-enhancing techniques.

WARNING

A warning tells you when a procedure may be dangerous—that is, when you run the risk of losing data, locking your system, or even damaging your hardware. Warnings generally tell you how to avoid such losses, or describe the steps you can take to remedy them.

Margin notes contain quick tips to speed you along in the discussion or references to other sections and chapters.

In addition to these special sidebars, you will see margin notes that contain helpful information for the paragraph or discussion.

New Riders Publishing

The staff of New Riders Publishing is committed to bringing you the very best in computer reference material. Each New Riders book is the result of months of work by authors and staff, who research and refine the information contained within its covers.

As part of this commitment to you, the NRP reader, New Riders invites your input. Please let us know if you enjoy this

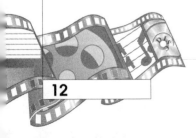

book, if you have trouble with the information and examples presented, or if you have a suggestion for the next edition.

Please note, however, that the New Riders staff cannot serve as a technical resource for Windows or Windows application-related questions, including hardware- or software-related problems. Refer to the documentation that accompanies your Windows or Windows application package for help with specific problems.

If you have a question or comment about any New Riders book, please write to NRP at the following address. We will respond to as many readers as we can. Your name, address, or phone number will never become part of a mailing list or be used for any other purpose than to help us continue to bring you the best books possible.

New Riders Publishing
Prentice Hall Computer Publishing
Attn: Associate Publisher
11711 N. College Avenue
Carmel, IN 46032
FAX: (317) 571-3484
CompuServe: 70031,2231

Thank you for selecting *A Guide To Multimedia!*

Part One:
Introducing Windows
Multimedia

A Multimedia Overview

*Changing the Way You Work
With Windows*

*Understanding Multimedia
Hardware Options*

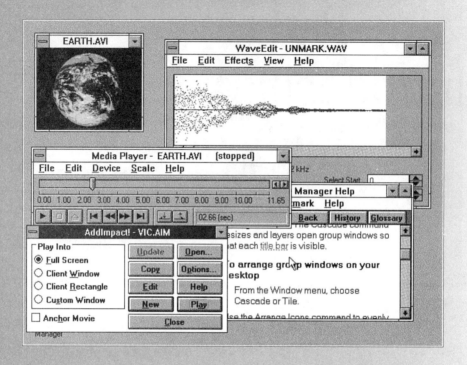

"Multimedia is a noun. It is not an adjective,
and using it as an adjective only contributes
to the confusion." -Quote from a report of the
ISO' Multimedia and Hypermedia Experts
Group.

Firstlight, 15353 N.E. 90th Street, Redmond, WA, 98052 (1-800-368-1488)

1

A Multimedia Overview

What is multimedia and why should you care about it? Today's common definition of *multimedia* is the incorporation of sound, animation, still images, hypertext, or video used in conjunction with computing technology. The definition "multimedia," however, is almost useless because multimedia continually becomes more integrated into common software. After a few years, you may not even notice separate multimedia elements such as sound and video. In the same way you expect graph capabilities to be part of today's spreadsheet programs, eventually you will expect word processors or electronic mail packages to incorporate sound or video capabilities.

Although the word "multimedia" is getting most of the press, many other terms are starting to work their way into technical jargon. "New media," "electronic publishing," and "personal digital computing," have slightly different meanings, but they all point to a growing trend—the incorporation of all types of digital information into the way we work and play (see fig. 1.1). Digital information can take the form of media (video, sound) or software "objects." An *object* is an encapsulated module of data that performs a function on related information.

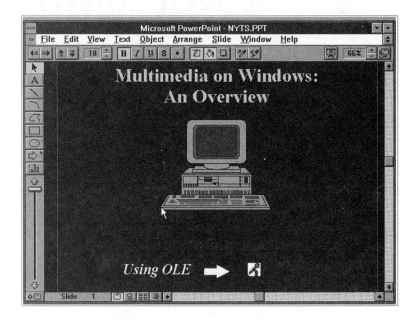

Figure 1.1:

Microsoft's Power Point lets you create presentations with Multimedia elements such as sound and video.

By integrating media elements and using object-oriented environments you can work with more information in more creative ways than ever before. Multimedia is the means by which personal computing will start to move off the desktop, and will be featured in new consumer appliances. Multimedia enables programmers to create more user-friendly interfaces. Through the use of images (in the form of frontends), sound (used to give instructions), and hypertext (used in on-line help systems), computer users do not have to

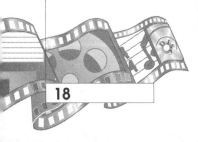

understand the underlying programming—they instead can concentrate on work or entertainment.

Gaming technology has been the leader in incorporating multimedia into desktop computing—games usually include images, animations, and sound to entertain the user. Multimedia is starting to integrate itself into business computing, however, through the use of sound annotation for spreadsheets, e-mail, and documents. Business multimedia also is taking off in the area of corporate presentations. Multimedia will hit the home market last, but this is the market with the largest potential for growth.

Multimedia also will affect mobile computing. Although the first crop of personal digital assistants is focusing on object oriented environments, pen-computing, and telecommunications, eventually the cellular phone you use to make calls also will be used to voice annotate a spreadsheet before you send it to another user on the network. Hand held CD-ROM players with color screens will be used to get travel information, as a training manual and for on-the-road entertainment.

Like any buzzword, "multimedia" is defined in a variety of ways and, as such, is in danger of being misused. Application developers and marketing departments may claim, for example, their new program uses multimedia just to boost their sales. Multimedia does, however, have a value other than being good marketing hype.

Why should you care about multimedia? If multimedia is used effectively, it can make you money, save you money, and make working with your computer much more enjoyable and intuitive. Mishandled multimedia ("muddymedia" in the hands of amateurs) can confuse a message, waste time, and irritate end users.

Some of the best "multimedia designers" come from the computer game companies because games were the first to include multimedia.

Like any tool, the way you use multimedia is more important than its features.

See Chapter 8 "Avoiding 'Muddymedia'" for tips on improving presentations and multimedia products.

Multimedia Through the Years

Computers evolved from mainframes and punch cards to terminals with command-intensive, character-based applications. Today, desktop computers with easy-to-use graphical user interfaces (GUI) are the standard. With the inclusion of digital signal processing (DSP) chips on the motherboard, the capability to decompress and use video and audio files will become standard for the next generation of PCs.

Before explaining more about what you can do with multimedia, review a little history about multimedia computing on PCs. What is thought of as "multimedia" has been available on the Mac platform for a number of years. Macs have always used sound in applications and had color monitors capable of displaying a minimum of 256 colors currently specified by the MPC standard. Despite these advantages, multimedia computing did not really surface with mainstream PC users until the announcement of the MPC specification.

The Multimedia PC hardware specification was developed by Microsoft in conjunction with a group of personal computer manufacturers. This group formed the Multimedia PC Marketing Council to create hardware standards, educate end users, and support developers of multimedia products. The original MPC Marketing Council members included CompuAdd, Creative Labs, Fujitsu, Headland Technology/ Video Seven Inc., Olivetti & Company, Media Vision, Microsoft Corporation, NCR, NEC Technologies, Philips Consumer Electronics, Tandy Corporation, and Zenith Data Systems.

Council activities were originally managed and coordinated by Microsoft, but later were transferred to the Software Publishers Association (SPA) in Washington, D.C. Although SPA is officially responsible for the MPC Marketing Council,

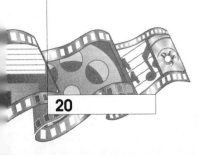

Microsoft still plays a role in helping to create marketing events and providing information to end users about the MPC.

In November 1990, the Multimedia PC specification was announced at the Microsoft Multimedia Developer's Conference. This specification describes the minimum set of standards for a Multimedia PC (or MPC). These standards include hardware devices that enable a minimally configured PC to access sound and data from a CD-ROM drive and to play sound in the form of wave and MIDI files. Included in the specification was the requirement that "MPC Titles" (applications designed to run on MPCs) run under Windows 3.0 with Multimedia extensions (the Multimedia extensions are currently supplied with Windows 3.1). This gave software developers confidence that a large base of installed users would be available for the titles. Users had the assurance that any title bearing the "MPC" logo (see fig. 1.2) would run on a personal computer designated as an MPC.

See the section "Defining the Multimedia PC (MPC)" for more information on MPC requirements.

Multimedia PC

Figure 1.2:
The MPC logo.

In December 1991, the MPC Marketing Council upgraded the base MPC specification, which was originally based on a 286. Although revising the specification meant that 22 percent of the upgradeable installed base would be lost, the Council opted to change the base PC configuration to feature a 386SX microprocessor. Because of the trends in personal computer buying, and the tendency of early adopters of new technologies to buy faster PCs, the change made a lot of sense. The majority of MPC upgrade kits sold today are for 386 and 486 windows-based systems.

Multimedia can help to create the "paperless office."

Although MPC computers are faster and easier to use, they have yet to fulfill promises of the late seventies and early eighties. One promise often heard in the seventies was that computers were supposed to eliminate the endless stream of documents by creating the "paperless" office. Corporate America is drowning in paper, and computers have done little to alleviate this paper "stream." If anything, personal computers and laser printers have given business people the ability to create more paper. Corporate America does not need more paper, or more computing, but a more effective means of navigating through the wealth of available information.

Multimedia PCs can help to replace mountains of paper with digital information that can be searched, edited, and copied. The increasing popularity of multimedia computing helps to promote better imaging standards. Because MPCs offer a minimum SVGA display, scanned documents can be read more easily on-screen. Users can scan paper files, and retain them on-line (instead of mountains of paper lying around the office). Rather than communicate via memos, co-workers can send each other e-mail. The e-mail can be compound documents, containing images, sounds and video (or animation). Pictures and video can be substituted for text, which decreases the use of paper. The cost of postage decreases as on-line information is more widely accepted.

Although multimedia computing can bring us closer to the reality of a "paperless" office, it presents new challenges. File security becomes a bigger issue than it is today, as corporations try to figure out new means of protecting confidential information. New networking protocols must be adopted to handle the bandwidth requirements of video and sound. Hardware costs increase (although this is offset by reduced printing costs) on a workstation-by-workstation basis; the

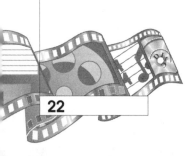

costs of file servers devoted to managing media also increases the price of installing a media-ready network.

Rights and permissions also may become a big issue if you begin to send multimedia mail; employees may unknowingly copy and alter digital images without thinking about copyright infringement. A new type of libel suit may appear from disgruntled people reacting to digitally-altered images of themselves. In some cases, productivity may go down, especially if people spend too much time compiling media presentations rather than presenting data and moving on to the next project.

A number of problems and lawsuits may result if multimedia is used more widely in the working environment.

Early technological prophets also said personal computing would make corporations more efficient and competitive in the marketplace. Studies have shown that personal computing has not increased effectively the nation's overall efficiency at all. Statistics for white collar employees show that the personal computer has not made the white-collar work force any more productive than they were 10 to 15 years ago. Instead of being more productive, this computerized work force simply spends more time creating and editing memos, business correspondence, and statistics, and crunching more numbers with spreadsheets that other employees must read.

With multimedia computing, executives may waste time videotaping themselves and editing the resulting clips, or working laboriously to produce the "perfect sound bite." Meetings start to eat up more time as each person conducts a full blown multimedia presentation. Until more "multimedia presentation templates" are developed, many good points may be lost amidst the soundtrack and dancing sprites of a presentation, created by an executive with a great deal of enthusiasm, but no sense of design.

Regardless of future potential problems, multimedia computing can give you a number of different media options to include in presentations and make your current applications more compelling. The media you use presents information or entertainment dynamically. The most important part of multimedia computing is the effective use of media. Not all media should be used in every "multimedia" application—some are more effective than others. The following sections examine the different media types and show how each element can be used in your work.

Adding Hypertext to Your Work

Open Windows Help to see hot links and other hypertext features (see fig. 1.3).

Hypertext is a new indexing technology that enables you to index every word in a document and to create "hot links" between different sections of a document. *Hot links*, which are part of hypertext, enables readers to jump from topic to topic intuitively and to display pop-up definitions. Other hot links enable users to hear sound or watch video associated with an electronic document.

Figure 1.3:

Every standard Windows Help System is a hyper-text document.

Program Manager Help

File Edit Bookmark Help

Contents | Search | Back | History | Glossary

title bar

The horizontal bar (at the top of a window) that contains the title of the window or dialog box. On many windows, the title bar also contains the Control-menu box and Maximize and Minimize buttons.

windows so that each title bar is visible.

To arrange group windows on your desktop

► From the Window menu, choose Cascade or Tile.

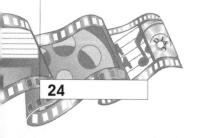

Suppose, for example, that this book is a hypertext document. You can click on the word "hypertext" in the preceding paragraph to see a definition of the term. If you already are familiar with the term, you can bypass the definition and continue reading the rest of this section without interruption. You can click on the word "sound" to hear a sound or click on the word "video" to see a short film clip. With hypertext you can examine information more quickly and have more fun interacting with a document. More importantly, you can interact with the document at your own pace and skill level.

Hypertext is the most important element of multimedia computing for a number of reasons. Instead of printing paper-based documents, you can create electronic documents that incorporate hypertext. Hypertext includes features, such as indexing and hot links, that you can use to maneuver more quickly through information.

If you create Windows applications, you are probably used to creating hypertext documents in the form of on-line help systems. An on-line help system can be a hypertext version of the user documentation, enhanced with hot links and indexing for easy search and retrieval of information. With the index, the user can quickly locate a particular topic, read the information, and then browse related topics (indicated by hot spots in the text.) Depending on how the on-line document was created, the user can click on an example to run a program, listen to an audio explanation of the information, or view a brief animated clip that shows the user how to perform key functions.

A number of tools on the market can be used to create hypertext and hypermedia documents. Unfortunately, many of the programs currently available do not contain an important feature—the capability to create indexes and links automatically, with little manual intervention. Without this automation, the creation of electronic documents from existing paper documents is difficult for businesses.

TIP

One available program that automatically indexes documents is SmarText by Lotus. SmarText uses algorithms that automate the creation of indexes and links. These features can save a hypertext author a great deal of time.

Printed text requires flipping through hundreds of pages to find information. Although hypertext documents still are time consuming to create, you can use their capabilities to search for words or phrases within a document in a matter of seconds. In addition, hypertext documents can store large amounts of material in a very small space. Companies can save time and effort by eliminating the process of printing and distributing paper-based documents . Hypertext documents can be updated and distributed more easily than paper-based documents, which need to be changed frequently.

Hypertext can be used to move reference manuals, human resource manuals, and other unwieldy documents from your shelf to the network. Hypertext also makes it easier to use software you are familiar with. Almost any good Windows application contains an on-line help system. These help programs are nothing more than hypertext documents. You can search for the information you need in a variety of ways—by looking for a term in the index, by browsing through related topics of information, or by clicking on topic headings to get more information.

To use hypertext files with Windows, you need the document and a runtime player so that the reader can access the file.

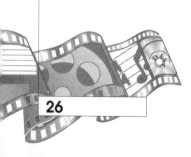

The hypertext runtime player is a program that comes with the authoring tool used to create the electronic hypertext document. After document creation and compilation (to create the links), you provide a copy of the document file, along with the runtime (or reader program) to the end user. The runtime program enables the end user to view your hypertext document, but not to modify the content.

The runtime version of the Lotus SmarText product is the SmarText Reader. The runtime version of the Windows Help System is WINHELP.EXE. Some programs have an unlimited runtime license agreement. This means you can freely distribute the runtime with every copy of your hypertext document. Other types of hypertext software (the SmarText Reader) have a runtime licensing agreement in which you are required to pay a royalty to Lotus every time you distribute a copy of the reader with your document.

Calculations of the number of copies you plan to distribute and the cost involved may affect which authoring system you use for creating hypertext documents.

Adding Sound to Your Work

Without sound, the world would be a much lonelier place. Sound enables us to communicate with others, get feedback from our environment (think about what a honking horn means), and experience pleasure (in the form of music.) The addition of sound capabilities to your PC enables you to communicate more effectively with others and get feedback while performing computing tasks.

Sound can be very useful in the business environment. Sound makes computers seem more human, which makes them more accessible—at least they seem more accessible with sound. The desktop computer seems more like an electronic assistant that can do as much as a personal secretary. PCs can track your appointments, help you write letters, manage your budget, and send messages to other employees in your organization.

With the addition of a sound board and voice recognition software, a PC can "proofread" the numbers you enter into a spreadsheet and accept spoken commands (instead of requiring input from the keyboard or a pointing device.) Sounds can be tied into Windows System events, alerting you to a command error, or chiming an alarm when you need a reminder.

Sound can be used as an effective means of making a point in a spreadsheet or text documents (see fig. 1.4). A sound file used to start a presentation wakes up the audience and makes them attentive. Sound, when incorporated into hypermedia training manuals, can serve to make a complicated point more clear.

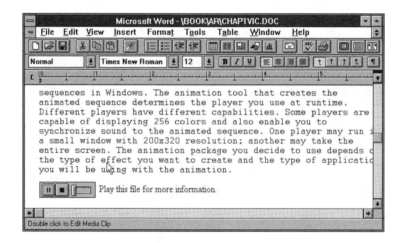

Figure 1.4:
Embedding a sound file into a Word document.

Sound enables you to annotate the work of others. After Post-it notes were introduced, corporate America experienced a blizzard of little yellow notes. It was easier to add your thoughts to someone else's work using Post-it notes than it was to scrawl all over the printed page. The only problem was that you had to take the time to write your message in long hand.

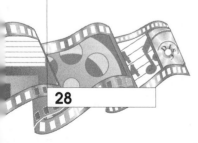

The sound capabilities of Windows 3.1 eliminates this problem. Now you can simply talk into a microphone and add a verbal comment to any work file, and use e-mail to send it over the network.

Sound is important not only because it communicates more effectively, but also because it makes computers more fun. Computers that are more fun to use are used more often. This helps to justify your hardware investment and helps to make employees more effective at computer related tasks. Sound helps new users become more comfortable with technology, and it enables users to customize the Windows environment (see fig. 1.5). You can play Bach when you power up, for example, or listen to Clint Eastwood say "Go ahead, make my day," when you make a typing error.

Sound makes computers seem more human and, as a result, more accessible.

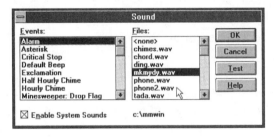

Figure 1.5:

Use the Sound applet in the Control Panel to attach sounds to Windows System Events.

TIP

Microsoft SoundBits is a sound clip collection designed to make using Windows more fun by giving the user sounds to attach to dozens of events in Windows. Three SoundBits sound clip collections are available: Musical Sounds from Around the Word, Classic Hollywood Movies, and Classic Cartoons from Hanna Barbara.

After you are used to sounds emanating from your PC you miss them when they are not there. When a computer has sound capabilities it seems more an extension of the way you work. Some people use PC sound to express their personality the same way others hang pictures on the walls of their offices.

NOTE

A few companies do not allow their employees to use sounds when computing because the company believes a computer should be a standardized environment. According to this type of philosophy, the same tools should be available for everyone so that the computer system is easier for the user to learn, and easier for MIS personnel to maintain. Although standardization has its benefits, sounds help to maintain the "personal" aspect of personal computing.

Sound makes the computer a more customizable, friendly tool that encourages play and exploration. When sound is implemented properly, it can teach novices how to use their computers, and how to find new means of getting their work done. More play and more creativity results in better computing.

Understanding Digital Audio

Computing with sound is possible today with Windows 3.1 and existing technology. Before you can take advantage of sound capabilities, however, you need to understand the three audio types available in Windows.

Waveform Audio

One type of audio recognized by Windows 3.1 is waveform audio. *Waveform* is audio that has been converted to a digital format by using a sound card. This digital information can be viewed and manipulated using waveform audio editor software. Waveform audio is played back through hardware in the sound card that takes the digital information, converts it to an analog audio signal, and plays it through an amp and speakers. Waveform files that can be played in Windows have a WAV extension.

Wave files can be created easily by plugging an audio source into the microphone input jack on your sound board. Audio sources can include a microphone, tape deck, audio CD player, or phonograph.

The Sound Recorder applet that comes with Windows (see fig. 1.6) enables you to record and digitize sounds at different sampling rates (11 or 22 KHz.)

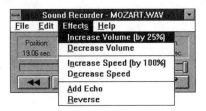

Figure 1.6:

The Sound Recorder enables you to edit wave files and add special effects.

The Waveform files most commonly used in business are voice snippets that you record yourself and use in compound documents. One product that may increase the popularity of business audio is the SoundXchange from InterActive (see fig. 1.7). This product uses the parallel port (you still can use a printer attached to the port as shown in figure 1.8) and uses a "telephone" for recording and listening to files. The telephone is more familiar than a microphone and less disruptive in an office environment with cubicles.

Figure 1.7:

SoundXchange is perfect for business environments.

Figure 1.8:

The SoundX-change connector provides printer throughput.

MIDI files that can be played from Windows have an MID extension.

MIDI Audio

The second audio type is MIDI, which is short for Musical Instrument Digital Interface. MIDI is an international standard established in 1982 that specifies the cabling and hardware for connecting computers and electronic musical

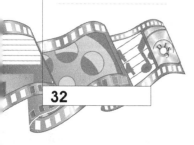

instruments. The MIDI standard also includes a communications protocol for passing sound from one device to another. A MIDI sound file contains information describing the notes to be played by a MIDI synthesizer.

If you use MIDI files, you need to select the correct MIDI setup for the device that plays the files. Windows supplies setups for a number of MIDI synthesizers. The manual supplied with your synthesizer should indicate whether it's a base-level synthesizer or an extended-level synthesizer, which MIDI channels it uses, and if it supports General MIDI Mode. Whether a synthesizer is base-level or extended-level depends on how many notes and the number of instruments the synthesizer can play simultaneously. Table 1.1 shows the requirements for base-level and extended-level synthesizers.

Table 1.1
Requirements for base-level
and extended-level synthesizers

Synthesizer type	Can play	Distributed among	
Melodic Instruments	Base	6 notes	3 instruments
	Extended	16 notes	9 instruments
Percussive Instruments	Base	3 notes	3 instruments
	Extended	16 notes	8 instruments

Base-level synthesizers can play six notes distributed among three melodic instruments and three notes on three percussive instruments. The melodic instruments are each on different MIDI channels, and all the percussive instruments are key-based on a single MIDI channel.

If Windows does not supply the setup for your synthesizer, or you want to connect your computer to a MIDI synthesizer that does not support General MIDI, you need to create a new MIDI setup.

WARNING

Do not try to create a new MIDI setup or modify an existing one unless you are familiar with MIDI synthesizers. If you are new to MIDI, contact the manufacturer of your MIDI board to obtain a Windows 3.1 MIDI setup.

Consult your Windows manual to see how to modify a new MIDI setup, or create a new one for your synthesizer. After selecting the correct MIDI setup from the MIDI Mapper applet (see fig. 1.9), you can use your MIDI synthesizer to play general MIDI files. Some synthesizers, when used in conjunction with MIDI software, enable you to create MIDI files. A keyboard synthesizer, for example, enables you to play notes (as though you were playing a piano) that can be captured and annotated by the software. The software enables you to edit the clip in different ways. When you are satisfied with the clip, you can save it as a General MIDI file.

	MIDI Patch Map: 'MT32'			

1 based patches

Src Patch	Src Patch Name	Dest Patch	Volume %	Key Map Name
0	Acoustic Grand Piano	0	100	[None]
1	Bright Acoustic Piano	1	100	[None]
2	Electric Grand Piano	3	100	[None]
3	Honky-tonk Piano	7	100	[None]
4	Rhodes Piano	5	100	[None]
5	Chorused Piano	6	100	[None]
6	Harpsichord	17	100	[None]
7	Clavinet	21	100	[None]
8	Celesta	22	100	[None]
9	Glockenspiel	101	100	[None]
10	Music Box	101	100	[None]
11	Vibraphone	98	100	[None]
12	Marimba	104	100	[None]
13	Xylophone	103	100	[None]
14	Tubular Bells	102	100	[None]
15	Dulcimer	105	100	[None]

OK   Cancel   Help

Figure 1.9:

The Windows MIDI Mapper.

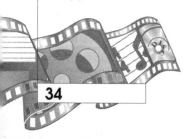

Musical talent is required to create MIDI files; they are not used often in business. MIDI is used more frequently in multimedia presentations, however. When presentations are made, the PC often is supplied, but the presenter has to bring floppy disks containing the slide show to install on the machine. MIDI files are much smaller than waveform files and preferably are for sparking up business presentations when music is needed.

Compact Disc Digital Audio

The third type of Windows-compatible audio is Compact Disc Digital Audio (CD-DA), which is the digital sound format used by standard audio CDs. CD-DA can be played from your CD-ROM drive while using Windows. Red book audio (an-other name for compact disk audio) does not come in a standard file format, but must be accessed from the compact disc through a Windows applet, such as the Media Player (see fig. 1.10).

Red book audio is discussed in the section "Looking at Compact-Disc Standards" in Chapter 3.

Figure 1.10:
The Windows Media Player.

Yankee Doodle Daffy Clip — Shields Archival, 6671 West Sunset Blvd., Hollywood, CA 90028 (213-962-1899)

CD-Audio can be used when your multimedia application requires top quality sound. Although Red Book audio sounds better than WAV files, it requires considerably more disc space—it should be used only when necessary. Because Red Book audio is not stored as a specific file on the disc, use of Red Book audio in an application requires a CD-ROM drive on the part of the end user's machine. This is not a problem when you produce an MPC-compatible title (because you can assume playback on an MPC). It may become a problem if you want to do a multimedia presentation incorporating CD audio sound.

TIP

The type of sound you can access in Windows depends on the devices you installed with Windows. To see a list of currently installed devices, use the Media Player applet. Click on the **D**evice menu, shown in figure 1.11, to see a list of the devices you have installed.

Figure 1.11:

Use the Media Player applet to see a list of installed media devices.

Adding Images to Your Work

An image, as compared to animation or video, can be defined as a static representation on-screen of an idea or concept and includes drawings, scanned photographs or line art, charts, maps and graphs (see fig. 1.12). Images have been used in computing since the day a bored programmer first

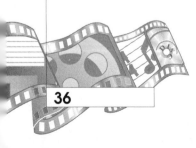

figured out how to make a smiley face on-screen by typing a series of Xs and Os. The use of images in computing did not take off, however, until desktop publishing became possible.

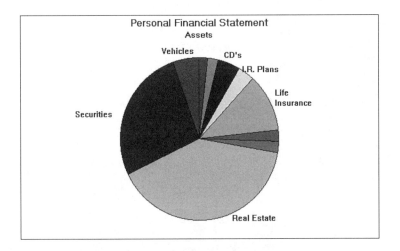

Figure 1.12:
If a picture's worth a thousand words, then a graph is worth a thousand numbers.

Images became an important part of business computing only after a computer user could crop a picture, scale it, wrap text around it, and then print it at 300 dots per inch (dpi) on a laser printer. The capability to graph spreadsheet data was another important factor in the increased use of images in computing. The final factor that led to the widespread use of images in business was "Macintosh envy."

Since 1981, corporate America has been doing some serious computing on the IBM PC and its compatible machines. Despite the effectiveness of their character-based applications, most business PC users suffered from a serious affliction every time they glimpsed the Macintosh computers in the graphics arts department. Mac-envy became so contagious that companies everywhere jumped on the Windows band-wagon when serious Windows applications became available.

Every graphical user interface (GUI), be it Mac, Windows, Presentation Manager, or some other interface, makes you more aware of images. The more you use GUIs, the more you are used to starting applications from icons, which are pictorial representations of programs. You can create a desktop environment on the computer that is as neat or as messy as your physical desktop. The more you work with a GUI, such as the one shown in figure 1.13, the more foreign a character-based environment such as DOS seems to you.

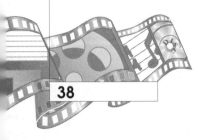

Figure 1.13:

A character-based application, compared to a graphical user interface.

As people became more "image aware," the video require-ments for visual computing increased. Five years ago an EGA board was state of the art. Today, some workstations include Targa boards capable of displaying millions of colors. Mi-crosoft lists the minimum requirement for running Windows 3.1 as a "display adapter that is supported by Windows." Actually many Windows users have SVGA displays, which is one of the requirements for multimedia computing. The type of display used on a computer influences greatly the integration of images into personal computing.

As the adapters for computers improve, both in resolution and in the number of colors they are capable of displaying, the quality of the images also improves. High-quality images require large amounts of storage, which makes the method for storing the images more important.

CD-ROM technology is capable of storing up to 600M of data. This large storage potential now enables users to include near-photo quality images with the rest of the data they use in day-to-day applications. High-quality images are part of database applications and standard documents. Recent improvements in network bandwidth also enable users to send images in a typical electronic mail message.

Examining Image File Formats

The images used in multimedia applications are either bitmaps or vector graphics. Each is discussed as follows:

➤ **Bitmaps.** Bitmap images are composed of sets of bits in the computer's memory that define the color and intensity of each pixel in an image. Although a number of different graphics packages can create and view different image file formats under Windows, the recommended formats for using images in multimedia Windows applications are standard bitmaps (files with a BMP extension), Microsoft device-independent bitmaps (files with a DIB extension), and files that have been compressed using a data compression technique, such as files with Run-Length Encoding (an RLE extension).

The Windows Paintbrush program creates bitmapped images, as do most screen capture utilities. The Microsoft

Multimedia Development Kit (MDK) comes with a BitEdit program. You cannot create new images with BitEdit, but it can convert images from other file formats, resize images, crop and rotate images, and change the palette used for a specific image.

Bitmaps comprise the majority of images used in the Windows environment and the majority of image files used in multimedia development. Vector graphics, described in the next section, are used in specialized circumstances.

NOTE
The terms "bitmap graphics" (as opposed to the BMP file format) and "vector graphics" describe how an image is created (a series of dots or instructions). PCX, GIF, and TGA are file formats; BMP is another file format. Although Windows enables users to work with these other file formats, the Microsoft Multimedia specification only recognizes BMP and DIB file formats. If you create a PCX image, you must convert it before using it in a multimedia title. Some authoring tools convert files for you.

> ➤ **Vector.** Vector graphics are images that are stored as a set of instructions. Vector graphics must be displayed in Windows metafile format (files with a CGM extension).

Vector graphics are used when the sections or dimensions of an image must be modified often. Software packages that create vector graphics usually portray a skeleton, or wire frame of the image. The individual components that make up the image can be moved or modified before the image is rendered. Rendering is the process that creates the colors and dimensions of the final images—imagine covering the

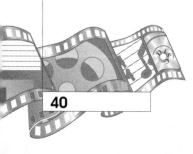

wire frame with cloth. Rendering can be very CPU-intensive and should be saved for the final stages of image editing.

Computer-Aided Design (CAD) packages use vector graphics, as do many of the 2D and 3D modeling and animation packages. Vector graphics have many uses in business: engineering, manufacturing, architecture, and graphic design.

Adding Animation to Your Work

Animation on a PC is a series of images that are displayed in rapid succession, fooling the eye into thinking it is seeing movement. Some of the most effective multimedia applications incorporate animated sequences. By adding animation to an application, you can simplify complex ideas and make them easier to understand.

To create computer animation you must use either frame animation or cast animation. *Frame animation* is the process of designing a separate frame for each screen view and then flipping through the frames in rapid succession. As you can see in figure 1.14, frame animation is similar to a film strip in that minimal changes occur from frame to frame.

Cast animation is the process of designing all the moving objects in a separate process, and then assigning character traits to each object. The character traits refer to the position pattern, size, and colorization of the objects. Composite picture frames are formed for each object, and the frames are flipped through in rapid succession to achieve the illusion of motion.

Animation makes complex ideas easier to understand.

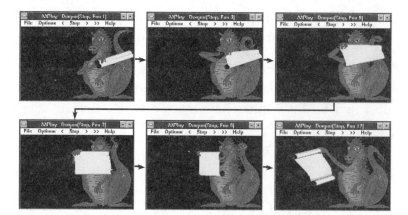

Figure 1.14:

Frame animation uses separate "cels" to create movement.

Gold disk's Animation Works product is an example of a cast animation package that makes it simple for novice artists to create animations, which can then be incorporated into multimedia efforts. Although the process of using cast animation is simpler than frame animation, from a design standpoint, both types of animation require time and creativity.

NOTE   Animation clip libraries are becoming more widespread. Soon clip animation will be as easy to use as clip art.

With a fair amount of design sense, the average business user can create some nice 2D (or two dimensional) animations, featuring flying corporate logos or moving bar graphs. These animated images may be exciting in a presentation, but they do not have the slick look and feel that can be obtained only from 3D animation. 3D animation is best left to experienced, professional graphic artists and animators. The process of building a 3D graphic involves creating a wire frame image, then rendering the image by mapping a texture onto the

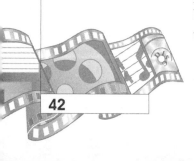

frame. Special effects may be applied to the image, such as providing a light source from a certain direction or mapping a mirrored image onto the wire frame, so that the rendered image reflects other objects in the picture. *Morphing*, or the merging of two images into a composite image, is a technique that has been receiving a lot of attention lately. Morphing was used in the *Terminator II* movie, and in Michael Jackson's *Black or White* video.

NOTE

Autodesk makes a series of tools that enable you to create 3D images and animations. Although Autodesk Animator requires you to create in DOS (not Windows), it comes with a Windows run-time player, capable of playing back FLI or FLC files, and attaching sound files to the animation files. Once installed the Animator run-time player becomes a multimedia device, accessible by any program that uses MCI commands (such as the Media Player).

Animation files depend on the player used to run the animated sequences in Windows. The animation tool that creates the animated sequence determines the player you use at runtime. Different players have different capabilities, as shown in figure 1.15. Some players are capable of displaying 256 colors and also enable you to synchronize sound to the animated sequence. One player may run in a small window with 200×320 resolution; another may take the entire screen. The animation package you decide to use depends on the type of effect you want to create and the type of application you are using with the animation.

Figure 1.15:

An animation running in a window.

 If you want to include an animated sequence in a compound document or in a corporate presentation, make sure the animation software produces compatible files.

NOTE

Adding Video to Your Work

Video differs from animation in that video describes images of real events stored in a digital form; animation is simply computer-generated images. Video image files usually contain audio tracks and are larger than animated images. Storage requirements for video files in turn prevent them from being loaded and played back from memory. As a result, video must be accessed from a hard disk or CD-ROM. Uncompressed, full motion video is impractical because 30

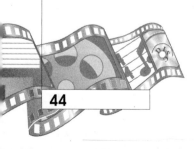

seconds of full motion video stored in an analog form requires over 500M of storage.

The problem with video is that it takes up so much room. To make video manageable, video files must be compressed using special software. Compression may be hardware-driven, with special boards required for video capture, compression, and playback. Video sequences also can be viewed and stored using software that decompresses the video frames when they run (at "runtime").

Although many good applications are created using images or animation or both, nothing is as impressive as seeing video running in a window on your PC. Video can be used for teleconferencing, the next generation of home movies, or sophisticated tutorials. The ways in which you can integrate video with your PC are even more varied than its uses.

NOTE

The most valuable use for video on a PC is teleconferencing. Although teleconferencing using the PC requires a considerable investment (for the network lines, hardware, and software) for a large corporation, it can save money in terms of travel costs. Additional information on video teleconferencing can be found in the Epilogue.

The most important thing to remember about video is that it is an expensive technology—development, integration into applications, and disk space are only a few considerations that require an investment of hardware and time. Another consideration is how the video itself is used. To have an impact, video must be used effectively and must enhance the overall application. Video cannot be tacked on as an afterthought.

Part of the Video for Windows development package includes a utility to convert Macintosh QuickTime files.

Two new products make it easier to incorporate video into your Windows computing efforts. Video for Windows (VFW), shown in figure 1.16, is a product from Microsoft that enables developers to capture, digitize, and compress (using a number of different compression algorithms) video. VFW is scalable; it can be played back on a user's PC, with an additional video decompression board. The quality of the video being played back depends on the processing power of the playback PC. The software drops frames, when necessary, to ensure that the audio stays synchronized to the video sequences. On a slow 386, the video may play back at 10 frames per second (fps). On a fast 486, the playback can be 24fps. VFW is installed as a multimedia device.

Figure 1.16:
Video for Windows.

CARE, Inc., 660 First Avenue, New York, NY, 10016 (212-686-3110)

QuickTime for Windows (QTW), from Apple, is similar to VFW in that it also offers scalable, "software only" playback of video clips. With QuickTime for Windows, users can access all of the QuickTime movies available for the Mac, without having to convert the files. For the developer, QTW offers an advantage. If you develop with an authoring tool capable of running your multimedia title on both Windows and the Mac, you can use the same QTW clips for both platforms and

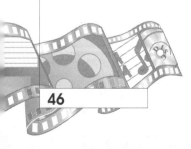

master only a single CD-ROM disc. The disadvantage to QTW is that it requires a separate runtime program.

What You Need To Create Multimedia Documents

Now that you are familiar with the diverse parts of multimedia, you probably are wondering what you need to begin creating true multimedia documents. Fortunately, the computer you already are using is probably powerful enough to be upgraded to a multimedia PC. As you can imagine, each part of multimedia places certain requirements on the computer. If the computer cannot produce 256 colors or does not have enough memory, a multimedia document or application does not run properly. This was the reason for development of the MPC specification. The following sections discuss the equipment you need for multimedia computing.

Defining the Multimedia PC (MPC)

The Multimedia PC, or MPC, is a traditional personal computer, that has been enhanced with special hardware and software to take advantage of multimedia elements. MPCs run any DOS or Windows applications currently available, plus titles and applications developed specifically for the MPC. The use of existing technology was important for the success of the MPC standard because users would not adopt the new technology if they could not leverage their existing investment in hardware and software. The MPC standard ensured millions of PC's could be upgraded to MPC status with the addition of a CD-ROM drive, sound board, and necessary software (see fig. 1.17).

Figure 1.17:

The hardware required for upgrading your PC to an MPC.

The minimum specifications for a multimedia PC (MPC) are as follows:

Hardware

● ●

Basic Computer Requirements

A PC featuring an 80386SX or higher processor

2M of RAM

30M or larger hard disk drive

VGA or SVGA Display

Two-button Mouse

101-key keyboard

● ●

The CD-ROM drive must have the following capabilities or features:

● ●

CD-ROM Drive

A transfer rate of at least 150K per second

A maximum seek time of 1 second

The drive cannot use more than 40 percent of the computer's CPU processing power

● ●

The audio board must provide the following capabilities or features:

• •
Audio Requirements

A music synthesizer

On-board analog mixing capabilities

Digitized sound in eight-bit samples at an 11KHz input sampling rate and eight-bit samples at both 11KHz and 22KHz output sampling rate

Serial and Parallel ports

MIDI I/O Port (most of the MPC-compatible audio boards feature a MIDI I/O port)

Joystick Port

Headphones or speakers connected to the computer system
• •

Ordinary speakers or headphones work with the MPC system, but speakers require an additional power source.

• •
Software

Microsoft Windows 3.1

MS-DOS or PC-DOS Version 3.1 or later

MS-DOS CD-ROM Extensions (MSCDEX) Version 2.2 or later
• •

NOTE Although the MPC specification includes a joystick port, a joystick certainly is not necessary for the integration of multimedia into business computing.

The MPC is not a single type of multimedia-enhanced PC, but a range of personal computers. The MPC Marketing Council (discussed in Chapter 3) assumed low-end MPCs would be bought for the home market and higher-end MPCs would be used in business and development. The initial MPC specification was based on an 80286 processor running at 10MHz. This base MPC specification was revised at the end of December, 1991, after it had been discovered that many of the MPC titles developed on much more powerful PC's were agonizingly slow on 80286-based computers.

If you already have a base PC that meets the minimum specifications, you can purchase an MPC Upgrade kit.

The average price of an MPC is between $1,700 (low-end) to $5,000 (high end). Shop around because clone manufacturers may have cheaper systems. The price for an MPC is well within the budget of most business departments, but may have to fall further before MPCs become a strong factor in the home marketplace.

Although hardware bearing the MPC trademark is 100 percent compatible with the MPC specification, software bearing this trademark may be more questionable. The Council does not test the applications or titles for compatibility; the developers are supposed to test their software. Most titles are compatible, but even in these cases, the MPC has yet to achieve plug-n-play ease.

MPCs can be purchased from a variety of manufacturers. Many of the original Council shareholders, including Tandy, CompuAdd, Fujitsu, NEC Technologies, NCR, Olivetti, Philips, and Zenith Data Systems, are currently shipping preconfigured multimedia systems. Many clone manufacturers also are starting to ship MPCs at attractive prices.

If you are shopping for an MPC system, make sure you buy the latest equipment; 80486 CPUs, CD-ROM XA drives, and DSP processors are or soon will be the standard for MPCs.

The current MPC specification of an 80386SX 16MHz computer already is beginning to show its age. This processor is not available from the mainstream computer manufacturers, and is much slower than the popular 80386SX 33MHz and 80486SX 25MHz processors. Companies such as Tandy now offer complete multimedia 486 PC systems for under $2,000—the base minimum of the future MPC has become a

486. A fast 486 PC is capable of playing scalable video at 24fps, making it a good choice for multimedia computing. If you have yet to buy other MPC components, consider these developments: CD-ROM XA drives soon will replace the current CD-ROM drives as the standard for multimedia computing. Expect to see sound boards being replaced by DSP chips capable of decompressing and displaying large image files, and playing sound and video clips.

Other Multimedia Equipment Options

In addition to the standard multimedia hardware requirements, you may want to add other hardware options to your system, depending on the design of the multimedia application. In most situations, when you design the multimedia application, you do not know anything about the user's playback machine other than it is an MPC. In other situations you may design a turnkey system in which you define (or provide) the playback machine and the special software. This occurs when you have created an application intended for a kiosk.

A *kiosk* is a multimedia PC (or other multimedia playback system) that has been encased in a cabinet—the system is a free-standing unit. The user is not aware a computer is inside the cabinet; figure 1.18 shows that he or she only needs to interact with the system by using an input device and reacting to the program's images and sound. Some kiosks even contain printers so that the user can print out information gained as a result of interacting with the system. Kiosks often are found in museums, or in shopping areas (in a store or in a mall setting) where it is used as an advertising vehicle.

Figure 1.18:
This CD-I kiosk shows consumers interacting with multimedia software. All the necessary equipment is hidden in the cabinet.

One technology that is becoming more important as kiosks become more prevalent is touch screens. Touch screens were treated as anomalies in the hardware world until very recently. Although they are good for specific applications, touch screens have not made it into executive offices, as was hoped by their manufacturers. Touch screens are the most important part of a kiosk systems. Multimedia tools currently available for authoring are making it easier and more cost effective to design point of sale kiosks for the general public. Touch screens are effective as a consumer input device; with them users do not need to know they are interacting with a computer.

The user interacts with the software by touching the surface of the screen to activate a hotspot. A touchscreen consists of two thin sheets of plastic, mounted on a thicker glass support

for stability. Each sheet features a transparent conductive coating on the facing surfaces. Between the two sheets are small transparent, separator dots, which are distributed evenly over the touch surface. When the user puts his or her finger on the touchscreen, the top conductive sheet makes contact with the bottom conductive sheet, causing voltages that vary in magnitude, depending on the position of the touch. An analog to digital converter electronically interprets these voltages into the X and Y coordinates of the touch screen monitor area.

Software must be specially designed for a touch screen. Because fingers are a less accurate pointing device than a mouse or pen, hot spot buttons must be much larger. The interface for a touch screen application should be much simpler than other software interfaces—the user should not need on screen help to be able to figure out the application. The application should promote quick use—no more than 5 minutes. Applications designed for kiosk use should start with a catchy animation or video clip, designed to draw the user's attention to the booth (if the kiosk is being used as a point of sale advertising vehicle). One good example of business kiosk use are the Citibank automated teller machines. In certain parts of the country, these money machines feature touch screens that let the user conduct all banking transactions and get information about his or her money with just a touch of the finger.

Another situation in which you should define the playback system is when you design a multimedia application for a personal information device or portable multimedia player. Although this hardware is not prevalent, it promises to become increasingly important because it moves personal computing out of the business environment and into the consumer marketplace. For mobile multimedia, you may be designing Windows-based software that requires pen input.

Pen computing is another technology that is becoming important to new media computing . Microsoft, Apple, and other companies are betting that personal assistants (PA), which use pen-based input to interact with the user, is important for the next generation of personal information managers. The PA hardware is a step up from computerized organizers, such as the Casio B.O.S.S. and Sharp Wizard. Personal assistants incorporate technologies such as a pen-like stylus and voice recognition for input. They may also feature cellular technology (see fig. 1.19) that enables the PA to communicate with desktop PCs at home or with networks at work.

Figure 1.19:

The EO personal digital assistant from AT&T is the first of what will be-come an important new trend in personal comput-ing. Although the EO is based on GO Corporation's PenPoint operating system, expect to see other PDAs announced that run Modular Windows.

NOTE

As our idea of what software is changes, so should our idea of a computer. A computer is not some-thing that sits on our desktop, but a set of instruc-tions that can be recognized by a processing chip. As chip technology improves (a new generation of chips is developed, on the average, every 18 months), their size decreases and the chip price drops. In the near future, computers as we know them will be part of personal assistants, smart

telephones, televisions, and VCRs. To keep up with these changes, we need to stop thinking in terms of "computer" and "software," and start thinking in terms of "equipment" and "interface."

Like touch screens, software designed to take advantage of pen input and cellular communications needs special designs. When designing for a PDA or mobile multimedia player, you need to decide if you want to take advantage of the hand writing recognition features of the pen software. You should design software that appends user-created images to the original application data files (pens enable users to create sketches that are stored as bitmap files). If you design software to be played back on a system that has cellular communications capability, you may want to design a Rolodex interface, or create a communications module in your software.

When you design a multimedia application for use on specialized multimedia hardware, hardware considerations determine the software's design. The manner in which the user interacts with the hardware also affects software design. If you design software for hardware that feature additions to the MPC specification (such as touch screens or video decompression boards) you may want to provide the hardware with the software for your end user. A turnkey solution gives you complete control over the playback environment and minimizes hardware incompatbility problems. If you are designing software to be used on a special consumer device, you may want to create your application using an operating environment designed for cross platform compatibility (such as Modular Windows)—this minimizes the amount of new code you have to write for each new platform. If you port an application from one platform (such as the MPC) to another (such as a PDA running Modular Windows) you may have to redesign parts of your interface, to take advantage of the new hardware options.

Multimedia Software Requirements

The MPC specification assures multimedia developers an installed base of machines exists for running multimedia titles. The last section discussed the hardware requirements for multimedia computing. This section discusses software requirements.

As with hardware, the needs of the end user differ from the needs of the developer. As long as MPC hardware is available, a user only needs Windows 3.1 for the simplest type of "multimedia" computing.

Windows 3.1 incorporates the Multimedia Extensions (MME), a collection of Dynamic Link Libraries (DLL's), device drivers, and applets that enable end users to access multimedia devices (such as sound boards and animation software players). Before the release of Windows 3.1, the MME were bundled as a separate product to be used with Windows 3.0.

For the end user, Windows 3.1 provides a number of device drivers that install multimedia devices through the Control Panel (see fig. 1.20). In addition, Windows 3.1 includes a few new applets to help users explore new media options. The driver that accesses your sound board and plays Waveform (WAV) files is called MCIWAV.DRV; the driver that accesses the MIDI sequencer is MCISEQ.DRV. The Windows driver that accesses the CD-ROM drive and enables you to play Red book audio and use disc-based data files is MCICDA.DRV.

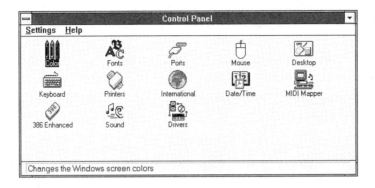

Windows 3.1 includes the following applets:

➤ **Control Panel icons.** Installs and configures multimedia devices

➤ **Media Player.** Plays multimedia files and enables you to control external multimedia devices

➤ **Sound Recorder.** Enables you to play, record, and edit Waveform files

With Windows 3.1 an end user can play Wave, MIDI, and video files. With OLE (Object Linking and Embedding), he or she can incorporate these media elements into other documents. As long as the user has an MPC, he or she can purchase any multimedia software marked "MPC-compatible" with the assurance that it works with the computer. A number of multimedia titles have been released on the market; more are expected in the coming year. A multimedia title may need drivers that have not been installed on the user's system (such as drivers for animation players). Although the majority of the title's software is accessed from the CD-ROM disc, most titles have a setup routine that installs software on the user's hard drive. This software is usually a collection of executables, drivers and other DLLs. They do not require a lot of disk space, but are necessary for executing the program.

For more information on OLE, see "Using Windows' Multimedia Software Tools" in Chapter 2.

A developer's software needs vary according to the type of multimedia development he or she is trying to accomplish. In addition to Windows 3.1, a developer needs a copy of the Microsoft Multimedia Developer's Kit (MDK) if he or she is going to create a title. If, on the other hand, a developer wants to add media elements to a standard Windows application, the Windows Software Developer's Kit (SDK) is suitable.

For the developer, the MDK provides data preparation tools (programs that prepare image and sound files), the Multimedia Viewer Author Toolkit (a multimedia authoring system), and the Multimedia Development Environment (a collection of programming libraries, source files, and debugging tools). The MDK also provides an Apple Macintosh utility that converts MacroMind Director files to MMM files. These animation files can be played if the user has an MMM animation player device installed. Microsoft Viewer multimedia titles install the MMM driver during the title setup routine.

Because the multimedia extensions have been incorporated into Windows 3.1, all developers creating multimedia titles have access to the following services:

The MCI is discussed in detail in "Interfacing with the Media Control Interface" in Chapter 6.

> **Media Control Interface (MCI).** MCI is a high level generalized interface that enables the developer to control media devices, such as audio boards, movie players, videodisc and videotape players.

> **Audio.** Audio services provide a device independent interface to audio hardware, enabling developers to add sound to multimedia applications. Developers can add Waveform, MIDI, or Red book sound to their applications, without worrying about the specific hardware required to provide the sound capability.

> **Multimedia File I/O.** Like other file I/O services, the multimedia file I/O services allow files to be opened,

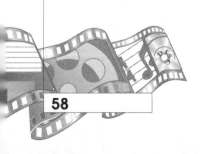

read or written to, and then closed. Multimedia File I/O services also support standard Resource Interchange File Format (RIFF) files, which are the preferred format for multimedia files.

➤ **Video, joystick, and timer.** Windows 3.1 supports special video modes, joysticks, and high-resolution event timing.

Developers who purchase the MDK receive the following data Preparation Tools:

➤ **BitEdit.** Enables you to edit bitmapped graphics

➤ **PalEdit.** Enables you to create or edit color palettes

➤ **WaveEdit.** Enables you to edit and play Waveform files (see fig. 1.21)

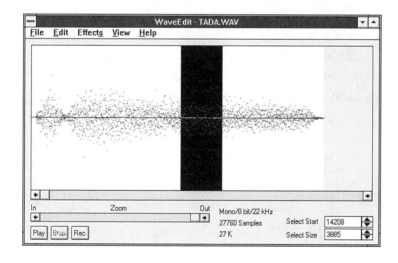

Figure 1.21:

The WaveEdit program from the MDK.

➤ **FileWalker.** Enables you to view and edit many types of files in different formats

➤ **Convert.** Enables you to covert data files from one format to another

In addition to data preparation tools, the MDK provides the Multimedia Viewer, an authoring tool you can use to create multimedia titles. Viewer enables you to incorporate media elements into the titles you create including sound, animation, and video. The most impressive part of Viewer is its powerful hypertext engine. You can use it to create cross-reference jumps for moving between related topics, and developers can use Viewer's text search capability for locating text strings within titles you create.

The Multimedia Development Environment also includes the following:

➤ **C header files and libraries.** The C header files contain multimedia specific definitions and declarations required by the C programming language source code.

➤ The debugging version of Windows.

➤ **Sample applications.** Some of the sample applications include Bouncer, a screen saver; Joytoy, a joystick demonstration application that shoots holes in your desktop; Lava, a lava flow simulator to demonstrate palette animation; MMPlay, for testing the Movie Player functions; and RLEApp, which creates a simple animation sequence from a series of bitmaps.

➤ **On-line reference files.** Provides complete information about multimedia functions, messages, commands, and data structures.

The most valuable part of the MDK is the documentation manuals; they explain fully the media control interface, high-level audio services, low-level audio services, special video topics, timer and joystick services, the Multimedia File I/O services, the multimedia functions, messages, data types and structures, command strings, and multimedia file formats.

This information is critical for any developer creating multimedia applications, regardless of the authoring tool or language used.

After the purchase of the MDK, a developer needs to select authoring software (to create the title) and media editing software (to develop or enhance the media clips to be incorporated into the authoring of the title). Many multimedia software development tools are available today. To determine the right tool for you depends on many factors. Chapter 7 "Planning Your Multimedia Project" addresses different authoring packages and shows you how to determine which is best for your needs.

"There is no 'Multimedia market.' Multimedia is a group of technologies that will have a profound effect on personal computing, making personal computers at least as important as communications tools as they are today as information tools." Nick Arnett, noted Multimedia Analyst

CHAPTER

2

Using Multimedia Windows at Work

T he common definition of multimedia describes software that incorporates voice, music, animation, still or video images, and text and data objects. As you read in Chapter 1, the addition of specialized hardware and integration of multimedia extensions into Windows 3.1 creates a "media aware" computing environment. Windows was designed to handle multiple drivers, enabling you to add different multimedia peripherals to your system. Although media aware computing has been available on the Mac for quite some time, it was not practical on the PC until the standardization of the MPC specification.

Traditionally, it was difficult to create media-rich applications that ran well under DOS. Multimedia under DOS meant that the application developer had to create drivers for all known peripherals. If you installed a new sound board into your computer, chances are it was not compatible with your existing software. Additionally, the DOS 640K memory limitation was inhibiting for multimedia developers. Because the MPC specification is based on Windows, problems with driver incompatibility and memory limitations have been resolved.

The Windows operating environment makes media aware computing possible for DOS-based PCs. This chapter examines the multimedia components included with Windows 3.1 and shows you how Windows 3.1 can help you take advantage of the many elements of multimedia.

New Opportunities for the Windows User

The greatest thing about the standardization of MPC hardware and software is that it takes multimedia out of the hands of specialists and makes it available to anyone. Multimedia makes computers more fun, more friendly, and more helpful. After you get used to using multimedia, you will not want to return to regular computing.

You can incorporate multimedia into your computing efforts in a number of ways. The easiest way is to try the multimedia version of your current word processing or spreadsheet program. Many major vendors are releasing enhanced versions of their software packages that enable you to use the product in a more efficient (and fun) manner. Multimedia enhancement is usually provided in the form of animated movies or sound added to the help system.

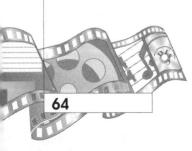

You can add multimedia elements to enhance your document or spreadsheet files. Microsoft has included two multimedia applets in Windows 3.1 that enable you to create and play back media files. The first applet is the Sound Recorder. With this applet, you can record waveform files by using a microphone, and use the resulting wave file in other applications. The Media Player applet enables you to play back all types of media files including waveform, MIDI, video, CD Audio, and movie (animation). Using the Sound Recorder or the Media Player along with the Object Linking and Embedding (OLE) feature that comes with Windows 3.1, you can easily add media to your other applications.

With OLE, you can use media creatively to improve corporate communications by creating compound documents. *Compound documents* are made up of objects from more than one source. These objects include media elements (such as sound or animation) in addition to the text and graphics typically found in a document file.

Because of multimedia, our perception of what the word "document" means will change, as will the purpose of documents. We currently think of a document as a text-based way to present information and ideas. In the future, we will think of a document as a way to present information and ideas, by using whatever media is most appropriate for the message. We currently distribute documents by delivering them on foot (sneaker-net) or through the postal service (snail-mail). In the future, most documents will be delivered over a network.

Because of Windows' multimedia capabilities, you can prepare for the future now. By using common Windows applications and your local area network, you can create compound documents and send them to others in your organization. This chapter explains more about the multimedia capabilities of Windows, how to use OLE with multimedia elements, and how to integrate media elements when using Windows at work. The chapter ends with a a discussion of how multimedia can be used to enhance Windows, and make working more enjoyable.

Examining Windows' Multimedia Capabilities

Read Chapter 3, "Making Multimedia Work with Your Hardware" to learn how to set up your MPC.

Setting up your multimedia PC MPC is the most difficult component of multimedia computing. After your MPC is configured properly, you are ready to experiment. The next few sections talk you through the process of playing with multimedia and creating a compound document.

How to Get Started

In the process of determining if your MPC was properly configured, you probably began playing with some of the media clips that come bundled with Windows or your MPC hardware. An easy way to get acquainted with multimedia and what you can do with it is to play with the Media Player and the Sound Recorder Accessories that come with Windows 3.1. The Media Player plays media clips of any type, by using the devices you have installed and configured for use under Windows. The Media Player also enables you to configure devices before playing a file. The Sound Recorder enables you to record, play back, and edit Wave files.

The Media Player

The Media player enables you to play sound, video, and animation clips. Audio CD Players, video disc players, animation players (runtime software is considered to be a "Media

device"), and VCRs are some of the devices that can be
controlled by the Media Player (see fig. 2.1).

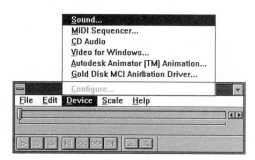

The following steps acquaint you with the Media Player's
capabilities and show you the different types of media clips
you can use with Windows.

1. From the Accessories Program Group, double-click on
   the Media Player icon or press Tab until the Media
   Player is highlighted, then press Enter.

2. The Media Player Applet opens, with the Media Player
   buttons grayed out.

3. Choose a specific file From the Media Player File menu,
   or select the particular media device to be used from the
   Device menu.

4. Select MIDI Sequencer from the Device menu by
   holding the right mouse button down until MIDI Sequencer is highlighted, then release the mouse button.

5. An Open dialog box appears showing a list of available
   MIDI files (files with a MID or RMI extension).

6. Select the CANYON.MID file that came bundled with Windows, by double-clicking on the file name in the list box.

7. The Media Player Applet shows the file name in the
   window title bar. Media Player buttons that pertain to
   MIDI files are no longer grayed out.

8. Click on the play button (located in the lower left-hand corner of the Media Player window). The MIDI clip begins to play.

9. To pause the music, click on the pause button (which has replaced the play button in the lower left-hand corner of the Window).

10. To resume play of the clip, click on the play button again.

The Media Player's buttons (see fig. 2.2) may be grayed out depending on the type of clip being played.

Figure 2.2:

The Media Player's buttons are similar to those on a CD or VCR.

Play   Stop   Eject

Experiment with the Media Player by selecting different types of clips to be played. In addition to playing clips, the Media Player can be used as an OLE server, enabling you to embed or link clips into other Windows applications. The Media Player's Options dialog box enables you to alter how the clip looks after being copied or linked to another application (see fig. 2.3).

The Sound Recorder

The Sound Recorder enables you to record, edit, and play back wave files. You also can use the Sound Recorder to embed or link wave files into other Windows applications.

NOTE   For more information on waveform (WAV) files, see the section "Waveform Audio" in Chapter 1, "A Multimedia Overview."

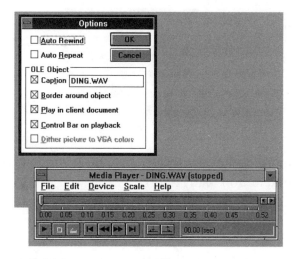

Figure 2.3:

The Media Player's Options dialog box.

Follow the steps to get acquainted with the Sound Recorder's capabilities:

1. From the Accessories Program Group, double-click on the Sound Recorder icon, or press Tab until the Sound Recorder is highlighted, then press Enter.

2. The Sound Recorder applet opens with the Sound Recorder buttons grayed out and the sound Wave line flat.

4. Select Open from the File menu by holding the right mouse button down until Open is highlighted, then release the mouse button.

5. The Open dialog box appears, showing a list of available Wave files (files with the WAV extension).

6. Select TADA.WAV which was bundled with Windows, by double-clicking on the file name in the list box.

7. The Sound Recorder Applet shows the file name in the window title bar. The Sound Recorder fast forward and play buttons are no longer grayed out.

8. Click on the play button, (the middle Button), to hear the file (see fig. 2.4).

Figure 2.4:

The Sound Recorder playing the TADA.WAV file.

9. To pause the music, click on the pause button (the second button to the right).

10. To resume play of the clip, click on the play button again.

Creating a Compound Document

Although experimenting with the Sound Recorder and the Media Player can be enjoyable, you still need to discover how multimedia can become useful in your business environment. Windows' Object Linking and Embedding utility (OLE) enables you to add media elements to Windows applications you use every day. With OLE, you can create compound documents. OLE is discussed in detail later on in this chapter, but first you learn how to create a compound document and what to do with it, once you have created it.

How Media Adds Value

We are accustomed to using a great deal of sound in business communication. We routinely conduct conference calls and make extensive use of voice mail. Sound is a powerful tool, but often it makes a confusing point more confusing.

Documents also are important in business communication. A document can be copied and distributed to a group of people easily. Documents can incorporate charts and graphics to clarify information or can be used as proof of a contrac-

tual relationship. Documents may take the form of text-based communication, but a document also can be a print-out of a spreadsheet.

The power of multimedia is the capability to combine both these forms of communication. Until now, you had to conduct a meeting to make use of both sound and documentation at the same time. Multimedia takes this one step further, by adding the capability to integrate video and animation. The usefulness of multimedia in the business environment ultimately depends on its capability to cut down on the number of meetings required for efficient business communication. If it takes you less time to create a compound document and distribute it than it does to hold a meeting— and if it takes the receiver of your document less time to "read" it—then multimedia ultimately can make you more efficient. If a compound document prevents extra travel for either party, then multimedia also can save you money.

You may have to conduct a little research to determine if multimedia can save you money or make you more efficient. Try the example in the next section as a test. It gives you a taste of business communication in the future.

Adding a Wavefile by Using OLE

Hopefully, you will enjoy this next exercise as much as you enjoyed experimenting with media clips. To conduct this test properly, you need an MPC configured with a microphone.

TIP   If your MPC did not come configured with a microphone, Radio Shack makes an inexpensive one for under $20. You also can use a microphone from any stereo system.

You also need a co-worker with access to an MPC. (In the event that you have the only MPC in the office, sit your co-worker down at your workstation when you are ready to conduct the test.) Ideally, both of you are on a local area network, but you also can copy the final file to a floppy and use sneaker-net, if necessary.

Finally, you need a Windows word processor, that can act as an OLE client. (This means that your Windows word processor has the capability to link and embed OLE objects. Check your documentation if you are not sure.) Microsoft's Word for Windows 2.0 is one.

Create a compound document by following these steps, but do not tell your co-worker what you are about to do. This test is most effective if you use a memo you are planning to send to that person anyway.

Select a passage of the document that contains difficult or complicated material. Use the Sound Recorder applet and the microphone connected to the input jack of your sound card to record an explanatory message. The message does not have to be lengthy, but it should clarify the point as if you were explaining something over the phone. Play back the resulting wavefile, and edit it with the Sound Recorder until you are satisfied.

NOTE

Do not take too long editing the clip—the idea of multimedia is to become more productive, not less. Do not take any more time than you would to leave voice mail in response to a question.

Use the following procedure to embed the clip into your memo.

1. Open the document into which you want to embed the sound file.

2. Choose **O**bject from the **I**nsert menu.

3. From the Insert Object dialog box, select **S**ound.

4. Choose OK. The Sound Recorder application opens.

5. From the Sound Recorder **F**ile menu, choose the **I**nsert File command.

6. From the Insert File dialog box, select the sound file you created to be incorporated into the document and choose OK.

7. From the Sound Recorder **F**ile menu, choose **U**pdate. This action embeds the selected sound file into the card in the Word document.

8. From the Sound Recorder **F**ile menu, choose E**x**it.

9. You return to the Word document, where the sound icon is placed at the cursor location. This icon indicates that a sound file has been embedded at this point.

10. Use your word processor to add this line underneath the sound icon: "Double-click on the icon shown above for additional information."

Deliver the file to the memo recipient, but do not say anything about the embedded sound file. After your recipient has had time to review the document, ask for his or her reaction. Try to find out if the embedded sound file helped to clarify the point, or was ignored, irritating, or difficult to use. The reaction of your recipient may tip you off as to how successful media can be when integrated into your communication efforts. Try the preceding experiment with a number of different people in your department, or with people in other departments. Some people will probably be open to the idea of compound documents, while others will dislike it, or will not care.

Although your company may be slow to adopt compound documentation and there may be a vocal group of people who hate the idea, it probably will be integrated into the corporate environment in the same way as voice mail. At first, many people hated voice mail and felt uncomfortable using the technology. But after only a few years, people wonder how they ever got along without it.

Using OLE with Multimedia

In the preceding section, you experimented with OLE and created a simple compound document—a document that contains objects from more than one source. These next few paragraphs explain more about OLE and what you can do with this new technology.

OLE is designed to let different applications communicate and share information. Although not a replacement for DDE (Dynamic Data Exchange), OLE makes data transfer between applications easier for the end user to implement. OLE-aware applications include a "Paste Link" or "Paste special" command for inserting data links to other OLE-aware applications.

OLE also enables users to embed objects via the Windows Clipboard. For example, the user can copy a bit map created by the Paintbrush program and use the clipboard to copy and embed the bit map into a Word for Windows document.

OLE is actually two different sets of services based on client and server applications. All OLE-ready applications fall into one of these two categories (some fall into both). The appli-

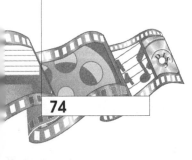

cation that creates and enables you to edit the object is the source application (server). The application into which the object is embedded is the client application. For example, if you place a bit-map graphic created with the Paintbrush program into a Word document file, Paintbrush is the server program and Word is the client program.

The difference between OLE and DDE is that Windows maintains a database of OLE server applications that you can use from within a client application. Using DDE to link two applications requires the end user to write code, while using OLE requires that he or she simply select the server application to be used (see fig. 2.5).

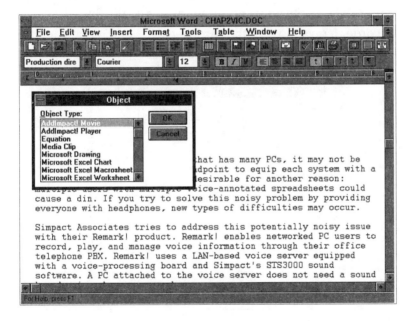

Figure 2.5:

OLE enables you to select from a list of server applications to embed an object in Word for Windows.

If you *link* an object, you create a pointer to the server data, telling the server program where that object resides on the hard disk. If you update an object linked into several compound documents, all the documents are updated automatically. If you *embed* the object, you store a copy of the data with the client program. By double-clicking on an embedded object, OLE copies the object's data into the source application, where you can edit it. If you update the embedded object, it is only changed in the compound document.

Documents with embedded objects result in much larger file sizes than those with linked objects. You can move a client document with embedded objects, however, away from the server. You can copy your document to a floppy disk, for example, without worrying about breaking a link.

If the server knows how to render the OLE object (in the case of a bit map), it does so. Otherwise, it displays the data in the form of an icon. If you link a WAV sound file into a card in Windows' cardfile application, for example, the Sound Recorder icon shows on the card (see fig. 2.6). To play the sound, simply double-click on the icon.

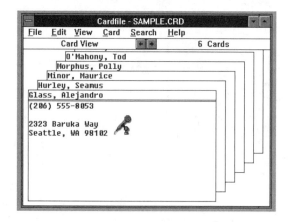

Figure 2.6:

Sound Recorder icon embedded in Cardfile.

NOTE Many applications can function either as a client or a server in OLE. A partial list of these applications includes Microsoft Word, Works, Excel, PowerPoint, Microsoft Mail, Project, Visual Basic,

the Sound Recorder, Gold Disk's AddImpact!,
Draw, Lotus 1-2-3 for Windows, Lotus Notes,
cc:Mail, and CorelDRAW!.

Using OLE with Sound Files

The capability to embed a sound file into a compound document along with text or numerical data is particularly useful in business. Compared to other media clips, sound files are easy to create, and OLE makes it simple to present your ideas more effectively.

In addition to recording your own, special sound effects can be obtained from sound libraries or downloaded from public-access bulletin boards, such as CompuServe and Prodigy. Since the release of Windows 3.1, the number of uploads and downloads of sound files to and from bulletin-board systems has exploded.

WARNING   Any file you download may be in violation of copyright-protection laws—especially sound clips obtained from albums, TV, or movies. If you add to a document a clip of Clint Eastwood saying "Go ahead, make my day," for example, and then distribute the document to a large number of people, you could be held liable for copyright violation.

If you work in a large office that has many PCs, it may not be practical from a financial standpoint to equip each system with a sound board. It also may be undesirable for another reason: multiple users with multiple voice-annotated spreadsheets could cause a din. If you try to solve this noisy prob-lem by providing everyone with headphones, new types of difficulties may occur.

Simpact Associates tries to address this potentially noisy issue with their Remark! product. Remark! enables net-worked PC users to record, play, and manage voice informa-tion through their office telephone PBX. Remark! uses a LAN-based voice server equipped with a voice-processing board and Simpact's STS3000 sound software. A PC attached to the voice server does not need a sound board, microphone, or speakers.

PC users who want to hear sounds that are not part of Remark!, such as CD Audio or MIDI files, still need sound boards for their PCs.

To add voice annotation to a compound document with Remark!, the user positions the cursor in the document in which the voice information should be stored. After the user selects the Insert Object option from the Windows applica-tion menu and double-clicks on the Remark! button, the Remark! window displays. The window enables the user to record, play, pause, restart, fast-forward, rewind, or stop the voice file. When the record button is selected, the STS3000 software instructs the voice server to ring the telephone on the user's desk. The user can then record a message into the phone and send the resulting compound document over the network. Anyone who clicks on a voice icon representing a message can listen to the message from the phone.

NOTE

Although the Remark! product has a number of advantages, it does not meet the needs of all cor-porate users with an interest in multimedia. Re-mark! requires a PBX and costs anywhere from $5,500 to $20,000 depending on the number of users. Aside from the cost, voice-annotation files can be very large—disk space may rapidly become a problem.

A product developed along the same idea as Remark! is SoundXchange from InterActive (see fig. 2.7). Instead of using a microphone and speakers, SoundXchange uses a handset resembling a speaker-phone (which is not connected to your company's internal phone system). If you already have a sound board, the SoundXchange Model A connects to the board with standard 1/8" mini plugs, which are included. SoundXchange Model A retails for $149.00. If you do not have a sound board installed, SoundXchange Model B incorporates a sound board that uses the PC's parallel port with the supplied smart parallel cable allowing a printer to share the port. The Model B retails for $289.00.

Figure 2.7:
InterActive's SoundXchange.

Another product created to meet the sound needs of a niche market is Monologue from First Byte, Inc. This product turns text files into speech in Windows applications. Monologue uses a rule-based approach to sound out the words you type. Although users can improve pronunciations by building their own sound dictionaries, the end result is still a computer-like voice.

To use Monologue with text, the user copies the text to the Windows Clipboard and clicks on the Monologue icon to hear the text "spoken" out loud. With Excel, the user highlights the columns and rows and then clicks on the Monologue icon to hear the figures. Although Monologue does not use OLE or WAV files, it is useful for anyone who wants auditory feedback of text or numbers. At $149, it is an inexpensive verbal "proofreader."

Using OLE with Video Files

Another type of media you can work with is video. *Video clips* are short, digitized, compressed video segments that you can view on-screen. Although Chapter 9 explains more about how to manage video clip development and editing, this section gives a brief overview of some of the ways you can use OLE and Video for Windows to bring excitement to your compound documents. You can use video to add impact to the documents, spreadsheets, and electronic mail you create with OLE client applications (see fig. 2.8).

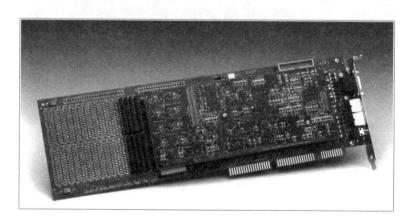

Figure 2.8:
Intel's RT (real-time) Video Developer's Kit, for Video For Windows.

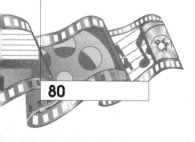

Video for Windows, described in Chapter 1 is a Microsoft technology enabling users to add video clips in their multimedia efforts. These clips are created by using Microsoft's Video for Windows tools. These tools enable you to capture a video image from an external source (such as a VCR), digitize and compress the data, and synchronize a sound track to the resulting "movie." For video capture, Video for Windows requires additional hardware (Creative Labs' Video Blaster or a Targa TrueVision board), but the resulting clips can be played back on any MPC. Although the image quality may be disappointing to anyone expecting full-motion video, these movies can be combined with other PC data to train, clarify, and present ideas to customers or employees.

In addition to clips created specifically for VFW, you can take advantage of the many movies created for the Mac with Apple's QuickTime technology. QuickTime, which preceded VFW, is a similar software-only decompression technology that plays movies with synchronized sound in a small window on your PC screen (see fig. 2.9). Windows users either can convert QuickTime movies to the .AVI file format required by VFW, or use the QuickTime for Windows runtime player available from Apple. Because QuickTime movies have been available for over a year, you can download them from bulletin boards, or purchase QuickTime movies in clip libraries.

With the release of Video for Windows, Microsoft makes it easy for a developer to capture, compress, and edit video clips that can be played back on a variety of machines. The capability to digitize and compress video requires a video capture board, discussed in the Chapter 3.

NOTE

Conversion of QuickTime movies to Video for Windows movies can be accomplished with a utility supplied with the Microsoft Multimedia Development Kit (MDK).

Figure 2.9:

Apple's QuickTime for Windows Player, with two QuickTime clips.

NOTE

Video for Windows will eventually become a part of the Windows operating environment—much as the sound drivers are today. Right now you can obtain the VFW drivers from OEMs selling video boards, and from Multimedia title developers who incorporate VFW into their applications. Quick-Time for Windows, on the other hand, requires runtime software to play back the QFW clips.

After you have a video clip, incorporating it into a compound document is as simple as incorporating a sound file. With OLE, you can embed or link any video clip by using the Media Player as an OLE server application. The Media Player contains several options that affect how the clip looks and behaves when played back from within a client document. The options—listed under the Edit menu—include auto rewind, auto repeat, adding a caption to the video window, putting a border around the video window, showing a control bar on playback and dithering the image for playback on a 16 color VGA monitor.

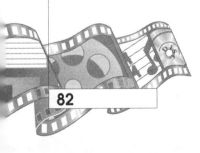

Because producing a quality video clip can be time consuming and the resulting file can be as large as 5M or more, you probably will not want to use video in everyday memos and business correspondence. Video clips should be used in documents in which you need to make a great impact, such as a sales presentation or an electronic annual report. Video clips make the biggest impression when used selectively. A compound document that incorporates too much video may resemble a corporate video tape.

Using OLE with Animation Files

You can use Windows' OLE capabilities to link or embed animations as long as the animation player functions as an OLE server application. A good example of this type of animation package is AddImpact! from Gold Disk, the maker of Animation Works InterActive.

AddImpact! is one of a growing trend of products designed to function not as a stand-alone application, but expressly as an OLE server. The animation package enables you to incorporate animation and sound in any document created by an OLE client application. You can include an animated man, for example, who runs across a spreadsheet when you click on the AddImpact! icon. You can combine this animation with a voice message embedded in a specific cell and send the file over the network to your manager or distribute it on a disk to your sales staff. Figure 2.10 is an example of an animated object created with AddImpact!.

Because they require less disk space, animations are a good alternative to video clips if you do not need a sound track synchronized to moving images.

Figure 2.10:
Using AddImpact!, the money bag seems to fly across the screen.

AddImpact! enables users to create and edit their own animations. In addition, over 100 clip animations have been included with the product. With AddImpact!, you can create and use multimedia in the corporate setting without the need for a CD-ROM drive because the server application and clip files are installed on a user's hard drive. The sound and animations that can be embedded have small file sizes; a one-minute animated sequence without sound may require as little as 20K of hard-disk space.

The Future of OLE: OLE 2.0

The current version of OLE, version 1.0, is a great way to create compound documents without special tools or programming skills. The next release of OLE (version 2.0) promises to be even more powerful. Microsoft has distributed beta copies of OLE 2.0 to developers; OLE 2.0 is scheduled to be released by second quarter 1993. Shortly after its release, expect to see the release of applications designed to be OLE 2.0-aware. Expect also to see OLE 2.0 featured in a Microsoft update to Windows 3.1. This update, which is being designed specifically for 80386 and higher CPUs, is code-named "Chicago" and expected to be released in the second half of 1993.

OLE 2.0 is designed to bring object-oriented features into Windows. Version 2.0 will incorporate many new APIs (application programming interfaces) and will feature improved inter-process communications, making data exchange more efficient than in OLE 1.0. OLE 2.0 will incorporate more drag-and-drop capabilities.

For users, the most evident feature of the OLE upgrade will be In-Place Activation. With OLE 1.0, you must either exit your current application or launch a new application to edit a linked or embedded object. In-Place Activation will enable you to edit the object without leaving your original application. The tool bar and main menu of the original application will change and be replaced by the tool bar and main menu of the server application, enabling you to edit the object. For example, when you want to edit an Excel spreadsheet embedded within a Word document, the Word application will remain open, but you will see the tool bar and main menu of Excel (see fig. 2.11).

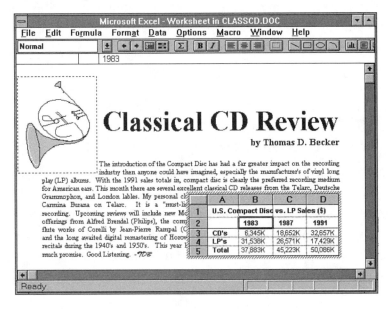

Figure 2.11:

An example of In-Place Activation in OLE 2.0.

OLE 2.0 will feature property inheritance. For example, if you embed a spreadsheet into a document, OLE 2.0 will enable you to export the properties (such as fonts and formatting) from the container document to the spreadsheet. OLE 2.0 will support nested objects—that is, you can embed a graph in a spreadsheet, then embed the spreadsheet in a document. OLE 2.0 also will provide developers with better cross-platform compatibility, as OLE 2.0 can be used with Windows 3.1, Windows NT, and the Apple Macintosh operating system.

OLE 2.0 will be included with the update to Windows 3.1. Code-named "Chicago," the update is expected to be released in the second half of 1993.

Applying Multimedia to Your Work

The earlier part of this chapter focused on the multimedia capabilities provided with Windows 3.1 and how to use OLE for easy integration of media into applications. The remainder of this chapter focuses on how you can effectively use multimedia in the corporate environment. In addition to discussing how you can use multimedia, applications that have already incorporated multimedia are examined so that you can see how they can help you work more effectively. If you have an interest in using multimedia authoring tools, the remainder of this chapter discusses business applications that can benefit from the addition of media clips. The next chapter describes specific authoring tools that can meet your development requirements.

The ways in which information is disseminated must change to accommodate our rapidly changing world. Today's office is drowning in paper. More efficient use of electronic mail and compound documents will help reduce paper. They also will help employees to prioritize and structure all the information that must be sifted through during the course of an average day.

NOTE Increased use of electronic mail and compound documents will help make employees more efficient by enabling them to prioritize, search through, and restructure information, and by reducing the amount of paper an employee must go through to get at pertinent data.

The technology needed to change the way we manage information is here. The use of OLE to substitute graphic, animation, audio, and video clips for text helps to streamline documents and make them more informative and engaging for the end user. Computers provide the capability to search through files for specific sections or terms, which reduces search time. Windows provides the capability to cut-and-paste text, reducing the amount of time it takes to draft new documents. "Electronic Post-it notes" in the form of text and voice annotation make it easier to respond to the ideas of another person. Better document-version control makes it easier for a group of people to co-author a document.

Like any new technology, multimedia document creation and dissemination will take some getting used to before it achieves widespread acceptance and integration into the corporate environment. The next few sections examine how to use multimedia with documents, spreadsheets, on-line help systems, and presentations. The sections demonstrate how you can use multimedia and describe multimedia-enhanced software packages.

Using Multimedia with Documents

By using OLE, the major word processing packages available today are multimedia capable. As you experiment with and distribute compound documents over networks, you will begin to think of new uses for a variety of electronic media.

Imagine that you have been on vacation for a week. When you get back to the office, your In-box is overflowing, and your chair is buried under a mound of paper. Your assistant welcomes you back, then informs you that you have a critical meeting scheduled for this afternoon.

The information you need to prepare for the meeting is buried somewhere in the stacks. You spend the remainder of the morning (and all of your lunch hour) trying to locate the document and assimilate its information in time for the meeting. Twenty minutes before you have to leave for the conference room, you find the document (stuck between the pages of *PC Magazine*). You have time to scan the contents, but do not feel fully prepared as you run down the hall. Any serenity you had from going on vacation is completely lost.

Contrast this scenario with how different things could have been if you worked for a company that used compound documents sent over the LAN. You would have gotten into the office Monday morning and seen that your in-box contained a few trade periodicals and some junk mail. After turning on your PC and logging in to the network, you would have seen that you had over 150 messages waiting. Normally, this would have been daunting, but you sort the messages so that you see those from your boss, your assistant, and any marked "Priority 1" first. A message from your assistant informs you of the afternoon meeting. You confirm it by looking at your office workgroup calendar.

To prepare for your meeting, you search through the email list for any messages that have files attached. You locate the report you need and begin to read through it. The report contains information about your company's quarterly results; a number of spreadsheets have been embedded into the document. A couple of voice annotations from your boss also are included asking you to chart the information for the afternoon meeting. Using OLE, you click on the spreadsheets to bring up Excel. It takes you only a couple of minutes to chart the data and embed these into the document as well. You record a wave file, telling your boss that you have completed the work and send the document to him, attached to a message marked "Priority 1." Satisfied that you are well

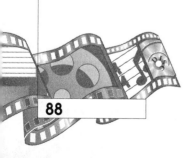

prepared for the meeting, you have time to read *PC Magazine* during lunch.

OLE is the simplest way to create a compound document, but you may need to create more elaborate documents incorporating hypertext for on-line manuals or computer-based training. A well-designed interface is critical to the success of a hypertext (or hypermedia) document to ensure that your user can find the information he or she needs without getting lost. One way to study ideas for the design of hypermedia documents is to investigate interactive on-line help systems with sound, video, or animation. These systems are bundled with many word processing packages. They are fun to use, but also show how training may be conducted in the future.

The first example of a multimedia business-productivity application was Microsoft Works for Windows (see fig. 2.12). This package incorporates a word processor, spreadsheet, database, drawing tool, and communications package. The on-line tutorial and reference sections of the help system use digital sound, animation, and high-quality graphics to make learning the software easy and fun. The Works multimedia help system is a good example of a hypertext document. You can design similar hypermedia documents by using the Microsoft Viewer product (discussed as an authoring tool in Chapter 7 "Planning Your Multimedia Project").

NOTE

Examine on-line hypermedia help systems to learn how a hypertext document is designed. More information on multimedia design and structure can be found in Chapter 8, "Avoiding Muddymedia."

Figure 2.12:

The opening animated sequence for the Microsoft Works product.

Microsoft Bookshelf is updated annually, to ensure that the books are kept as current and accurate as possible.

Word for Windows, Multimedia Edition, includes a help system that resembles Works for Windows. It incorporates the 1992 edition of Microsoft Bookshelf. Bookshelf is a series of reference works that includes multimedia versions of *The American Heritage Dictionary and Electronic Thesaurus, Bartlett's Familiar Quotations, The Concise Columbia Encyclopedia, Hammond Intermediate World Atlas*, and *The World Almanac and Book of Facts*.

The Bookshelf product, accessible from the Word ToolBar, turns Word for Windows, Multimedia Edition into a complete writing and reference application (see fig. 2.13). By combining this version of Word with the power offered by many different OLE servers, you are limited only by your imagination.

Storing and retrieving documents in digital format instead of printed paper can help you manage information more efficiently, no matter where you are. PaperWorks, from Xerox Corporation, enables you to retrieve information stored as a document on your PC from any Fax machine.

Bookshelf icon

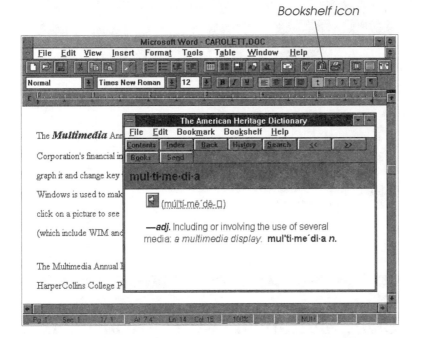

Figure 2.13:
Word for Windows, Multimedia Edition provides access to the Bookshelf reference materials.

TIP

One product that is using multimedia capabilities to redefine the purpose of documents is Paper-Works by Xerox Corporation. With this software and a fax board in your computer, you can perform the following functions from any fax machine: fax documents already stored on your PC to a single person or many people; fax documents to your computer for storage; obtain a list of all fax mail sent to your PC and retrieve any or all of it; have documents stored on your PC delivered to the fax machine; get new PaperWorks forms from the PC; and delete documents on the PC to free up space (see fig. 2.14).

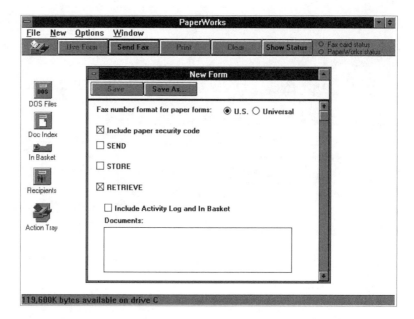

Figure 2.14:

PaperWorks, from Xerox, enables fax machines to communicate with your desktop PC.

Using Multimedia with Spreadsheets

Spreadsheets also benefit greatly from multimedia capabilities. You already are accustomed to the impact added to spreadsheets by good graphing capabilities (see fig. 2.15). Sound annotation will become the next important feature of spreadsheets—especially as businesses move into enterprise-wide computing. In *enterprise-wide computing*, many different people contribute data that is rolled into a single compound workgroup spreadsheet. The capability to click on a cell and see text or hear a voice explaining what that number means becomes critical in understanding the information.

Lotus designed their Notes product based on the idea of workgroups sharing common access to data, with the capability to update dynamically data stored in different locations on a network. Microsoft is moving in the same direction, with the announcement of their peer-to-peer networking product, Windows for Workgroups. As workgroup computing increases in importance in the corporation, so will the capabil-

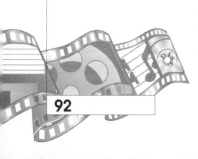

ity to explain the meaning of the contents of a spreadsheet. Although the capability to chart the information helps, it does not explain to another person why the numbers have changed from the previous month, or what a particular bar on a graph means within a larger corporate context. Voice annotation is a good way to explain data, without crowding a spreadsheet with written annotations.

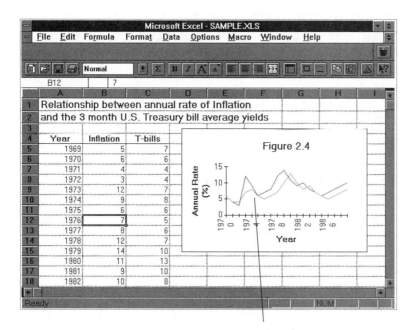

Embedded graphic

Figure 2.15:

An Excel spreadsheet with an embedded graph.

Windows database packages (such as Borland's Paradox for Windows or Microsoft's Access) can be annotated like spreadsheets. Specialized databases designed to manage media clips will become prevalent as users begin collecting large clip libraries.

Video and Animation are other good ways to annotate a spreadsheet or database report. Video clips showing how a product is manufactured are good additions to help someone understand a spreadsheet with manufacturing cost informa-

93

tion. Animation is effective in drawing the user's attention to specific cells on a spreadsheet. When the user clicks on the animation icon, the animation plays within the spreadsheet program. AddImpact! has a number of animations that relate well to numerical data including an adding machine, a cash register, dollar bills, and a flying money bag.

The only Spreadsheet program that specifically incorporates multimedia elements is Lotus 1-2-3 for Windows, featuring SmartHelp. The on-line help system incorporates multimedia movies to tutor spreadsheet users.

Using Multimedia Help

In the future, many more software vendors will offer multimedia help systems with their software packages. If you are responsible for in-house software development and you create Windows applications for the rest of your company, you may want to consider a multimedia on-line help system as a means of getting your feet wet in multimedia software development.

Lotus 1-2-3 for Windows with Multimedia SmartHelp is a good example of how media can be used to enhance on-line help systems and can serve as a model for your multimedia design efforts.

An impressive example of a multimedia on-line Help system is Lotus 1-2-3 for Windows' Multimedia SmartHelp. The help system was created jointly by Lotus and the HyperMedia Group (a small firm located in Silicon Valley that specializes in multimedia development). The help system incorporates a hypertext engine based in part on the Lotus SmarText product.

Multimedia SmartHelp features an animated and narrated guided tour and entertaining "show me" movies that interactively educate users on how to use 1-2-3 (see fig. 2.16). It also provides on-line books with full documentation and help.

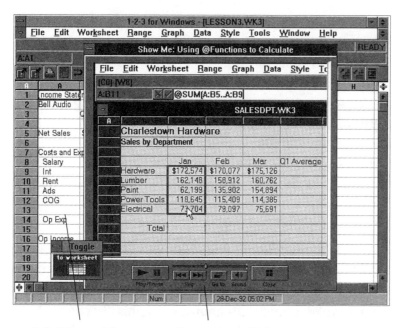

1-2-3 Spreadsheet   Lotus SmartHelp

Figure 2.16:
A SmartHelp movie for Lotus 1-2-3 users showing how to use @Functions to Calculate.

NOTE

Although all multimedia help systems are fun, informative, and entertaining, SmartHelp stands out because of its high-quality animation and interactive linking of help to specific spreadsheet functions. SmartHelp provides on-demand and just-in-time training. You can request help for a function whenever you need it, and stop the help movie as soon as you have the information you need.

Using Multimedia for Corporate Training (Arthur Andersen Case Study)

One of the most beneficial ways to integrate multimedia into your company is to replace your current training methods with computer-based training incorporating a variety of media elements. One company that has tried this with spectacular results is Arthur Andersen & Co, one of the world's leading providers of professional services. Andersen's Center for Professional Education provides training and performance improvement strategies for all of Andersen's approximately 60,000 personnel, which amounts to more than 6.5 million hours of student training per year. This training costs Andersen more than $340 million each year; the company reinvests six to eight percent of annual revenues in employee training.

Jeff Howell, Director of Technology Services for the Professional Education Division is responsible for supervising the design and development of computer-based training and interactive multimedia programs. Under his direction, Andersen has completed 11 interactive multimedia training courses, and has plans to develop another 14 or 15. These courses vary in length from four to 40 hours and focus on student self-paced instruction.

The Arthur Andersen Business Practices Course is an entry-level course used for all new hires in Andersen's consulting division. More than 3,000 people a year take the course. Other Andersen computer-based courses include the A+ Tax 1040 Software Course, the Network Solutions Course, and the Model-based Design Simulation.

Andersen Interactive multimedia courses feature video, audio, and software simulation in addition to hypertext. The courses are activity driven with no traditional tests. When a student has completed the activities for all course modules, they have learned the required material.

The Andersen courses all run under Windows (except the A+ 1040 Course which is being upgraded to Windows) and are taken by students at individual PC workstations equipped

with IBM Action Media II boards (for full motion video) and CD-ROM drives. Andersen opted to use video decompression boards because they felt the quality provided by software-only solutions (like Video for Windows) was not of a high enough quality to meet their training needs. In the future, Andersen hopes to provide interactive multimedia courses on laptops so that they can offer on-demand and just-in-time training. They envision a future when students will be able to download course updates from a network.

The Andersen courses have been developed using Macromedia's AuthorWare, Microsoft's Windows Help System, and Asymetrix's ToolBook. Andersen software developers also wrote a number of device drivers and DLLs (Dynamic Link Libraries) in C to expand the functionality of the authoring tools.

Before Andersen implemented computer-based training, they required trainees to come to the Center for Professional Education for a week to take the Business Practices Course. Andersen Managers and Partners provided course instruction. Arthur Andersen Instructional Designers developed all course materials. As escalating numbers of students took the course, the cost of providing the training increased dramatically in terms of travel costs and printed material (not to mention a week's lost productivity for the students and the instructors).

When deciding to convert the Business Practices Course to computer-based training, Jeff built a business case for the conversion that examined the costs for traditional course delivery versus the technology costs over the five year life cycle of the course (Andersen courses are updated every five years, on average). Based on his calculations, conversion of the Business Practices course will result in a ten to one return on investment. Andersen expects a $30 million savings over the life of the course. Not only will Andersen get a high ROI,

For more information on authoring tools like Author-Ware or ToolBook see Chapter 4, "Using Multimedia in the Corporate Environment."

In converting the Business Practices Course to Computer-based training, Jeff Howell will save Arthur Andersen over $30 million. Students taking the interactive multimedia course achieve a forty percent reduction in training time and remember more of the course material.

their research shows that students are better trained and remember more with computer-based instruction. The computer-based training has resulted in a forty percent reduction of training time (measured by the time it takes the average student to complete the course).

Integrating Multimedia and Corporate Communications

Large corporations traditionally have had in-house graphics or "corporate communications" departments develop their brochures, presentation materials, direct-mail materials, and newsletters. One of the first places multimedia made a big impact was in these departments.

As high-level media editing tools were adopted, software vendors began producing "lite" versions of these tools targeted towards the business end user who has minimal graphic skills. The idea behind these products is that middle-level managers, using clip media and presentation templates, can produce their own multimedia presentations without the help of a graphic arts department (see fig. 2.17). The popularity of these packages indicates the impact of business presentations is becoming more competitive. Employees try to outdo each other by using many "bells and whistles" to dazzle their audience.

The criticism voiced against business presentation packages is that the message is often lost behind all the media. This is not a fair criticism. Better presentation tools help grab the attention of an audience used to MTV and bombarded with thousands of advertisements daily.

The tools themselves are not responsible for empty presentations. The problem may be that no message was there to

Presentation software packages like Microsoft PowerPoint or MacroMedia's Action! enable you to create professional looking presentations, but do not require that you become a graphic artist. You type in the text for your presentation; the software formats the text, adds bullets, and enables you to import clip media.

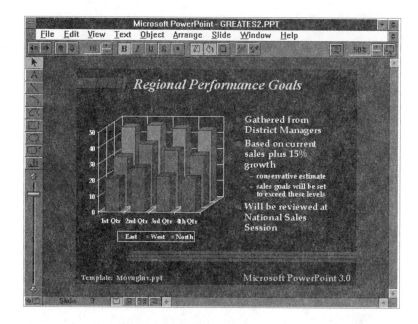

Figure 2.17:

A Microsoft PowerPoint slide, designed with a template.

begin with. Managers may spend too much time creating the "show" and not enough time developing the content of the message.

NOTE

When using multimedia techniques in a presentation, it is important to remember that less media can make the impact more effective and that information is still the most important part of a presentation.

Creating Effective Multimedia Presentations

If you have to give a presentation in front of a large group of people, and it is important to your career that things go well, you may want to consider a multimedia presentation. You can blow away the competition with a couple of well-placed sound files, animations, or video clips. The presentation tool you choose is as important as a number of other factors discussed in this section.

First, ask yourself these key questions:

➤ What type of PC will you use to play back the presentation?

➤ Is the PC you will be showing the presentation on different from the PC you used to create the presentation?

➤ What projection system will you be using?

➤ How large is the audience?

TIP

When you are shopping for the multimedia software you want to use, the most important factor to consider is the stability of the software. Make sure that the presentation software will not crash or fail while you give your speech. No other single feature matters as much.

Something always goes wrong with a multimedia presentation. This is not one of Murphy's laws—it is a fact. Multimedia is complicated enough on a stand-alone PC designed to run the multimedia software. The addition of other factors (large speakers, microphones, and unfamiliar computers) can be a nightmare when you already are nervous. If your microphone dies, you can always yell; if your software crashes, you are dead.

Aside from product stability (this is not the time to test beta products), determine how many multimedia elements you want to include (sound, animation, or video) and how interactive you want the presentation to be. Do you want a slide show, or do you need buttons so that you can jump around the presentation? How technically sophisticated are you? Unless you are accustomed to multimedia development, ease of use should be a big factor in the selection of the authoring tool.

TIP
If you are not a qualified graphic artist, consider buying a product that has a lot of templates and clip media. Many people make the mistake of thinking they know what looks good—do not be one of them.

TIP
Try to curb your desire to throw every available element on the first screen. To avoid this temptation, use a good template for the entire presentation.

Many good multimedia packages are out there; they are reviewed on a regular basis in computer trade periodicals such as *PC Magazine* or *InfoWorld*. Do a little research on the product you intend to use.

TIP
A good general package for presentations is Animation Works InterActive by Gold Disk (see fig. 2.18). It makes animation easy by enabling you to drag an animated image (called an *actor*) along a path. It offers the capability to create text and titles, edit actors and backgrounds, create visual effects such as wipes and fades, include sounds, and create buttons for interactive presentations.

This product also comes with a runtime movie player.

Animation Works InterActive is easy to use, but you pay the price in terms of performance. Sometimes the animations tend to be slow. On the positive side, the actors you create with this product can be used in the AddImpact! product mentioned earlier in the chapter.

Figure 2.18:

Animation Works Interactive enables you to create high-impact multimedia presentations easily.

Preparing for Off-Site Presentations

When you give a presentation away from your home office, you may be forced to use a PC leased for the occasion. MPCs still are relatively new. For this reason, check (and double-check) to ensure that the computer you will be using has the peripherals you need for the presentation. In addition, examine these items:

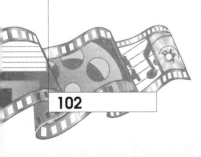

➤ If you are demonstrating software running off a CD-ROM, make sure the CD-ROM drive meets the minimum MPC specifications for speed and make sure the PC has a copy of Microsoft MSCDEX Version 2.2 or later installed

➤ Make sure that the PC is running Windows 3.1

➤ Make sure the multimedia drivers for the sound board and CD audio have been installed by using the Control Panel (read Chapter 3 if you need help setting up the hardware.)

If you plan to use a portable PC, keep in mind these suggestions:

➤ Make sure the portable has a sound board installed or portable audio device attached.

➤ Make sure enough room is on the hard drive for the presentation files to load.

➤ If you use a portable audio device, test it a few times.

➤ Make sure the PC speakers you use are adequate for the size of your audience.

➤ Test the sound board with the amplifier provided in the presentation room.

TIP

Media Vision makes a portable audio device that can be plugged into a parallel port.

Find out the speed of the PC you will be using. Nothing is more embarrassing than developing a presentation on a zippy 486, including lots of animation and video, and then watching it crawl on the 386SX you have to use on the big day.

The best way to ensure that off-site presentations go smoothly is to use your own laptop computer with the addition of a portable sound adapter. By using your own laptop, you can be sure that you have the video adapter, audio capabilities, and hard disk space needed to make your presentation go smoothly.

Determine whether your presentation looks good projected against a large background (avoid detailed graphics).

What type of monitor does the PC use? If you create a presentation with 256-color graphics, you need a SuperVGA graphics adapter. A standard VGA adapter will not work because it displays only 16 colors. In addition, make sure you test the PC using the projection device for the screen.

Finally, determine the pointing device you will use (and the type of microphone). Make sure you can use the mouse easily while giving your speech so that your cables do not get tangled.

TIP

When you must give a speech that uses a mouse to move from slide to slide, consider having someone else "mouse" for you while you stand up and talk. That way, you can focus on the important points in your presentation.

Creating Electronic Corporate Information

One area in which you will see an increase in multimedia development is the delivery of internal and external corporate reports. As more companies connect through networks, it becomes cheaper to produce documents electronically instead of printing them on paper.

This section focuses on two potential applications: the company newsletter and the electronic annual report. Each is a good multimedia application, but for different reasons.

Multimedia Corporate Newsletters

Large corporations publish corporate newsletters to keep their employees in touch with what is going on and to foster a sense of belonging to a group. Much time and effort is taken to make these documents look attractive, and a great deal of money is spent on production and distribution. These newsletters, however, are not revenue generators because they do not include advertising. Despite all the effort that goes into producing and distributing them, corporate newsletters are not always read (they tend to be lost in overloaded IN baskets) and usually are not saved.

If these newsletters are circulated as compound multimedia documents, money can be saved in printing and distribution. Multimedia documents also might have greater readership if they employ animation, video, and sound to make them more interesting.

Such "newsdocs" can be updated easily. Users do not need to save the newsletter on a hard drive; old editions can be saved on a file server. A number of companies have started experimenting with distributing company news in this way. Expect to see the trend grow as more organizations expand to include a networked PC on everyone's desk.

Multimedia Annual Reports

You read in earlier sections how compound spreadsheets and text documents can be created for distribution over a network. Multimedia can be used in the creation of reports specifically designed for this type of distribution. Digital annual reports can include a number of interesting elements, including a video speech from the CEO, voice-annotated explanations of the financial data, or a custom spreadsheet for playing with the company's bottom line.

High-quality scanned images can be used to show pictures of the corporate officers, a sound track can accompany movement from section to section, and short animated clips can be used to show the company's plans for the coming year. In addition to being an informational tool for stockholders, the digital annual report can make a great advertising piece (see fig. 2.19).

Annual Report navigation buttons

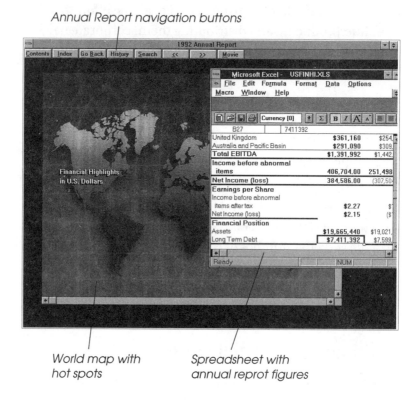

Figure 2.19:

A prototype for an Annual Report.

World map with hot spots

Spreadsheet with annual reprot figures

Given the file sizes of the media clips involved, a multimedia annual report created today would need to be distributed on CD-ROM. Because most people do not have access to a CD-ROM drive, widespread development of corporate reports in digital format has not yet occurred. This will change in the future as we start to have numerous means of accessing

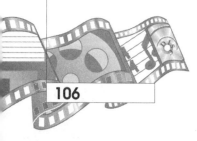

digital information. Soon we may view annual reports on handheld personal informational devices. There will be many different flavors of these units (personal digital assistants, portable CD players, and other portable devices) that will retrieve data in a variety of ways, such as by cellular communication, CD discs, or flashcards. These devices will make it easier for consumers to access digital information, prompting more companies to offer information in a multimedia format.

NOTE

Personal information devices can be found in the Epilogue, "The Future of Multimedia."

Electronic Information and Cross-Platform Compatibility

One of the most important parts of creating compound documents is the capability to retrieve and view them on a variety of platforms. Most wide-area networks comprise a mix of PCs, Macs, and workstations. To date, only ASCII text files can be viewed on all platforms. Other files lose the formatting or the fonts that made the document easy to read on a monitor. Interleaf and Adobe are working on products to address this problem. The Interleaf product is available today; the Adobe product is under development.

Working with Interleaf's WorldView

Interleaf Corporation, a developer of high-end publishing systems for mini and mainframe UNIX systems, is developing WorldView, a product that enables organizations to take text and graphics from any platform and view them on any other platform. The WorldView system has two components. WorldView Press reformats documents from a source format (a partial list includes PostScript, WordPerfect, Microsoft Word RTF, HPGL, PICT, and SGML), compresses the files, and adds hyperlinks and a full text index. The resulting documents can be viewed on a variety of platforms (PCs, Macs, workstations, and mainframes). By using Interleaf's WorldViewer tool, a user can view the document, attach electronic Post-it notes, use the hyperlinks and full-text search capabilities, and zoom in and print a copy of the document on a standard printer (see fig. 2.20).

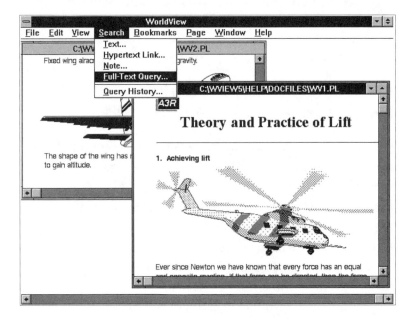

Figure 2.20:

An example of the WorldViewer Tool, from Interleaf.

Interleaf plans to support Adobe's Carousel (see the next section of this chapter) when it becomes available. The WorldViewer will be capable of viewing Carousel files; Interleaf 5 (the document-creation product) will be capable of outputting files in Carousel format.

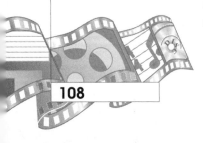

NOTE

Unlike Adobe's Carousel, which is not available yet, a number of companies are already using the WorldView product. These companies include Allen Bradley, Sprint International, the British Royal Navy, Saab Aircraft, and Lockheed Missiles & Space Company, Inc.

Interleaf provides prospective clients with some interesting statistics, gathered from Xerox Corporation, AIIM Studies, and the Gartner Group. Here are some facts to consider if you still want to stay with a paper-based distribution of information:

➤ 92 billion original paper documents are produced each year.

➤ Active files grow at a compound annual growth rate of 25 percent in major corporations; corporate files double every 3.5 years.

➤ In the United States, the average business document is copied 19 times during its life.

➤ The cost of floor space has gone up 300 percent in the last decade.

➤ Three percent of documents are misfiled; on the average it costs $200 to recover each file.

Adobe's Carousel

Adobe, developers of the PostScript language, have created a new document technology code-named "Carousel." The word "PostScript" currently describes the layout and font descriptions of any PostScript-formatted page that can be printed on a PostScript printer. Adobe is expanding on the

PostScript language to create what they hope is the first step towards portable documents (bringing us one step closer to a paperless office). By creating specialized printer drivers for each environment, they capture the PostScript-formatted output from an application and convert it to a single uniform document-interchange format.

A series of document viewers and printing utilities using this document-interchange format can be written for each platform. In essence, you can take a document written in this common format and read it on any machine that has the necessary document viewer and printer.

Carousel is more powerful than the printed page. The document viewers enable you to attach electronic notes to any page, search for specific words or phrases, and create active links between an outline and different parts of the document.

To ensure readability, Carousel incorporates Adobe's Multiple Master font technology. This technology is much like Windows 3.1 TrueType font formatting—fonts are created on the fly to retain the look of the original document. Carousel documents retain graphics and color in addition to fonts and formatting.

A number of publishers have pledged support to Adobe's Carousel. If this technology is adopted on a wide-scale basis, books and periodicals currently available in a paper-based form may be delivered electronically. With the additional functionality offered by a computer, people may prefer to receive documents on-line because they are easier to use. Corporations can benefit the most from the reduction in overhead costs associated with paper-based distribution of information.

In addition to the Carousel "viewable" PostScript, Adobe is working with DEC on an "editable" PostScript. Future plans

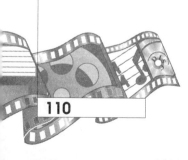

also include a product for fax machines, animated PostScript, and audio PostScript. Because PostScript is currently in use with over 5,000 applications, Adobe is in a key position to set a standard for a new cross-platform technology.

Using Multimedia To Enhance Windows

With the introduction of Windows 3.1, sales of sound boards took off. It did not have anything to do with increased productivity, reduction of paper flow, or the capability to share information across platforms. People started buying sound boards because it is fun to use sounds with Windows. You may want to begin to use multimedia because it is the future or because it can make your company more profitable. You will stay with multimedia computing because anything less seems boring after you get used to sound, animation, and video.

In a business environment, you have to temper fun with practicality (you do not want to be caught playing Battle Chess at your desk). Nevertheless, you can have fun with sound in a number of ways. One of the most enjoyable (and justifiable) software packages is Berkeley Systems' After Dark 2.0 for Windows. This collection of visually stunning screen savers keeps images from burning into your screen and provides password protection when you are away from your desk. The package comes with sound support, which means that you can hear bubbling fish with the Aquatic Rcalm screen saver (see fig. 2.21), or howling coyotes and thunder in the Creepy Night screen saver.

After Dark for Windows 2.0 makes multimedia enjoyable without being obtrusive.

Figure 2.21:

The Aquatic Realm screen saver from Berkeley Systems' After Dark collection.

Adding Sound to Windows Events

If you attach sounds to Windows events you can experience multimedia computing the moment you fire up Windows. The Sound icon in the Windows 3.1 Control Panel (see fig. 2.22) enables you to attach WAV files to the following system events: Windows Start, Windows Exit, Asterisk, Critical Stop, Default Beep, Exclamation, and Question.

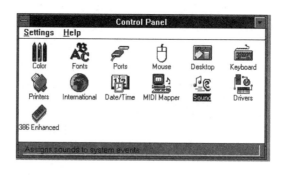

Figure 2.22:

The Sound Icon highlighted on the Windows 3.1 Control Panel.

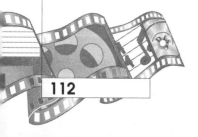

If you want to replace the default beep with a toilet flushing sound, for example, follow these simple steps:

1. Choose the Sound icon from the Control Panel window. The Sound dialog box opens.

2. Make sure that the Enable System Sounds checkbox is checked.

3. Assign the sound by highlighting the default beep in the Events list.

4. Select TOILET.WAV from the Files list in the Sound dialog box, by clicking on it once. This highlights the file name. (You also have the option to search for different sounds on any drive and directory in your system.)

5. Test the sound by clicking on the Test button.

6. Click on OK to finish.

You also have the option of turning off every sound by clearing the Enable System Sounds check box in the Sound dialog box. Figure 2.23 shows the Sounds dialog box.

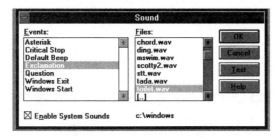

Figure 2.23:

Selecting a wave file to go with the Windows Exclamation system event.

NOTE

If your PC does not have a sound board installed and you clear the Enable System Sounds check box, you will turn off the standard Windows warning beep.

Applications are available that enable you to define sound events for applications, other Windows system events, and Message Box icons. One such program is Whoop It Up!, a shareware program published by Starlite Software. In addition to giving you more sound events, Whoop It Up! enables you to attach MIDI files to events.

Playing Redbook Audio Using the CD-ROM Drive

A nice benefit of owning an MPC is the capability to play a CD audio disc in the office. You can play regular CDs in the CD-ROM drive in addition to CD-ROM-based applications that use Redbook (CD audio quality) audio. Although the sound quality through the sound board (if you have a SCSI cable that connects the sound board to the CD drive) or directly through the drive may not be as good as your home stereo, it still is impressive. The quality of the PC speaker you attach to your system greatly affects the sound quality you can achieve with your MPC. A number of options are available on the market with prices ranging from under $25 to over $400.

Creating New Opportunities for the Windows User

Windows 3.1 incorporates multimedia elements to give you a richer computing environment. After you get used to sound, video, and animation, you will want to incorporate these media into applications you develop for your company. You will start thinking of new ways to present information and begin to prototype media-aware applications by using tools such as Microsoft Visual Basic 2.0 and Asymetrix Multimedia ToolBook. You will create databases that incorporate video and sound, develop on-line help systems that show animated explanations of procedures, and find yourself sending compound status reports to upper-level management.

The addition of different media elements is a simple task, thanks to Windows 3.1 capabilities such as OLE and the Media Control Interface (MCI). The MCI enables you to control media devices such as audio boards and video-disc players with high-level string commands. The addition of sound to a Visual Basic application, for example, can be as simple as adding a few lines of code. In Chapter 10, you see examples of code that show you how playing sound files can be accomplished. The rest is up to your imagination.

MCI is discussed in detail in Chapter 6.

Multimedia Computing...just hotwire a PC,

and you're ready to Rock-n-Roll.

3

Making Multimedia Work with Your Hardware

How do you use multimedia successfully? Successful use of multimedia requires the right combination of tools and talent. As you read in Chapter 1, multimedia capabilities can vary, based on the hardware tools available.

This chapter gives you an idea of what tools are available, when they are appropriate, and how to use them effectively. Do not be discouraged if you do not have the hardware described here. This chapter shows you how to make the most of what you do have and serves as a reference when the time comes to expand those capabilities.

Deciding on Multimedia Hardware

What is multimedia hardware? When asked this question most people say sound boards or CD-ROM drives. Multimedia hardware really refers to any hardware that solves a multimedia problem. Consider, for example, the CD-ROM drive. No magical quality makes the CD-ROM drive a "multimedia" peripheral. It simply solves a common multimedia problem: providing mass storage at a relatively low cost. The same can be said of any multimedia peripheral. It simply fulfills a particular multimedia need.

Now that you understand what multimedia hardware really is, think about the specific problems surrounding multimedia. What problems are unique to the multimedia developer? What problems does the multimedia user experience? It does not take long to see that these two groups may have very different needs. For practical purposes, these needs are divided into the following two categories: the developer's MPC and the user's MPC.

Understanding the Developer's MPC

The multimedia developer or author can have very demanding MPC hardware requirements. The computer user's MPC is meant for playing multimedia titles; the developer's MPC must be capable of creating or authoring multimedia titles, resulting in the need for a much more powerful computing environment. The basic developer's MPC should include a 33MHz 80386 processor, 8M RAM, and a 100M hard disk. From this starting point, goals for the multimedia title help you further refine your hardware requirements.

If you are (or will be) a multimedia developer, you first must determine your specific hardware needs. The following points may help you with these decisions:

➤ **End-User's Hardware.** You should be able to duplicate the minimum and maximum hardware requirements for the end user of your multimedia tool. This enables you to experience the application the same way the user will experience it. This is important; the user may not have your sophisticated, speedy hardware. If your product does not run well on the "least common denominator," it is not ready to be released.

➤ **Sound.** Are sound effects, music, or voice narration a part of your product? Do you need CD-quality sound in your application or will FM stereo-quality sound suffice? Sound can add to a multimedia project, but first you need to determine the type of sound you want to use. What will the playback capabilities of your end user's system be? The way in which you create sound also helps determine the hardware you need. Will you be using Redbook audio, waveform files or MIDI files?

➤ **Animation.** Animation is eye-catching, but can carry a heavy disk-space requirement. Do you want to add 2D animation, or will you require 3D rendering for the application? What types of animation software will you be using? What type of resolution will you require on the part of your end user's monitor?

➤ **Video.** Is live-motion video to be integrated in your project? From what source? Video can be digitally recorded, compressed, and played from a CD-ROM or hard drive, or queued from a video laser disc. What type of video compression will you use? How will your end user play back the video clips?

As a developer, you can safely assume a 386SX processor as the minimum hardware configuration for the end users of your application.

MIDI files are discussed in "Understanding MIDI Synthesizers," Redbook audio in "Looking at Compact-Disc Standard," and WAV files in Chapter 1 under "Waveform Audio."

The amount of storage your development system requires depends heavily on the amount of video you plan to incorporate into the application.

➤ **Interaction**. How is the user to interact with your multimedia application ? Will he or she use a desktop computer; a touch-screen; a remote control? The means by which users interact with the application influences the tools you need for development.

➤ **Storage.** During development of your multimedia project, you probably will require many times the final storage requirements of your project; you may need gigabytes of space! The working storage medium for developing the application differs from the distribution medium for the application and depends on your total storage requirements, budget, and patience. One key question to ask yourself is: how many media clips do I plan to include in the product?

These are the basic questions you must answer before beginning a multimedia project. As you consider the questions, you begin to see your specific needs. The developer's MPC requirements resemble the user's requirements (see fig. 3.1). The primary differences are speed and high-end capabilities in all areas. You can do a considerable amount of multimedia authoring on a basic MPC, but if multimedia authoring is your profession, you need more power and storage to get things done in a timely manner.

Another key difference between the developer's and the end user's system is the developer's need for tools to create various media clips. The user's MPC plays back multimedia titles; a multimedia developer or author requires special software and hardware tools to create the basic elements used in a multimedia title.

A developer may require video grabbers, scanners, MIDI instruments, and even CD-ROM mastering hardware.

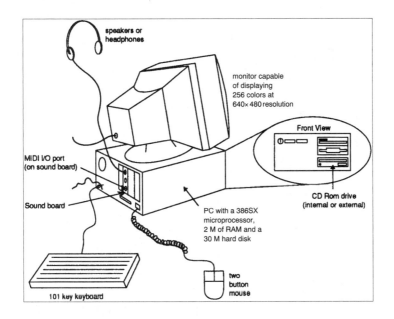

speakers or
headphones

monitor capable
of displaying
256 colors at
640×480 resolution

Front View

MIDI I/O port
(on sound board)

Sound board

CD Rom drive
(internal or external)

PC with a 386SX
microprocessor,
2 M of RAM and a
30 M hard disk

two
button
mouse

101 key keyboard

Figure 3.1:

The components
that make up an
MPC.

Understanding the User's MPC

The main difference between a user's MPC and a developer's
MPC is that the user's MPC focuses on playing multimedia
titles. As a result, the user's MPC requirements are determined by the applications (or multimedia titles) it uses.
Many multimedia peripherals (the sound board, for example)
may be the same for the developer and the user. Fortunately
for the end user, most multimedia titles support a full-range
of hardware—from the basic MPC standard to the high-end
MPCs for developers.

What are the basic components of the user's multimedia PC?
The Multimedia PC Marketing Council has defined the
minimum set of standards for a multimedia PC as follows:

PC with a 386SX microprocessor

2M of RAM

30M hard disk

Most PCs ca-
pable of running
Windows 3.1 can
be upgraded to
meet the MPC
specification with
the addition of a
sound board and
a CD-ROM drive
(as long as the PC
is equipped with a
SVGA monitor.)

VGA or VGA+ display

Two-button mouse

101-key keyboard

Serial port

Parallel port

MIDI I/O port

Joystick port

CD-ROM drive

Audio board with speakers or headphones

TIP

The MPC spec is a suggested minimum. If you are investing in a MPC, consider the Tandy Sensation, a 486SX, 25MHz MPC, which sells at a street price of about $1700.

Few multimedia titles actually require all the features listed in the requirements; some require more.

Fortunately, many of these MPC elements are commonly found in most 386-based and 486-based computers on the market today. Some exceptions are the audio board (which should include a MIDI synthesizer and port) and the CD-ROM drive. This situation is rapidly changing, however—Compaq and other computers now include built-in audio capabilities.

A number of PC manufacturers sell ready-to-run MPCs (look for the MPC logo, shown in fig. 3.2). If you already have a PC with a 386 (or better) processor, you can upgrade your system for MPC compatibility. A number of multimedia upgrade kits are available that usually consist of an MPC-compatible audio board and CD-ROM drive. Some kits even include speakers, headphones, and a microphone, enabling

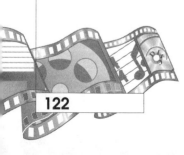

you to create a complete multimedia upgrade in a simple 30-minute operation.

Multimedia PC

Figure 3.2:
The MPC logo.

Whether you buy a ready-to-run MPC, purchase an upgrade kit, or upgrade the computer yourself using separate components, here are some key requirements to make an audio board and CD-ROM drive MPC-compatible:

➤ The audio board must feature a music synthesizer, on-board capabilities and compliance for providing digitized sound in eight-bit samples at an 11KHz input sampling rate, and eight-bit samples at both 11KHz and 22KHz output sampling rates.

TIP

Creative Labs (SoundBlaster 16, SoundBlaster Pro) and Media Vision (Pro Audio Spectrum 16, Pro Audio Spectrum Plus) make MPC-compatible sound boards. Another option to consider is the Microsoft Windows Sound System, which, although not MPC-compatible, comes bundled with voice-recognition software.

➤ The CD-ROM drive must have a transfer rate of at least 150K-per second, a maximum seek time of one second, and must use no more than 40 percent of the computer's CPU processing power.

You may want to purchase a CD-ROM XA drive because this probably will become the new standard.

NOTE

CD-ROM drive standards are changing so rapidly that it's easy to become confused. If you purchase a standard CD-ROM drive, make sure it has at least single session Kodak PhotoCD compatibility (although multisession is preferable.)

With so many component options available, the selection of the right hardware can be a challenge. As with PCs, quality and performance of components vary—look closely at what each component can do and determine what your budget allows.

Choosing an MPC Upgrade Kit

If you want to upgrade a PC so that it is multimedia-ready, you can choose from a number of MPC upgrade kits. These kits provide a CD-ROM drive and Waveform/MIDI audio capabilities. Only those kits carrying the MPC logo can promise complete MPC compatibility.

Many hardware manufacturers are now offering MPC upgrade kits. With prices starting at $750, these kits provide a CD-ROM drive, an audio board, and the necessary system software. Upgrade kits require that you install the audio board into one of your PC's expansion slots and install an internal or external CD-ROM drive (depending on the type of kit you purchase.)

NOTE

The Pro 16 Multimedia Upgrade Kit from Media Vision is a good multimedia upgrade. Although slightly more expensive, it comes with a cable that enables you to connect the CD-ROM drive to the

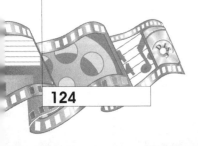

sound board. This cable enables both CD Audio and WAV or MIDI file sound to be played through the sound board. (You will only need to attach a single set of PC speakers to the system.)

NOTE
The conversion of a standard PC to an MPC occasionally is difficult, even with prepackaged MPC upgrade kits. A good way to determine whether all the multimedia components are working together is to purchase software that takes advantage of every feature. Although it does not contain waveform files, Microsoft's Multimedia Beethoven is a good test package to determine if your MIDI synthesizer and CD audio capabilities are working.

Quality can vary considerably from vendor to vendor. During your comparison of different upgrade kits, remember that the most important component is also the most expensive—the CD-ROM drive. Make sure the CD-ROM drive has a continuous transfer rate of 150K-per-second and provides audio output so that you can play standard audio CD's.

TIP
Most of the CD-ROM drives used in the MPC upgrade kits have a data transfer rate of 150K-per-second. Two manufacturers, Media Resources and NEC Technologies, offer the new double-speed drives, with a transfer rate of 300K-per-second.

The audio card included in an MPC upgrade kit must be capable of recording sounds from an input device, such as a microphone, and converting the sounds to digital format. The sound board also must be capable of transferring digital sounds (stored in the form of Waveform or MIDI files) back to analog (or audio) for output to speakers connected to the card.

Sound quality is determined by sampling rate and the size of the sampled file. At a minimum, your sound board should meet the MPC standards. This means that it needs to feature:

➤ A music synthesizer

➤ A MIDI I/O port

➤ On-board audio-mixing capabilities (or an external audio mixer)

Your board must be capable of recording digitized sound in eight-bit samples at an 11KHz input sampling rate and play back eight-bit samples at an output sampling rate of 11KHz or 22KHz.

Companies currently offering MPC Upgrade kits include CompuAdd, Creative Labs, Media Vision, NEC Technologies, Procom Technology, Tandy, and Turtle Beach, with more companies planning upgrade kits in the near future.

Building Your Own MPC

An MPC Upgrade kit is the easiest and fastest way to make your PC multimedia-ready. MPC upgrade kits also are the most efficient in terms of your computing resources. Many upgrade kits offer single-slot solutions for the audio board and CD-ROM drive.

What if you already have one (or more) components found in an MPC Upgrade Kit? The following sections describe what to look for in the separate components.

Purchasing a Sound Board

If you already have a CD-ROM drive that meets the MPC specifications, you may want to purchase a sound board to start using multimedia. Many companies produce sound boards at prices ranging from $149 to $995. Some companies to look for include: ATI Technologies, Creative Labs, Media Vision, Microsoft, ProMedia Technologies, Roland Corp., and Turtle Beach.

NOTE
InterActive's SoundXchange (see fig. 3.3) can be connected to the PC's parallel port and does not require an extra slot. Its telephone-like attachment is perfect for crowded office environments.

Figure 3.3:
SoundXchange.

The most important purchasing factor for a sound board is whether a driver is available for running the hardware under Windows. A *driver* is the software that enables Windows to recognize your peripheral device. Drivers must be installed through the Drivers applet in the Windows Control Panel.

Another factor to consider when shopping for a sound board is the number of available Direct Memory Access (DMA) channels on your PC. Most sound boards use these channels to transfer audio data between RAM and the computer's hard drive. Most boards can use a number of different channels, but you need to know which channels are currently being used by other devices. If necessary, you can share the sound board's channel with another device (network cards, tape backup drives, SCSI controllers, or PostScript controllers), but you cannot use the sound card and the secondary device at the same time.

You also have to set your PC's interrupt request level (IRQ) so that the sound card can send an interrupt when it needs computer resources. As with the DMA channel, you need to determine which IRQ is not being used by another device, and then set up your sound card to access the unused IRQ.

IRQs are set through DIP switches on the sound board, or through software that comes with the board's installation program (which differs from installing the board through the Windows Control Panel). More refined installation programs let you know which IRQs are available. If not, you need to determine this through trial-and-error (often by swapping boards in and out of the PC).

TIP

After you determine which DMAs and IRQs are in use, write this information down and keep it in a handy place. You will need it for your next installtion.

Finally, some sound boards enable you to use an SCSI cable to connect your CD-ROM drive directly to the sound board. With this connection, you can play CD audio directly from the speakers connected to your sound board; otherwise, you would have to attach a separate pair of speakers to the CD-ROM drive. After you install the CD-ROM drive (if it is internal), install the sound card, and then set the appropriate DMA channels and IRQs, you need to connect the small SCSI cable from the CD-ROM drive to a connector pin on the audio board (see fig. 3.4).

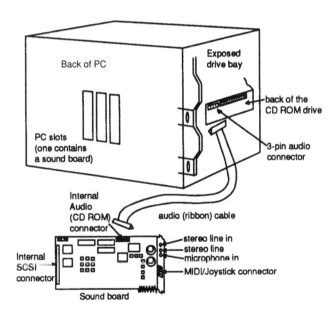

Figure 3.4:

How to connect the audio cable between a sound board and an internal CD-ROM drive.

Obtaining Speakers and A Microphone

In addition to a sound board, you need speakers or head-phones for listening to the sound files. If you choose speakers, you need an external power source (usually batteries or an adapter.) If you want to record your own sound files, you also need a microphone. Audio boards have an input jack for the microphone that you plug in the same way you would a tape recorder.

TIP

The microphone's quality can affect greatly the final sound quality of the file. For this reason, do not skimp on the microphone. Rather than purchase your microphone from a computer retail store, you should consider going to a store that specializes in audio equipment.

Using the PC Speaker

If you plan to play sounds on a regular basis, the use of your PC's speaker is not recommended.

You also can play sounds through your internal PC speaker, if you have access to the proper software driver (drivers are available through public bulletin boards). You may be able to load these drivers into Windows through the Control Panel, depending on how they are written.

Although sound files play through the internal PC speaker, you cannot access other PC devices, such as a keyboard. In addition, internal PC speakers do not have a standard sound quality (some sound OK, others do not), and they are unable to play MIDI files because they lack the internal MIDI synthesizer chip found on sound boards. Use the PC speaker as a test to see if listening to sound files is something you want to do with your PC. If you want the sound capability, make the investment in a sound board.

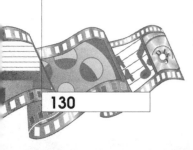

If you are a power user, or want to create professional quality sound files for integration into multimedia titles, you may want to investigate higher end sound boards and MIDI synthesizers. These give you much tighter control over the sound quality of your files, and enable you to perform professional-quality sampling and mixing.

TIP

One good sound board to consider is the MultiSound board from Turtle Beach. This $995 board can record and play stereo Waveform audio at CD audio quality (16-bit samples at 44.1KHz.) The board can accept an audio output jack from a CD-ROM drive and mix the CD audio sound with Waveform audio and MIDI sound sources. The Media Vision Pro Audio Spectrum 16 card also samples at 16-bit, 44.1 KHz at a price of $299.

What To Look for in a CD-ROM Drive

If your PC already has sound capability and SVGA, all you need to add is a CD-ROM drive. CD-ROM drives can be internal (requiring a spare drive bay) or external. If you purchase an external drive, make sure it has a SCSI interface. The SCSI interface is faster than a serial connection and enables you to daisy-chain other external SCSI devices.

Your primary consideration when purchasing a drive should be speed. Two factors affect the speed of the drive: transfer rate and access time. Most drives on the market transfer data at 150K-per-second (kbps). Some manufacturers have begun shipping "double speed" drives with a transfer rate of 300kbps. The double speed drives provide smoother playback of audio and video files, but are more expensive than the standard rate drives.

The access (or seek) time required by the MPC specification is under one second (1,000 milliseconds, or ms.) This is the average amount of time the drive should take in locating data on the disc. The MPC spec is slow; most drives on the market have an access time of approximately 380ms—the better drives clock in at 280ms.

In addition to compatibility with the MPC spec, you should consider compatibility with future standards, primarily PhotoCD and CD-ROM XA. A number of drives have single session PhotoCD compatibility—some have multisession compatibility. With a PhotoCD compatible drive, you can drop off a roll of 35mm film at a Kodak developer and get back the images recorded on a compact disc for about $20. With single session PhotoCD, you can only record on the CD once. With multisession, you can add new images until the disc is full (approximately 100 images.)

With the proper software, CD-ROM XA drives are capable of playing PhotoCD images.

CD-ROM Extended Architecture (CD-ROM XA) is an extension of the CD-ROM specification, and is expected to replace the CD-ROM as the future standard. On CD-ROM XA discs, the audio and text/image/video information is interleaved (or read and played simultaneously) in a single data stream, which provides much smoother playback and synchronization.

Although it should not be the most important factor in your decision, most CD-ROM drives are bundled with titles worth hundreds of dollars if purchased separately.

NOTE Some of the titles bundled with different drives include: *Nautilus Magazine, Compton's Encyclopedia, Microsoft Bookshelf,* and *National Geographic's Mammals.*

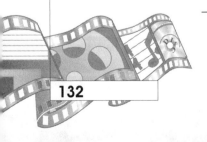

Examining Multimedia Hardware for Windows 3.1

The components defined in the Multimedia PC Marketing Council's minimum standard MPC configuration are not all the hardware you may need to work with multimedia. Additional hardware peripherals, such as CD-ROM drives and MIDI synthesizers, supplement multimedia title creation and playback. Each of the peripherals performs a special function. To understand the way each of these hardware peripherals can be used, you first must be familiar with the peripherals and their capabilities.

Many MPC peripherals work in concert with one another. The following sections give you an in-depth look at each component, what to look for, and what the component can do for you.

Understanding Compact Discs (CDs)

Audio CDs have been around since 1979. An audio CD can hold up to 76 minutes of stereo music sampled at 16 bits and 44.1KHz. Although audio CD players gained widespread acceptance among consumers, the compact disc (CD-ROM) was not introduced into the technical marketplace until 1984.

Multimedia computing efforts require sound and image files, which need a great deal of storage space. The MPC Marketing Council members realized this and decided some type of large storage device would be required if multimedia computing was to be successful. The compact disc was a strong contender because it can hold 650M of data. The standard CD-ROM drive supported by the MPC specification requires a sustained transfer rate of 150K-per-second. This transfer rate enables the user to access either sound or data from a single disc, but with a standard CD-ROM, both cannot be accessed at the same time. This is the reason a number of applications need to copy data files to the user's hard drive before the application can access the music from the CD-ROM drive.

CD-ROMs can provide from 650M to 5.8 gigabytes of data at your fingertips.

Compact discs are a great mass-storage device for multimedia. CD-ROMs are such affordable mass-storage media that it now is possible to incorporate extensive sounds, graphics, and even full-motion video in multimedia titles. In addition, CD-ROM discs are removable (unlike hard drives), enabling you to replace the data as easily as you replace an audio CD.

More and more software products and multimedia titles are recognizing the benefits of CD-ROM technology. Some products, such as the CorelDRAW! clip art library, are available only as CDs, enabling you to install or run the program directly from a CD-ROM drive (no floppy-swapping). As disk-space requirements for programs continue to grow, CD-ROM versions provide a great way to access large programs or databases without investing in a large hard disk drive.

TIP

For more information on compact discs and new standards, read New Riders Publishing's *Technology Edge: Guide to CD-ROM*, written by Dana Parker and Bob Starrett.

Looking at Compact-Disc Standards

Compact discs can contain different types of data, including audio, data, and video. The specifications that describe the

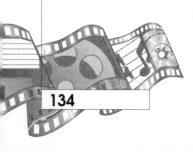

physical characteristics of the disc (including the size and placement of the pits representing data) were jointly developed by Philips and Sony. The specifications for the different types of discs are known by the colors of each of their specification manuals, such as the Red, Yellow, and Orange Books.

These specifications provide hardware and software developers with complete descriptions of data format, encoding, physical dimensions, and all aspects of compact-disc technology. Different CD technologies include:

➤ **Red Book.** The common name for the *Compact Disc Digital Audio Standard.* Most Red Book standard discs have "Digital Audio" printed below the disc logo. Digital music for the Red Book Audio standard is sampled at 16 bit, 44.1KHz. The Red Book standard applies to how music is sampled and digitized. Standard audio CDs contain only Red Book Audio, but CD-ROM discs may contain a mix of Red Book Audio and other media or data.

Music CDs conform to the Red Book standard.

➤ **Yellow Book.** The standard for Compact Disc Read-Only Memory, or CD-ROM. CDs made to the Yellow book specifications contain digital information read by a computer and typically have the label "Data Storage" printed below the disc logo. This is the type of disc most commonly used in multimedia applications.

CD-ROM discs are read only; once the disc has been pressed, you can't modify the data.

NOTE

Most currently available multimedia titles conform to the Yellow Book standard (CD-ROM), although CD-ROM XA is expected to become the future standard. If you understand the differences between these standards, it will help you select the best drive for your needs.

CD-ROM discs can contain multiple media data in addition to text. A disadvantage of CD-ROM discs is that only one type of data can be accessed from the drive at a single time. To synchronize two types of data (animation and audio, for example) you would need to copy one type of data to the hard drive or memory before accessing the second data type from the CD.

TIP

You can get the Red Book and Yellow Book standards from ANSI, Attn: Sales, 11 West 42nd Street, New York, NY 10036, (212) 642-4900. For the Red Book, order #CEIIEC 908; for the Yellow Book, order #ISO 10149:1989. ANSI stands for the American National Standards Institute, which is an organization that publishes software and hardware standards.

The purchase of a CD-ROM XA drive may be your best bet because a CD-ROM XA drive reads CD-ROM discs, single-session PhotoCD discs (with the proper software), and CD-ROM XA discs.

➤ **CD-ROM/XA.** An extension to the Yellow Book standard that incorporates the capability to combine computer data, compressed audio data, and video or picture data on one track. Most popular CD-ROM drives are not capable of supporting CD-ROM/XA.

➤ **Green Book.** The standard for Compact Disc-Interactive, or CD-I. This format was developed by Philips for a hybrid type of consumer hardware unit, designed to be hooked up to a television (see fig. 3.5). Philips is calling its CD-I player "The Imagination Machine." Special CD-I titles must be created for the player, which cannot play standard CD-ROM discs (although the unit can play Red Book Audio discs.) The lack of compatibility and the small amount of authoring tools has made CD-I unpopular with software developers.

Figure 3.5:

Philips' CD-Interactive player and remote.

TIP

Order a copy of the Green Book standard from the American CD-I Association, 11111 Santa Monica, Suite 750, Los Angeles, CA 90025, (213) 444-6619.

➤ **Orange Book.** This is the popular name for the *Compact Disc Recordable System*, the standard for recordable CD technology, also known as CD-R. The Orange Book standard is divided into two parts. The first part is devoted to rewritable magneto-optical discs; the second part covers optical WORM (Write Once, Read Many) discs. Many companies are using WORM discs to create "masters" for CD titles they plan to distribute or sell. After the company is satisified with the master, the master can be sent to a CD disc duplication facility.

CD-WORM drives conforming to Part II of the Orange Book standard enable you to master your own audio or data CDs that then can be read by any CD-ROM drive. Although the drives ($8,000 to $12,000) and discs may seem expensive (at about $25 to $40 each), when you consider the cost per megabyte, CD-WORM becomes an economical solution for mass-storage requirements.

➤ **Blue Book**. This is the standard for the video laser disc. Some laser-disc players include a serial port interface for software control. Video disc is an analog, not digital, technology and is expected to become obsolete in the coming years.

Today, the Yellow Book standard's Compact Disc-Read Only Memory, or CD-ROM, is most commonly used in multimedia applications. CD-ROM drives also are a part of the basic MPC configuration. As the name implies, CD-ROM drives are read-only; that is, you can read from the disc but you cannot write to the disc.

CD-ROM discs generally must conform to one additional standard: ISO-9660. ISO-9660 is an international standard that defines a file system for CD-ROM discs. This standard comes in two types:

➤ **Level One ISO-9660.** Provides DOS compatibility.

➤ **Level Two ISO-9660.** Allows longer file names (up to 32 characters), but sacrifices cross-platform compatibility.

Understanding CD-ROM Drives

Like record players, CD-ROM drives are read-only devices. CD-ROM drives use a technology similar to audio CD players, which have virtually replaced record players. CD-ROM drives can even read an audio CD of your favorite music because audio compact discs and CD-ROM data discs store information in digital format.

The average access time of a hard disk drive is 16ms; the access time of an MPC-compatible CD-ROM drive is one second, although you can purchase faster CD-ROM drives (280 to 380ms.)

You can order a copy of ISO-9660 from ANSI, Attn: Sales, 11 West 42nd Street, New York, NY 10036, (212) 642-4900.

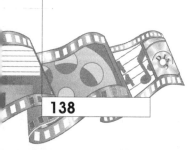

CD-ROM drives are available in internal, external, and transportable configurations, with prices ranging from $200 to over $1000. Internal CD-ROMs are ideal when you have limited desktop "real estate" and have a free drive bay in your computer. If you do not have free space in your computer, an external drive may be your only choice. External drives are housed in their own box and require a SCSI interface.

CD-ROM drives usually feature a SCSI (pronounced *scuzzy*) interface. SCSI stands for "small computer system interface." Most external CD-ROM drives and multimedia kits (with external drives) provide the necessary SCSI interface board, but be sure to verify this first. The advantage of a SCSI device is that it can be daisy-chained to other SCSI devices using a single interface card in a single PC slot.

Transportable CD-ROM drives are similar to external drives, but because the SCSI interface is built-in, they can be transported easily from one PC to another without opening the PC and adding an interface card. These drives typically connect with a serial or parallel port and generally operate at slower speeds than standard CD-ROM drives. Transportable drives, such as NEC's CDR-36M (see fig. 3.6), make excellent choices when the drive must be shared among a number of PCs at various locations.

Regardless of which CD-ROM configuration best suits your needs, make sure the CD-ROM drive you have or want to puchase meets or exceeds MPC specifications. Consider how it will be used: if you intend to access libraries of CD-ROM data, speed may not be critical. If a CD-ROM is integral to your multimedia presentation, however, performance is a serious issue. If you need to play animation or digital video from the CD-ROM, the speed of the drive is critical. The best advice is to get the fastest CD-ROM drive your budget allows.

CD-ROM drives are considerably slower than the average hard disk drive.

Most MCP audio cards have SCSI built into them.

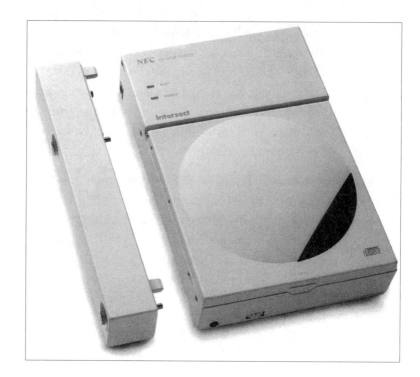

Figure 3.6:

NEC's CDR-36M, a portable CD-ROM reader.

NOTE

If performance is your most important requirement for playing multimedia, purchase a double speed CD-ROM drive. If future compatbility is important, purchase a CD-ROM XA drive.

Comparing CD XA, CD-I, and PhotoCD

New CD player standards continue to enter the marketplace, and they are not compatible with the MPC specifications. As mentioned earlier in this chapter, new technologies are starting to become the new standard.

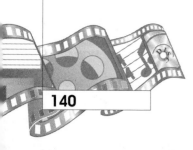

CD XA

The next generation of CD-ROM drives are the CD-ROM XA. These drives interleave audio and data sectors when they access discs. The IBM Ultimedia machine uses a CD-ROM XA drive, but few titles are currently available to use the power of the XA technology. Microsoft calls the CD-ROM XA drive its Level 2 Standard for MPCs. All the users who purchased MPCs and Upgrade kits with Level 1 drives (plain vanilla CD-ROM) have a problem if the rest of the industry decides to accept the XA standard. Kodak is supporting the CD-ROM XA standard by enabling these drives to read the new Kodak PhotoCD.

IBM is not the only company using the XA standard. At the Seventh Annual Multimedia and CD-ROM Conference, Sony Corporation announced the Sony Portable CD-ROM XA Player. This handheld device, now sold as the MMCD (see fig. 3.7), is capable of playing multimedia titles. Sony is finding support for the Bookman from companies such as Apple and Microsoft. Microsoft is adapting a version of the Multimedia Viewer so that developers can create titles specially for the Bookman.

Sony is positioning the MMCD as a reference tool for Business people who travel. Among the titles currently available for the unit is the *Zagat-Axxis City Guide*, which incorporates mapping technology with restaurant reviews. You can pinpoint your location on a city map, and get information on local restaurants. Newsweek is developing *Newsweek Interactive*, a quarterly multimedia supplement to *Newsweek Magazine*, which plays on the MMCD.

The MMCD is a stand-alone unit; it should not be confused with CD-ROM XA drives designed for the PC.

Sony envisions corporations putting manuals and training materials on MMCD discs, which can be distributed easily and cheaply to field offices or personnel on the road. MMCD player monitors are currently monochrome, but can be connected to a standard television monitor for viewing the multimedia information in color.

Figure 3.7:

Sony's MMCD
Player.

CDI

Compact Disc Interactive (CDI) is another CD format
launched in late 1991 by Philips. The CDI player is a stand-
alone reader designed for the general consumer marketplace
that plays when connected to a television set. CDI can
feature multimedia elements and is interactive. CDI titles are
available and are distributed through such outlets as Sears,
Radio Shack, and the Home Shopping Network.

PhotoCD

The PhotoCD system, developed by Eastman Kodak and
Philips, stores 35mm photographs, text, graphics, and sound
on compact discs. PhotoCD images are created by scanning

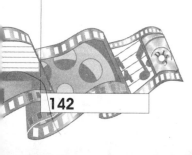

conventional photographs or film and digitally recording the images on specially-encoded compact discs. The PhotoCD is housed in a CD jewel case; the cover of the case displays "thumbnails," which are index prints of all the images on the CD. To view the PhotoCD, a consumer needs to purchase a PhotoCD Player, which connects to a television. These players also can play standard Redbook audio CDs. Other compact disc players, such as the CDI or CD-ROM XA, are capable of playing the PhotoCDs.

Currently, PhotoCDs are used just for displaying photo images; as video compression and decompression standards continue to emerge, PhotoCDs will be used to store home videos (or corporate videos) as well.

PhotoCD images can be loaded into a properly configured computer. To do so, the PC must have a CD-ROM XA drive that is capable of reading new CD standards. The PC also must be equipped with a display capable of handling bit-mapped images (Kodak recommends 24-bit color display adapters for the best image representation). Finally, the PC must have PhotoCD Access end-user software so that the computer user can view the images.

NOTE   Because of the marketing strength of a company as large as Kodak, the CD-ROM XA standard may replace the current MPC CD-ROM standard if the PhotoCD starts to gain market acceptance. Computer users who already have Level 1 CD-ROM drives—which are incompatible with CD-ROM XA—would have to decide whether they want to upgrade or stay with their current drive.

Mastering a CD-ROM

Multimedia developers have two choices when mastering CD-ROM discs: they can make their own or contract with a CD-ROM manufacturer. Mastering a CD-ROM requires special hardware because CD-ROM disc drives are read-only.

Recordable CD drives are becoming more popular as prices continue to drop.

If you plan low-volume CD production, you can master your own CDs with a recordable CD drive. These drives cost between $8000 and $13,000 and are available from JVC, Philips, and Sony. With these drives, you can create your own CD discs, although the process is time-consuming. It takes an average of two hours to master a typical CD-ROM. This technique works well for small batches or prototyping.

TIP

For more information from any of these three manufacturers, call the following service numbers:

The JVC Personal ROM-Maker, JVC Product Information: (714) 965-2610.

The Philips CDD 521, Philips Consumer Electronics: (615) 475-8869.

The Sony CDW-900E, Sony Computer Peripheral products: (800) 352-7669.

When you need to make hundreds or thousands of CDs, or if you cannot afford the CD mastering hardware, you can contact a CD-ROM manufacturer. The cost to produce CDs varies depending on the number of discs you want. If you want 3000 discs, for example, the cost may be $1000 for the master and $1.25 for each copy—your total cost may be $4749 for 3000 discs (about $1.58 each).

Smaller quantities generally cost more per disc, but it pays to shop around. Manufacturers often run special promotional offers that enable you to run small quantities at a reasonable cost.

TIP

The following CD-ROM manufacturers are suggested resources; contact them for estimates and information:

Digital Audio Disc Corporation
1800 North Fruitridge Avenue
Terre Haute, IN 47803
(812) 462-8100
(812) 466-9125 fax

Disc Manufacturing Inc. (DMI)
4905 Moores Mill Road
Huntsville, AL 35810
(800) 433-DISC
(205) 859-9042
(205) 859-9932 fax

As you can see, CD-ROMs are an integral part of both the developer's MPC and the user's MPC. Like CD-ROMs, sound boards are an important component of the MPC.

Understanding Sound Boards

Sound boards, once considered a novelty for game-playing youngsters, have made inroads in corporate America. Large PC manufacturers, known primarily for their corporate presence, have begun to include MPC sound capabilities on their newest computers.

Why has sound become important in the corporate world? As advertisers have known for years, sound can have a dramatic effect on your perception of any presentation. Sound can reinforce a message, stir a memory, or evoke an emotion. Sounds can include voice, sound effects, music, or any combination of the three.

With an MPC-compatible sound board, you can do the following:

➤ Annotate a spreadsheet with verbal comments

➤ Record music from a CD or tape player

➤ Add sound effects and music to enliven a business presentation

With a sound board, you can create the type of impact that advertisers have had for years.

To decide what you need from your sound card, you may need to look into the future. Although you now may be content with using sound to dress up your Windows environment, eventually you may want to use voice to proof the numbers you enter into a spreadsheet.

NOTE Some sound boards not only reproduce sound but also include voice-recognition capabilities that enable the computer to respond to your spoken commands. These capabilities are included in the new Microsoft Windows Sound System, which is capable recognizing spoken commands.

One way to determine the capabilities of a sound card is to compare its sampling rate against standard sampling rates. *Sampling* is the conversion of sound from analog signals to a digital format. Sampling rates are measured in KHz and bits; the higher the number for these measurements, the better the quality. Standard sampling rates are 11KHz, 22KHz, and

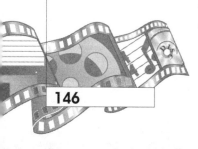

44KHz; sample sizes are 8, 12, and 16 bits. The resulting recordings are stored in waveform format with a WAV extension. Sound that is sampled at 16-bit, 44.1 KHz is stored in Red Book audio format on the CD.

MPC-compatible sound boards must have a music synthesizer, on-board capabilities and compliance for providing digitized sound in eight-bit samples at an 11KHz input-sampling rate, and eight-bit samples at both 11KHz and 22KHz output-sampling rates. Some boards, such as the Media Vision PAS Plus offer 16-bit sampling that produces a stereophonic (as opposed to monophonic) sound. You may want to invest in a better quality board, depending on how important sound quality is to you.

MPC-compatible sound boards are divided into three categories: monophonic boards, stereophonic boards, and specialized MIDI boards. The basic difference between these categories is the sound quality. Sound quality can be measured by the sampling capability, monophonic versus stereophonic sound, and the number of voices. The sound quality of each type of board serves different purposes:

> **Monophonic sound boards.** The SoundBlaster sound board, made by Creative Labs, Inc., offers affordable sound that is compatible with most multimedia software. Although some versions of SoundBlaster are monophonic, the board produces surprisingly good sound. SoundBlaster and other types of monophonic boards are an excellent entry-level sound board for the MPC end user.

> **Stereophonic sound boards.** The SoundBlaster Pro 16 and the ProAudio Spectrum 16, made by Media Vision, provide true stereo sound. Some of these sound boards offer 16-bit samples at up to a 44KHz sampling rate, which is equivalent to CD-quality audio sound in true stereo.

Portable, external sound devices are monophonic. Although you lose some of the sound quality, you gain portability, which is important if you are doing presentations on a laptop.

➤ **Specialized MIDI boards.** Turtle Beach System's MultiSound offers the high-end sound quality of stereo boards and high-quality MIDI synthesis. The best boards use sampled MIDI voices, which are sounds taken from actual instruments. When a MIDI file calls for the voice of a grand piano, for example, the sound board plays the sound actually sampled from a grand piano, which provides a realism not otherwise possible.

When you shop for a sound board, consider the purpose for which you will use it. If you plan to make music, get a 16-bit board with a 44KHz sampling rate and MIDI in/out capabilities. If you need the board for a combination of voice and occasional music, a basic sound board should suffice. As with most hardware, the software you choose can determine the capabilities you need. Check that the audio board you choose fully supports all the software you will use it with.

TIP

If you need sound for your laptop, consider one of the portable sound adapters, such as Media Vision's Audioport. These devices usually plug into your PC's standard parallel port, enabling you to take your show on the road. Not all adapters include a microphone port, and some do not allow parallel port pass-through (you may have to unplug the sound adapter when you want to use the printer).

Another consideration when you shop for a sound board is how you plan to use it. How do you get sound into or out of the board? The next two sections introduce the various input and output options that can affect your sound-board decisions.

Sound-Board Input Options

Although sound boards generally are tools for producing sound, do not overlook their capability to accept sound from other sources. Sound boards can offer as many as four different means to input sound to your MPC: microphone, RCA line-in, MIDI, and CD-Digital Audio.

The MPC specification defines microphone input as a necessary component; the sound board most often is used for this input. Microphone input enables you to use Windows' Sound Recorder to record any sound captured by a microphone. You can add voice annotation to a spreadsheet or create special sound effects for your multimedia title.

No matter what use you have for sound input, make sure you get a decent microphone ($30 and up).

TIP

Microsoft's new sound board has voice recognition, a feature that enables the computer to respond to your spoken instructions. You can use voice recognition to train your computer to recognize certain words or phrases. You then can assign these learned words and phrases to specific commands or macros. You can tell your computer to print or save, for example, simply by talking to it. Watch for this capability to be used more and more in the future.

WARNING

When you connect music components, such as receivers and tape decks, make sure you follow the directions provided by the sound-board manufacturer or you may damage your computer.

Although voice recognition can be very useful, you should use it with a degree of caution. With an early version of the

Microsoft Windows Sound System, one user's pronunication of the word "delete" sounded like a door slamming. As a result, every time he shut his door too firmly, he lost a file!

MIDI is another capability often provided by the sound board. MIDI is a standard for musical devices (both instruments and equipment) that enables instruments to communicate with each other. MIDI is covered in detail later in this chapter.

The fourth form of input is CD-DA, or Compact Disc-Digital Audio. Some sound boards, such as Creative Labs' Sound-Blaster Pro, enable you to listen to audio CDs played in a CD-ROM drive and record music using the sound board. In Windows, you can use the Media Player applet to play audio CDs in the background with no performance penalty.

TIP

Before the Media Player applet can recognize your CD-ROM drive, you must set up the CD-ROM using the Drivers applet in Window's Control Panel. Select [MCI] CD Audio (the Media Control Interface driver for a CD audio drive), and then choose Setup. Your CD-ROM drive is added automatically to the Media Player's list of devices. See the section "Editing SYSTEM.INI" later in this chapter. If you do not see [MCI] CD Audio, choose Add and select [MCI] CD and press OK.

Sound-Board Output Options

Another important issue often overlooked in the selection of sound boards is sound output. If you are creating professional multimedia presentations, good sound quality is essential. Sound quality suffers unless you have acceptable speakers or headphones, regardless of the quality of your sound board.

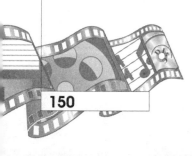

If you are shopping for a sound board, consider how you intend to play the output. Without any additional board, you can play sounds through the speaker built into your PC, but usually built-in speakers are tinny sounding at best and are not an acceptable option. Unpowered speakers are a step up, but they will not work with some sound boards because the boards require amplification. Generally, you need either headphones or powered speakers.

Most sound boards have a 1/8-inch headphone jack, popular with most personal stereos. Any headphones can be used if you have the proper adapters. Headphones are a good low-cost solution for single users in an environment in which noise can be disruptive to others. If a group must hear your message, amplified sound through speakers is a must.

Powered speakers can be battery or AC-powered. Some more advanced speakers include equalizer capabilities. Speaker manufacturers such as BOSE and Altec (see fig. 3.8) now make speakers that are targeted specifically for the MPC market, but you do not necessarily need special computer speakers. The important concern is magnetic shielding. Inadequately-shielded speakers can distort your monitor's display if they are placed too close to your monitor. Get speakers with adequate magnetic shielding. If possible, first test them.

Make sure the powered speakers you buy have volume control.

TIP

Although special computer speakers generally have magnetic shielding, they are expensive. If you are on a low budget, you can reduce shielding problems in two ways. The first way is simple: place the speakers away from your monitor. If you cannot, buy speakers made for use with video equipment (such as a stereo television). If the speaker does not distort a television, it usually does not distort your monitor.

Figure 3.8:

Altec Lansing Computer Speakers.

You can also hook up most sound boards to an external stereo amplifier using standard RCA stereo accessory cables. These cables connect to the amplifier's line-in jacks. This arrangement gives you the additional option of using the equalizer and mixing capabilities of your sound equipment to sculpt the sound for your environment. This arrangement offers a cost-effective solution with excellent sound quality (if you already have the proper sound equipment within cable's reach).

When shopping for a sound board to add to your computer, make sure alternate DMA channels and IRQs can be used in the event that you have a conflict with boards already installed in your system.

Hardware Conflicts

Another important consideration when choosing a sound board is compatibility with existing hardware. This is only an issue when you are upgrading an existing PC. Sound boards require that a Direct Memory Access (DMA) channel be available so that it can transfer audio data between the computer's RAM (memory) and its hard drive. Many devices—including network adapters and tape-drive controllers—use DMA channels, but only one device can use a DMA channel at a time.

Your PC also must have an IRQ (Interrupt Request Level) available so that the sound board can send an interrupt when it needs the computer's resources. Most sound boards make use of little-used DMA channels and IRQs, but, to be safe, make sure your sound board can be reconfigured to avoid conflicts.

Understanding MIDI Synthesizers

The Musical Instrument Device Interface, or MIDI, is a standard format for digital reproduction of sound. The MIDI "language" enables digital equipment and instruments to communicate. A wide variety of MIDI devices are available, from black boxes and keyboards to guitars and wind instruments. Many MIDI devices can serve double duty as both an input and an output device.

If you have a MIDI keyboard, you can play a song into your MPC and then print out the musical notation of your composition. You then can edit the notation and change the key, or just fine-tune the melody and then replay it through the keyboard.

MIDI quality varies tremendously because it is the digital reproduction of sound. The MPC specification requires that sound boards include MIDI support through Frequency Modulation Synthesis (FM synthesis). FM synthesis has a decidedly electronic sound. Other boards, such as Turtle Beach System's MultiSound, provide digital recordings of the actual instruments. The effect of these boards is dramatic, rivaling the sound of high-end synthesizers.

If you want to use sound to enhance a presentation, or as a background effect for other media, MIDI files may meet your needs—these files also conserve file space.

NOTE

MIDI offers a strong advantage to multimedia developers. Storage requirements for MIDI files are a fraction of that for comparable WAV files. On the down side, MIDI sound-reproduction quality is directly related to the sound board's capabilities. If sound-reproduction quality is important, test your MIDI files using several sound boards to get a feel for how they play. A simple solution to MIDI sound concerns is to use WAV files.

Check to make sure your graphics board and monitor are capable of displaying 256 colors at 640×480 resolution; this is required by most multimedia applications.

Understanding Graphics Boards

Graphic boards work in concert with your monitor to provide the visual images required by multimedia. Graphic boards are available in many configurations, but for the multimedia developer, a Super-VGA (SVGA) board with 1M of video RAM is essential. This configuration enables you to display 256 colors simultaneously at resolutions ranging from 640×480 to 1024×768 pixels (columns×rows). See figure 3.9 for a comparison.

Figure 3.9:
The difference between a 256 and a 16 color image.

Produced by Pinnacle Effects, 2334 Elliot Avenue, Seattle, WA 98121

In some applications, even 256 colors are insufficient. Photorealistic imagery requires greater color depth that only 24-bit color can provide. 24-bit color can display 16 million colors.

When you plan your multimedia project, consider the following items:

➤ **Windows support.** Not all high-color graphics boards provide Windows drivers. Make sure the board has drivers available for the latest version of Windows.

➤ **Application support.** Even when a Windows driver is available, not all Windows applications can take advantage of more than 256 colors. Make sure the applications you are using support additional colors.

➤ **Title distribution.** Determine whether your multimedia title will be mass-distributed or developed for a specific type of hardware. If distribution is important, know that the additional color depth you have on your developer's MPC could cause problems when viewing the title with less-sophisticated graphic boards.

➤ **Input/output needs.** Do you need to capture video images or output to video tape? Any type of video input or output needs require special consideration when selecting a graphics board.

Three Types of Graphics Boards

Three basic types of graphics boards are available: the dumb frame buffer, the graphics coprocessor, and the graphics processor.

➤ **The dumb frame buffer.** This board uses the computer's CPU to perform the necessary calculations for updating the display you see on your monitor. Because these calculations require CPU time, these boards are the slowest of the three categories. Most standard VGA video boards fall into this category; they also are the most compatible boards.

Make sure the coprocessor or processor board you want to use for multimedia in-cludes support for Windows 3.1.

➤ **The graphics coprocessor board.** Processor boards are a step up in performance from frame buffers. Graphics coprocessor boards greatly cut down the amount of work the CPU must do to update the screen. This is accomplished by offloading specific commands to the graphics coprocessor. XVGA (Accelerated VGA), 8514/A, and IBM's new XGA boards are all examples of graphics coprocessor boards. Most of these boards require special software drivers to take advantage of their enhanced performance.

➤ **The graphics processor board.** This type of board is the fastest of the three types but also is the least compatible. Processor boards are used mostly for specific high-end graphics applications. Most of these boards are based on the TI 34010 processor from Texas Instruments. Prices range from $400 to $1000. The graphics processor board can be very useful, particularly for high-end graphics or animation work.

Other Graphics Performance Issues

Most graphics boards are built for the eight-bit or 16-bit ISA bus. A few graphics boards are made for the 32-bit EISA or MCA bus. More recently, another bus type, called *local bus*, has surfaced. Local bus is making news because it has much greater performance. The better the throughput, the faster your screen refreshes.

For comparison of ISA boards and local bus video, examine the transfer rates of the typical ISA bus compared to the

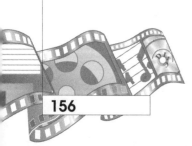

newer local bus. The traditional ISA bus transfers data at 1M to 2M-per-second; the local bus transfers data as much as 25M to 50M-per-second, or the rate at which the video circuitry can access CPU memory.

NOTE

If you opt for a local bus, you may need a new PC. The PC's motherboard must be specifically designed to support local bus boards. Until recently, no standard for local bus boards existed. Fortunately, VESA recently created a standard for local bus video. Dubbed VL-Bus (VESA Local Bus), this new standard can help you find compatible motherboards and graphics adapter boards.

Understanding Scanners

Much of the information in today's corporations is still paper-based (analog format), which raises the costs of re-creating information. A high quality scanner is critical if you intend to use a lot of existing imagery in your application. A scanner, combined with optical character recognition (OCR) software, is useful if you plan on importing a lot of existing text.

Scanners enable you to capture graphics and text so that you can add them to multimedia documents or applications. When a document is scanned, a *raster image* is produced, which is made up of a series of dots. Raster images differ from *vector images*, which are made up of lines, arcs, and other geometric entities. Because of this type of image, scanned-image files can be quite large.

If you buy a hand-held scanner, make sure your scanner software can "stitch" together several separate small images to form a larger composite image. "Stitching" is described in the next section.

Scanners come in many shapes and sizes, but can be broken down into categories based on their capabilities:

- ➤ Black-and-white, line-art scanners
- ➤ 256-color grayscale and halftone scanners
- ➤ Color scanners

These capabilities are available in a variety of resolutions, from 300dpi (dots per inch) to 800dpi, and in configurations ranging from digital cameras to flatbed to hand-held scanners. Scanners typically require an interface board and software for scanning and image editing. OCR software is used with a scanner to convert scanned text into a format that your word processor can understand.

The best scanner for your work depends on your needs and your budget. The simplest and least-expensive scanner is the line-art scanner. Most of these scanners are hand-held. You usually can find black-and-white line-art scanners starting around $100. These scanners are great for capturing simple line art in a digital format. Most clip art is line art. Crisp, black-and-white line art scans nicely, but color or photographic images do not scan well.

One step up from line-art scanners are grayscale scanners. These scanners capture photographic images in addition to line art, but convert all colors to shades of gray. This type of scanner is available in hand-held, flatbed, and, more recently, digital-camera configurations such as Logitech's Fotoman. Line-art and grayscale scanners are most useful for desktop publishing.

Color scanners capture full-color images and provide the greatest utility for producing multimedia titles. Color images take longer to scan and the resulting files are considerably

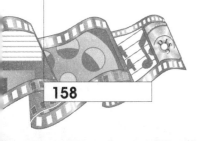

larger than either line-art or grayscale images. Color scanners are available in both hand-held and flatbed models.

The higher the resolution of a scanner, the higher the image quality and the larger the resulting file. Keep in mind that most graphics boards are not capable of displaying the resolutions that most scanners are capable of capturing. To put this in perspective, consider the effective resolution of a full 8-1/2-by-11-inch page scanned at 300dpi. The resolution of the final image is 3300×2550! On a standard VGA display (640×480), you hardly see a portion of the entire image. You need the resolution of a high quality scanner if you plan to rescale the size of the images you are capturing.

NOTE

For multimedia production, color (and color depth) are far more important than resolution. A low-resolution image with higher color depth looks better than a high-resolution image with low (or no) color depth.

Hand-Held versus Flatbed Scanners

Hand-held scanners offer several advantages over flatbed scanners, the most notable being the price. Hand-held scanners range in price from $100 to $700; flatbed (and drum) scanners cost from $500 to $5000. Hand-held models also take up less space and can be tucked away when not in use.

On the down side, hand-held scanners generally are less accurate because they are more susceptible to shifting during the scan. Shifting can cause blurring or distortion of your image. Hand-held scanners also are limited in scan width;

A hand-held color scanner is an inexpensive addition to any multimedia development system, but should not be used for professional-level imaging needs.

most can scan only a strip about 4" wide. Some models come with software that enables you to "stitch" together multiple passes, creating a single composite image. If your scanning needs dictate that you regularly scan images larger than 4" in width, you are better off with a flatbed or drum scanner.

TIP

If you choose a hand-held scanner, invest in (or build) a simple accessory for guiding the scanner. These devices help keep the scanner in-line during a scan, improving your chances for a good scan the first time.

Flatbed scanners, although more expensive than their hand-held counterparts, are more accurate. Because neither the hardware nor the image actually moves, blurring or distortion does not occur. Most flatbed scanners handle 8-1/2-by-11-inch media with no problem, and some handle even larger sizes. If you have a lot of scanning to do (and the sheets are the same size), you can add a sheet feeder to many flatbed scanners for automated scanning.

Alternatives to Scanning

If you have no scanner, do not despair. A number of options are available to get your images into your computer. You can use a service bureau, for example, or a DTP (desktop publishing) service bureau. You can get one or one hundred images scanned and saved in whatever format you require.

PhotoCD is another method for getting images into digital format, although it is not useful for line art. Given the costs involved in purchasing a PhotoCD compatible drive, the cost of the additional software, and the $20 cost for developing each roll of 35mm film, you may be better off investing in a medium quality scanner.

If you have a fax and a modem, you can use them as a low-budget scanner. Fax software such as WinFax Pro from Delrina enables you to convert received faxes to a PCX or TIF format for use in your multimedia titles. The resolution is not too good (only 150 to 200dpi), and you do not get colors or shades of gray, but this method works in a pinch.

Raster-to-Vector Conversion

As you have already seen, scanned images are stored in a *raster format*, meaning they are made up of a series of small dots. *Vector format* stores images as a series of geometric objects, and can save a tremendous amount of disk space for line-art images. To convert an image from raster to vector format requires some work, but you can produce more efficient files and scale and stretch the image to suit your needs.

A number of raster-to-vector conversion programs are available, such as CorelTRACE! (bundled with CorelDRAW!). Some scanners come with conversion programs as well. Typically, you have to experiment with the settings to get the results you want, and even then you have to edit the resulting vector image manually.

Exploring Alternative Multimedia Hardware

As personal computers are used in more situations, peripheral hardware for the PC is becoming increasingly specialized. Additional hardware you may need for your multimedia setup depends on your application and audience. If you create a great deal of multimedia presentations, you may want to invest in a projection device. One type projects the monitor image onto a screen or white wall using an overhead projector. One good product is the Smart 2000 Conferencing System from Smart Technologies, which was designed to let users interactively discuss and annotate spreadsheets, documents, graphics and charts. The Smart Board (a presentation screen that shows the image from the PC monitor) can be connected to a network; by using your finger or a Smart Board pen, you can make electronic marks on the image. These annotations appear immediately at every site connected to the board.

Touch screens are used in multimedia kiosks because they are more intuitive than mice (or other pointing devices) and are less intimidating to the user. Pen devices are useful for applications that are used by mobile professionals. The next two sections cover touch screen and pen input devices in greater detail.

Touch Screens

Touch screens are special input devices that take the place of a keyboard or mouse. Touch screens are used almost exclusively in environments in which the end user has little or no knowledge of computers, such as an information kiosk in an airport or an order-entry system at a catalog showroom.

Touch screens enable the user to interact with the program by simply pointing and touching the monitor screen with the finger. In such circumstances, the computer, keyboard, and other peripherals may be concealed within cabinets, providing the user with a simple, easy-to-understand interface.

Touch screens come in two basic varieties. *Special-purpose* touch-screen monitors have the necessary tactile sensors built into the display. These monitors are made especially for touch-screen environments (such as a kiosk), and may not be suitable for the dual-purpose use required when developing a multimedia title.

The second type of touch screen is the overlay. The *overlay* attaches to the front of your existing monitor and communicates to your PC through a serial port. This device is useful for the developer who needs to test the final interface because the overlay works in conjunction with a standard monitor. The overlay can also be disconnected and transferred to another MPC, which makes it more transportable than an entire monitor.

TIP

The following manufacturers are suggested as resources for touch-screen monitors and overlays:

TruePoint Touch Screen Monitor
MicroTouch
(800) 866-6873

TouchWindow (touch-screen overlay)
S.C.T., Inc.
Lilburn, GA
(800) 753-2441

To design an application for a touch-screen device, you need a little extra thought and planning. The typical touch-screen application requires that almost all commands and program controls are accessible through the touch screen. Generally, the keyboard is hidden within cabinets. The host PC should be configured to start the touch-screen application automatically when the unit is turned on, making a keyboard completely unnecessary except for system maintenance and reconfiguration.

Touch screen devices are used mainly for multimedia application development. Occasionally, they are used in executive information systems.

NOTE

When designing an application for a touch-screen interface, keep it simple. Remember that a finger does not have the precision of a mouse pointer. Judicious use of a few generous, well-placed buttons goes a long way. Keep the language simple enough for a child to understand, and your application will be well received.

When do you use a touch screen? Use one whenever the end-user environment is unpredictable, if supervision is minimal or nonexistent, or if the end user has little or no knowledge of computers. How do you use a touch screen? Keep in mind the environment, and design your multimedia title or application accordingly.

Pen Input Devices

Pen Windows, the Windows-compatible link to pen-based PC computing, provides a new way to interface with your computer. Pen-based PCs often do not have a mouse or a keyboard; they use only a pen, or stylus, with a cable attached to the computer. The display surface doubles as a digitizer, enabling you to input instructions directly over the display. These hand-held computers enable the pen to act like a mouse; make menu selections and press buttons. Pen-based computers also feature character recognition, which enables the computer to interpret your hand-written instructions and gestures. Most pen-based PCs use a 386 microprocessor.

Pen Windows is an extension of Windows 3.1, with approximately 70 new system calls added for the pen interface and handwriting analysis. Pen Windows shines when used with

pen-based applications, but Pen Windows also can be used to run standard Windows applications.

Pen-based computing may be part of your multimedia title. Pen-based applications already are appearing for work in remote locations in which data cannot be entered using keyboards. Pen-based applications have been developed for everything from order-entry at grocery stores to automated ticket writing for police.

The limitations of pen-based PCs also are their advantage: character recognition. Currently, character recognition requires that you carefully form letters in a consistent pattern. In addition, the recognition process can be sluggish, with a delay that ranges from a minor nuisance to a major inconvenience.

Pen-based input works best with form-based applications in which you can use lots of check lists and boxes to minimize the amount of actual handwriting.

Understanding Video Technology

Video and computer technologies have recently begun to overlap each other. More and more often, computers edit video and video is used to help communicate a message through computers.

Video can grab your attention like nothing else on a computer, partly because it surprises you. People do not expect to see video images or full-motion video on a computer. Although desktop video—the marriage of video and computers—still is in its infancy, you can use it in a number of ways.

Microsoft's release of Video for Windows is critical for integrating video into computer applications because it does not require de-compression hardware to play back a video clip.

The term *desktop video* means different things to different people. It can include the capture of still video images, the input and display of full-motion video from a VCR, the taping of computer images overlaid on one video source and re-corded on a VCR, and the digital storage (and retrieval) of compressed video signals.

These capabilities are possible because of a number of standards affecting video technology, currently available hardware, and other components that fit into the multimedia picture.

Examining Video Standards

The most notable difference between video and computer signals is that video signals are analog; a computer monitor receives digital signals. This incompatibility necessitates special hardware for both video input and output. *Codec* (compression/decompression) is the term that describes a series of standards used in compression of video capture and playback. Here is an overview of the standards governing PC/video connections:

➤ **NTSC (National Television Standards Committee).** NTSC is the established standard for video signals in Northern America. Signals from any tuner, VCR, or laser-disc player purchased in the U.S. conform to the NTSC standard.

➤ **PAL.** PAL is the European community's equivalent of NTSC. Unfortunately, PAL is incompatible with NTSC, necessitating a different version of hardware for each standard. If some or all of your potential audience is based in Europe, be prepared to work with PAL; make sure your hardware provides PAL input or output options.

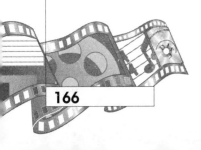

➤ **AVI (Audio Video Interleave).** AVI is a technology developed by Microsoft in its video for Windows products, for software-only playback of full-motion video. Video capture for authoring requires special hardware compression but decompression, and playback are software-only tasks, enabling AVI video to be viewed without special hardware.

➤ **DVI (Digital Video Interactive).** DVI is a combination of software and hardware developed by Intel and IBM in conjunction with other hardware and software vendors. Because it relies on special hardware, DVI can obtain greater compression ratios (as much as 150:1) and smoother playback. Indeo, Intel's new scalable video-compression technology, enables video to be compressed and played back on a wide variety of different platforms.

➤ **JPEG (Joint Photographic Experts Group).** JPEG is a compression standard for still images.

➤ **MPEG (Motion Picture Experts Group).** MPEG is a compression standard for video (motion) images.

➤ **QuickTime.** QuickTime is the video codec playback technology developed by Apple for the Macintosh computer. QuickTime video players have also been written for Windows, enabling video to be played back on MPCs as well.

Currently, Intel's Indeo (which is supported by QuickTime and Video for Windows) is emerging as the video compression standard. MPEG Compression (the MPEG algorithm is being included on a number of DSP chips) will probably become the compression standard of the future.

Most video digitizing boards are compatible with NTSC and PAL signals. You will probably need two different VCRs, however, to work with both standards.

Understanding Video Frame Grabbers

Although real motion video is the holy grail of multimedia, it still is impractical using today's technology. The current method for working with video is by capturing and converting the analog signal from a video source and either manipulating the image's data (which is written to video tape) or compressing the data using compression techniques (either software-only compression or a combination of hardware and software compression).

To display or capture a single screen of an NTSC signal, you must have a video frame grabber. These are lowest on the rungs of the video ladder, in that they have less capability than boards that capture streaming video. These cards enable you to grab a single frame of video from a Laser Disk or a VCR. Video frame grabbers come in two varieties: single-frame capture and real-time capture. *Single-frame capture* boards enable you to freeze a selected frame and record it to your hard disk. In this function, single-frame boards are similar to scanners—they provide a means of capturing an image and saving it for use in a multimedia title.

Frame grabbers typically work in conjunction with the normal graphics board by connecting through the VGA board's feature connector. The *feature connector* is connected to the frame-grabber board with a ribbon cable, and enables the two boards to work together. You can connect a variety of NTSC sources to the frame grabber, including cable TV, VCRs, and video-disc players.

Low-end single-frame capture boards convert captured images to grayscale images; better boards capture full-color images. A few examples include the ComputerEyes board (B&W) and Creative Labs' VideoBlaster (color), shown in figure 3.10.

When you use video capture boards with video editing software, you have the same editing capabilities that formerly only were available at professional editing suites.

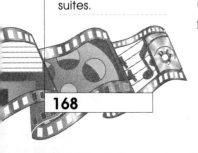

Figure 3.10:
Creative Lab's Video Blaster Board.

Real-time frame grabbers *capture* full-motion video at a rate between 15 and 30 frames-per-second using video compression (video compression is described in the following section).

NOTE

The real motion video you see on television plays at 30 frames-per-second. At least 24 frames-per-second is required to fool the eye into believing it is seeing motion—anything less than 24 frames appears "choppy."

NTSC-to-VGA adapters take the composite NTSC signal, overlay computer graphics on the live video, and then write the combined output to a television monitor or VCR. Other boards use "genlocking" to control video input. A *genlock* device synchronizes the VGA signal with the NTSC signal, enabling you to view live video in a window on a PC monitor. You cannot use genlock devices to store or manipulate video images.

Most video frame grabbers allow real-time display of live video images, either in a window or full screen. This capability can provide a high degree of interaction in multimedia titles, particularly when combined with serial-controlled laser-disc input. In this configuration, the multimedia title can have random access to any point on the laser disc, giving you access to up to one hour of video. You learn more about how to incorporate laser-disc players later in this chapter.

WARNING Although using a video disc player in conjunction with multimedia software enables you to play realtime video sequences in a window, it requires a lot of hardware: PC, CD-ROM drive, sound board, video disc player, genlock board, and optional NTSC monitor.

If you need to include video tape or input broadcast from a network or cable station, some boards now include a built-in tuner. Cheaper tuner boards require full-screen display, but enable you to toggle between the computer's working screen and the video display with a hot key. Better boards display a resizable video window, which is particularly useful for viewing video tutorials while working in the program you are learning.

Looking at Video Compression and Playback Boards

A single second of video captured directly to disk requires about 33M of storage space. At that rate, your hardware can quickly become bottlenecked. Several techniques are available that enable you to get around this seemingly insurmountable barrier.

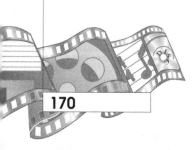

One of the easiest solutions is to reduce the size of the play-back window. The fewer pixels displayed, the less data required. A 100×100 pixel window takes 1/30th the data of a 640×480 window.

Another solution is to reduce the playback rate. Although standard video playback is 30 frames per second (fps), you often can reduce the playback to 15fps or even 10fps with acceptable results. Compton's Multimedia Encyclopedia, for example, plays video clips at rates ranging from 10 to 30fps.

NOTE

One difficulty in creating multimedia applications that use software-only compression is ensuring that the audio portion is synchronized with the video segment. Video for Windows is *scalable*, which means it drops frames (if necessary) when playing back on a PC with less processing power, to ensure that the audio remains synchronized.

If video is an important part of your multimedia title, you will need a window of adequate size and a playback rate of at least 24fps. If you plan to use video sparingly, a rate of 15fps is fine (15fps is the rate of an average QuickTime movie).

The best way to reduce file size is video compression. Video compression and playback can be performed in either software-only or hardware-assisted mode. Software-only decompression and playback of videos is starting to enter the marketplace. Apple again led the way with the development of QuickTime. IBM produced a similar technology for DOS called Photo Motion, and Microsoft introduced Video for Windows technology. These technologies use hardware decompression to capture, manipulate, and store the video, but require only software for playback on the end user's PC.

QuickTime

QuickTime, written for Apple's Macintosh computers and now available for Windows, provides scalable video compression. *Scalable compression* takes advantage of your computer hardware—the better your hardware, the better the playback quality. Now that QuickTime is available for Windows, you can access the large libraries of video clips available in the QuickTime format.

Video for Windows (VFW)

By comparison, Microsoft's Video for Windows format is optimized for a 256-color, 160×120 pixel playback window, using video clips stored on a CD-ROM. The result, when played back in this configuration, should look better than a comparable QuickTime video clip. An additional advantage of VFW is software compatibility. VFW installs as an MCI device, which makes it accessible instantly to any application capable of calling Media Control Interface (MCI) devices (such as Asymetrix Toolbook).

As with QuickTime, VFW is somewhat choppy, however,— the memory and speed limitations of today's technology cannot produce a clean picture.

Hardware Compression

Hardware-compression boards offer the smoothest video playback at the highest cost. Hardware-compression boards are still a young field and no clear standards are defined. A variety of common video standards are supported by hardware boards, including DVI (Digital Video Interactive format), JPEG (Joint Photographic Experts Group), and MPEG (Motion Picture Experts Group). Although standards have not been established, two hot standards are emerging: JPEG and MPEG. JPEG is a standard for still video that eliminates redundant data within a single frame to compress it. The JPEG compression chip is used in some boards such as

Fluent Machines' CL-550 to achieve quarter-screen video at 30fps from an MPC-compatible CD-ROM. MPEG is the emerging standard for full-motion video; it describes what can be compressed within a fame and between frames. DSP chips that provide JPEG or MPEG technology are becoming available from a variety of vendors.

Another hardware prospect is Intel's DVI chip set. DVI can compress video at rates of 150 to 1. The DVI protocol supports a variety of standards and can process video at various quality levels. DVI technology is provided on special adapter boards for the PC that currently are sold by IBM and Intel. Although DVI is an expensive technology (compared to software-only decompression), prices always decrease for computer chips. The next generation of MPCs may feature DVI chips that make real motion (30fps) video a reality. Intel currently offers the ActionMedia II board with video playback (video capture is optional); other manufacturers such as Fluent Machines are expected to come out with compatible boards.

Hardware-compression boards are still expensive—generally over $1000. Their cost puts them out of reach of most MPC users, but they still can be a valuable tool to the developer of video clips. Intel claims that the DVI chip set eventually will be priced to make video-compression boards as affordable (and as common) as sound boards are now.

Understanding Video Discs

Video-disc players have been around for years, but only in recent years have PC-ready video-disc players come to market. PC-ready video-disc players (called Level 3 video disc) are essentially the same as their standard video siblings (Level 1 video disc), but they include an RS-232 serial interface. Pioneer and Sony both make PC-ready video-disc players at costs under $1000.

The serial interface gives the software control over video playback. Unlike video tapes, video discs are random-access devices that enable near-instant access to any point on the video disc. With software control, multimedia titles can access enormous libraries of video clips in a nonsequential manner.

TIP

Although PC-ready video-disc players are available, how do you record the initial video discs? Currently, video-disc mastering hardware costs between $14,000 and $20,000. A more reasonable option is to have your video disc mastered by a service bureau.

Looking at Multimedia Drivers and Applets

Windows 3.1 includes multimedia drivers to provide control over the various Media Control Interface (MCI) devices. MCI software drivers enable hardware devices, such as sound boards and video players, to communicate with Windows. Each hardware manufacturer is responsible for writing device drivers compatible with Windows 3.1. All a user needs to do is install the device. The Windows MCI commands then can recognize the new device.

Windows applications, such as Asymetrix Toolbook, can call MCI-controlled devices without any specific knowledge of particular hardware. The MCI driver handles communication

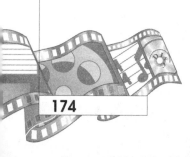

between Windows and the hardware device transparently—
the calling application is not involved.

Several common MCI drivers exist to control sound boards,
MIDI interface, MIDI mapping, and CD-ROM audio playback. Software developers also create additional MCI drivers,
such as Autodesk's animation driver that plays FLI and FLC
animations. Here is a closer look at the more common MCI
drivers:

> **Sound driver (MCIWAVE.DRV).** This driver provides
  installation and configuration of waveform audio sound
  players.

> **Sequencer driver (MCISEQ.DRV).** This driver provides
  installation and configuration of MIDI devices, both
  internal (sound cards) and external (MIDI synthesizers).

> **CD-ROM driver (MCICDA.DRV).** This driver enables
  you to configure a CD-ROM drive to play audio CDs.

> **MIDI Mapper driver (MIDIMAP.DRV).** This driver
  enables you to reconfigure the mapping of a MIDI
  device's instruments.

You can install, edit, and remove an MCI driver by selecting
the Drivers icon from the Control Panel (see fig.3.11). This
opens the Drivers dialog box, shown in figure 3.12. This
dialog box displays the currently installed drivers and offers
options for adding, removing, and setting up drivers.

Drivers

Figure 3.11:

The Drivers applet
icon.

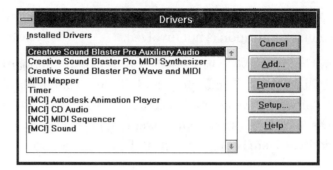

Figure 3.12

The Drivers dialog box.

Windows 3.1 comes with a number of MCI drivers, including drivers for several sound boards. If your particular hardware device is not listed in the Drivers dialog box, the installation software for your board should contain the driver. If not, contact the manufacturer of your sound board for a driver.

After you install and set up your multimedia devices, Windows provides several *applets* (mini-applications) for them. These applets are selected through the Control Panel to control MIDI setup, MIDI mapping, and system-event sounds.

Using the MIDI Mapper Applet

The MIDI Mapper applet (see figures 3.13 and 3.14) enables you to edit the key maps for your MIDI device. General MIDI standards specify that certain instruments are used to supply the voice on certain channels. If your MIDI device does not support those instruments or channels, you must "rekey" the instruments by editing the map. In some cases, the manufacturer of your MIDI device can supply the necessary customized key map, but even then you may want to reconfigure the key map or just experiment with it.

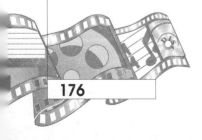

MIDI Mapper

Figure 3.13:

The MIDI Mapper applet icon.

Figure 3.14:

The MIDI Mapper dialog box.

MIDI key maps can be saved with a unique name and a description. It is highly recommended that you leave the General MIDI key map alone and avoid creating new maps with descriptive names.

When you edit a key map, you use the MIDI Key Map dialog box shown in figure 3.15. This dialog box lists the source key, the source key name, and the current destination key for the percussive sounds as designated by general MIDI standards. You can edit the destination key.

Understanding the Sound Applet

After installing your sound board, you can use the Sound applet (click on the Sound applet icon in fig. 3.16) to assign waveform files (WAV) to certain system events, such as system startup, exit, and warnings. You can also use the Sound applet to enable or disable the system sounds.

The sound applet can be used with any installed sound board.

Windows 3.1 comes with a number of sample waveform files preassigned to system events. If you have a sound board installed and configured, you can check the Enable System Sounds box in the Sound dialog box to activate them (see fig. 3.17).

Src Key	Src Key Name	Dest Key
35	Acoustic Bass Drum	47
36	Bass Drum 1	48
37	Side Stick	49
38	Acoustic Snare	50
39	Hand Clap	51
40	Electric Snare	52
41	Low Floor Tom	53
42	Closed Hi Hat	54
43	High Floor Tom	55
44	Pedal Hi Hat	56
45	Low Tom	57
46	Open Hi Hat	58
47	Low-Mid Tom	59
48	High-Mid Tom	60
49	Crash Cymbal 1	61
50	High Tom	62

MIDI Key Map: '+1 octave'

OK   Cancel   Help

Figure 3.15:
The MIDI Key Map dialog box.

Figure 3.16:
The Sound applet icon.

Sound

Figure 3.17:
Use the Sound dialog box to assign sounds to system events.

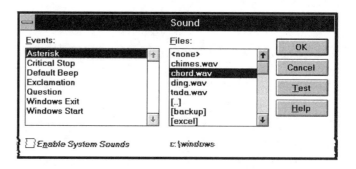

As you configure system sounds, you can test them before you commit to them. Of course, you can always change your mind and reconfigure or even disable the sounds at any time.

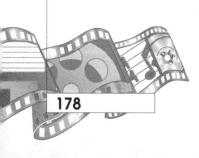

Editing INI Files Manually

When you install, uninstall, or reconfigure a driver, Windows automatically updates the necessary INI files. For further fine-tuning, you can edit these files yourself. You can use Notepad, your own text editor, or SYSEDIT—the Windows-supplied system editor (see fig. 3.18)—to edit INI files.

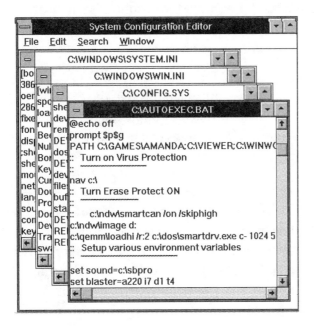

Figure 3.18:

SYSEDIT is one way to edit the WIN.INI and SYSTEM.INI files.

TIP

SYSEDIT is a helpful editor that is not installed automatically in any program group, even though it comes with Windows. SYSEDIT works much like Notepad but automatically opens four edit windows for WIN.INI, SYSTEM.INI, CONFIG.SYS, and AUTOEXEC.BAT. You can find SYSEDIT in the C:\WINDOWS\SYSTEM directory. (Substitute the appropriate drive and directory name for your Windows directory.)

You may want to edit or simply view your INI files to determine the default values or debug a special hardware item.

Editing WIN.INI

The WIN.INI file contains preference settings for controlling the Windows environment. Many applications automatically add sections to the WIN.INI file to control their environment. WIN.INI is a dynamic file—it constantly changes as your Windows environment evolves.

Direct editing of the WIN.INI file is seldom necessary. Many of its settings can be controlled through the Control Panel. Other settings are controlled by application software, such as Word for Windows. All settings can be manually edited for fine tuning.

TIP

Always back up the INI files before you manually edit them. If you do not get the results you want or, worse yet, if disaster strikes, you can recover by copying the original INI files and restarting Windows.

Two sections of WIN.INI are of particular interest when configuring your MPC. The first, [mci extensions], associates media-file extensions with a specific MCI driver. Special extensions may be installed with new hardware, but the standard extensions are as follows:

```
[mci extensions]
wav=wavaudio
mid=sequencer
rmi=sequencer
```

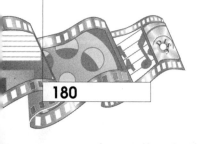

The other section in the WIN.INI file that can affect your MPC hardware is the [sounds] section. This section enables you to assign WAV or MID files to system events such as starting and exiting Windows. The following is a sample [sounds] section, showing different wave files assigned to the Windows system events:

```
[sounds]
SystemAsterisk=chord.wav,Asterisk
SystemHand=C:\WINDOWS\MUSIC\RIFF.WAV,Critical Stop
SystemDefault=ding.wav,Default Beep
SystemExclamation=C:\WINDOWS\MUSIC\BAM.WAV,Exclamation
SystemQuestion=C:\WINDOWS\CHORD.WAV,Question
SystemExit=C:\WINDOWS\CHIMES.WAV,Windows Exit
SystemStart=C:\WINDOWS\MUSIC\INTERLUD.WAV,Windows
Start
```

All these options are configurable through the Sound applet described earlier in this chapter. You should edit these settings manually only if you know that the files exist, are in the stated directories, and that your hardware is capable of playing them.

Editing SYSTEM.INI

The SYSTEM.INI file contains numerous sections affecting your MPC configuration. Some of these settings are configurable through the Control Panel.

The first section of SYSTEM.INI that is of interest to multimedia developers is [mci]. This section defines the names of the actual MCI drivers. Only installed devices appear here; if you do not have a CD-ROM drive or animation player, you do not see the lines (and should not add them manually). The following is a sample [mci] section for a system configured with a sound board, MIDI sequencer, CD-ROM drive, and an animation player:

Please note that these file settings are examples. Your sound board may differ.

```
[mci]
WaveAudio=mciwave.drv
Sequencer=mciseq.drv
CDAudio=mcicda.drv
Animation1=mciaap.drv
```

The [drivers], [mciseq.drv], and [midi] sections in SYSTEM.INI cover specific hardware drivers, such as the SoundBlaster Pro or Media Vision PAS Plus sound boards. Installation of some hardware drivers may cause new sections to be appended to the SYSTEM.INI file. A SYSTEM.INI may appear as follows:

```
[drivers]
MidiMapper=midimap.drv
Timer=timer.drv
AUX=sbpaux.drv
MIDI=sbp2fm.drv
Wave=sbpsnd.drv
MIDI1=sbpsnd.drv

[mciseq.drv]
disablewarning=true

[sndblst.drv]
port=220
int=7
dmachannel=1
MasterVolume=10, 10
FmVolume=10, 10
CDVolume=14, 14
LineVolume=10, 10
VoiceVolume=14, 14

[midi]
BufferSize=32
MidiMap=0
```

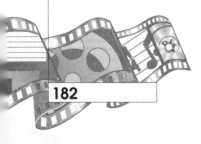

NOTE The [mciseq.drv] section outlines settings specific to the sequencer driver of the author's sound board. All these settings are configurable from either the Drivers applet or, in this case, from the SoundBlaster Mixer applet supplied by the sound-board manufacturer.

Part Two: Multimedia in a Business Environment

Using Multimedia in the Corporate Environment

Multimedia from an End-User's Perspective

Multimedia from the Developer's Perspective

"In the 90's, Multimedia is to our culture as the personal computer was in the 80's—an opportunity not to be missed."—Thomas Lopez, Chairman, Mammoth Micro Productions

CHAPTER

4

Using Multimedia in the Corporate Environment

Business use of multimedia can make corporate life more "fun and interesting." Although most businesses frown on this use of multimedia, it can be used to make corporations more inviting and enjoyable places to work—therefore making them more effective.

Businesses use multimedia to be more effective. The primary focus of this chapter is to provide a foundation for your company's effective use of multimedia to train, communicate, and sell.

Multimedia, like most other enabling technologies, finds its place in the corporate environment in one of three ways:

➤ Creating businesses focused on multimedia technology

➤ Making businesses more effective in their primary activities

➤ Making business life more "fun and interesting"

Businesses focus on technology. Many corporations have adopted multimedia products as one of the many reasons for their existence. These companies include the following:

➤ Tool vendors: Asymetrix Corporation or Macromedia, for example

➤ Publishers of traditional media that have expanded into electronic publishing: Time Warner Inc. and Britannica Software, for example

➤ Companies that explore the multimedia frontier: Continuum Productions, for example

Hypertext Information Systems

Business runs on paper. One of the most important kinds of paper for business is reference material. From dictionaries to encyclopedias and from software documentation to policy manuals, a businessperson is surrounded by information on paper, most of which is relatively inaccessible. The best type of information on paper is indexed or alphabetized, with one, or perhaps two, forms of linear access.

The business world has promised for many years that we are entering a paperless society. Instead, with the ubiquitous

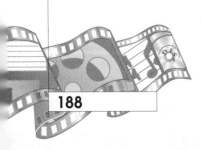

laser printer, we generate on paper more inaccessible information than ever. All this paper continues to demand to be
read from beginning to end and to follow authors' arguments
in the order in which they are made. In a *hypertext* document, nonlinear navigation from place to place and from
topic to topic is not only possible but also part of the design.
Although hypertext documents normally are electronically
based, you also can print them. The children's book series
Choose Your Own Adventure is an example of paper-based
hypertext, as are several novels by William Gibson. Hypertext
information systems attempt to solve both storage and
access problems in our modern information overload.

One of the most common hypertext information systems is
the set of on-line manuals supplied with many commercial
software products. Word for Windows, for example, includes
the help shown in figure 4.1.

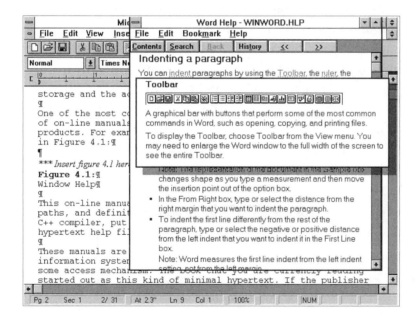

Figure 4.1:
A Windows Help
screen.

This on-line manual provides indexing, multiple navigation paths, and definitions. Some programs, such as the Borland C++ compiler, put virtually their entire printed manuals in hypertext help files.

These manuals are examples of the most basic hypertext information system: an on-line text document provided by an access mechanism. Some computer books now include a disk that includes all the book's text in a word processing document. With hypertext, you can search the text for a particular word or outlined topic area. If you read that an ANSI committee is working on a standard for hypertext SGML, for example, you can search within this document for another reference that defines the acronyms. You can suppress all the text and look at the book as an outline, and navigate quickly to any particular topic.

An on-line hypertext form of the preceding paragraph might have two forms of navigation embedded in it. The first is *definitional look-up.* If you do not know what ANSI means, you can simply click on the word *ANSI* with your mouse; the hypertext program finds the definition and pops it up on your screen (see fig. 4.2). In another example of hypertext navigation, shown in figure 4.3, you might be interested in other information about hypertext. When you click on the phrase "hypertext information system," a menu of other articles is displayed.

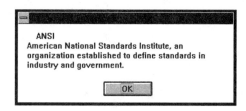

Figure 4.2:

A definition in a hypertext document.

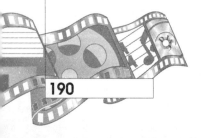

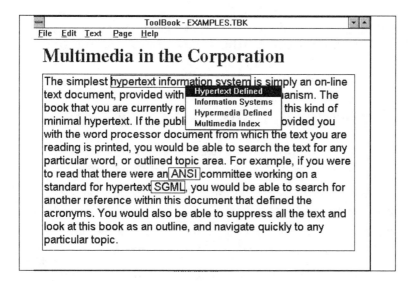

Figure 4.3:

Chapter selection in a hypertext document.

The most long-lived standard for hypertext documents is the Standard Graphical Markup Language (SGML). *SGML* is a set of rules for tagging parts of a document, such as headings, cross-references, and figures. It has been in use since the early 1980s, most often in the aerospace industry for aircraft maintenance manuals. Although SGML was designed for paper-document production, several companies—most notably, TMS, Inc., and Owl International—have developed systems for reading SGML documents (or their analogs) as on-line hypertext documents.

Although SGML extensions support graphics, hypertext documents use only one channel of information communication: text. Text communicates only about 10 percent of the information potentially present in a document or presentation. Sound, graphics, and motion all contribute to a much richer communications environment. With the addition of these elements, hypertext becomes hypermedia. Several dictionaries broaden their spectrum by including audio pronunciations of terms. Encyclopedias include animations that show how things work. Within a corporation, a policy manual can be made much more effective if it includes an audio message from the CEO or an animation of exit routes for emergencies.

Hypermedia Information Systems

The movement from simple hypertext to hypermedia demands more sophisticated software and some effort in program development so that content specialists can use the software to produce reference material. Two of the most commonly used software tools for hypermedia development are Microsoft Viewer and Asymetrix's ToolBook.

Simpler hypertext material can be implemented on DOS-based 8088- and 80286-class computers, as long as graphics demands are minimal. As complexity increases, an 80386-based Windows computer or a Macintosh becomes de rigeur. The majority of corporate reference material translated into hypertext form is in document sizes of less than 5M, with many documents only 500K in size. Although documents of this size can be stored easily on individual users' workstations, the retention of this material on a network server has significant advantages. When items are stored on a network, only a single copy is necessary, and local storage is left free for other uses. A much more important reason for storing corporate reference material on a network, however, is version control. All "copies" of a company policy manual can be updated in one simple installation, and all workstations then are guaranteed to have the correct copy.

Commercial reference material is being supplied more frequently on CD-ROM. The richness of hypermedia often can require large amounts of data for audio, video, and animation; therefore necessitating the larger data-storage format of a CD-ROM. Other information suppliers deal with so much text data that CD-ROM is the only economical distribution method.

Material based on CD-ROM requires that individual copies of the documents be accessed primarily from individual workstation CD-ROM readers. Most reference material, however, is used only intermittently by individuals. Companies can benefit, therefore, by exploring site-licensing possibilities for CD-ROM products so that large numbers of users can have access to a single reference source through their in-house network. Pioneer, Sony, and Hitachi supply network-oriented CD-ROM servers; the Pioneer CD-ROM cartridges and carousels are the most economical, particularly for multidisk sets. Users can get frustrated, however, as they wait in line for access to their disk while other users rotate the carousel. Ganged single-disk CD-ROM readers provide faster access with a corresponding increase in both cost and network resource loading.

NOTE Many CD-ROM publishers assume that their title will be used on a local workstation. The users access to the CD-ROM data is through either the Macintosh System 7 extensions or the MSCDEX DOS extensions rather than through the file system. These titles cannot be used on network servers. Titles that make heavy use of CD audio rather than digital-file audio become much less useful across a network. This type of title plays its audio to the other CD-ROM readers in the server room rather than on your workstation.

Hypertext information services demand an investment in both equipment and effort. The payback is large: less use of paper, more uniform and accessible information, and a better focus on the task.

Video Teleconferencing: the Multimedia Backbone

When most people think about multimedia, they think about a CD-ROM or videodisc connected to a stand-alone computer. Although these certainly are examples of multimedia, single-user multimedia in the corporate world is being replaced rapidly by networked multimedia. The effort to generate and implement multimedia applications can be justified only if it is shared by many users. Some types of multimedia must be shared—it is difficult to imagine stand-alone video conferencing, and most uses of multimedia can be made more effective by sharing—networked multimedia can create, for example, a "virtual classroom."

Because networking and telecommunications are such an important part of future-think multimedia, you must have some background in the arcane world of telecommunications technology to make the best use of multimedia. Acronyms abound: after you have decided, for example, to place multimedia across a WAN rather than a LAN, you must decide whether you will purchase your POTS from the RBOCs or obtain ISDN from an ATV. You should recognize some of these basic acronyms to understand conversations about telecommunications (see table 4.1).

Table 4.1
Telecommunications Acronyms

Acronym	Meaning
ADSL	Asymmetrical digital subscriber line (signal-enhanced high-speed T-1)
ATM	Asynchronous transfer mode (broad-band ISDN)
ATV	Alternative telephone vendor; telephone network vendors that have sprung up since the breakup of AT&T (MCI and Sprint are well-known examples)

continues

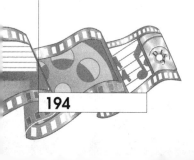

Table 4.1
Continued

Acronym	Meaning
CATV	Community antenna television (cable TV)
CCITT	Comité Consultatif International Telephonique et Télégraphique, an international standards organization for telecommunications
CO	Central office; the local telephone exchange
FDDI	Fiber-distributed data interface (fiber-optic token ring)
gbps	Gigabits per second (1 billion bits)
ISDN	Integrated services digital network; 56 kilobit-per-second digital lines
JPEG	Joint Photographic Experts Group, an international committee focused on compression standards for images (JPEG is a short form of JPEG compression, an efficient form of lossy compression)
kbps	Kilobits per second (1 thousand bits)
LAN	Local area network
mbps	Megabits per second (1 million bits)
MPEG	Motion-JPEG-compression, a form of the JPEG compression algorithm optimized for motion video
NTSC	National Television Standards Committee; "NTSC signal" describes normal U.S. television signals
PBX	Private branch exchange; typically, an in-house telephone network
POTS	Plain old telephone service; normal business lines
RBOC	Regional Bell operating company (known also as the "baby Bells"); the parts of the Bell Telephone System after the court-ordered divestiture
T-1	Primary-rate ISDN
T-3	Telephone network backbone (inter-CO connections)
WAN	Wide area network
X.25	The CCITT packet network protocol

Telephone Network-Based Services

When you pick up your office telephone, you are listening to an analog audio signal. Many parts of the telephone system simply switch and amplify that signal between telephones. Analog signals can be noisy and have dropouts not related to the phone system. If your phone line runs next to a large electric motor, for example, the electromagnetic energy of the motor can be picked up in the phone wires and cause interference in your conversation. Analog signals also degrade over distance, and the bandwidth of an analog signal on simple copper wire is limited.

To get around these problems, vendors have adopted various forms of digital technology. Rather than operate your phone system like a phonograph record, these vendors operate it like a compact disc. Audio signals are converted to their digital representation, sent down the line, and converted back to analog signals. This translation can occur at the local telephone exchange (in the case of "plain old telephone service"), at the PBX (as is typical in most T-1 installations), or at the telephone (in many of the newer PBXs). The multimedia equipment you can use—and the effectiveness of its use—depends on how your telephone system is built and how you are connected to it.

Plain Old Telephone Service (POTS)

The basic telephone service for which most businesses pay about $60 per month per line is "plain old telephone service" over switched copper wire. POTS has the lowest bandwidth of all the telecommunications services. It was designed for voice communication, and because human speech has such a large amount of redundancy, telephone-system vendors were able to *multiplex*, or share, lines between several conversations. The number of switches, or telephone exchanges, a signal must go through between two network users typically degrades POTS quality.

With all these limitations, the bandwidth available on POTS is about 100 kbps (or about 10,000 characters per second). The current effective limitation is between approximately 20 and 30 kbps. Fast V.32bis modems coupled with V.42bis compression (V.32bis and V.42bis are CCITT-established standards) theoretically could transmit data at 57.6 kbps; noise, switching latency, and simple line quality, however, limit data-transmission speeds to about half the theoretical limit. An emerging standard, known informally as V-fast, describes a transmission and compression standard that should bring POTS to a real-world 70 kbps. This transmission rate is almost fast enough for small-sized Video for Windows or QuickTime video with "telephone-quality" audio (see table 4.2).

Table 4.2
Transmission Bandwidths

Kilobits per second	Material
10	Text
15	POTS
20	JPEG-compressed full-screen still images
30	"Telephone-quality" sound, from 300 to 3,000 Hz bandwidth
50	"AM radio" sound, from 100 to 10,000 Hz bandwidth
56	Basic-rate ISDN, Switched 56
100	1/4-screen, 10 frame per second Video for Windows or QuickTime

continues

Table 4.2
Continued

● ●

Kilobits per second	Material
150	"FM radio" sound, from 50 to 15,000 Hz bandwidth
384	Fractional T-1, Switched 384, FrameRelay
400	1/4-screen, 30-frame-per-second Video for Windows or QuickTime
500	Full-screen, 20-frame-per-second JPEG-compressed video
600	"CD quality" monophonic sound, from 20 to 20,000 Hz bandwidth
1000	Full-screen, 30-frame-per-second Video for Windows or QuickTime
1200	"CD quality" stereo sound, from 20 to 20,000 Hz bandwidth
1540	T-1, primary-rate ISDN
4000	Low-speed token ring
8000	"High quality" compressed video
10000	Ethernet
15000	Full-screen, uncompressed NTSC-quality video
16000	High-speed token ring
30000	High-definition television (HDTV)
46mbps	T-3
100mbps	FDDI
150mbps-1.2 gbps	ATM

● ●

The AT&T VideoPhone uses V.32bis over POTS to provide
between 5 and 10 frames per second on a 3-inch screen.
ShareVision Technology also uses POTS for its Desktop
Visual Communications system for approximately the same
image quality.

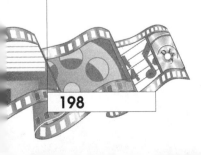

Pure videoconferencing technology over POTS is great for Christmas calls from Grandma, but it lacks the technological power for effective messages to (or from) your CEO. The combination of low-grade video over POTS and other forms of synchronous and asynchronous multimedia, however, can be an effective part of a multimedia presentation.

Integrated Services Digital Network (ISDN)

The next step on the telephone ladder is ISDN. Two key differences exist between basic-rate ISDN and POTS: ISDN is both digital and multichannel.

Basic-rate ISDN provides two 56-kbps channels, normally used for digital voice transmission, and one 16-kbps channel, normally used for signaling or low-speed data transmission. Between 250,000 and 300,000 ISDN lines now are installed, primarily within corporate campuses. In addition to RBOC-provided ISDN service, most PBX providers supply digital-signal PBXs that are functionally equivalent to ISDN, even if they are not protocol transparent. The advantage to you, as a multimedia provider, is that a large installed base of digital-capable distribution systems exists, probably including your company.

With clean digital channels, the use of alternating channels, and compression, basic-rate ISDN can push 200 kbps, easily in the QuickTime range. As with POTS, compression technologies are emerging: the most significant is the reduction of the CCITT H.261 video compression-decompression (*codec*) standard to chip sets. These codecs enable video to be produced at 15 frames per second across an ISDN 56-kbps channel.

Although the increased ISDN video throughput is significant, the multichannel character is more important for video-conferencing. The three channels enable you to establish a multiperson conference, and to transmit data, both machine-readable and fax.

Fractional T-1 (Packet-switched 384)

Fractional T-1 brings videoconferencing data-transmission rates to the magic number of 384 kbps, which is the throughput required for minimal 30-frame-per-second video. PictureTel and Compression Labs provide sophisticated codecs for high-quality, small-group videoconferencing. The RBOCs provide in many localities a FrameRelay service, an X.25-based version of fractional T-1.

Primary-Rate ISDN (T-1)

T-1 is the medium of choice for television-quality teleconferencing. It provides 23 56-kbps channels, and 2 16-kbps control channels. Most larger businesses use T-1 tie-lines into their PBXs, which makes T-1 available (with some effort) inside large corporations. Bell Communications Research has proposed a new copper standard, the asymmetrical digital subscriber line (ADSL). It will run at 1.54mbps, on 18,000-foot runs on standard telephone lines.

As compression technology improves and its acceptance lowers the cost of ISDN, and as CATV becomes more interactive, the stage is set for an interesting conflict between the CATV vendors and the telephone companies. Who will be first to provide communications that have high bandwidth (the CATV companies' specialty with hundreds of TV channels) and that also is interactive (the telephone companies' specialty with a century of real-time communications experience)? The quantum CATV division of Time-Warner, Inc., is using fiber-optic backbones to put multigigabit-per-second signals into blocks of 500 houses in Queens, New York; significant parts of Toronto, Ontario, have fiber-optic subscriber connections to residential customers.

T-3

T-3 is the backbone network between telephone central offices (COs). Customers have made limited use of this technology, although some large installations (typically with more than 25,000 network connections in a relatively small area) use T-3 to connect to their PBXs. Some supercomputer users, such as Lawrence Livermore Laboratories and Los Alamos National Laboratories, use T-3 for system interconnectivity.

Local Area Network Technology

Local area networks (LANs) are an obvious choice for sharing multimedia. They are fast enough for compressed video transfer, they have large storage capacity for images and audio, and they are installed and ready for use. LANs are designed for small packets of data, however, and concurrent video and audio requires large streams of synchronous data.

Ethernet

Ethernet, the most common business LAN topology, provides a theoretical throughput of 10mbps. With its contention-management schemes and packet overhead, however, it is more realistic to think of it as having a "real-world" limit of about half that amount. A single Ethernet bus can carry four or five concurrent digital video interactive (DVI) sessions when it is used with an optimized server, such as the video server from Starlight Networks.

Ethernet has a maximum bus length of about 10,000 feet without the use of repeaters.

Token Ring

IBM's high-speed Token Ring network is slightly faster than Ethernet, at a theoretical throughput of 16mbps and an actual throughput of approximately 9mbps. IBM has developed a multimedia server that will run from five to seven DVI sessions on a single ring.

Token Ring has a maximum ring perimeter of about 1,500 feet without the use of a repeater. Token Ring therefore has a maximum station-to-station distance of 750 feet on a ring.

Fast WANs (or big LANs)

As LANs add repeaters and increase the distance they can cover, and as WANs become increasingly faster, the two technologies have begun to merge. The first products of this merger are FDDI and broad-band ISDN.

FDDI

FDDI is an enhancement of IBM's Token Ring topology based on fiber optics. FDDI moves data at 100mbps, and with its optical-based technology, has little performance overhead. The FluentLinks system, from Fluent Machines, Inc., can provide from 15 to 20 simultaneous video sessions. FDDI has a maximum ring perimeter of 500 miles.

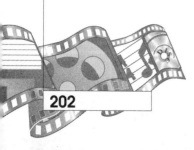

ATM (broad-band ISDN)

Asynchronous transfer mode is the most promising broad-band ISDN technology. ATM's purpose is to integrate different data types and speeds in one coherent and flexible transmission system. Adaptive Technologies and NEC both are building ATM switches that move data at a speed of as much as 154mbps, and IBM is working on a similar solution that utilizes digital transmission over cable TV.

NOTE

The next step is faster, pure light-frequency systems known as *photonic switched systems.* Because these systems do not have to convert traffic down to radio-frequency signals for amplification and redirection, they can maintain network throughput that approaches 1 terabit per second (a terabit is 1 million megabits) and node speeds of as much as 10gbps. This speed enables users to "attend" meetings in which 3-D images of participants "sit around" virtual tables—no one has to be in the physical presence of anyone else.

Using the Video Teleconferencing Backbone

Video teleconferencing is private television typically transported over a telephone network and more and more often over a local-area digital network (LAN). It hardly qualifies as multimedia. In that simple form, teleconferencing does not sound exciting until you stop to think that a picture is worth a thousand words. A recent study of business communications produced the following results:

➤ 7 percent of the meaning of a conversation is carried by the words

➤ 38 percent is carried by intonation

➤ 55 percent is carried by visual cues

You pick up the phone to get 45 percent of the message across; teleconferencing is a tool for conveying the other 55 percent.

Two basic types of teleconferencing exist: simple video with voice (and occasional data) and true multimedia teleconferencing, in which the voice and picture are only one path of communications. The second form requires more effort and planning, but it has the potential to reap significant benefits. Almost all the types of multimedia discussed in this chapter can benefit from the addition of live video.

Simple Teleconferencing

The use of simple video teleconferencing can be as simple as using the AT&T VideoPhone 2500 between two offices. The VideoPhone costs about $1,500 and plugs into standard telephone lines (POTS). It has a 3-inch screen and displays images from 5 to 10 frames-per-second, depending on their complexity. In computer terms, this video is at the level of QuickTime on a medium-performance Macintosh. Because the VideoPhone can be installed anywhere a standard analog telephone is installed, you easily can use the VideoPhone as part of a prototype in a video teleconferencing system.

At the opposite end of the spectrum is NEC's experimental virtual-reality teleconferencing system. This system enables you to work in 3-D across T-3 or ATM lines; when (and if) it comes to market, you should expect to pay at least $150,000 per station.

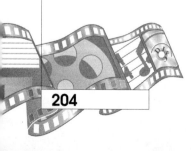

In the middle of the simple video teleconferencing spectrum is the Hitachi DP-200 videophone. At $15,000, this product provides 11-inch images at as much as 15 frames-per-second. You must use it on a digital network (either ISDN or Switched 56); it gets its throughput by using the CCITT H.261 compression standard. The DP-200 also has connections for fax and modem using the data subchannel of basic-rate ISDN.

The use of the DP-200 begins to cross over into multimedia conferencing. Although a modem connected to a videophone is not an integrated multimedia solution, it is a beginning.

Multimedia Conferencing

Some of the most interesting multimedia conferencing does not use real-time video. The Virtual Meeting (TVM), from RTZ Software, is a Macintosh-based conferencing system that controls multiple computers across a wide area. TVM can incorporate the following elements:

➤ Sound

➤ Graphics

➤ Program information, such as spreadsheets, word-processor documents, and schedules

➤ QuickTime video

Although all this data must be resident on each computer at the beginning of the conference, control of the data is provided in real-time so that each user sees the same screen display. TVM includes a white board so that participants can create and display annotations and sketches in real-time during the conference.

The other half of the multimedia conferencing equation is computer-hosted videophones. Macintosh-based solutions seem to be leading the pack.

Because video teleconferencing uses more data than can be transmitted over existing networks, data-stream reduction systems must be used. The most common systems are sampling and compression. The following list shows the three primary types of sampling:

➤ Frame reduction

➤ Difference analysis

➤ Color reduction

Frame-reduction sampling works by reducing the number of frames from the 20 to 30 frames-per-second required for full-motion perception to as few as 5 to 10 frames per second by dropping intermediate frames. (Moving pictures typically are displayed at 24 frames-per-second, and television is displayed at 30 frames per second.) Frame reduction results in jerky images, not unlike the images in early silent films. Although these jerky images often are irritating and incomplete, they can convey the key features of visual cues—a brief smile or a raised eyebrow, for example.

Difference-analysis sampling transmits only the differences between frames. Often, less than 5 percent of a frame differs from the previous frame, and just transmitting the differences allows for more realistic video with less data. Difference analysis requires more sophisticated and powerful hardware for interpreting the data stream; Intel's Digital Video Interactive (DVI) hardware, for example, may be required to generate or resolve the difference in data in real time. Microsoft's Video for Windows and Apple's QuickTime both operate fundamentally by difference-analysis sampling.

Color reduction is a third sampling technique. The human eye can resolve nearly 16 million colors (24-bit color), but it can be satisfied with between 16 colors (4-bit color) and 256 colors (8-bit color). By reducing the amount of color from 24 bits per pixel to 8 bits per pixel, an image can be cut to one-third its original size.

Orthogonal to sampling is compression: a video stream can be compressed as well as sampled, but neither implies the other. Video images have much redundant information in patterns and in large areas of consistent colors. The following list shows three of the most common types of graphics compression:

➤ Lossy

➤ Lossless

➤ Edge-capturing

JPEG/MPEG is the most well-known lossy-compression scheme. You often can recognize a real-world visual image that has considerable distortion or loss of image. JPEG compression can produce compression ratios of 5:1 or 6:1 when it is allowed to lose 10 percent of the image being compressed.

The PKZIP program uses a lossless compression. Whatever goes in comes out—exactly. The trade-off is that typical compression ratios are only 2:1.

Fractal Compression, developed by Iterative Systems, Inc., is one of the most promising edge-capturing compression schemes. By mathematically analyzing the transition maps from color to color, fractal compression can decompress to scalable, smooth images with compression ratios approaching 100:1. Such compression demands significant special-purpose hardware, and it is just beginning to be fast enough to do real-time compression.

Multimedia teleconferencing puts you firmly on the "bleeding edge" of technology. Just to experiment demands a considerable investment in hardware, and to use the technology can require major changes in a corporation's telecommunications infrastructure. The experimental technology, however, costs little more than the expense of travel and lost time for two executives going from coast to coast to a meeting. After teleconferencing is implemented, it can continue to save travel costs and increase communication bandwidth. Teleconferencing has an unmistakable "gee whiz" characteristic for customers that often can reduce the effort necessary to make a sale.

Increasing Productivity with Multimedia

Multimedia is fundamentally a way to increase communication levels over time and space. A multimedia application can approach and sometimes exceed the communication content of person-to-person conversation—and it can free that communication from time constraints. Support, training, and information sharing are major tasks in the modern information-based corporation. By using multimedia in this area, you can reduce costs and increase performance.

Corporate Training

Imagine an infinitely patient trainer, one who—no matter how tired—always teaches with the same clarity and emphasis and always toes the "party line"; this person can even be in 2 (or 20) places at a time. This type of instructor is the goal of multimedia corporate training.

Traditional stand-up corporate training is expensive. Each hour of classroom presentation time can take 40 hours of preclass development time and extra refresher time every

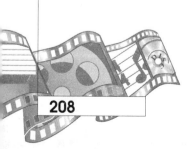

time the class is taught. Classes must be large to justify the cost of hiring a trainer, and this requirement precludes effective one-on-one instruction. A good corporate trainer must possess specialized, in-depth subject knowledge and must be a skilled communicator comfortable with—and energized by—teaching a sizable group of people in an "artificial" classroom situation. People who have this combination of skills and abilities are hard to find and therefore are in high demand; the cost of their expertise, teaching and travel time, and meals and accommodations is high. In addition, because of the stresses corporate trainers bear, they eventually can become tired and less effective.

Two solutions to these problems of trainer expense and effectiveness often are sought in the areas of video training tapes and printed training manuals. To create a tape, a class is taped, and the video is shipped to corporate sites and shown to numerous classes. The cost of trainer time and travel therefore is eliminated, and pacing problems are solved by repeating sections of the video and skipping to more relevant material as dictated by student need. Sometimes printed manuals are distributed to students, and the same difficulties of cost and presentation pacing similarly are resolved. In both cases, however, it is difficult to customize the material for classes in which needs vary from those addressed by the existing video or manual. When the course content changes (because of company hardware or software upgrades, for example), it is difficult to make necessary modifications to the videotapes or printed manuals.

To avoid the static nature of video and printed training materials, companies sometimes turn to computer-based training (CBT). CBT tends to consist primarily of presentation and practice, with little flexibility or the capability to accommodate individual trainee needs. Corporate trainers cannot tailor a stand-up course to meet the individual needs of people at different knowledge levels within a single group:

if one person cannot keep up with other students, the trainer cannot take the time to repeat material or provide individual help. If another student already is conversant with the material being discussed, the instructor cannot skip ahead to more interesting or more challenging material, and the student grows bored and impatient and feels that valuable time is being wasted. CBT can solve this problem.

These three nonpersonal solutions to corporate training problems follow the same paradigm: reduce the communication bandwidth so that the information can be encapsulated in a manageable and affordable form. Multimedia corporate training removes significantly the bandwidth limitation.

Multimedia-based training can be used to perform both affective training and cognitive training. You will want to train customer service representatives (CSRs) for your company. You normally write a text-based course, and, in a series of stand-up training sessions and workshops, teach new CSRs how your company responds to customer needs. Multimedia training development is the same at the beginning: you define what you want to teach, your goals for the course, and how you intend to teach it. The multimedia training class trains the CSRs in a simulated work environment: they pick up the phone, request information from the customer, receive data from the corporate computer system, and act on the conversation. The remainder of this section explains how the multimedia class is designed and constructed.

A trainee picks up the telephone

First, you tell the trainee your objectives and state that a trial telephone call is coming in "at any moment." You have recorded a sound file of your company's telephone ringing, and, after a random period, you play that sound through the computer's speakers. Your MIS department already has built telephone simulators, controlled through your computer's serial ports; when the trainee picks up the phone, your program is notified. You can present a list of possible greetings to the trainee, and that person can select and use one to begin the conversation. Your program then does a simple format analysis on the student's voice to pick up signs of stress.

The trainee requests information from the customer

Your company has specific methods, described in the policy manual, of interacting with customers. Without prompting, the CSR can ask for the customer's identification code, and you can record for later evaluation the information requested. A customer's recorded voice can provide an identification number and a request, and a combination of computer-screen simulation and directed questions can test the student's understanding of the request. As lessons become more advanced, the program can simulate different accents, line conditions, and customer attitudes, in addition to more complex problems.

The trainee obtains data from the corporate computer system

The CSRs must enter all calls in a tracking system that also is used to suggest possible resolutions. Because you have chosen a multimedia authoring system rather than just a CBT development system, you can simulate (or even use) the corporate computer system. The trainee examines the screen and enters data as necessary. If the trainee takes too long, the customer can even express impatience.

Critically important to both of these training stages is the use of multiple modes of help and training. If a trainee does not ask correct questions of the training system, the system can provide an audio prompt and on-screen textual prompting. Responses can be used to identify trainees who are "visually" or "audially" oriented.

The trainee takes action based on the conversation

In the last step, the CSR takes some action on the problem, and enters it in the corporate computer simulation. The trainee's response can be recorded again for analysis, and a chosen response can be self-compared.

In many ways, this process is traditional CBT, enhanced with multimedia to create a more realistic simulation of the work environment. If more affective training is the object, you can add Video for Windows clips of the customers; to add a more personal note, you can add instructions on videodisc, overlaid on the training screen. This system only touches on the possibilities of multimedia training. When CBT is combined with teleconferencing, CATV, networking, and multimedia, you begin to touch on the possibilities of The Virtual Classroom, a concept developed by Interactive Generation. One instructor can control multiple local multimedia devices in classrooms, in addition to a "live" on-camera instructor who can modify the instructional process based on trainee feedback. The Virtual Classroom uses multimedia and networking to provide much of the "high touch" of instructed training with CBT self-pacing.

Multimedia CBT demands large amounts of storage for a training system's audio and video components. Because the majority of this data is static, it can be stored on CD-ROM. The use of CD-ROM makes it much more difficult, however,

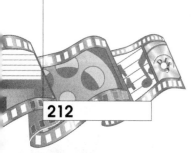

to change content or affect. CD-ROMs have many of the same versioning problems as other forms of program distribution. In the ideal method of distributing multimedia CBT, you store analog video segments on custom videodiscs and distribute all the rest of the segments and the CBT across the network.

Computer-based training requires a sizeable investment for its substantial payback. You can use multimedia in CBT to multiply the rate of return by increasing the following elements:

➤ Realism

➤ Learning modes

➤ "Friendliness" of the learning environment

Companies that use the best training methods in the '90s will clearly be the companies that win in the global battle. CBT can bring your company to the training table, but you must use multimedia to be a winner.

Interactive On-line Help Systems (Training on Demand)

Computer-based training is half of the support equation; the other part is on-line help, or training on demand. After you have learned to use a computer system, company procedure, or management skill, the need always exists for rapid access to details and techniques for doing a job better.

Regardless of whether training consists of the most advanced type of computer-based multimedia simulations or one-on-one personal training, it is best at providing the overview and the concepts and structures. Most people do not retain training details; even if someone retained every detail from a training session, certain details are best discovered in a real workday situation. It is the task of help systems to provide that detailed support.

The root of on-line help is a hypertext environment. Information navigation and presentation is under the control of the user rather than the other way around. Help systems present information in small chunks: when you use the help system in Word for Windows, for example, you do not want to learn all about formatting—you want to learn only how to apply a double underline. This presentation style makes on-line help systems an ideal environment for training.

NOTE

The most important factor in a good on-line help system is its availability. Like the infinitely patient CBT instructor, the instantaneously available support person is the icon of on-line help. The help system never tires of answering the same question about double underlining.

A simple help system is only a partial implementation. Users continually cry, "Don't tell me—show me!" A multimedia help system can show a user how to complete a task. Animations can clarify individual tasks, from setting international rates on a postage machine to adjusting control points on Bezier curves. You can provide examples of affective speech through audio integrated into the help system, and a short video clip can demonstrate a complex procedure. The key to effective help is small, flexible chunks of information that can be used instantly.

A side effect of the atomic nature of an effective help system is that it is flexible and multipurpose. You may want to know how to underline; another person may want to know what "formatting" means. You do not want to wander through a discussion on formatting, and the other person does not want to understand underlining. Neither a printed-paper help book nor the monolithic electronic text help that is

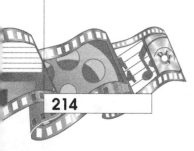

typical in UNIX systems enables both of you to access the information effectively. Like most electronic information, you can modify help systems incrementally; you must redistribute the files after you make changes, but the cost of production is negligible compared to that of paper help.

If you combine the reference characteristics of on-line help with the instructional features of CBT, you obtain an important and powerful new training tool: just-in-time training. Multimedia on-line help enables you to build training systems that provide instruction when the trainee wants it rather than when you want to provide it. You have a much more effective training system, therefore, with fully engaged and interested trainees focused on solving the problem at hand with the information you provide. You are much more likely to remember how to do double underlining in Windows when you learn how to do it at the time you need it rather than in a class in which you ask, "When will I ever need to double underline?"

In the example of the CSR in the preceding section, suppose that a call comes in and the CSR processes it—but not in a satisfactory manner. An on-line help system provides the CSR with ready and rapid access to the policies and procedures relevant to that call. Just-in-time training enables the student to find a situation similar to the one encountered, to see how it should be resolved, and to practice making that resolution in a strongly receptive learning state. The phrase "Show me, don't tell me" is critical in this case. The use of multimedia helps the CSR to suspend disbelief and to practice as though a call situation really exists. Text can never do this.

To corporate bean counters, one of the best characteristics of just-in-time training is that it is free (or almost free). After you have developed training materials and on-line help (both necessary to simply stay alive in the contemporary corporate environment), it is a relatively simple task to combine the two to produce just-in-time training and greatly increase their effectiveness.

Although just-in-time training has obvious uses inside a corporation, its uses extend far beyond internal ones. Many large corporations require financial transactions to be made through electronic data interchange (EDI). Although EDI data formats are uniform, procedures for processing the information are not. If your company provided its suppliers with your own internal just-in-time training for your side of EDI, it would be better able to do its part by "second guess-ing" the way your data is used.

Another example of just-in-time training is in education, in a traditional public school setting or a corporate remedial-training situation, for example. Suppose that your child cannot solve a homework problem in geometry because she does not remember the point-slope formula she supposedly learned in the "training class" (algebra) the previous year. You help her derive the formula, and she then can see its use and immediately apply it in the geometry problem. On her exam the following day, she remembers and applies the formula correctly because she understood the concept and applied it when she needed it for the homework exercise.

Corporate-wide Databases and Shared Resources

The personal computer has encouraged the creation of "personal data" (spreadsheet models, word-processor templates, reports, and proposals, for example), which leads to problems when the data is corporate data. The data gets lost or forgotten and often is underused. The sheer volume of multimedia data leads you to recognize again that data must be shared to avoid unnecessary duplication. Although multimedia data occupies much computer storage space, its flexibility and powers of indirect "multichannel" communication make the investment in extra storage a wise decision. No reason exists, however, for the amount of duplication that is typical with text data.

Much of the audio and even some of the video for the CSR training-class example is equally applicable for training, software-support technicians, bill collectors, and receptionists—indeed, anyone whose primary contact with your company's public is through the telephone. All departments that need these training services can share the cost of developing high-quality sound resources and keeping them on-line, and therefore significantly reduce the cost to any single department.

Consider that CSR training might well require 500 megabytes of data for every class. The cost of equipping every workstation in a classroom with hard disk storage for just one class easily can be prohibitive. The cost of equipping all CSRs in a corporation with enough hard disk storage space to provide just-in-time training in all aspects of their job easily can exceed your payroll budget. These costs can make unavailable one of the most powerful tools you can use for increased employee productivity. When you keep multimedia data on a network server, you make this type of sharing financially feasible and even technically easy.

The data-transmission bandwidth of most LANs is high enough to make multimedia data sharing relatively straightforward. Effective sharing requires some planning, however. Digital video demands the most capacity; token-ring networks with special servers that run unencumbered can support only seven or eight simultaneous sessions. CD-quality digital audio demands a data stream of 100 kilobytes per second. With packet overhead, Ethernet is limited to no more than 40 to 50 simultaneous sessions. At first, this limitation seems to restrict the use of multimedia on networks; you cannot forget, however, that training sessions and presentations—the two most important multimedia applications in today's corporations—are not movies, and they do not demand fully continuous data. In the CSR example, a video clip of the customer's side of a conversation might be only 3M of compressed video, and a telephone conversation can be replicated with 100 kilobytes of "telephone quality" audio.

The solution to the network bandwidth problem has two parts. One consideration is the allocation of hardware resources on the network, which is critical for effective multimedia work. Optimized servers connected with high-speed fiber-optic or FDDI backbones are essential, not only for multimedia but also for general high-speed corporate computing. The more effective your infrastructure, the easier it is to implement corporation-wide multimedia. The other consideration is the planning of presentations, help, and training so that they use small, discrete chunks of multimedia data rather than long, monolithic streams. This approach provides several benefits include the following:

➤ Reduces network traffic and enables more sessions to function across a single network

➤ Reduces data contention because a user is less likely to have to wait for a smaller piece of data

➤ Increases performance because many multimedia devices attempt to load all their data at one time and because smaller chunks of data load faster

➤ Increases the ease of repurposing, or using existing small "building blocks" of data for new structures

If your company shares multimedia resources on networks, it might be able to take advantage of the many benefits that multichannel communication can provide to employees. It needs only the following ingredients:

➤ Careful planning

➤ Interdepartmental cooperation

➤ A willingness to experiment

Multimedia Memos and Electronic Mail

At some point in your career, you no doubt have wanted to write a memo that says, "Read me!" With electronic-mail multimedia services, you can—almost—accomplish that goal.

Electronic mail has been a boon to modern corporations, and, because of some of its limitations, a bane. Because electronic mail typically consists of unformatted text, it is difficult to convey nuances in meaning and emphasis. Because of this limitation, an entire language of "emoticons" has been created to carry nonverbal meanings that unform-atted text alone cannot convey. <g> stands for grinning or "Take this as a joke," for example, and : - (represents a sad face on its side that indicates dissatisfaction or unhappiness. The capability to tell your funny story in your own voice or to convey your sadness through facial expressions is much more satisfactory. Multimedia embedding enables you to add these missing dimensions to your electronic- mail communications.

One of the most common, and most difficult, tasks in internal corporate communications is the conveyance of a process or the development of an idea. As video capture and playback become available more readily across a corporation, you will be able to send, as a memo, a video clip of yourself explaining a concept at your office white board. You no longer will have to reduce your ideas and diagrams to dead words on paper. Electronic mail will become, in effect, time-delayed video conferencing. This increased bandwidth of communication will speed up product development and increase interoffice productivity.

Making Money with Multimedia

Multimedia clearly has the potential to make a company much more functional and agile in its internal operations by increasing the effectiveness of internal communications and training. It can make your company more profitable by increasing the effectiveness of your communication with the outside world.

Corporate Presentations

Corporate presentations provide, above all other consider-ations, the opportunity to educate your public about your company and its products. You can demonstrate your company's effective use of leading-edge technology and show potential customers why they should do business with you.

Until the advent of desktop multimedia, a corporate pre-senter had three choices: bland, black-and-white view foils presented on overhead projectors; numerous trays of slides produced by the art department on three months' notice; or expensive, glitzy, content-free Las Vegas-style videotape shows. Now you can balance production values, costs, and content to present your company and your concept as both media-savvy and fiscally responsible.

Presentations are a means to communicate information in both an affective and cognitive manner. Like all communications, they should have the following elements:

➤ An opening that demands attention

➤ A message to convey

➤ A conclusion that makes emotive contact and calls for action

Multimedia can enhance each of these areas in a presentation. Multimedia does not help define the message, but it is particularly adept at sharpening message clarity. For multimedia to work for you in a presentation, you must be able to define your message clearly and concisely. You should be able to show a slide that states in one sentence what you want to say, and everything in the presentation should support that statement of purpose. With that clarity, the tools of multimedia presentation work for you rather than against your company's goals.

The Opening

Multimedia still has a "glitz factor": sound and motion attract attention by themselves, and you want to use one or both of these elements to strengthen the beginning of your presentation. If you take the time to write your own music, record your own sound effects, and tape your own video, these tasks probably are unjustified within your presentation's goals. Many sources of "standard" sound and video exist. A search of such multimedia periodicals as *MPC World*, *Multimedia World*, and *New Media* can turn up many vendors of MIDI files, wave files, and QuickTime, AVI, or DVI clips. Each of these items has its benefits in a corporate presentation.

MIDI provides a flexible and compact storage format for music and effects. Because MIDI reproduction makes light demands on a computer system, it is ideal when you use music or effects simultaneously with CPU-intensive forms of media. More than any other media, the reproduction quality of MIDI files depends on the hardware that plays it—its greatest weakness. A specific MIDI synthesizer or sound board may or may not have the patches or sound colors you have sequenced or programmed into the MIDI file.

MIDI synthesis hardware can range in price and capability from $200 sound cards from MediaVision (ProAudio Spectrum) and Creative Laboratories (SoundBlaster) to banks of keyboards, samplers, and synthesizers from Ensonix and Yamaha. Two of the best choices for corporate multimedia are the ESS-1 MIDI synthesis board from Roland (at about $500) and the ProAudio Spectrum 16 (at about $400).

Wave audio is now the only effective way to include speech in multimedia applications. Current desktop sampling technology makes it easy for you to record sound and voice digitally at CD quality. Digital audio comes at a price, however; it demands a great deal of storage space, and it requires a substantial amount of CPU and data-bus power for both recording and reproduction.

A large variety of wave-audio reproduction hardware is available. The ubiquitous—and unacceptable—PC speaker is everywhere; it can be used with Microsoft driver software to reproduce barely recognizable speech. The next step up is a toy-store refugee: Disney's Sound Source. At approximately $30, it provides AM-radio sound quality from a PC's parallel printer port. The Sound Source is effective for large-scale distribution of wave audio at a relatively low cost; the low-end for most corporate multimedia, however, is any sound board in the $150 range, such as Windows Sound System, or the ProAudio Spectrum 8. The best of the mid-range ($400) multipurpose boards is the ProAudio Spectrum 16. The top of the line begins with the $900 Turtle Beach MultiSound, a wave-audio-only interface board for CD-quality sampling.

Animation can provide most of the affect of video at a much lower cost for storage, CPU overhead, and production time. Animation devices are available more readily from third-party suppliers than are video devices, and they often are less encumbered by copyright and licensing restrictions. Animation often is less realistic than video and has a lower glitz factor, although its relative simplicity frequently carries your message more effectively.

In the world of business presentations, animation is a software-only domain. The two primary providers of animation software for PCs, Autodesk and Macromedia, both provide Media Control Interface (MCI) drivers for Windows. These drivers make it easy to implement animation within an authoring environment such as the Asymetrix ToolBook. A recent addition to animation technology is Microsoft's FileConverter, supplied as part of Video for Windows. It allows animation file formats to be converted to the Video for Windows (.AVI) file format.

Video clips provide the greatest realism, and, therefore, the greatest potential presentation effect. That effect, however, causes high storage and other hardware costs. Third-party video also is fraught with ownership and copyright problems; even the simplest use of video clips in a corporate environment involves synchronization rights, which can be difficult to obtain as the entertainment industry enters the digital age. You should use locally produced video for presentations, even though it can be costly.

The minimal playback of video clips has been made easy with the release of Video for Windows. As long as you have a

486-class CPU, you can produce small-image playback at 15 frames-per-second with the Indio codec. Larger or higher-quality video must be assisted by hardware. The least expensive level of hardware includes SuperVideo Windows, from New Media Graphics, and VideoBlaster video overlay boards, from Creative Laboratories. Full-motion, full-screen video playback requires boards in the class of Intel/IBM Action-Media/II. It is not clear whether the payback from the use of higher-end boards for presentation purposes justifies their cost.

Video playback is only half the story, of course. Before you can play back video, someone must digitize it. The Super-Video Motion Compression board, from New Media Graphics, and the IBM ActionMedia/II board are the most effective desktop boards for video recording. Both boards must be used in fast computers with large amounts of memory and massive amounts of free hard disk storage space.

The Message

Traditional business presentations are direct, cognitive, and text-oriented. This situation corresponds with the supposed purpose of a business presentation: to convey information, mind to mind, about a company or an idea. In the current business climate, however, the traditional method for conveying information is not enough; relationships, feelings, and emotions enter into the business decision-making process more frequently. You no longer can just try to convince a client or a financier intellectually that you have the best idea. You must make them believe that you are the best person, or organization, with which to work. To accomplish this second task with a one-dimensional presentation is nearly impossible. A presentation must involve the "whole listener," and it must be flexible enough to accommodate the exploration of

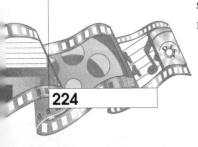

ideas during the presentation. Hypermedia techniques, in addition to pictures (both still and moving), are powerful vehicles for carrying multidimensional messages.

When you build hypermedia links into a presentation, you can layer levels of information and hide and reveal details as necessary. This capability keeps your presentation directed yet flexible. Hypermedia demands more preparation than does a traditional view foil presentation, and it requires on-line computer resources. It is the least expensive multimedia application, however, for presentations.

Any number of tools can be used to create hypermedia presentations. The most frequently used tools are enhanced slide shows, such as Microsoft PowerPoint and Persuasion, from Aldus. Although these tools are easy to use, they lack the sophistication to produce a true hypermedia presentation. They provide the following capabilities, however:

➤ Slide-to-slide navigation

➤ Sequential production of differing media (they provide access to audio and visual information files in any order, but one at a time)

➤ Limited support for pop-ups

Neither PowerPoint nor Persuasion, however, supports the concept of navigating webs of information (nonsequential navigation), and neither allows complex actions or the concurrent display of differing media (playing audio and video "tracks" simultaneously, for example). Multiple media synchronization normally is done in programming languages, which has made this level of multimedia difficult to produce. Multimedia ToolBook, however, combines many features of slide-show presentation applications with the power of a programming language and preprogrammed "widgets" to enable presenters to do their own multimedia synchronization.

A series of still images often can communicate effectively. They can motivate viewers to focus directly on points being made and exercise their imagination on omitted details. Still images are easy to incorporate into presentations and are inexpensive to produce. You can capture them by scanning or using video capture systems.

The Conclusion

Many presenters fall into the trap of making their endings Broadway productions. Presentations are not shows; they do not need a heartwarming denouement. You must carefully choose media to end business presentations. A short sound or video clip that shows the viewer performing the desired action is often all that is necessary to elicit appropriate audience behavior. The subliminal message in a presentation's conclusion should be, "To make the show go on, you must become part of it." Keep the conclusion light on entertainment and heavy on the commitment you want, and use multimedia sparingly without letting glitz appear (leave the curtain up on the set).

Although presentations are best made person-to-person, such "live" presentations are not always possible. A significant advantage of a multimedia presentation is that another presenter often can provide it with much the same effect. Although hypermedia provides more room to explore concepts, the inherent structure of a multimedia presentation and its richness of noncognitive content reduce the importance of the presenter. A presentation often can be videotaped from the computer's sound and video outputs for a high-quality and highly portable presentation. Jovian Logic Corporation produces several high-quality scan converters that can be used to produce S-VHS videotapes.

Point-of-Sale Presentations

Point-of-sale presentations are brief, stand-alone business presentations that can deliver a message and elicit an action in approximately the time it takes to view a TV commercial: from 30 seconds to one minute. Customers who have no training in the system at hand must be able to operate these presentations. Two fundamental types of point-of-sale presentations exist: the product demonstration, whether it is interactive or self-running, and the kiosk, which is always interactive. Although demonstrations and kiosks can use the full range of multimedia technology, including live video, videodisc, and networked media access, for reasons of simplicity, reliability, and maintenance, you should use software-only multimedia as much as possible. A CD-ROM drive and an audio card are generally all that is necessary.

Product Demonstrations

The most effective product demonstrations employ nothing more than animation and audio. In a period of 30 seconds to one minute, well-executed animation captures a potential customer's attention, and sound delivers a message that the person will not have time to read and understand. If "fancier" technology is used, the viewer begins to focus on the demon-stration rather than on the product. Again, simpler is better. A demonstration should not require viewer interaction to achieve its goal; in other words, all product demonstrations are self-running. A viewer always should be able to interrupt a self-running demonstration to obtain more information, repeat a portion, or even purchase the product being demon-strated.

Kiosks

Unlike product demonstrations, kiosks invite viewer exploration. People use kiosks in one of the two following modes:

> ➤ **To acquire information quickly.** In this case, viewers should be on and off the system in about 30 seconds

> ➤ **To engage a patient, consistent, and knowledgeable salesperson.** In this case, a typical session may last from two to three minutes

Although a kiosk may include a certain amount of self-running information presentation to attract attention, its fundamental mode is interactivity. Because of the way in which people tend to use kiosks, the chunks of information they deliver must be smaller (typically from 10 to 15 seconds long) in comparison to the 30- to 60-second chunks a product demonstration delivers. Kiosks are hypermedia by nature—they are nonlinear explorations of a subject area.

Because of the response-time constraints in a kiosk program, you should limit your use of them to only digital media and, ideally, store data on a large, fast hard disk. Optical media, such as CD-ROMs or videodiscs, is too slow to meet rigorous kiosk demands.

In addition, kiosks often are in exposed and unsupervised locations. A pointing device, such as a mouse, is quickly and easily damaged, often misused, and sometimes stolen. The only reasonable pointing device for use in a kiosk situation is a finger on a touch screen.

Touch screens impose significant constraints on a screen's visual design. The daintiest finger on the largest screen has an activation area of between 10 and 20 pixels, and a mouse has a "hot spot" of a single pixel. Mice often convey information through their motion and position; in kiosk applications, however, a touch screen is a true point-and-click device that conveys position and activation, not motion.

A well-planned kiosk program should include a way to produce information presented in hard-copy form. When you use a kiosk, you often have neither pen nor paper, and no surface on which to write.

Two particularly effective types of kiosks are on opposite sides of the North American continent:

➤ **World Financial Center, in New York City.** These relatively simple kiosks use still photographs, animation, and multilingual sound to tell you not only how to find a shop, but also why you ought to shop there

➤ **The Seattle Art Museum.** This information kiosk uses stereo sound, full-motion video, text, animation, and 24-bit full-screen color photographs to guide viewers in an in-depth exploration of the museum's collection and its exhibits.

The museum's kiosk invites viewers to understand its place in Seattle's cultural life and to commit to an active and supporting relationship through understanding. The average amount of time spent on this kiosk is between 5 and 10 minutes. In contrast, the World Financial Center kiosks call for direct action—go to this shop—and average interaction time seems to be less than 20 seconds. Although these kiosks are very different, they serve their business purposes well.

Looking at Multimedia As an Industry

Multimedia is both a set of tools and a new way to present information. This statement is not much different from what someone might have said about the printing press in the 15th century. Both Gutenberg's press and Aldus' type were tools that made possible the production of printed books—the printing press was a new way to present information that redefined the way Europe looked at its world. In the new publishing world, "books" are similar in many ways to printed books:

➤ **They tend to be heavily text-oriented,** but they consist of hypertext

➤ **They include graphics,** but the graphics move

➤ **They are built of words,** but those words speak

The remainder of this chapter discusses some of the "new books" toolmakers and publishers, and provides addresses for contacting the tool companies.

Multimedia Tool Companies

Asymetrix Corporation built ToolBook, one of the first multimedia-capable authoring systems for the Windows platform. Since then, the company has focused on developing advanced tools for multimedia developers, such as Multimedia ToolBook, and tools for end users, such as MediaBlitz!

> Asymetrix Corporation
> Suite 700
> 110 110th Avenue NE
> Bellevue, WA 98004

AimTech Corporation makes IconAuthor, a visual programming system that supports multimedia extensions. It focuses primarily on CBT applications, enhanced by multimedia, rather than on presentations or "pure" multimedia titles.

AimTech Corporation
20 Trafalgar Square
Nashua, NH 03063

Macromedia Inc. makes Authorware Professional, which provides nearly transparent compatibility for Macintosh and Windows multimedia applications.

Macromedia Inc.
600 Townsend Street
San Francisco, CA 94103

Microsoft Corporation's Visual Basic Professional provides a set of multimedia controls for building multimedia-aware applications for the Windows, VIS, and Sony CD player platforms.

Microsoft Corporation
1 Microsoft Way
Redmond, WA 98052

Multimedia Publishers

Reference books are the current primary focus of the multimedia publishing industry. Encyclopedias and dictionaries abound. Two of the most significant dictionary publishers—Oxford University Press, publisher of the *Oxford English Dictionary*, and Maxwell Electronic Publishing, publisher of the *Macmillan Dictionary for Children*—span the spectrum of a dictionary's purpose. Although the venerable Oxford dictionary is not strictly a multimedia product, it is notable for its use of hypertext and the ease with which users can trace definitions. Macmillan's children's dictionary uses an innovative combination of still pictures, animation, audio, and games to define words and to get children interested in and excited about the words.

Electronic encyclopedias form another class of multimedia references. One of the best of this genre is *The New Grolier Multimedia Encyclopedia* (Grolier Electronic Publishing), and *Compton's Multimedia Encyclopedia* (Britannica Software) also is a good example. Multimedia encyclopedias feature Boolean and proximity searching, in addition to the following features:

➤ Hypertext navigation

➤ Animation

➤ Color photographs

➤ Sounds

The Grolier encyclopedia also includes video. Microsoft recently announced Encarta, a reinterpretation of the encyclopedia. It should be interesting to see the results of its research into information-access patterns.

An interesting variation on the encyclopedia theme is *Explorer—The Video Encyclopedia of the 20th Century* (CEL Educational Resources). This product combines a multiple-videodisc system with a searchable full-text database that covers this century's major media events.

Multimedia Bookshelf (Microsoft) is an example of a composite reference set that contains the following items:

➤ Dictionary

➤ Thesaurus

➤ Quotation books

➤ Business references

A third category of multimedia resources is multimedia magazines. *Nautilus* is a compendium of multimedia tools, techniques, and applications published monthly on CD-

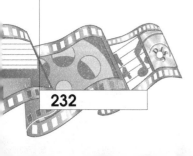

ROM (METATEC/Discovery Systems Corporation). You can almost consider Nautilus the *Popular Science* of the PC multimedia industry. Warner New Media (a division of Time-Warner Inc.) publishes CD-ROM compendia of major news-worthy events. The most significant of these publications is *Desert Storm*, a multimedia history of the Persian Gulf War, drawn from articles and dispatches in *TIME* magazine.

Summary

Multimedia is a powerful tool for increasing a modern corporation's viability: it increases the power of communication within a company and helps it declare more forcefully its message to the public. With all this multimedia power, a company easily can pour money down a hole with great abandon and few results. Because multimedia often is just expensive glitz, your addition of it to a presentation or training system that lacks real substance does not create that substance. Multimedia does not have to be either glitzy or expensive, however. The most effective multimedia often is the simplest and least expensive to produce. As in many new technologies, less is more, and the use of multimedia "special effects" cannot substitute for careful thought, creativity, and innovation.

Multimedia is about sharing information. The infrastructure necessary to make that sharing possible can make all of a company's functions more effective. Multimedia can motivate a company to focus on its basic issues of communication and innovation, and it can provide the tools for building that communication.

"Multimedia is a synthesis: a hybrid offering the advantages of the user-driven book with the wonders of electronic technology."

—Robert Winter, The 1990 UCLA Roundtable in Multimedia

CHAPTER 5

Multimedia from an End-User's Perspective

I f you have been a Windows user for any length of time, you probably have had at least a simple hypertext encounter with multimedia. Many Windows Help programs, for instance, use hotwords and linking to assist the user. If you have used that type of help, you have already seen multimedia from an end-user's perspective.

This chapter discusses some of the interface behaviors that end users typically see, and what their expectations might be. Aside from the informational content of your multimedia document, these "interface expectations" are an important part of your planning.

This chapter assumes that you are an experienced Windows user and that detailed instruction about the graphical user interface is unnecessary. As much as you may know about it, though, it might be a good idea to do some real homework with Windows GUI documentation if you plan to develop multimedia applications. There might be a few designs and standards that you are unaware of (or that you need to be reminded about). Considering the number of Windows-style controls present in multimedia applications, the GUI is an excellent model.

The controls of a multimedia application are similar to the controls of a Windows application. Buttons, dialog boxes, list boxes—these are all common objects that a user encounters in a typical multimedia document.

If you have never used a multimedia application, you can learn a lot about multimedia by installing and running the sample application that accompanies this book. The application is by no means complex, but you will see buttons in a different light. You probably are familiar with buttons (such as OK or Cancel) that serve as procedural tools in a "let's get on with it" environment. In multimedia, however, buttons serve many different purposes, they are tools for retrieving information, viewing it, and acting upon it.

Chapter 10, "Authoring a Multimedia Document" walks you through the process of creating a multimedia document.

Multimedia's Interface

The vitality of the new, multimedia data types such as pictures and sound always seem to grab center stage in discussions of multimedia technology. These elements, however, are only part of the multimedia story. Multimedia applications organize data for presentation, and the interface plays a very important role.

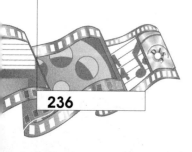

Multimedia, after all, inherits a great deal from its hypertext roots. Hypertext is a way of making lots of data available to the user. It usually operates in a nonlinear fashion, which means that the user must be able to jump to other places and call up multiple linked topics. The interface makes these actions possible.

You should be aware that multimedia promises to alter radically the way we use computers—just by providing intelligent access to monumental amounts of data. Information-rich multimedia components are already available in some common Windows applications, including:

➤ Microsoft Works for Windows now features a multimedia Help system (Help features are common examples of a hypermedia system)

➤ A multimedia version of Microsoft Word for Windows is available, which provides embedded access to Microsoft Bookshelf on CD-ROM

➤ Microsoft Project for Windows comes with a special type of Help that you can use to work your way through an unfamiliar process using a hypertext system that operates on your own data

The evolution of multimedia has definitely affected the graphical user interface. The clicks and keyboard entries that used to modify the screen are now capable of providing sophisticated feedback: stereophonic sound, text-to-speech synthesis, photos and photorealistic still images, animation, and even full-motion video. Even voice recognition is on the horizon.

Most of the old interface standards are still at work in multimedia, though—archetypal enough to be around for a long time:

➤ Icons will always be an intuitive navigation aid.

➤ The basic window is now able to bring you the score of music being played on your system, photos from a flower-identification field guide, and video of Hank Aaron's record-breaking home run.

➤ Multimedia makes dynamic use of multiple windows.

➤ Menus do not have to be text only (think of color palettes in paint and draw programs).

➤ The keyboard will become a less and less attractive alternative to the mouse.

Those are just some examples of the role that the user interface plays in multimedia. It will be your job as a developer to think like a user.

TIP

Your interface should always be designed so that users can get out of a situation if it fails to hold their interest. They should be able to escape without losing data or losing ground. Users should never be penalized for exploring!

Controlling Multimedia Applications

By now you are aware that controlling a multimedia application is not very different from controlling a standard Windows application.

You are not likely to encounter much that is new—particularly at the level of individual interface controls. A notable change is the increased emphasis on using a pointing device.

The behavioral differences between multimedia and standard applications are most distinctive in their overall purpose and in the results of user actions.

Applications are called applications because they are traditionally used as tools for performing workaday tasks: bookkeeping, word processing, and project management. Even database applications (which in some respects behave more like multimedia applications), presuppose that users are engaged in business-type activities.

Multimedia applications, on the other hand, are often personal information tools—like books. Their purpose is to manage lots of data simply and intelligently, regardless of whether the data is for business, education, or entertainment. Multimedia applications feature controls that are called upon to facilitate retrieving and viewing much less than data-input and formatting.

Another distinction must be made as you compare applications as tools and applications as information sources. It underscores an important point that might otherwise be overlooked in a book dedicated to multimedia documents. Multimedia does not always have to be the primary function of a document. It can be very useful in a supporting role. Take Microsoft Works, for example.

Some tool applications have multimedia components, like Microsoft Works with multimedia Help; some are full-blown multimedia applications, like Multimedia Beethoven. Multimedia Works performs functions similar to those of the traditional working applications. It operates identically to its non-multimedia version. It looks and feels like any standard Windows application, and you only become aware of multimedia when its Help is called.

An application whose primary goal is interactive communication looks different from the outset. The appearance of the interface invites exploration and promise information.

What exactly does the user see?

Buttons

The staple control of most multimedia applications is the command button. The face of a command button usually has a caption or icon that defines its purpose for the user. A single click issues a command. In the case of multimedia, buttons are used to execute commands and to follow through with links to other objects such as pages or text fields.

As much as possible, users should see some consistency between tool-application buttons and multimedia-application buttons.

Like menu options, buttons ideally should reflect a Windows standard when executing commands or options. Just as menu items are disabled when they represent an invalid choice, buttons should be disabled when they are not valid. This is a useful way to guide users away from disappointing or useless paths.

Last of all, but perhaps most important, buttons should provide navigation options that anticipates users' desires and possible paths of interest. Aside from the standard options of moving forward or back one page at a time, backtracking, and so on, special buttons should be provided for special circumstances. Some users want a way to escape a long side trip, and it is the developer's job to provide transportation.

Text Hotspots

The most common multimedia behavior is a response to active words in an application's client area. Clicking on certain text strings causes a new linked screen of information to appear. In multimedia applications, the text strings are commonly referred to as *hotwords* or *hotspots*. The result of clicking on a hotword is a *jump*.

There are no absolute standards for hotword jumps and pop-ups, so use your best judgment on a case-by-case basis. The only thing the user should expect in that situation is an easy way out of the side trip. A good multimedia application never penalizes a user for exploring.

Picture Hotspots

Picture hotspots are analogous to text hotspots. Pictures can contain one or more hotspots that cause jumps and pop-ups as a result of a single click.

Again, there is no current standard for jumps or pop-ups. It should, however, be clear to the user that a hotspot is there; picture hotspots can be transparent and very subtle.

It is obvious that pictures communicate different things to different people. The meaning contained in pictures is bound by experience and culture. Picture meanings are also age-bound. (Remember that if you intend to develop multimedia for children or for specific age groups.) How do these limitations effect the behavior of hot-spot pictures?

In an application like the atlas, pictures most likely reinforced with and cross-referenced to textual elements present on the screen at the same time. There is a text key to the countries. A click on a number in the picture is equivalent to a click on the same text number in the key.

But you cannot always count on text-to-picture redundancy and cross-referencing. In an application like Broderbund's "Grandma and Me," the richness of the screen and the level of its interactivity will amaze you. But due to the young target audience, it is not navigable with text at all—children in that age group are not likely to be reading yet. This is an extreme example of pictures having to carry the meaning of an application, but you should be prepared for any eventuality as multimedia grows in its application.

Buttons, hotwords, and picture hotspots are the principle multimedia controls. Buttons come directly from Windows user-interface design standards. Active text and picture hotspots are inherited from hypertext. The next portion of this chapter provides more information about hypertext and give you ideas for presenting it to users in an effective way.

Hypertext: The Roots of Multimedia

Hypertext has evolved steadily since the advent of multimedia, yet it is still firmly grounded in the same principles. Here is a brief look at the theory behind hypertext past and present, and suggestions for creating a good hypertext document.

Hypertext, as its name implies, began as a text retrieval system. A standard document (a book, for example) is constructed so that it can be easily read beginning to end. A hypertext document might contain exactly the same content as the book, but it is constructed in an entirely different way. It facilitates retrieval of information on topics that are linked together in parallel.

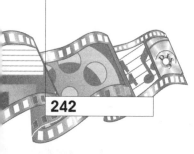

In contrast to the book's linear trip through the information, the hypertext document can provide the user with a nonlinear look. From the outset, theorists and users realized that flexibility and ease of access were hypertext's main benefits. You can, of course, read a book by paging around in whatever order you wish; it is just not very convenient, and it is not likely to offer a sense of continuity.

If you look at a book's table of contents—particularly a reference book—you can get an idea of how hypertext works. The book is usually organized around a few main ideas. In most cases, those ideas are collective topics made up of subparts that may or may not build upon one another, logically or chronologically. Each subpart, in turn, may be developed into multiple subparts in an increasingly branched, parallel structure. In a book, the author assigns a sequence to these ideas, whether or not there is any logical need to order them.

If a reader decides to follow a nonlinear path through the book, reading parts out of sequence, there is always a lot of flipping back to the table of contents for direction. In a hypertext document, content is organized in a tree structure as the "logical" table of contents would be. Each node in the tree (or topic of content where multiple branches originate) is called a *page*, even though it may be as lengthy as many of the book's pages.

NOTE

In the Windows environment, scrolling allows users to display more information than can be displayed in a static area.

Good hypertext design takes screen-size into account. Whenever possible, a hypertext page should fit on your display in its entirety. Because the number of possible jumps to and from a page is unlimited, it is usually possible to break a topic's content into small enough chunks so that pages can display their entire contents within the space of a screen.

Integrating Early Hypertext Features

In a hypertext document, the table of contents, an index of key words, a table of figures, and any other organizing element, is always on-line. You can tell at a glance where you are in relation to the length of the entire book. You can view the book at any level of abstraction if you need to make a big jump. Each hypertext page features hotwords that hint at additional information.

It should be as easy to move backward to the pages you viewed previously (even if they are not sequential pages) as it is to move forward. In fact, the notion of sequential pages is nearly irrelevant. The hypertext system keeps a history of all the moves you make in case you want to backtrack out of a topic one step at a time.

The Evolution of Interfaces and Hypertext

The earliest forms of hypertext evolved as interfaces evolved. After the graphical user interface was developed, hypertext sprouted wings and flew. The first major step was color. Jumps, keywords, and functional elements of any kind could be color-coded to hint at the results of a mouse-click.

Typography was another important step. Topic headers and subheaders could be identified just by their fonts. Different

textual content could be displayed in meaningful ways. For example, Microsoft produces a hypertext system for programmers that supports its computer languages. You can get conceptual information about a particular statement, the syntax it requires, and the options that each parameter accepts. The concepts are in a proportional font that is easy to read, while the code itself appears in a monospace code-setting font. This is an example of how design can be used to organize and clearly present information.

Context sensitivity was the next step in the evolution. It was incorporated as on-line Helps were being developed. An application's Help is the archetypal PC hypertext system.

In most Windows applications, if you need help about a command or procedure, you just highlight the command in question and press the F1 function key. (This is a Windows standard.) The Help automatically searches for the entry and displays the appropriate Help page.

NOTE

Helps have become a very valuable asset for application developers. Some of the Helps display code samples and allow developers to cut and paste code examples.

Some Helps also let you annotate their contents. You can display all your own notes on a subject at the click of a button. This opens up the potential for using hypertext systems as a classroom learning tool.

Pictures were the next major augmentation. As the GUI developed in its graphical capabilities, graphics became part of the hypertext lexicon. You could navigate around in a hypertext document by selecting from a series of pictures. At first, each picture was equivalent to a piece of active text. As

Windows Helps became more sophisticated, a designer could identify a series of hotspots on the same picture. A click detected on an individual spot would cause a jump to a different page or make its own pop-up appear.

In Windows 3.1, hypertext took another giant step. You could run a program from within a hypertext Help. This meant that you could execute a different program without ever having to leave Help.

And now multimedia is having an impact on hypertext. The Windows Multimedia Viewer supports everything discussed so far. In addition, it plays back sound files, runs command macros, plays back full-motion video and animation, and does full text searches.

NOTE

As Viewer evolves, it will not only become a more vital sensory experience, it will become more intelligent.

In Windows, Helps are woven directly into the thread of the application itself. Multimedia applications can make program calls directly to Windows so that they can do just about anything Windows can.

On-Line Helps

You have just had a look at the qualities of hypertext that have been borrowed by modern multimedia applications. In this section, you are given the basics of on-line help design so that you can better accommodate users. It provides some insight into how multimedia applications are organized, as well.

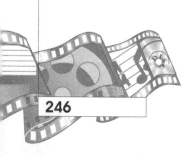

A help is organized in what is called a level-of-abstraction structured text. Engineers call this the *top-down* view. The first page of a hypertext document is usually a main menu that contains a short list of the topics that are covered. Each time you make a choice, you drop down to a more concrete level.

Most Windows applications have on-line, context-sensitive Helps. Helps themselves are miniature applications that can be executed from within the parent applications. (Helps are specific to an application. They contain information equivalent to an application's documentation.) When you are finished, you can put it away and close it, or leave it running.

The kind of information accessible from a Help is very important to daily application use:

➤ command assistance

➤ prompting

➤ an on-line tutor

➤ on-line documentation

➤ and software version information

NOTE There are some standards for Helps, though multimedia developers do not always adhere to them strictly.

For example, the finger is pretty standard among multimedia developers. When the finger appears over a highlighted word, you have found a hotspot that is activated by clicking.

Clicking on a solid green underlined word jumps you to another part of the Help for more information. You can quickly return by clicking on the "Back" button at the top of the Help window.

Clicking on a dotted green underline signifies a topic keyword. Holding the mouse button down on a topic word brings up a special message box with more information on the keyword.

By now, you have had a look at the multimedia interface elements that are commonly seen by users. There are some other aspects that are not so readily visible, but that are important to you as a developer.

Windows Behind the Scenes

One of the purposes of this chapter is to teach you what is going on with Windows as things unfold on the screen. Here, then, are some transparent but important points about what happens when you run a multimedia application.

Multimedia Viewer

When you execute a multimedia application using any of the standard methods, Windows does something behind the scenes. It runs a built-in multimedia presentation program called Viewer and then loads your multimedia application into the Viewer—much like a word processor loading a document.

Why does Windows do this? Viewer is like a database manager that knows how to make jumps to linked topics and

search on text strings. Like a presentation program, Viewer also can display images, play sound files, and even play back full-motion video or animation. Without a program like Viewer, every multimedia application would have to contain a lot of program code to perform those functions. Viewer merely abstracts out these functions so that multimedia applications can contain mostly data.

Viewer's operation is invisible to the user. It is automatic, and you generally do not see it running by itself without a specific application loaded (unless an error occurs during the start-up process). When your multimedia application is installed, its icon is added to a group in the Windows Program Manager.

Multimedia applications appear to be the same as standard Windows applications. The user double-clicks on an icon, and the application is loaded. If you are a beginner, that is all you need to know. If you find that you want to run Viewer directly, however, Windows provides an icon in the Accessories Group.

You should also be aware (and so should the user) that Windows often looks for data files on a CD-ROM diskette when it starts multimedia applications.

Before you attempt to run a multimedia application that accesses CD-ROM material, you must place the CD-ROM diskette into the CD-ROM drive. If you do not do this, you get an error when the application attempts to load itself into Viewer. Viewer cannot find the necessary files and it terminates the loading process.

When this happens, Viewer is left running, but no multimedia file is loaded. To rectify this situation, place the CD-ROM diskette in the CD-ROM drive and open the multimedia application from Viewer's File menu.

NOTE

To best meet the potential of multimedia, as much data as possible should be on a CD-ROM diskette.

Most multimedia applications are data-intensive. That is, they usually have vast quantities of text, pictures, and sound files associated with a relatively small amount of executing code.

This is the opposite of most common applications where the program part (the executable EXE file) is big, but the data files you produce with them do not get very big.

It is best to allocate as much as possible to the CD-ROM diskette. Though it is not an absolute multimedia PC requirement, a PC without a CD-ROM drive does not approach its full multimedia potential.

Not all multimedia applications require large amounts of data on-line when they are running. For example, the Multimedia Sound Mixer runs automatically when Windows is started. Its program is stored entirely on the PC's hard disk, and it can open sound files regardless of where they are located. It does not require that a CD-ROM diskette be loaded.

The Sound Mixer is also a good example of how multimedia controls are just variations on the standard Windows themes. The Sound Mixer has a control menu, Minimize and Maximize buttons, and a main menu. It has customized controls in its client area (the area inside its frame). If you have ever used a real audio mixer board, you know that slider bars are used to control the volume of the various input and output channels and other mix components. In keeping with the Windows philosophy of interface graphics that look like their

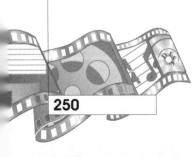

physical counterparts, mixing is done with sliders in this application. As it happens, Windows has a standard control that fills that need: the scroll bar. Because users are probably familiar with scroll bars, it is likely that they can intuitively grasp the function of the slider.

States and Modes

Both states and modes are alternate behaviors that the application can assume in response to your commands (or in response to input from the system). The difference between a state and a mode is subtle—often indistinguishable—and generally of little consequence to the user. It is worth mentioning because of that little consequence. State and mode changes may be pertinent to your user interface.

A *state* is a response to an event. A *mode* is a switchable change in control behavior. The concepts are inextricably intertwined. The following examples should make the distinction more clear.

State Change

The most common state change you see in Windows applications is a waiting state. A good application's interface always indicates when the application has gone into a special state. In Microsoft Word, saving a document triggers a waiting state. Word turns the cursor into an hourglass. This hourglass is standard. Every application behaves the same way. The hourglass you see as you wait for Windows to boot up is exactly the same as when Word is saving documents—it just happens in response to a different event.

Some states are unique to an application. Broderbund's Playroom, for example, contains a little dice game that kids can play. When the dice are being shaken, the PC makes a special sound, but does not let you make a move on the board until it is done.

Mode Change

A mode change is just a bit different from a state change. You generally have to toggle your application into a different mode by taking some action. For example, figure 5.1 shows Windows Paintbrush.

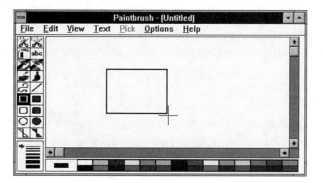

Figure 5.1:

Windows Paint-brush.

When a brush tool is selected, dragging causes the brush to color the client area under its path. Selecting a box-drawing tool changes Paintbrush's dragging behavior. Paintbrush reflects this change in mode by changing the cursor from an arrow into a set of crosshairs.

Dragging the crosshairs creates a "rubber-band" box (shown in the figure as a rectangular set of dotted lines). Releasing the mouse button draws the box with the dimensions indicated by the rubber-band lines.

Multimedia applications can contain command buttons called state buttons. *State buttons* assume different visual appearances or states when they are clicked; they often have pictures on their faces to represent changes of state. For

example, a state button may have a traffic light depicted on it. As you click it, the picture cycles from a red light to a green light, indicating whether the state of the application is moving or static. Clicking on a state button usually places the application in a different mode.

States or modes do not have to be associated with just button clicks. It is common for multimedia applications to change modes by having the cursor move from one part of the screen to another.

A left mouse-button click causes a pop-up window to appear with information about the topic that the cursor is on top of. Moving the cursor off of the keyword causes the application to return to a state where the cursor is an arrow, and to a mode where a left mouse-button press is ignored.

This chapter has presented a range of background information that will be useful to you as a developer. The concept and use of controls is important to you as a multimedia author and as a user.

Now you know what sophisticated users might expect from a good application, and you know what to give them. The information should be useful to you as a consumer, too. You now have at least a few evaluation tools to work with as you examine competing products. After all, an application that has accomplished an admirable level of detail in its interface standards has probably had a comparable level of detail devoted to its design.

"We are at a point in our society when opportunity and crisis come together. The Chinese pictograph symbols for these two ideas, in fact, are the same. —Robert Abel, The 1990 UCLA Roundtable in Multimedia

6

Multimedia from the Developer's Perspective

C hapter 5 discussed multimedia from an end user's per spective; in other words, how end users take advantage of media-aware applications. This chapter is for readers who are interested in multimedia development. Multimedia is the computer developers' answer to the entertainment industry—it provides plenty of "glitter." You can develop serious media-aware applications, but they should also be fun, entertaining, and exciting for users. If not, rethink your software design.

Much careful planning and structure are necessary to make effective multimedia applications. The media you add must have value; you are on the wrong track if you add media elements just to show that you can do it.

If you decide a multimedia application is best for your organization, you first must convince your management team to pay for the project. Afterward, you must cope with the inevitable learning curve involved in developing your first media-aware application; give yourself time and expect to be confused, especially if your application involves hypertext linking. A number of resources can help you handle the learning curve, including seminars, sample code, reference books, and the technical-support centers for the tools you use. This chapter discusses these resources and other sources you can turn to for help.

See Chapter 8, "Avoiding 'Muddy-media'" for detailed information on multimedia design.

This chapter also discusses briefly how to design effectively. It discusses the type of person who makes a good multimedia developer and compares the skills other disciplines bring to multimedia. The chapter concludes with an overview of what is involved in programming with Windows multimedia by discussing the media control interface (MCI), low-level MCI coding tools, and high-level command-interface strings.

Justifying the Cost of Multimedia to Upper-level Management

You may have difficulty justifying the cost of multimedia development. When Microsoft first evangelized Windows, it was easy to obtain reprints of studies that proved it was cost-effective to convert users to a graphical user interface. Unfor-

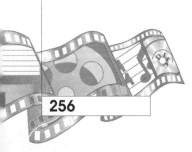

tunately, leading edge companies tend to keep their research secret to maintain competitive advantages, and thus few similar studies exist for multimedia. To convince upper-level management to fund the initial development costs of a multimedia project, each cost must be outlined. Some companies are open to multimedia development and want to "get their feet wet"; they feel that multimedia is the computing arena of the future and want to face the learning process now.

Other companies do not see why the "bells and whistles" are worth the increase in hardware expenditures and retraining. If you work for a company resistant to multimedia development, the following suggestions may help:

> **Make people understand what multimedia is.** Offer to give a demonstration—with multimedia, showing is much better than telling. People often are resistant because they do not understand the technology and what it can do, and they do not want to appear ignorant by admitting it. To enthuse a group of people about the technology is relatively easy, even if they are not ready to provide funding.

> **Start small.** Never perform a demonstration for more than ten people at a time. Gather participants around a desktop and let them use the mouse to experience interaction for themselves. Bring a variety of different software packages and try to get the members to enjoy themselves. Do not direct the demonstration—you want to encourage people to focus on what they find interesting.

> **Collect a variety of packages designed for different purposes and created with different tools.** When you are planning a demonstration, try to include a reference package (Microsoft Bookshelf is a good choice), an

> Contact the Multimedia PC Marketing Council at 202-331-0494 for help with your multimedia project.

example of using OLE for voice annotation of a spread-sheet, a multimedia help system (the Lotus Multimedia SmartHelp is a great example), and a game or a children's multimedia storybook (Chessmaster 3000 from Software Toolworks is awesome).

➤ **After showing examples of available products, show examples of what can be done in-house.** Create a small, focused, and limited applet or two using a visual programming environment such as Microsoft's Visual Basic or Asymetrix's Toolbook. Make the applet specific to your line of business and include an example of every media element, including hypertext. If you do not have the capability in-house to create sound or video clips, take the time to download a couple from a BBS. Make sure that you include an example of Video for Windows or QuickTime; video is the most impressive part of any demonstration. QuickTime clips are available from many forums on CompuServe and can be included in your application using the Apple QuickTime Player for Windows. AVI clips can be obtained from a number of sources and can be played back by using the Video for Windows drivers. Be impressive, but not too impressive; too impressive a demonstration easily can lead management to unrealistic and unrealizable expectations. Remember that you are just showing the technical feasibility and appropriateness of multimedia.

When your presentation succeeds, the participants are excited by multimedia, begin to understand it, and know you can use it to meet their needs. People usually spontaneously generate ideas for how this new technology can support their part of the business. They become your allies in pioneering new technology.

For a difficult crowd, offer to create a multimedia demonstration the next time your boss has to deliver a presentation.

Most companies are accustomed to spending significant amounts of money for corporate presentations. If you can show your boss how cost-effective and impressive a multimedia "slide show" can be, you may get the go-ahead on other multimedia efforts.

To convince your superiors of the need for multimedia development tools, you may need specific reasons. Fortunately, each reason is simple to understand and persuasive.

Making Software Easy to Use

Well-designed multimedia software is easier to use than other types of software. Features such as on-line help systems with hypertext or voice annotation make using the software more intuitive for the end user. To take advantage of this multimedia benefit, find out how much money your company spends annually for computer training and show how multimedia can make that investment more productive.

Are a number of your company's employees trained to use spreadsheets? If spreadsheet training is frequent and costly, it may be cheaper to provide users with a Multimedia PC upgrade kit and a copy of Lotus SmartHelp.

Does your company have an internal help desk or other forms of company based software support? Analyze the frequency of calls and the type of help requested. You may be able to design a hypertext-based tutorial that can answer many of the most frequently asked questions.

Can you use products such as Word Basic (Microsoft Word's macro language) or Visual Basic to design media-enhanced executive information systems? If you can design an effective application for upper management, you may get funding for products that help the rest of the company.

Try to show your management team videos of recent trade shows that feature "information at your fingertips" solutions. Let your team members know that this technology is not "blue sky" thinking—it is available right now.

TIP

For additional help with your in-house multimedia promotional efforts, contact the Multimedia PC Marketing Council. This group can help you promote the use of multimedia and educate consumers and developers about multimedia. The Council may be able to supply you with videotapes, multimedia demos, and other useful materials.

Reducing Paper Use

When you use a common application (a spreadsheet or word processor) and you need information about a special feature, what do you do? With many packages you must stop what you are doing, save your work, get up from your desk, go to the bookshelf, and shuffle through the shelves until you find your documentation manual. Then you have to look through the table of contents or the index and read about the new feature. You then bring the manual back to the desk and balance it on your lap while you type, point, and click to test whether you understand the new feature. After you think you know what to do, you save your work (again) and walk back to the bookshelf to put away the manual, unless, of course, you already lost it in a pile of papers on your desk. If your program has on-line help, however, you can press the F1 key to access the most relevant parts of the manuals right where you need to—on your computer screen.

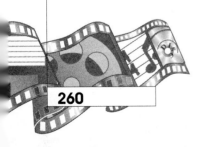

If your package offers on-line, context-sensitive help, a better method exists. Rather than hunt for the printed documentation, you can click on the Help menu and use the index to find the subject you want. You even can leave the help information open while you work on the application.

If you have ever used Windows Help (see fig. 6.1) you already know of the power of hypertext. With well-designed Help systems, a manual is not necessary (unless you just want to have it around). If you can demonstrate this concept to your management team, you may be able to secure funds for hypertext versions of in-house documents.

If your program has Help, try pressing the F1 key (or Ctrl-F1) to access information on the feature you are using.

If your promotion of multimedia lacks examples, consider using hypertext Help—it is well known and powerful.

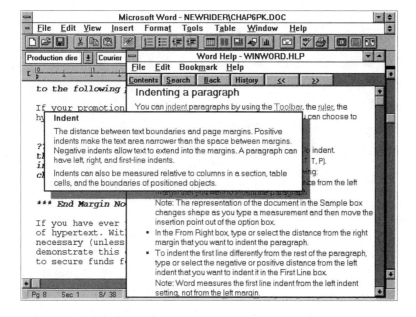

Figure 6.1:
Word for Windows Help.

Many documents used by large corporations are expensive to update because of their size, and are used infrequently. When was the last time you consulted your personnel manual? Such documents are more effective if you store them in a database that can be accessed through a corporate network. Many jobs require workers to carry documentation for procedures performed infrequently (mechanics need this type of information). These manuals are easier to carry if you store them on CD-ROM discs. The discs, which are easier to store than paper and are not affected by negative weather conditions, also can include video or animation sequences.

If you can do a small project well, your company may be willing to pay for larger efforts.

When you explain to your management team that hypermedia and multimedia are easier to use and update, and are more informative and cheaper (in terms of reducing production and storage costs), you have an effective argument for receiving funding for a test project.

Increasing Productivity

Well-designed multimedia applications lead to increased productivity for the end user. Poorly-designed multimedia applications take more time to learn and use. For this reason, it is important that you study design elements before you use the productivity argument with your management team. If you know what multimedia elements are beneficial to your company, you ensure management that you will use multimedia effectively.

The most convincing example of how multimedia can be used for greater learning, increased understanding, and greater productivity can be seen in schools that have incorporated technology as a teaching aid. Students with access to multimedia tutorials are more interested in the learning process, pay more attention, and have greater retention rates than students who learn by more conventional methods. The same principles would seem to be true with an adult audience.

Multimedia is useful for helping people understand more than what is represented initially by a linear problem. When

you look up something with an electronic reference, you may have to take an extra second or two to explore links that pertain to the research you were doing, or stop to see or hear a sound, video, or animation clip. The end result, however, is that you end up with more overall knowledge—a plus in a corporate standpoint.

If you experiment with multimedia in creating better work applications, the Windows environment enables you to apply, across multiple applications, knowledge you have gained. If you use a Wizard—Microsoft's term for context-sensitive help— within a spreadsheet to help you understand OLE, that knowledge makes you more productive when you use a Windows-based database.

Multimedia also can increase productivity by reducing the amount of meetings you must attend. Rather than meet to discuss issues, you can send multimedia, or compound documents, through electronic mail. You can send a document to everyone in a project group, for example, and ask each recipient to annotate their spoken comments and return them to you. This method is especially cost-effective in communicating with people at different corporate locations.

Multimedia also can save money when you use teleconferencing rather than meetings. Analyze the cost savings for your company: although the equipment may be expensive, it probably can pay for itself after a couple of months, depending on how often your company meets.

Creating Happier Employees

It is difficult to quantify employee satisfaction to upper-level management. You may have to collect information about how much employee turnover costs your company and then show how much fun it is to work in an environment that uses multimedia technology. Perhaps the best way to convince management on this issue is to install some "zippy" executive information systems and let the software speak for itself.

Technology often is considered to be a perk in some companies, but technology is less expensive than giving a monetary bonus. A bonus usually is given annually. If you provide new technology as a bonus, you probably will not have to upgrade the new systems for 18 months to two years. Technology also can be written off as a capital expenditure. It may be as effective to give someone a multimedia-ready 486 as it is to give a bonus; the end result is that the employee will do more for the company and be less eager to leave.

Learning To Develop Media-Aware Applications

After your management team gives you the go ahead, you must figure out what you need to do and how to do it. The process of creating a multimedia application is the same as creating any other software application. You must create project specifications, select a development team, start developing code, test the code, and develop documentation. You also must collect media elements, or clips, determine the links (in the creation of a hypertext document), and create an on-line help system.

Multimedia applications often incorporate hypertext and extensive linking; creating specifications for these projects can be daunting. You have to think through the logic and interface of a hypertext application more thoroughly than for other types of software. The design of a multimedia application should take as much time, if not more, as the coding.

You may have to experiment with a number of different interfaces and metaphors before you find one that makes sense.

A well-designed interface is possible if you work closely with users during the design stage. In addition, use tools that let you develop prototypes, and be willing to change the look and feel as many times as necessary. Give your project twice as much time as you normally would for projects, and expect to be confused during the process.

TIP

It may be helpful for your first project to hire an outside consultant or to work with a firm that designs only multimedia applications. Look closely at other firms' efforts to determine what works.

The development team you choose may require you to have the application coding done by another company. A number of programming firms have created beautiful multimedia titles and specialize in certain development tools, or in cross-platform development. You should team up with an experienced firm if:

➤ This is your first development project

➤ The project you are in charge of is a mission-critical application

➤ The project will be distributed outside the company

It is not difficult to add media elements to an application, but it is difficult to design a media-rich application that works. If you decide to do everything in-house, make sure that at least one key member of the development team has experience.

If your multimedia project uses hypertext, make sure you assign twice as much time to its design as you would for a normal application.

> **T**o create media clips in-house, you need expensive hardware, expensive software, and well-trained graphics or media experts.

Coding, testing, and documentation are probably familiar to you; media acquisition may be entirely new. As multimedia development increases in popularity, media licensing becomes a critical issue. Media licensing is vastly different from software licensing, and it is oriented to the entertainment value of the media, rather than its information value. Media owners also tend to set prices based on the assumption that your next corporate report will be *Batman Returns*. But license you must. Media developers take their property seriously, and lawsuits already have started making news.

A good strategy is to acquire clip media libraries (similar to clip-art libraries) and then spend extra money to create one or two custom clips featuring your corporate logo or other company-specific information. If you select your clips carefully, you still can provide a well-integrated media product. Many companies that sell the clips enable you to modify them for your own use.

NOTE

Chapter 8, "Managing Different Types of Media" discusses clip acquisition in depth.

Using Valuable Reference Tools

The most valuable reference tools for multimedia development are the manuals that accompany the Microsoft Multimedia Development Kit. These manuals, in addition to the media-editing applets, are well worth the $495 price tag, even if you never develop with the Viewer authoring tool included with the package. If you decide against buying the complete kit, much of the same information in the manuals is available

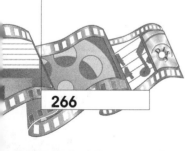

in the *Multimedia Programmer's Reference Library,* a three-book series available from Microsoft Press.

Another good reference is *Multimedia Applications Development Using DVI Technology,* by Mark Bunzel and Sandra Morris. Bunzel is president of Avtek, Inc., a Silicon Valley-based firm that specializes in multimedia development. Even if you do not have an interest in including full-motion video in your application, this publication provides an overview of the production process.

Another reference you should have is the *Multimedia Producer's Legal Survival Guide* (Multimedia Computing Corporation). This guide provides a solid overview of the legal issues involved with media copyrights and licensing. Without acquiring the proper permissions, you leave yourself (and your company) open to litigation. This guide explains the differences between joint work agreements, work-for-hire agreements, licensing agreements, collective and derivative works, and how to navigate through the legalese to get the media clips you need.

The *Multimedia Producer's Legal Survival Guide* is an invaluable resource. Contact Multimedia Computing Corporation at 408-737-7575 to order a copy.

You even can attend a course for multimedia development. Microsoft University offers a multimedia publishing course targeted to general business and technology professionals responsible for managing large document-publishing projects. Call MSU at 206-828-1507 for more information.

Attending Seminars and Conventions

The quickest way to become proficient in multimedia development is to attend multimedia trade shows. You can attend informative breakout sessions, acquire software at discounted rates, and network with experienced multimedia developers. Fortunately, most people in this business are friendly and willing to help beginners because multimedia is still new.

Trade shows you should consider attending include:

> **FOSE CD-ROM and Multimedia Conference.** Held in August in Washington, D.C. Call 703-683-8500 for more information.

> **Image World.** Held in New York in the fall, and Atlanta in the winter. Call 914-328-9157 for more information.

> **Intermedia.** Formerly the Annual Conference and Exposition on Multimedia and CD-ROM. Held in the spring in San Jose or San Francisco. Call Reed Exhibition Companies at 203-964-0000.

> **Multimedia Expo.** Held in New York in May and Santa Clara in October. Contact American Expositions, Inc. at 212-226-4141.

NOTE

Intermedia and Multimedia Expo are the most significant multimedia trade shows. If you are interested in the more esoteric aspects of computer graphics, Siggraph is the show.

> **Multimedia.** Held in Chicago in October. Call 703-836-6363 for more information.

> **Siggraph.** The major computer graphics show. Held in Chicago in the summer. For more information, call ACMSiggraph at 312-644-6610.

> **The CD-ROM Exposition and Conference.** Held in Boston in the fall. Call 617-362-2001 for more information.

Fall COMDEX now includes a multimedia track and the Multimedia Pavilion, where vendors have numerous booths offering multimedia products and future technologies.

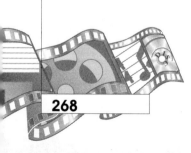

NOTE

Unless you have another business reason for attending COMDEX, this show may not be your best opportunity to become familiar with multimedia. With the crush of more than 130,000 attendants, you easily can be overwhelmed in the crowd. The sheer volume of things to do and see makes it easy to lose track of the information you need. A smaller multimedia-specific trade show can help you prepare more for your development efforts.

Using BBSs and Forums

Information obtained from public-access bulletin boards and CompuServe can save you time and money. You can communicate with other multimedia developers, learn about beta software, find information about bugs in hardware or software you may be using, download current versions of software drivers, download sample applications and media clips, and read reviews about current products.

Some major on-line services include CompuServe, GEnie, America On-line, and Prodigy. In addition, most multimedia vendors (including Microsoft, Creative Labs, and Media Vision) have BBS services for their customers.

The CompuServe multimedia and multivendor forums are a good place to start looking for information. The company representatives that "hang out" on the forums are usually product managers and developers. You can ask questions about product use or report bugs to them. You can post questions for other forum members about specific products or even how to get started. The members were beginners too, and they are more than happy to make hardware and software recommendations and to relate their experiences. You can get good information about how other people are using the technology, the types of applications they are creating, and the issues they face. The forums are also a good place to get the latest gossip.

One of the best resources on the Multimedia Forum is Sysop Nick Arnett. As the president of Multimedia Computing Corporation, he has a wealth of information about who's who and what is going on in the industry. If you ask Nick a question or just read his response to the questions asked by other forum members, you can save hours of time and research.

You can call any of these numbers to find information about multimedia forums and bulletin boards:

On-line service	Phone Number
CompuServe	800-848-8990
America On-line	800-827-6364
BIX/WIX	800-695-4882
GEnie	800-638-9636

BBS	Phone Number
Microsoft Multimedia BBS	206-936-4082
National PC/MIDI Databank	708-593-8703
Creative Labs	408-986-1488
Media Vision BBS	510-770-0968

Studying Sample Code

A good way to learn more about developing multimedia applications is to study sample code someone else developed. Fortunately, some authoring tools enable you to get code from a number of places.

The Asymetrix ToolBook Multimedia Development Kit, for example, comes with "multimedia widgets," which are sample objects that make it easy for you to add multimedia elements to the books you produce. As figure 6.2 illustrates, you can study the scripts used to create these widgets to learn how to code using the MCI.

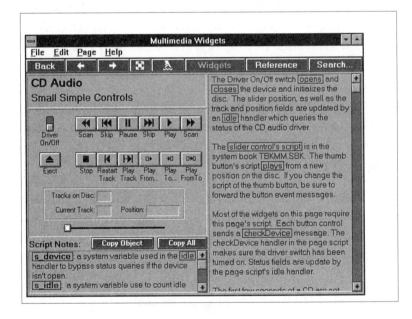

Figure 6.2:

ToolBook Widgets for CD Audio.

NOTE See the section "Interfacing with the Media Control Interface" later in this chapter to learn more about the MCI.

Visual Basic can be used in conjunction with custom controls to add multimedia elements. A *custom control* is a special dynamic link library (DLL) that adds an icon to the Visual Basic Toolbar. When you click on the icon, you can add the control's functionality to your Visual Basic application. Custom control packages are available from a number of third-party vendors. If you want to see sample Visual Basic code that enables you to access the MCI directly, you can download code from CompuServe's MSBASIC forum. Forum members often put sample code in the MSBASIC Visual Basic library to share coding techniques with other developers.

The MS Viewer is a simple, Windows-help-like player for relatively simple multimedia. The development kit for the MS Viewer is included in the Windows Multimedia Developer's Kit. Viewer run-time files are first created as Rich Text Format (RTF) files and then compiled to an indexed machine-readable format for viewing. The MDK comes with a sample application called USA. The USA demo includes the RTF files used to create the document, the MVP files used in compiling the documents, and a sample setup script (SETUP.INF) that passes instructions to the MS setup program.

TIP
No matter what package you use for multimedia development, you should study the SETUP.INF file. At some point, when you want to offer your users a well-behaved installation program, the SETUP.EXE program may be useful to you.

Learning to Design Effectively

The most difficult part of creating a multimedia application is the design. Thanks to the capabilities of hypertext, you now

have more power than ever to confuse users. You can lead users in a quest for information and then abandon them. You can frustrate users by providing a document structure that promises a wealth of information but only gives a shallow amount of data. You even can incorporate sound and video clips that are poorly planned and implemented—a great way to irritate and confuse.

It may not be easy to find material that helps you design a multimedia application. Multimedia still is a new area of software design, and most guides focus on getting the hardware to work properly with your software.

Chapter 7 gives you some general advice about design and structure. You also may want to look at books that address multimedia and hypermedia generally. Books that address multimedia issues on the Macintosh may provide examples that you can apply to your MPC software efforts.

Using Reference Guides

➤ *From Ventura to Hypertext.* (Knowledge Management Associates). This book discusses the types of documents that should be converted to hypertext and then explains the conversion process. Although the book focuses on Ventura Publisher, the techniques can apply to any authoring tool. For more information, contact KMA at 804-496-8682.

➤ *Hyperdocuments and How to Create Them.* (Prentice Hall). An entire section in this book discusses organizing documents, and another section provides guidelines for authors. Although the author does not focus on a single platform, he stresses that clarity is the most important feature of a well-designed application.

➤ *Multimedia Interface Design.* (Addison Wesley) This recent book provides detailed and academic studies of interface design. The extensive bibliography of studies is particularly valuable when you are facing difficult interface decisions in a complex application.

➤ *The Visual Display of Quantitative Information.* (Graphics Press). This book is for applications that require a great deal of graphing of numerical information. This classic covers everything about the most effective ways of presenting numerical information in a manner that is both effective and accurate.

Using HyperCard Lessons

HyperCard, from Claris, was the first objected-oriented software development tool available for a large nonprogramming audience. It was introduced in 1988, two years before the first similar product on Windows. Hyper-Card took advantage of the Mac's sound support, which has been standard on the Mac since its release. When HyperCard was introduced, the Mac community was flooded with stacks designed by novices. Some applications met specific business needs very well; others were just plain horrible.

To address HyperCard design problems, a number of guidelines were developed and published for Mac HyperCard developers. One good reference is Danny Goodman's *Hyper-Card Developer's Guide* (Bantam Computer Books). Although information on the Mac operating environment is not of interest to Windows developers, the stack model and the overall design principles of HyperCard stacks is useful information.

Using Structure over "Creative Expression"

When you think about how to design your application, begin with a copy of *The Windows Interface: An Application Design Guide* (ADG), supplied with the Microsoft Windows Software Development Kit. The ADG describes how Microsoft wants to see Windows used and is the result of much user interface testing. The rules for interface development are the same, whether or not you are using multimedia. If your application follows the principles of good Windows design, your users can use your application effectively and with little, if any, training and support. Standard Windows user interfaces do not automatically make a hypertext application usable, but at least your users will not have to relearn the basics.

NOTE

One of the advantages of using Windows is that it is easier for the user and requires less training. Think about your application first as a Windows program before you add the media elements that make it multimedia. Key Windows features that your application should support are on-line Help from the F1 key and clipboard support for text.

Try creating a prototype of your ideas using ToolBook or Visual Basic, then let volunteers try it. Nothing points out glaring design flaws as effectively as a novice user who walks through your application while you watch. Do not coach users; just watch to see whether they can navigate the program without your assistance. If users get lost, your program may have a major design flaw. Good multimedia software enables users to choose where to go; great multimedia software leads users so subtly that they may never realize a navigation strategy existed.

You may want to consider the following questions during your design stage:

➤ What information do you want to provide?

➤ How do you want to provide the information?

➤ How will users interact with the multimedia elements in your application?

➤ Is the media the primary focus of the program, or is it there to enhance the text?

➤ Is the purpose of the software to educate, entertain, or meet a specific data requirement?

With the creativity available through the inclusion of media clips, it is easy to get carried away. A good way to determine whether your design is solid is to envision all the media replaced with text. Does the structure hold together? Is the application still useful? If so, you are probably on the right track. If the entire thing falls apart, think about redesigning the interface.

Recognizing When You Have Gone Overboard

John Murdoch, a software designer and author, became disgusted one night with the confusion of the interface in a large shareware project and wrote a Visual Basic application called "The Lurker's Guide to Bad Design." This humorous application points out some obvious design flaws novice developers often make when they create Windows software. Figure 6.3 illustrates just one example.

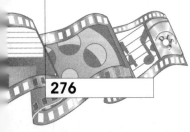

276

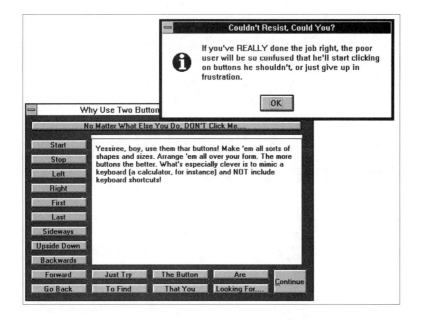

Figure 6.3:

The Lurker's Guide to Bad Design.

Although the Lurker's Guide is not multimedia-specific, his guidelines are perfect for truly bad multimedia software:

➤ Ridiculously garish windows and loud colors are a must.

➤ Make sure that button sizes are not consistent.

➤ Why use two buttons when you can have 30?

➤ Make sure that all the screens in your application look different. Consistency is for the unimaginative.

➤ Assume that users' machines are just like yours. Feel free to use a variety of fonts. Why worry about whether users have the same fonts on their machines?

➤ Do not let users in on the secret of how to use your application. Use cryptic labels for your buttons and fields. Better yet, do not use labels.

➤ Make sure that you leave out what everyone else forgets—menus! A sure sign of a novice application is a wealth of buttons, without a single menu.

If you would rather create a useful application, the Lurker's Guide to Bad Design comes with a Windows Help file that gives design tips. A final point to remember: truly bad software does not include a help system.

People: Designing Good Multimedia Software

You can tell what profession a person is in by looking at the multimedia applications he or she creates. This section discusses several types of multimedia developers and their strengths and weaknesses in this new form of communication. Each profession has pros and cons associated with it. Remember the points made in the following sections when you develop your own multimedia software, or when you interview multimedia development shops for contract work.

Working with Writers

Many different types of writers exist; some are well-suited for multimedia development; others are not. A multimedia author with a strong writing background can bring many strengths to applications design, including the ability to articulate thoughts in a clear and structured manner. Remember that the purpose of multimedia is to provide information, regardless of which media element is best suited for the job.

Some applications are text-intensive, such as those structured around a hypertext or hypermedia document. A writer probably should be the driving force behind the structure and creation of these types of programs. Technical writers, especially people with a background in creating on-line help

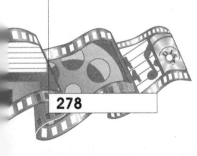

systems, make the best "writer-type" developers. Their abilities are helpful in these areas:

➤ Technical writers can explain technical terms in a way that end users can understand.

➤ Technical writers have strong technical skills.

➤ Technical writers are accustomed to structuring information in a logical, linear fashion.

NOTE A number of hypertext tools (Lotus SmarText and MS Viewer) start the creation process as text documents in a word processor.

The problem with writers is that not all multimedia applications are (or should be) based on a book or document metaphor. Some multimedia applications need to be more freeflowing, such as those that follow the model of an interactive movie. Applications based on graphics, animation, or video certainly should include writers on the creative team, but not as leaders in the creative process.

Working with Programmers

No matter how complete an authoring tool is, at some point you probably will need add to it to suit your application's purposes. To do so, you will need the services of a programmer on your creative team. Some authoring tools were designed with programmers in mind. Other tools you use may meet most of your needs, but you still may need programming help to design an installation program.

Programming support is critical for all applications except the smallest media-aware programs. Programmers are well-acquainted with the software project-management life cycle.

In addition to helping to structure the logic behind the code, programmers can help devise a testing plan to make sure that your application runs smoothly on a variety of machines.

An advantage to having a programmer lead the design team is that the resulting application is tightly structured and runs more efficiently. A drawback is the skills that are so useful in general software design really do not help in designing and integrating the media to be embedded in the software.

Working with Graphic Artists

Graphic artists who create designs on a computer often make the best multimedia designers if they can use tools that do not require much programming. The resulting software usually is visually impressive, but it might not be as interactive as software designed by someone with more technical skills.

Another problem in using a graphical designer is that most graphics shops are heavily Mac-oriented. In some ways, this Mac orientation can be an advantage because many wonderful media authoring and graphics-manipulation tools run on the Mac. In addition, many of these programs can create applications that run in Windows. A problem with ported applications, however, is their color palettes do not transfer well—the application runs with no problems, but the colors are no longer balanced and accurate. If you have spent a lot of time and money creating software that is visually stunning, the cost of color correction can be significant.

Working with Multimedia Generalists

The best multimedia designers have a range of skills and are experienced with a number of different disciplines. A graph-

ics designer who has learned to program Toolbook scripts or a technical writer with a fine arts background may be your best bet as the person who should head the development team. Among the best people to have on a team are professional programmers who are active performers in music or theater. People from any type of artistic background usually can provide interesting skills. Consider unusual mixes: someone with a background in theater can provide a strong narrative sense that your application might need.

The most important factor in hiring someone is how well he or she understands the technology. The applicant, however, does not have to be a programmer. A well thought-out structure can be programmed by any competent programmer. To design a creative application that is compelling and exciting to use is an art form.

When you are interviewing prospective designers, ask to see samples of their work. See if you like the "look and feel" of their products. Try to get a sense of how intuitive the product is to use and its functionality. Determine whether using the product seems boring after only a couple of minutes (a sure sign there is not enough depth to the amount of information provided). Does the design of the product show a sense of humor? Determine whether the media is used as an integral part of the product or whether it seems tacked on as an afterthought.

When you evaluate someone's work, it is relatively easy to see who has talent. To hire development talent still is somewhat expensive because not many experts are available. If you must choose between the design and the developer, spend more money on the initial design. You can manage and train a junior programmer if your design and layout is thorough and impressive.

Setting Up Development Hardware

Many multimedia development shops use both Macs and PCs running Windows. One of the most frustrating experiences a Windows junkie can have is setting up a multimedia-ready PC and then watching a Mac-fanatic cohort set up a workstation. The reason for the anguish is the PC setup.

NOTE

Two key acronyms that are part of hardware setup drive PC users crazy and cause Mac users to smile:

Direct Memory Access (DMA). A peripheral can write directly to memory if it has access to a DMA channel. Access to a DMA channel is required for quality audio and video capture. Most 486 PCs have seven DMA channels to share, but only three are available to most peripherals

Interrupt ReQuest (IRQ). A command sent to the CPU to load a special piece of code (an interrupt service routine) to send data to or process data from a peripheral.

Suppose that you install a sound board and a CD-ROM drive in your existing workstation, and then a DMA channel conflict occurs. The friendly voice on the end of the tech-support line suggests that you pull out every board but the video board (if your computer uses one) and re-install each board one by one to locate the conflict. Afterward, you discover a conflict with your tape backup. You find the cause of this new problem—backups cannot occur while listening

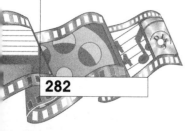

to a music CD—and decide the two peripherals can coexist peacefully and share the same channel when the music is off.

With that problem solved, you start to install software drivers for the new devices from within Windows 3.1. You discover, however, that the sound board's manufacturer has not included a Windows 3.1 driver, although the old driver works well with Windows 3.0 and the Multimedia Extensions. The friendly voice on the end of the tech-support line suggests that you call its bulletin board and download the new driver. After numerous attempts to get through (the line seems to be perpetually busy), you finally connect and download the file. You unzip (decompress) the driver and are ready to install it using the drivers applet supplied with the Windows Control Panel (see fig. 6.4). During the installation of the new driver, you are prompted for your original Windows 3.1 disks. After rummaging around in your desk, you manage to find them, and the remainder of the driver installation proceeds smoothly.

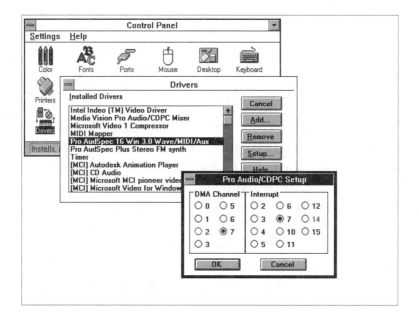

Figure 6.4:

Installing a driver in the Control Panel Drivers Applet.

With that task finished, you plug in your PC stereo speakers on the back of the sound board and make a quick trip to the electronics store for a power adapter (the speakers do not work without them). When you turn on the speakers and start Windows, you finally are rewarded with the "Ta-da!" sound.

What happened to your Mac-loving friend? He left the office hours ago, right after he took the Mac out of the box and plugged in the peripherals.

Know beforehand that it takes time and patience to prepare your PC for multimedia Windows. The good news is that the first upgrade is the worst. After you have completed one multimedia upgrade, you know what to look for. Give yourself lots of time and be patient.

NOTE

The next generation of PCs will have sound capability built in (even those that are not classified as MPC.) Compaq Corporation is leading the way with sound boards and microphones as standard equipment on its new class of business machines. Other clone manufacturers are following suit.

When you prepare to make your corporation media aware, remember to factor in the time and expense involved in upgrading a number of PCs for multimedia. If you plan to replace old and obsolete equipment, consider purchasing complete MPC solutions instead of upgrade kits. You may want to implement a multimedia network, which features a number of workstations connected to a media server. Companies such as Fluent are working on compression technology that will make it possible to send large compound documents over a network. The multimedia network may be more

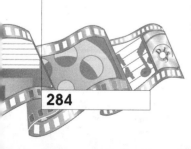

cost-effective in terms of hardware requirements and end-user support.

Finding Technical Support

Technical support is a valuable resource when you set up hardware or need to learn more about the use of new software for multimedia development. In addition to calling the tech-support phone number supplied with your documentation, you can address many tech-support questions directly to companies through CompuServe forums.

If you have difficulty reaching the tech-support department, or if you have complicated questions, try to contact the company switchboard rather than use the 800 number—you may get to speak directly to the product manager. Acquaint yourself with product managers—it is a wonderful way to find out about future upgrade plans. You have the opportunity to make suggestions for improvements you want to see, and you might be invited to participate in a beta test.

Programming with Multimedia

This last section of the chapter provides a brief overview of the Media Control Interface (MCI) and explains how you can control media devices connected to your PC. This section is intended to be a "high-level" summary. You will not learn the details of controlling media devices in Windows, but you will be able to understand how a programmer goes about making it all work together.

NOTE

For more detail about the Media Control Interface, see *The Microsoft Windows Multimedia Programmer's Workbook* and *Multimedia Programmer's Reference.* Both of these books come as part of the documentation for the Multimedia Development Kit for Microsoft Windows (MDK), a set of tools and programs for C and Assembler programmers to use for creating multimedia applications.

Both of these books are available in bookstores or from Microsoft Press.

The Media Control Interface is a part of Microsoft's strategy for layered, object-oriented, and device-independent development in Windows. As a user of multimedia authoring tools, you probably will be concerned only with the very top and bottom layers of this software Dobosch torte: the *MCI String Interface* and the multimedia hardware itself.

Interfacing with the MCI String Interface

Microsoft's goal in building the MCI string interface is to make it easy for multimedia authors to control media devices—without having to resort to arcane programming—and to a great extent they have succeeded. MCI sets out a standard to which all device manufacturers should write drivers, and when the standard is clear and everyone follows the standard, controlling a media device can be straightforward. For example, to play the second track of a music CD, the MCI commands would be as follows:

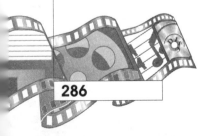

MCI command string	What it does
open cdaudio	tells the driver to get ready
set cdaudio time format tms	fuse tracks, minutes, seconds and frames to measure time
play cdaudio from 2 to 3	plays the CD from the beginning of track 2 to the beginning of track 3

To play a MIDI sequencer file through a MIDI device, the commands would be much the same:

MCI command string	What it does
open "mytune.mid" alias MIDI	tells the driver to get ready and load mytune.mid for playing
set MIDI time format song pointer	use sixteenth-notes to measure time
play MIDI to 128	play the first 8 bars (128 sixteenth notes of the song

The same holds true for any device that has an MCI driver: most, if not all of their functionality can be controlled by a relatively simple set of text commands. Some of the devices that have MCI drivers are as follows:

CD audio players

Digital audiotape players

Digital video in a window

Animation "movies"

Analog video overlay devices

Image scanners

MIDI sequencers

VCRs

Video disc players

Video camcorders

Sound boards capable of playing waveform files

Windows 3.1 comes standard with certain common device drivers, including a CD audio driver, a MIDI sequencer driver, and a device driver for playing and recording waveform audio. The MCI driver interface is open, so you can write an MCI driver (or have one written) for almost any device. Custom drivers have been written for slide projectors, video switches, and audio and video mixers among many other devices.

 For information about writing MCI drivers, consult Microsoft's Multimedia Device Driver Kit's documentation. Writing MCI drivers, like writing any other driver demands an ample knowledge of C and 8086 assembler, compiler theory, and a thorough understanding of how both Windows and the device being driven work.

Authoring software developers have followed through on their part of the deal as well and made simple interfaces to the MCI string interface. For example, Multimedia ToolBook provides fully functioning control objects that can be copied into an application as well as a function call supporting MCI, and Visual Basic provides a custom control for MCI support.

Interfacing with the Lower-level Interface of Multimedia Extensions

In addition to the MCI string interface, the Multimedia Extensions to Windows provides two other levels of interface to media devices, the MCI message interface and the Low-level interface. Both of these interfaces provide more control for the programmer and more information back to the programmer than does the MCI string interface. These interfaces are designed for C programmers, not for "real people," and they take much more effort to use. The MIDI example in the previous section takes three lines to play the first eight bars of a piece; in the MCI message interface, it would take about thirty lines of code to accomplish the same task, and in the low-level interface it would take one hundred.

NOTE

You can use the lower-level interfaces in two ways: by extending authoring software and by developing in C. Most authoring software enables you to link to the functions in mmsystem.dll, and then use them just like functions in the authoring software itself. Some functionality in the lower-level interfaces is unavailable in authoring software, because authoring software does not normally provide functions that can be called by other programs (callback functions) and because most authoring software cannot process the special messages sent by mmsystem.dll.

To get the full power of the lower-level interfaces, you will need to use C. Borland's C++ 3.1 has all the help files, header files, and libraries required, but you still will need the documentation for the Multimedia Developer's Kit (MDK). With other compilers, you need to purchase the complete MDK.

Why would anyone use these lower-level interfaces? Within corporate multimedia, there is little reason to use them. But they are powerful—with ten more lines in either low-level interface you could change notes during playback—something that is completely impossible with the MCI string interface. With the lower-level interfaces you can change window characteristics, such as transparency and size, that may not be possible within the string interface, and with the lower-level interfaces it is possible to perform more careful synchronization of multiple media events. Multimedia ToolBook's MCI interface straddles the string and message interfaces and is often a good choice when you need more control, but do not want to end up coding in C.

Part Three: Managing Multimedia

Planning Your Multimedia Project

Avoiding "Muddymedia"

Managing Different Types of Media

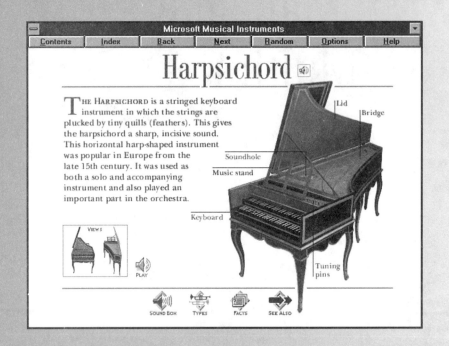

"Creating multimedia is easy: you just sit down at the keyboard and open several veins." — Ian Martin, Assistant Sysop, Multimedia Forum on CompuServe

Planning Your Multimedia Project

More than any other type of software, multimedia title development requires careful planning and project management. With your first multimedia effort, it's difficult to know what resources to devote to the project, how much to budget, and how to develop or license the necessary media clips.

Even for an experienced project manager, new media development can seem daunting, because media acquisition provides a whole new dimension of complexity. Few experts are around to help you, and fewer models are available to help you to plan your effort. Yet without a clear understanding of the tasks involved, and the resources required, your project risks running out of control and over budget.

This chapter will explain the steps involved in developing a multimedia title. Much of the process resembles straightforward software development, but those steps that pertain to media will require most of the development budget and the largest part of your effort. Multimedia development involves the following:

1. Selecting a Project: Starting Small
2. Estimating Development Costs
3. Designing the Project and Developing a Prototype
4. Selecting an Authoring Tool for the Job
5. Structuring the Text-based Data
6. Collecting Media Elements
7. Tagging and Coding Documents
8. Compiling
9. Testing the Product
10. Including Documentation and On-Line Help
11. Distributing the Product

This chapter examines the process of creating multimedia software and provides information about the costs to expect during project development. Advice also is given about designing and prototyping the software, selecting an authoring tool, collecting and preparing the media for inclusion in your multimedia title, and distributing the product after you create it. the following sections discuss the ins and outs of each step and show you how to minimize costs and reduce the time it takes to produce a quality title.

Selecting a Project: Starting Small

Earlier chapters suggested that you get accustomed to new media by using OLE to add media clips to applications you use everyday. If you followed this suggestion, you're probably eager to go farther. Perhaps you want to convert an in-house training seminar to interactive multimedia courseware. Maybe you want to put together an electronic brochure as a sales vehicle for your company's products. Perhaps you have been inspired to create a multimedia entertainment title for distribution to the consumer marketplace.

The nice thing about using multimedia is that it inspires your creativity—the more you see media being used, the more ideas you get about products you want to create. The problem is often not one of "what can I do," but "where do I start?"

With any new project, it makes sense to start with something small; your first multimedia application is not the time to experiment with a large scale project. Every multimedia developer can tell you that the process of creating multimedia software takes more work and time than expected. It will ease your development pains considerably if you scale back to begin with.

Good multimedia software offers a lot of information to the user. The user should have the opportunity to browse, explore related topics, and then go back to the main line of inquiry. To give the user this type of rich media experience, the software you design must have a lot of "depth." Users who work with an application that has breadth but no depth soon become bored and frustrated.

Most first-time multimedia developers either are not aware of the need for much depth (and never include it, creating a shallow product) or discover the need during the prototyping process. With your first application, try to create a small application with a lot of depth. The end result is liable to be more impressive, and you will be better prepared to tackle something larger.

If you are unsure about spending development time and money on a multimedia application, a good way to get started is to try a few corporate presentations. Although multimedia presentations are often nothing more than zippy slide shows, you can experiment without any pressure. With software such as Gold Disk's Animation Works, you have the opportunity to create a presentation featuring animation, sound, interaction (the product enables you to add buttons to each screen and attach scripts to the buttons), as well as other media clips. Presentations enable you to experiment with media clips (you will find yourself scrambling for the perfect sound file), learn the fundamentals of animation, and play with fonts, images, colors, and backgrounds.

Other areas of multimedia you may want to begin working with are small promotional pieces to be sent to clients, in-house newsletters, and custom in-house software tutorials.

If you still are eager to create something larger, remember that you'll need a lot of data. For this reason, look to develop in areas where you have access to significant amounts of information. If the application will be mostly hypertext, present large amounts of textual data. If the application is largely media oriented, make sure that you offer enough sound, animation, or video to make the project engaging, while providing enough solid information to ensure that the application is meaningful.

TIP

A well-designed multimedia application seems to have only one-third to one-half the information actually available. If you are creating a hypertext version of a report, you would need to include at least two or three times the information featured in a printed report to make the report seem as informative. (Optimally, you would want to include much more than two or three times the data.)

Finally, image also is important. High-quality multimedia should have a slick look and feel. Many talented graphic artists are drawn to this new field, and are able to use their design skills in developing great interfaces. If you do not have the graphic skills to develop a really great-looking product, consider hiring professionals to help you.

Consider your first multimedia effort as an training investment; do not expect it to make money; consider it technological investments in learning to apply a new technology. Beginning efforts always require an investment in education. Multimedia development will become more cost effective (and potentially profitable) when you have gone through the learning curve involved with learning a new authoring tool and how to manage media. Multimedia development also will benefit from economies of scale, if you can develop a few products simultaneously (perhaps the same title for different platforms, or similar titles focused around a theme), if you can re-use media clips, or if you can start accumulating clip libraries.

Even if you start with a small project, your first effort (unless you are just putting together a presentation) will involve a lot of work for all members of the development team. It will require learning on the part of everyone, not just learning how to use the new tools, but learning new ways of coordinating efforts. As you go through the process, remind yourself that the second project will be easier, and the one after that easier still.

Estimating Development Costs

Multimedia development costs have good news and bad news. The bad news is that developing a top-quality multimedia title is very expensive. The good news is that the price is decreasing almost monthly as hardware and peripheral prices continue to drop and as software tools become more sophisticated.

Price also depends on the type of title you want to create. Full-scale multimedia productions created for the consumer marketplace can cost as much as a million dollars (although this compares favorably to the cost of a major two-hour motion picture). Software game developers can provide a model in helping you determine how much money to budget for a large multimedia title. Electronic Arts produces approximately 100 titles a year. These titles, which incorporate interactivity, graphics, sound and animation, require the efforts of five to 20 people each and take a year to develop. A typical title costs between $200,000 and $500,000 to produce.

Remember that these are the costs for consumer titles expected to sell many thousands of copies. Your effort, especially if you are creating a product for in-house use, can be accomplished with a very modest budget. (Another compelling argument for starting small and working your way to large production efforts.)

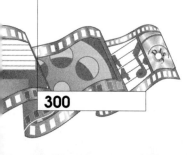

The cost of an interactive multimedia presentation (to be used when making a speech) may be no more than the price of the presentation tool and the cost of a few hours of time to learn the tool.

Asymetrix now sells multimedia presentation tools priced under $100.

If you know that you want to develop a title but have no idea how much to budget for the type of title you want to create, it helps to check with one or all of the following:

➤ You can hire an outside consultant to specify the project and create rough cost estimates.

➤ You can ask a special multimedia development firm for an estimate (it pays to shop around).

➤ You can post a message on a BBS or CompuServe forum asking others how much they have paid for development of similar projects.

Although the investment in development hardware can be significant, the bulk of multimedia development costs come from hiring the right designers and programmers and the cost of media acquisition (whether through custom development or licensing). The more "visual" the application, the more money it costs to have someone develop, or acquire, the required animation or video.

NOTE

I approached the legal counsel of a large publishing firm with the idea of developing one of their fantasy/science fiction novels as a multimedia title. As we discussed the idea, I expressed concern about what it would cost to develop the program properly. The author's estate was concerned about the quality of anything connected with the work, so I knew the project would require a large development budget. When I told the legal counsel my estimate (roughly a quarter of a million dollars), he just laughed. The company had already spent considerably more than that in legal fees to buy back the rights to the work from another publishing house.

You may have to write additional DLLs to expand the functionality of the authoring tool you select. Understand when planning your budget that this may be necessary, and add in the cost for extra programming expertise.

You may have to customize your project's authoring tool to suit your needs (or you may need to develop an authoring tool for your specifications). To tweak an authoring tool can be expensive because good programmers can demand top dollar; make sure that you save the bulk of your budget for the media development. If you spend too much on the tool, the end result may be technically impressive, but the user will not be impressed because the "glitter" part of multimedia is not apparent.

NOTE

A good general rule to follow is total project programming costs should be only 50 percent of what you spend on media acquisition.

Considering Hardware Resources

You may wind up spending $8,000 to $11,000 for a completely equipped Multimedia development system; MPCs for users, however, can be purchased for under $2,000.

The price of computer hardware drops so rapidly that to provide specific prices here would be useless. What is more helpful is to describe the caliber of equipment in which you should be investing—if better equipment is available by the time you read this, try it.

With multimedia, the greater the amount of processing speed, memory, hard disk capacity, and compression capabilities the better (see fig. 7.1). To be outfitted completely for all types of multimedia production (video, sound, rendering, and others), consider spending $8,000 to $11,000 per com-

puter. You can get by with a smaller investment, but it involves trade-offs. Workstation costs drops significantly with a network, however—you can share resources such as printers, video-capture boards, and scanners.

Figure 7.1:

The hardware components of an MPC.

Chapter 3 explains the differences between a user's PC and a developer's MPC. Although you can develop on any Windows-ready PC featuring a sound board and a CD-ROM drive, you really need a powerful machine to avoid complete frustration. Any office PC is fine for playback purposes if you tack on a multimedia upgrade kit, but to develop multimedia applications you need to invest in a new MPC.

When it comes to hardware investment, go for the best you can afford. The sheer size of media files puts a heavy strain on a PC's resources. At a minimum, choose a 486 50MHz PC, with at least 16M of RAM. You need a 500M hard drive (at a minimum) if you plan to create video clips; a gigabyte or more is probably desirable.

If you plan on creating a lot of 3D animation, a math coprocessor is essential in reducing the amount of time it takes to render the final image.

NOTE

As you assemble your multimedia development team, let the team members help you make up your hardware "shopping list." Very often, established programmers, illustrators, and animators have strong preferences, which are the result of trial and error on prior projects. These experts also may know where to get substantial discounts on the hardware.

Some of the best illustrators and animators insist on the Macintosh platform for development. This does not have to be a problem if all the machines are on a network. It is easy to transfer the media files and convert them (using editing tools that come with the Microsoft MDK) to file formats required for Windows multimedia. In the event your team is not networked, you can get a copy of MacLink Plus (which comes with cables that connect to the serial port of the PC and the communications port of the Mac) for transferring the media files.

Sound that is sampled at 44KHz, 16-bit is CD audio quality.

In addition to the computer, try to find the best sound card you can afford (see fig. 7.2). The optimum card is one that enables you to capture samples at 44KHz, 16-bit sound. Although a user's MPC plays back sound at 11KHz or 22KHz, if you capture and archive sound at the highest level, the audio clips can be reused in the future (perhaps the base-level audio card will have improved).

When purchasing your development hardware, you need to take a long term perspective, as opposed to planning for just one product. If possible, leverage the cost of better quality audio equipment (sound card, speakers, microphone, equalizer) over a few projects. By purchasing the best equipment

you can afford, you will be able to capture and archive CD quality audio samples, which will form the basis for a corporate clip library.

Figure 7.2:
Creative Lab's Sound Blaster Pro.

In time, these libraries will be far more valuable than the original cost of the equipment. By creating original media clips, you'll save money that otherwise would have been spent on licensing media content. You have the opportunity to reuse clips, or license them to other developers.

As more people get into multimedia development, the demand for high quality clips will rise. For this reason, get your content in the best form possible and be willing to invest in the hardware that makes it possible to do so. In the case of audio, this means capturing and storing your CD audio quality clips.

You may want to make the investment in a flatbed color scanner to acquire images.

For video development, invest in the best video-capture board possible—one that enables you to save clips in a variety of compression formats including DVI, JPEG, MPEG, and AVI. That way, no matter what format emerges as the standard in the future, your video archives are ready. In addition, capture graphics in 24-bit color and then dither to 8-bit if necessary.

NOTE

What if you only want to get your feet wet in multimedia, and you are not ready to become a full-service production shop? The minimum development MPC should be a 486 50MHz machine with 16M of RAM and a 200M hard drive. You probably will want to invest in a video-capture board, a flatbed color scanner, and a modem. A modem is critical because it enables you to download clips from bulletin boards.

Considering Software Resources

Compared to the cost of purchasing development hardware, software costs are relatively minimal, depending on how you plan to acquire your media. If you plan to license all the media or if you have access to in-house clip libraries, an authoring tool may be the only software you need to consider.

At a minimum, you probably should acquire the Multimedia Development Kit from Microsoft. In addition to providing the Viewer authoring tool, the Multimedia Development Kit provides a series of media-editing tools that enable you to manipulate bitmaps, palettes, and wave files. This $495

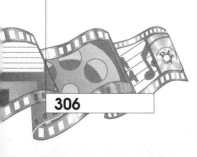

package may be all you need, depending on how you plan to create your software.

Other authoring tools can range in price from $199 (the price for Visual Basic, standard edition) to many thousands of dollars. The cost of tools to create or edit the media also varies greatly. A number of authoring tools have already been described in Chapter 4; this section will give a brief synopsis of some of the most common authoring tools and factors to consider when making your selection.

Another consideration is the time you estimate it will take to develop your product. In addition to the purchase of the primary authoring tool and the initial media-editing tools, budget an extra thousand dollars for media-editing software. It may take several months to a year to develop a large multimedia product. During that time, a number of new tools may appear that can significantly shorten and ease your development effort. Rather than buy all your software tools at a single time, buy only the tools you need when you need them. That way, you can take advantage of the most powerful and most recent editing capabilities available in your price range.

TIP

The less experience your staff has, the less sophisticated the software you need. Fortunately, less powerful software also is cheaper. Do not spend thousand of dollars for sound-editing tools or MIDI synthesizers unless you have a highly experienced staff. It makes more sense to have the clips made professionally (for a product you plan to sell) or to record and edit them using a simple wave-edit tool (for in-house products).

Plan to spend an average of $1,000 to $2,000 per workstation for media-editing software (less if you have specialized workstations, such as one for sound production and one for video), in addition to the cost of the authoring tool. These software costs should be eliminated if you farm out most of your media development work.

Considering the Cost of Document Tagging

If you plan to produce a hypertext or hypermedia application, a structure for your program's data is essential. The information you plan to use often needs to be prepared before it can be compiled by a hypertext authoring tool.

The first stage in document preparation is to get all text into ASCII text format. For older data, this may involve scanning printed pages and using OCR (optical character recognition) software. Scanned pages require extensive proofreading. Newer documents are usually stored in a file format that can be converted to ASCII. Then the document must be tagged, often using SGML (Standard General Markup Language, an ASCII text-coding scheme). SGML tagging involves inserting special codes into the document, which indicate the physical layout of a page. On a very simple level, SGML tagging can be used to distinguish Level One headings from Level Two headings, and Level Two headings from the main body of the text.

Tagging for the physical structure of a document is a quick and simple process. The physical structure of a document refers to page layout, the fonts used, line lengths, and other aspects of the physical appearance of the text. Tagging for a hypertext document is considerably more complex because the logical structure of the document is more important than the physical structure. The logical structure refers to the hierarchical arrangement of topics of information—how topics are linked to each other, how the table of contents should be laid out, which topics should appear in the primary indexing scheme, and if the document should have more than one index. Tagging a document for the logical structure is an extensive editorial task that needs to be conducted by someone familiar with the content.

The larger the amount of data, the more difficult and lengthy the tagging labor becomes. CDs offer up to 600M of storage, or roughly 250,000 pages of print. For a large hypertext effort (like an encyclopedia), the tagging can take longer than any other part of the development process, including media creation.

Document tagging, when sourced out to other firms, can get expensive, with prices ranging from $75,000 to $200,000 or more for moderate to large projects. The advantage to spending this money is that you do not need to hire the staff to tag the product. The disadvantage is that your company never develops in-house expertise in production of hypertext titles, and you must pay a similar cost for every title you develop.

If you decide to tag and code documents in-house, plan on devoting one to two full-time people for a large project (two or more book volumes of material.) Although many hypertext authoring tools accept SGML tags, and use them to compile the document, other authoring tools require a different format. The Microsoft Viewer product, for example, will compile only RTF (Rich Text Format) files. Convert documents in SGML format.

A less-expensive way to "tag" the logical structure of a document is to use the SmarText 2.0 product from Lotus Development Corporation. For $495, the SmarText Builder simplifies the process of indexing a document and creating hypertext links by constructing links based on the frequency of words and the page layout of the word-processed document you import. Although SmarText enables you to import graphics, full multimedia capabilities are not yet offered. The expensive part of the product is the SmarText Reader (which enables others to view but not edit the documents you create); the Reader comes with a runtime license of $99. For hypertext documents distributed to a large audience, the Reader cost is prohibitive.

Considering Personnel Costs

The personnel costs associated with multimedia development make up the largest part of the budget. Large multimedia projects take hundreds, if not thousands, of hours. Whether you hire people for in-house development or contract much of the work, personnel is what makes multimedia expensive.

Costs vary widely depending on the skill sets you need and where you are located. Qualified personnel are more prevalent (and therefore less expensive) on the West Coast. Top multimedia analysts can command consulting rates of $1,000 to $2,500 a day. These people can help your organization develop marketplace strategies, put together business plans, and identify key products and marketplace segmentation. They also can conduct competitive strategies, help you determine the types of products being developed by your competition, and recommend new multimedia personnel.

Multimedia producers are responsible for directing and managing the overall project—from the design of the specifications, to acquisition of the media, to programming and testing of the product, to creation of documentation, to production and package design. If you hire a full-time person, expect to pay a salary of $60,000 to $100,000, depending on the person's experience. If you hire a consultant for a specific project, expect to pay $75 to $150 for each hour of time. In addition to managing the project, the project leader generally takes a lead role in coding or creating media.

The prices of programmers and media-development specialists can vary so much that it is difficult to estimate how much to budget. Generally, it makes sense to hire experienced people because it takes them far less time to accomplish a task than a couple of moderately experienced people. The cost of the best development personnel is $50 to $100 per hour (consulting rates) or $40,000 to $70,000 per year (annual salary). For experts in certain tasks (production of high-quality video, for example), expect to pay more; so few experts are in this new field that they command top dollar.

Considering Media Rights Licensing Costs

If you plan to save money by not hiring in-house people to develop media, you must spend money licensing existing media clips for your application. You probably spend more in the long run with this method because you do not develop in-house expertise or your own clip library. To license media may be cheaper if you are developing a single product or if you need to acquire a specific work for your title.

Certain multimedia titles do not require much licensing because you may already have the material available (an electronic corporate report is one example). Other titles, especially those you plan on selling to a mass market, require extensive licensing.

The more valuable the property, the more money you have to pay—not only for the rights to use the material, but in legal fees while you negotiate for the rights. A number of lawyers are starting to develop expertise in this hot new area of contract law. If you are unfamiliar with the legal issues involved in licensing, pay the money to hire someone who is. Before you start paying to digitize and edit the material, you should feel confident that you have the right to distribute the material, in the form you want to the area (United States? Worldwide?) you want. Negotiate for as many rights as you can possibly get, especially if you think you may want to reuse the material again at some later date.

If you find a video clip you want to use, for example, negotiate for the right to use the electronic (digitized) version of that clip in all works produced by your company for a certain number of years. Make sure that you have the right to edit the clip, in case you need to. Ensure that you have the right to use still images captured from the clip.

Another consideration is to ensure (have your lawyer make sure), that the company licensing the material to you has the right to license the material in the way you plan to use it. If you want to make an animation of a famous work of art, for example, make sure that the original artist will not sue you for tampering with his or her work in the future.

TIP

Try to negotiate an exclusive agreement if you can. You do not want to go to the expense of developing a title only to find that three other companies have developed similar products based on the same original material. When you can, try to use works in the public domain; this can lessen the cost of your overall project.

Designing the Project and Developing a Prototype

Too often, novice multimedia developers make the mistake of selecting an authoring tool before considering how they want their project to look and how the user should interact with the product. The authoring tool's capabilities wind up driving the product design, instead of the design requirements determining the choice of authoring tool.

The first and most critical point in designing the project is figuring out the user's needs and building the product to meet those needs. Write out an initial product concept, which describes the need to be filled, the target audience, the plot (or hook), and preliminary media requirements (or how you envision presenting the information to your user). From the concept, develop a script around your idea. Many times, because of the nature of multimedia, your "script" may actually look like a story board, or a flow chart—or a hybrid, incorporating aspects of all three.

The script should clearly chart all the paths the title can take during the course of user interaction. It should list all the required data elements—text, image, voice, music, animation, video, and any additional interactive elements. From the script, you are ready to develop a prototype. Never start to code before the script is complete; this is the surest route to a project management, muddymedia nightmare.

 NOTE More information about how to design your product can be found in the next chapter, "Avoiding Muddymedia."

Your prototype does not need to be developed with the authoring tool you eventually choose for actual product development; a program that enables you to put together screens quickly is preferable. You want something that enables you to develop the interface, without worrying about software robustness or easy programming extendibility.

Good choices of prototyping tools include Microsoft's Visual Basic and Asymetrix's ToolBook. Each of these applications enables you to design screens quickly and easily by creating forms and adding objects (such as buttons, icons, and menu bars). Many companies have used these for development of consumer products in addition to prototyping.

After you develop your prototype, show it to potential users to get feedback before continuing development. Ask them to evaluate the design in terms of ease of use, and how well it meets their needs. Ask for a critique of the amount of information available; if the users are not satisfied, work on collecting and indexing more data and redesigning the interface.

Novice users may compare your product to the sleek applications that receive attention in the trade press; make sure that your prototype has a professional look and feel. Assess whether volunteers can navigate through the application without having to ask questions (if a user is able to navigate through the end product without referring to the documentation, then the application is well-designed). Ask users to suggest improvements or enhancements to the design. After working with users to finalize your design, you are ready to select the authoring tool that will best enable you to complete the design concepts portrayed in the prototype.

Selecting an Authoring Tool for the Job

Although it is possible to develop a multimedia title using a programming language such as C, a high-level authoring tool is better. An authoring tool is a program designed to help you build a multimedia title. The authoring tool provides a basic framework for creating a multimedia title, and gives the developer building blocks for creating a title, element by element.

Some authoring tools do not require any programming knowledge on the part of the user; creating a title is as simple as drawing a flowchart and dropping in media elements. Other tools come with a sophisticated programming language that offers a high degree of creativity and flexibility, but also demands a certain level of technical ability on the part of the developer. Some tools (such as Visual Basic) were designed primarily as a programming tool, but are being used by multimedia developers who like the product's flexibility. Authoring tools are available for as little as $100; others can cost many thousands of dollars.

Although many tools are available to choose from, after you have put together your preliminary design specifications, certain features will stand out as more or less important. One or two tools will seem the logical choice, depending on the type of product you want to create, the type of media that dominates the product, the expertise of your staff (or the company you want to hire), and the amount of money you have budgeted.

It may be helpful to poll other people to determine the tool to use for a specific project. Ask firms that specialize in multimedia development what tools they use for certain projects and why they prefer those tools. Many firms are eager to build business relationships and do not charge if you ask in an informal manner. What you discover is that most firms specialize in a single tool or two and shun others. If you work with an outside firm, make sure that the requirements of your product are mentioned before your contractor discusses their familiarity with a certain authoring tool.

The Multimedia Forum on Compu-Serve is a great place to ask for opinions about the advantages of one tool over another. Representatives from companies such as Microsoft and Asymetrix are responsive to specific questions about their products' capabilities.

Another way to determine whether a tool is right for you is to post questions on the CompuServe forums. Although you may get a lot of answers (and start a few flame wars in the process), you learn about what tools are out there and why people use them. The best part about getting information from on-line forums is that you learn about tools from people who actually use them. This approach is different from reading an article written by an editor who evaluated five different tools in a single month and then picked an "editor's choice" based on the best set of features. The other useful thing about forum opinions is that you often get information from people evaluating tools in the beta-test stage that have not yet been released. You can find out when it is better to wait to purchase one tool because a better tool will be released within the month.

Many authoring tools currently are on the market, and more will be available in the coming months. Each tool has specific strengths and weaknesses, and each is right for a certain type of software. The following sections provide overviews of some of the tools now available.

Looking at Microsoft's Multimedia Development Kit and Multimedia Viewer

Many reasons make the expense ($495) of acquiring the Multimedia Development Kit (MDK) worth it, not the least of which is the Viewer tool that Microsoft includes as part of the package. If you plan on extending the capabilities of your authoring tool by writing C code, you will need the MDK's header files, import libraries, sample applications, and editing tools. In addition, you will want the documentation that comes with the CD-ROM disc. The MDK also comes with a utility that enables you to convert MacroMedia Director movies created on the Macintosh to an MMM format (MultiMedia Movie, an animation file format) that can be played in Windows.

If you need to create an application that is text-intensive but with full multimedia capabilities, you may want to author with Viewer (see fig. 7.3). This tool is similar to the Windows Help program; the process of creating a Viewer file is much like that of creating a help file. With a word processor (such as Word for Windows) capable of creating Rich Text Format (RTF) files, you create the document using context strings to tag Topics. A *topic* is the basic informational block used by Viewer titles. After the topics have been tagged you can jump from topic to topic. Topics can be linked to words within the text. Links also can be made to graphics, sounds, animations, and video sequences.

Viewer gives you the ability to access other executables and DLLs, embed graphics (that can feature hot spots), and build links across other Viewer documents. As a part of the compilation process, every word in the Viewer file is indexed, which gives flexibility to the final product—the user can even do Boolean searches on the textual material.

If you are comfortable creating Windows help files, you easily can create multimedia applications with the Microsoft Viewer authoring tool.

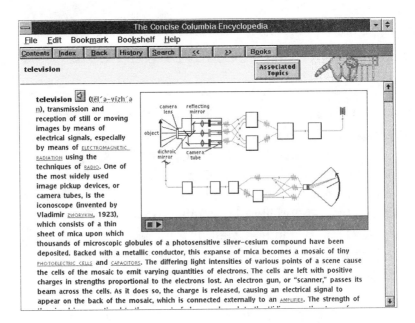

Figure 7.3:

The Columbia Encyclopedia product was designed with Viewer.

Viewer is a powerful tool but it is not designed for quick development work. Most linking must be done manually, and, with Version 1.0 of the product, you are forced to use a rather primitive DOS compiler to create Viewer documents (see fig. 7.4). Nevertheless, Viewer is powerful and can produce a nice end product—if you are willing to invest the time and patience.

Looking at Asymetrix's Multimedia ToolBook

At $695, Multimedia ToolBook is not the cheapest product on the market, but it is one of the simplest to learn. ToolBook resembles closely the Claris Hypercard product created for the Mac (see fig. 7.5). ToolBook follows an object-oriented approach to software design. Users can place objects (buttons, bit maps, and so on) on the screen and attach a script to each object.

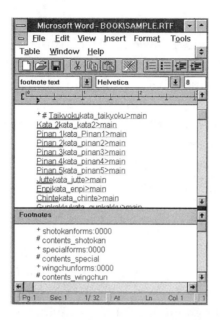

Figure 7.4:

A sample RTF file that will be compiled into a Viewer title.

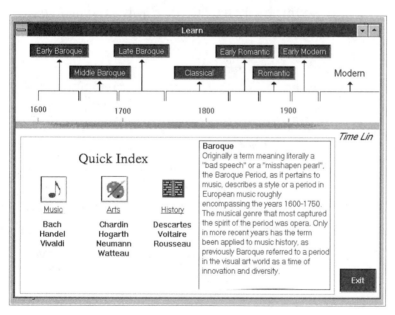

Figure 7.5:

Composer Quest, from Dr. T's Music Software, was designed with ToolBook.

See the section in Chapter 6 titled "Programming with Multimedia" for information on the Media Control Interface (MCI).

ToolBook follows a book metaphor (as compared to the index card metaphor followed by Hypercard on the Mac). Each "book" consists of a series of pages, which the user can scroll through or jump between. Multimedia functionality is easy to add by using the multimedia widgets that come with the multimedia version of ToolBook. *Widgets* are objects that come with scripts to access the Windows MCI. Unskilled programmers can cut and paste widgets into a book to control CD-ROM drives, sound boards, and other media devices.

Asymetrix has an unlimited runtime distribution policy. A developer can distribute a book, along with a copy of the runtime version of ToolBook, without any additional cost. Although ToolBook is easy to use and does not require a knowledge of programming to build a multimedia application, the resulting books tend to run slowly as compared to products developed with other tools.

NOTE

Ironically, ToolBook's greatest strength (ease of development) also can be one of its greatest drawbacks. ToolBook does not require programming skills to develop an application, which is beneficial for people with little or no experience with software design. As a result, many horrible multimedia books have been created and many more surely will follow (see fig. 7.6).

If you develop with ToolBook, make sure that you follow the design guidelines in Chapter 8 "Avoiding "Muddymedia" and other reference manuals to avoid a "Mickey Mouse" look and feel.

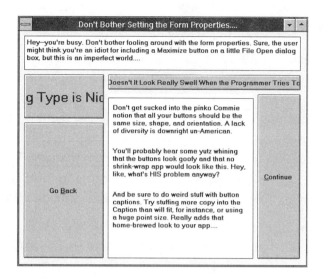

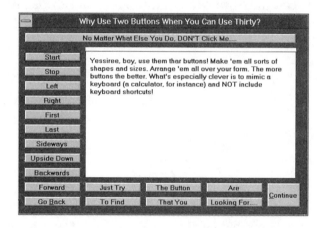

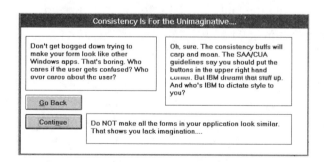

Figure 7.6:

John Murdoch's "Lurker's Guide to Bad Design", a Visual Basic application designed to showcase inter-face flaws made by novice developers.

Looking at Microsoft's Visual Basic

Visual Basic programming example that shows how to play wave and MIDI files by clicking on a button is found in Chapter 10.

Visual Basic 2.0, $199 standard edition, $495 professional edition, from Microsoft, enables you to place objects on-screen (in a Windows form) and attach BASIC code to the objects. Although Visual Basic was designed so that non-C programmers could create Windows applications, it serves as a good multimedia development tool. Access to the MCI with Visual Basic requires more knowledge of programming but you can better control the look and feel of the final product.

The following example shows you how to design a Visual Basic application that can play a MIDI file when the user presses a button.

In addition to an MPC, you need a copy of Microsoft Visual Basic 2.0 to program this application.

This application assumes that you are familiar with Visual Basic programming techniques. Refer to your Microsoft Visual Basic Programmer's Guide if you need additional assistance.

Create a Visual Basic form that looks like the one in figure 7.7.

Name the form "BACH.FRM" and give it the following properties:

Control	CtlName Property	Caption Property
Top Command button	PlayBach	Play Music
Middle Left Com. button	BTN_Pause	Pause
Middle Right Com. button	BTN_Resume	Resume
Bottom Command button	Command1	End

You must call the mciExecute routine in the MMSYSTEM.DLL to pass MCI string commands to your MIDI synthesizer. When calling any DLL from Visual Basic, you need to place a Declare statement in the global module of your MAK file. You will declare a variable called "midi" as an integer. This will allow VB to pass the value of the "midi" integer to the DLL.

You also will need to declare a global variable called "Sound" as a string.

Your global module should look like this:

```
Declare Function mciExecute Lib "mmsystem.dll" (ByVal
midi$) As Integer

Global Sound As String
```

Rename your global module to "BACH.BAS."

Returning to BACH.FRM, create a general procedure to pass mci command strings to mciExecute and to enable the Pause button after the music starts playing:

```
Sub PlayMidi ()
    Tune$ = "Close All"
    i = mciExecute(Tune$)

    Tune$ = "Open " + Sound
    i = mciExecute(Tune$)

    Tune$ = "Play " + Sound
    i = mciExecute(Tune$)

    BTN_Pause.Enabled = -1
End Sub
```

When loading the BACH.FRM, set the values of the Pause and Resume buttons to off:

```
Sub Form_Load ()
    BTN_Pause.Enabled = 0
    BTN_Resume.Enabled = 0
End Sub
```

If the user clicks the "Play Music" button, set the value of the Sound variable to the name of the MIDI file to be played and call the "PlayMidi" Sub Procedure:

```
Sub PlayBach_Click ()
   Sound = "bach.mid"
   PlayMidi
End Sub
```

If the user clicks the "Pause" button, send an mci string to pause the sound, enable the "Resume" button, and disable the "Pause" button:

```
Sub BTN_Pause_Click ()
   Dim i As integer

   Tune$ = "Pause " + Sound
   i = mciExecute(Tune$)

   If i = 1 Then
      BTN_Resume.Enabled = -1
      BTN_Pause.Enabled = 0
   End If
End Sub
```

If the user clicks the "Resume" button, send an mci string to resume playing the sound, enable the "Pause" button, and disable the "Resume" button:

```
Sub BTN_Resume_Click ()
   Dim i As integer

   Tune$ = "Play " + Sound
   i = mciExecute(Tune$)

   If i = 1 Then
      BTN_Pause.Enabled = -1
      BTN_Resume.Enabled = 0
   End If
End Sub
```

If the user clicks the "End" button, send an mci string to close all devices:

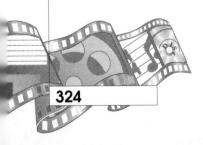

```
Sub Command1_Click ()
   Tune$ = "Close All"
   i = mciExecute(Tune$)
End Sub
```

When unloading the BACH.FRM, make sure that all mci devices have been closed:

```
Sub Form_Unload ()
   Tune$ = "Close All"
   i = mciExecute(Tune$)
End Sub
```

Compile the application and test it.

Visual Basic comes with custom controls, which are special dynamic link libraries (DLLs) that act as an extension to the Microsoft Visual Basic Toolbox. When you add a custom control to the program, it becomes a part of the VB development environment and provides added functionality to your programs. Visual Basic contains, among other things, a custom MCI control for the recording and playback of multimedia files. This control produces a media playback panel (with Previous, Next, Play, Pause, Back, Step, Stop, Record, and Eject buttons) on your Visual Basic application form (see fig. 7.8).

Although Visual Basic gives you full programming functionality and enables you to create a single executable file (that must be distributed with the VBRUN200.DLL file), it does require some programming ability on the part of the developer. Because Visual Basic offers flexibility to developers, it's easy to create problematic applications if you don't know what you're doing.

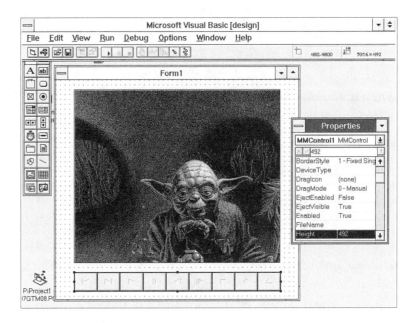

Figure 7.8:

Visual Basic's custom MCI control produces a media playback panel at runtime.

Many novice VB programmers create applications that do not return memory back to Windows after the VB application is closed. Other VB programs that create Child windows forget to close them when the main Window is closed. If you are careless, you can create an application that looks great at 640× 480 resolution, but looks terrible when displayed at 600× 800. Although Visual Basic is a superb prototyping tool, do not try to develop a full scale multimedia application with it, unless you're an experienced programmer.

Looking at Owl International's Guide

Guide, from Owl International, was designed for managing large amounts of text. You can create hypertext documents and then add media elements to the final product. The $495 product enables you to import text files from a number of word processing packages and then mark the text to create buttons that link to other parts of the application. One product that was developed with Owl is shown in figure 7.9.

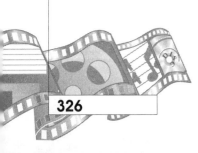

Figure 7.9:

InterOptica's Multimedia Travel Guide, Great Cities of the World, was developed with Guide.

To add media elements to the Guide document—or to get full functionality from the product—you program using Guide's proprietary language, LOGiiX.

To play back books created with the Guide development product, you must purchase a separate Guide Reader. The price of the Reader must be negotiated with Owl on a site-by-site basis.

Although Guide handles text well, it cannot manage media elements as well as other authoring tools. The need to negotiate a license agreement for the Reader is cumbersome and should be considered when choosing a development tool if you are distributing to a large number of users.

Looking at AimTech's IconAuthor

The $4,995 price of IconAuthor suggests that this product is a professional-level development tool. As the name implies, IconAuthor offers an icon-driven approach to creating multimedia applications. You select icons from the IconAuthor toolbar and drag-and-drop to the application work area. Numerous icons are available to control flow, input, output, and data. IconAuthor enables you to extend the functionality of the authoring program by adding external dynamic link libraries.

By continuing to drag-and-drop icons, a visual flowchart is created in the work area, charting the dynamics of your multimedia application. This charting feature makes it easy to see the flow of the application and makes editing easier than with other authoring tools. A double-click on any icon in the flowchart shows its content window or dialog box, which enables you to assign media-related details, such as the names of files to be incorporated or the type of event that can trigger the next step in the process.

Despite its flexibility, power, and simple to use icon-oriented interface, IconAuthor may be too expensive because each runtime player costs $50.

Although development using IconAuthor is graphically driven, the program is not easy to use. Four days of training are included as part of the IconAuthor purchase price. Given the strength of the product and the fact that training is included in the package, it may be easy to justify the high price tag. The problem with the price of IconAuthor is the $50 fee for each copy of the runtime module you must distribute with anything you create. If you are planning to create a multimedia title for widespread distribution, or if you are trying to create an application priced for the impulse buyer, the runtime fee certainly prices your product out of most users' budgets.

Looking at MacroMedia's Authorware Professional for Windows

Another product, priced strictly for the professional developer, is Authorware Professional for Windows, which costs

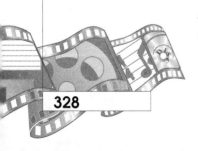

$8,000. One feature that may make the cost more palatable is programs you develop using Authorware for Windows also can be executed on the Macintosh. As the number of multimedia playback platforms increases, cross-platform capability becomes a critical factor in tool selection.

Like IconAuthor, Authorware uses a flow-chart structure for multimedia development. After creating an application, you can compile the final product into a single executable file, which makes distribution significantly easier (the resulting EXE file may become very large, however). The package comes with a number of sample applications and something Authorware calls "models"—segments of code that can be added to your own applications—similar to the multimedia widgets offered by ToolBook.

Although $8,000 is a sizable investment for an authoring tool, it may well be worth the cost, if it saves you from having to write two sets of code—one for the Windows platform and another for the Macintosh.

Structuring the Text-based Data

Although the words *multimedia*, *hypertext*, and *hypermedia* are used somewhat interchangeably, a big difference exists among the three. *Multimedia* focuses primarily on media that is nontextual in nature. Imagery, sound, and video or animation are the most important components of multimedia. Text, when it is included, tends to be directional in nature (for example, "Press Enter") or is designed to add value (for example, when you request more information about an animated process, the information is provided in the form of an article). Products meant to entertain are best suited to multimedia, as are corporate presentations and advertising and marketing materials (see fig. 7.10).

Hypertext is text that has been indexed, and linked topically. The user reads the resulting document with the use of a hypertext-retrieval engine. Better designed for research, hypertext gives the user the ability to search for data through conceptual links or keywords. Hypertext enables the user to add customized search-and-retrieval mechanisms such as bookmarks and annotations. Common or most-recent searches can be stored and used at a later time with an updated version of the hypertext database. Hypertext products are well suited to encyclopedias, reference materials, corporate training manuals, documentation, and anthologies of information. Although hypertext can include other media elements (most often graphics), the media is not the primary focus; the text provides the information (see fig. 7.11).

Hypertext products must be carefully planned. No matter how good the monitor, most people do not want to do a significant amount of reading on screen. For this reason, hypertext products are best suited for research materials—the user may want to browse through the material for information but would prefer to print the data, after it is located, to read at a later time.

Educational products are good choices for hypermedia, as are corporate reports.

Hypermedia combines the best of both worlds by featuring heavily indexed textual databases with a wealth of supporting information. In hypermedia, the flashy media and the interface are still the primary focus for the end user. The idea behind well-thought-out hypermedia applications is that the user can enjoy the slick interface but have depth in the form of text (see fig. 7.12).

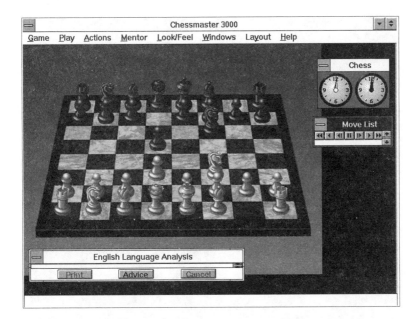

Figure 7.10:

The Software Toolworks' Chessmaster 3000 is a multimedia game.

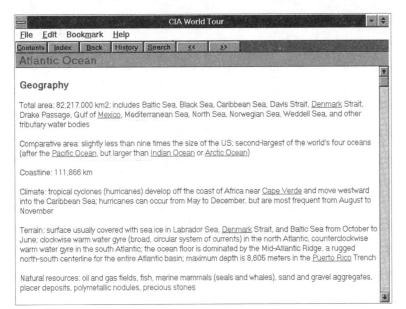

Figure 7.11:

The CIA World Tour, from the Bureau of Electronic Development, is an example of a Hypertext document.

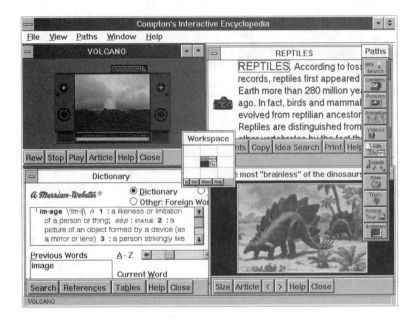

Figure 7.12:

Compton's Inter-active Encyclope-dia is a hyper-media application.

If you create your application using specialized fonts, you need to acquire the licensing rights to distribute those fonts. Unless a certain font is critical to the look of your title, stick with system fonts.

Obviously, hypertext and hypermedia applications require the greatest amount of text. Most companies (unless they are creating a great deal of new material for inclusion in a product) put little thought into how they plan to use the text files they have on hand. Many people naively assume that just because the text is in a digital format, it will be easy to include it in a hypertext product. The format in which your text is stored is important to the development process. Text must be in a format that can be imported into the authoring tool. Certain tagged formats, like SGML make it much easier to index and compile your data into the final document.

If your original documents feature a large number of fonts, this may be problematic when you want to distribute your application. You must ensure that when the final product is delivered, only system fonts are used; otherwise, you must distribute the fonts with the application. Distribution of fonts can be costly in terms of file space and finances—you may be required to license the font and pay a royalty for each copy of the application you distribute.

TIP

One advantage to the TrueType fonts bundled with Windows 3.1 is that they give you a much greater selection of fonts to work with. Take advantage of these fonts when you create your application's design.

If you know what type of product you want to create, you probably have a good idea where to get the information. If you need backup materials to create a more thorough product, however, look into acquiring material from the public domain. You may also need to license text from other parties to supplement original material you provide. Supplemental material, even material that requires paying licensing fees, can make the difference between success and failure in the commercial market.

Information (at your fingertips or elsewhere) is money. The more you can provide, the more you can charge.

If the information you need is available and in a format you can use, the most difficult task still lies ahead. You need to determine where and how the information links should be incorporated. Certain logical rules apply. You should have an electronic table of contents, an index, and a glossary at a minimum. Beyond this, where and how you place text in the application depends on the density of your data, the structure of your product, and how you want the user to navigate around the product.

Some authoring tools can help ease the process of indexing and linking text by performing a "first pass" of the data. Algorithms are used to count the number of words overall and then rank the words by frequency. This list helps you pinpoint key words to you used in the linking process. Other packages force you to do the entire process yourself. Regardless of the level of automation, you still must perform a great deal of checking, error correction, and manual indexing.

A great deal of creativity is involved in the process of structuring and linking a hypertext or hypermedia document. If you have organized your information and project specifications carefully, logical links will be obvious to you and the software's users. Occasionally, however, you may have to create a series of links to lead your user down a particular path—to get the user to see things a certain way or to point out conceptual connections that are not intuitive. Today's applications generally offer links that mimic the index of a book. As more talented and creative multimedia designers enter the marketplace, expect more interesting ways of indexing to occur in new applications.

Indexing, linking, and structuring are the means by which you can offer more value to a user, making hypertext/hypermedia a more intuitive and valuable way to get information. The planning of indexing—and then linking that information—is a part of the information preparation process. This area can be one of the most challenging, as you will see when you begin to test the links during the testing phase of product development.

TIP

Give yourself twice as much time as you think you will need to structure the data, create the index, and create the conceptual links.

Collecting Media Elements

Media acquisition is, in some ways, the most fun, exciting, and creative part of the multimedia process. You are the director of your own movie—you evaluate actors and actresses and then manipulate them on screen to create the best possible performance.

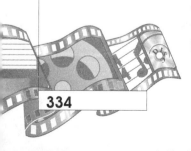

If your application is media driven (as opposed to being text-oriented), try to structure your use of media as much as possible. Focus on visual and audio themes and stick to them whenever possible. Your development and the acquisition process will be more focused and there will be less chance of overwhelming the user. Thematic use of media also yields a more professional, polished-looking product. An example of "theme media" is to use sound as a directional device to help the user know where he or she is when navigating through the program. A musical sound bite can play, for example, when the user reaches a primary topic, and a different sound bite for reaching a secondary topic.

Try to feature a similar "look and feel" for your graphics, animation, and video. Try to maintain consistency in using icons and use one or two (at most) thematic colors through-out the application. A good strategy might be to coordinate everything around the use of your company logo.

NOTE   If you are designing an application around a text base, media is meant to enhance—not overwhelm. If you are trying to provide information, do not lose the message by wrapping it in too much media. Media should be used only when it can add value and enhance the overall product. When in doubt, take it out.

Media is demanding in terms of storage. Even with a 600M CD-ROM disc, space can be filled at an alarming rate, especially with video. Try to go for maximum effect whenever you use a sound, animation, or video clip. Try to reuse clips whenever possible. Optimize your media clips before including them in the final application. If a picture is worth a thousand words, how much is a 15 second video worth? If the

Media acquisition is covered in depth in Chapter 8. This section summarizes some of the key points to help you plan for media acquisition .

With OLE (discussed in Chapter 2), you can link any type of data object to a compound multimedia document. These are not limited to sound or video—they can include embedded charts, spreadsheets and other types of data objects.

use of a video clip does not reduce or replace text, do not include it.

In addition to the media described so far in this chapter, you can incorporate other types of data into your application. The term "multimedia application" is a misnomer; "multiobject application" is more appropriate. When you want to annotate a thought or link additional information, you do not need to limit yourself to text, sound, image, animation, or video. You can add emphasis to a document by linking in a spreadsheet by using OLE. The spreadsheet can then be annotated with sound (linked to specific cells). The sounds can be accompanied by animation. You can create layers and layers of media experience (or object experience), all driven by the parent document. Other parts of the document can contain links to databases, other documents, and communication packages (as well as the capability to send electronic mail). The only limitation to media incorporation, acquisition, and development is your budget.

Tagging and Coding Documents

After you have collected text to be incorporated into your application, structured the information, and determined links for connecting the data, you may want to tag the document before writing the code and compiling the final program. *Tagging* is the process of using special codes to "tag" certain parts of the raw text, indicating sectional divisions (for example, chapter headings and topical headings) and links between specified sections.

Tagging is appropriate for hypertext or hypermedia applications in which the text represents the primary form of data.

After the document is tagged it can be compiled into the final product. A number of different tagging schemes are available; as you read earlier, one of the most common is SGML. Many authoring tools enable you to import data that has been tagged in SGML format.

Sometimes you need to use a third-party product to convert a tagged document into a format you can use with your authoring tool. Exoterica's XGML product converts a number of different tagging formats (including SGML) for use with various compilers. Although Exoterica's product is expensive ($10,000 for the low-level conversion tool) and requires you to write code for the conversion process, it provides a great deal of flexibility. Microsoft used the XGML product to create the Multimedia Bookshelf product. XGML converted data in SGML format to the RTF format required when using the Viewer authoring tool.

Major publishing houses are in the process of converting all their editorial products to SGML format. This leads to interesting marketing opportunities. By creating SGML databases that contain all sections of all editorial products, a publisher can sell "custom books" comprised of various sections required by the buyer. This replaces the traditional method of creating specific pages, chapters, and volumes through the standard editorial process. Books need not be printed at all—the information currently obtained through books may be sold on-line, in CD-ROM databases, or combined with other media to be sold in multimedia applications.

If your interest is in-house multimedia development, consider storing the data you plan to use for development in a tagged format, especially if you plan on updating the data often. After the data is tagged, you have the option of importing the tagged files into your authoring tool and including other media or data objects.

As you begin to create new data, start to think in terms of modular information. Begin to write (or have your authors write) with modular topics in mind, instead of more traditional paragraphs, sections and chapters.

NOTE

Not only do you want your authors to write in a modular fashion, you should ensure that your programmers create code in the same way. If you plan on developing a number of titles, it is important to start creating libraries of code that can be re-used many times. If your team programs in this manner, each new title you develop will cost less than the one before.

The process of writing code for a multimedia document is similar to writing code for any large program. Try to modularize the process of writing the code and use software libraries whenever possible. If you code in a language such as Visual Basic, write custom controls to minimize the amount of coding or purchase custom controls from third-party vendors. If you use ToolBook, make use of multimedia widgets whenever possible.

Authoring tools that create hypertext documents usually do not require you to write programming code in the same fashion as other tools. These authoring systems require you to insert codes (text-based strings) within the body of the text, which indicate topics, headings, and where hot links should be included. The compiler for the authoring tool uses the coded information to break up the body of the text into the topics, index, and links.

If your data has already been tagged (a necessary step for very large text files), then you only need to convert the tags to the code strings used by your tool and compile. If your data has not been tagged, or if you plan on inserting the codes manually while you create the document, several methods can help speed the process.

If you use Microsoft's Viewer, try to write Word Basic macros to minimize much of the tedium of "coding" the RTF document. A number of third-party tools have been developed to create Windows help files—these products also can be used to create RTF files and then compile them with the Viewer compiler. A good tool is RoboHelp from Blue Sky Software.

If your company is not set up to handle the creation and conversion of large text databases, you can work with other companies to create a hypertext or hypermedia publishing product. R.R. Donnelley, a company that handles document management and production for many major publishing houses, has the capability to create hypermedia products for their clients by storing the publishing data in SGML format and working with numerous authoring tools to meet their clients' design needs.

One of the tools Donnelley has licensed for multimedia development is SmarTrieve. Working with a company like Donnelley may be a good option for companies who want to get into multimedia development, but who are not prepared to make a large investment is developing in-house production capabilities.

NOTE SmarTrieve offers sophisticated searching algorithms that enable the user to search using natural language queries. With a natural language query, searching for information is more like asking a question. Contrast this with the Boolean search capabilities of most tools, in which the user must structure a query as "trees NOT apple" to find all topics that contain the word "trees" but do not contain the word "apple."

Creating installation scripts can be a frustrating programming task, but it is important to do it properly. It is the first example of your programming skills that the user sees.

In the future, well-designed installation scripts will enable the user to de-install the application, when desired—removing not only the program files, but restoring WIN.INI and other system files to their original state.

If you are creating a multimedia product for a large audience, you must write an installation script. Installation scripts are the SETUP.EXE or INSTALL.EXE programs that come with every Windows application. The installation script installs necessary files to the user's hard drive, modifies necessary system files, and creates a program group and icon for the newly installed application. Installation scripts are more important for multimedia applications than for other programs because a multimedia application needs to know where to look for the media clips included with the end product.

Well-designed, professional-quality installation scripts have certain things in common: they install through Windows (shelling out to DOS is amateurish), and they enable the user to specify the drive and directory for installation. Good quality scripts also enable the user to exit from the installation process at any time; they modify the AUTOEXEC.BAT file (if necessary) but enable the user to override this change; modify the WIN.INI file if necessary (really top-rate scripts create an application-specific INI file); and installation scripts create a program group and icon for the installed application.

From a developer's standpoint, writing an installation script can be a royal pain. The process of creating a script is seemingly simple; you write an ASCII text file, called SETUP.INF. This file contains the information that the SETUP.EXE program needs for installation. The difficult part about creating a setup script is making it "bullet proof"; unless you know the exact configuration of every user's machine, any number of things can go wrong during an installation. Even when the setup script works perfectly on the developer's PC, extensive testing on a variety of platforms is necessary before the setup script is ready to be released.

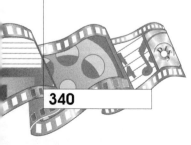

You can use the SETUP.EXE program that comes with the MDK or the SETUP program that comes bundled with the Microsoft SDK, to use with the SETUP.INF script you write. The SDK's SETUP program also includes a utility to compress files to be installed. You also can try the InstallShield program from Stirling. Both the Microsoft and the Stirling programs function in pretty much the same way; but the scripting language you use to write the INF file for each is slightly different.

Compiling Your Program's Code

After you import your text and clips and add any other required coding, you are ready to compile the document and start testing. The way in which the document is compiled obviously depends on the authoring tool, but no matter what tool you use, you should keep in mind a few things.

Develop and compile a small-scale version of the product before going into full-scale production. These test runs are important, especially with multimedia—you want to make sure that all the media elements work together before you code the final product.

Testing Your Product

Testing multimedia can be an extremely difficult part of the product-creation cycle—but very critical. So many different combinations of hardware and software are involved with multimedia that the chances of something going wrong are greater than with most programs.

Develop a thorough test plan, before you begin. The test plan should clearly lay out all the components to be tested, and the order in which testing will occur. The test plan should specify how bugs will be documented and classified, and how errors will be resolved. When possible, test the program in batches. Multimedia applications get very large; compiling the entire application can take more than a day. By testing modules of the program over the course of development, you minimize the number of times you have to compile the entire product.

Test your application on a number of different systems configured with different peripheral devices. Be sure to test your application by modifying the directory and drive listed in the path statement of the user's AUTOEXEC.BAT file. Make sure that the application still works if a drive letter changes.

NOTE   With the multitude of SCSI devices on the market, the CD-ROM drive designated as drive D today can easily be designated as drive K tomorrow. Make sure that your application still can play back sound files when this happens.

Test to make sure that the media you use is accessible on different machines with different device configurations. MIDI files created on one type of MIDI synthesizer, for example, may not be compatible with other MIDI devices. Test the quality of media clips on different devices. WAV files sampled and played back at 22KHz may sound terrible when played back on a sound board that can only play back at 11KHz. As with any testing, run your application on as many different platforms and with as many multimedia devices as possible.

Test all your links to see whether they are complete and logical. Test all paths to ensure that the user does not hit a dead end from which he or she cannot return. In addition, test all the index and glossary entries.

Test your application using as many different monitor resolutions as possible (see fig. 7.13). An application that looks great at 640× 480 may feature off-centered buttons or text when displayed at 600× 800 (or greater). In addition, if you create images on a machine with 24-bit color, make sure that the images are dithered properly in case a user has only 8-bit color (256 colors). Even test resolutions you do not anticipate supporting (like grayscale monitors, or standard VGA)—someone at some point may use it with your application, and it is helpful to know how your application behaves in such instances.

Test your application on VGA grayscale monitors if you anticipate someone using the application on a laptop, even if you specify that your product should only be used on an MPC.

Figures 7.13:

A comparison of Chessmaster 3000 at SVGA and VGA resolutions.

Like any serious developer, you create applications on a powerful PC optimized for performance. You know the application will run slower on a typical end user's machine. For this reason, test the application on the lowest-level machine recommended by the MPC specification. You may be in for a shock (the MPC Marketing Council certainly was; that is why they amended the original specification for a baseline MPC machine). Multimedia on a slow machine is agonizingly slow—sound files have a tendency to break up and the illusion of interactivity is completely lost as the user waits and waits for the system to respond. Tests on a slow machine may make you realize that you need to optimize your code.

Well-behaved Windows applications return all system resources after a session and close all child windows. Not all multimedia authoring tools are well-behaved, which means the applications you create with them are not well-behaved either (Visual Basic is notorious for this). It is embarrassing when your application crashes a user's machine. As with any application, test your product thoroughly in this area.

Applications created using multimedia authoring tools put a big drain on available system resources. When you combine tools to create a single end product (shelling out from ToolBook to run an animation runtime player, for example), the final product requires a lot of memory on the end user's machine (and probably will be very slow). Be careful when combing authoring tools, and test for the amount of memory the final product requires.

Including Documentation and On-Line Help

Any product used by a large audience needs documentation and a Windows Help system. Although creating and producing documentation is an expensive proposition, thorough help manuals can pay for themselves by decreasing the amount of system support you have to provide.

Consider making the printed documentation minimal if you plan on offering extensive on-line help and tutorials. Some documentation for multimedia products consists of little more than installation instructions and a "cheat sheet" of navigational tips. If you followed standard Windows programming conventions, your documentation can make reference to the Windows users' manual for many common Windows functions, like how to navigate with the mouse, or what it means to "double-click."

Help systems and documentation for currently available commercial applications can be used as a guideline for your product's materials. The USA demo, included with the Microsoft Multimedia Development Kit's Viewer application and shown in figure 7.14, contains a sample Windows Help system that you can modify and adapt to meet your application's needs.

If you plan carefully, the information presented in the documentation also can be used in the Windows Help system (which should be just as interactive and media rich as the rest of your product). As mentioned earlier in the chapter, products on the market are available to help you create the RTF files needed for use with the Windows Help compiler.

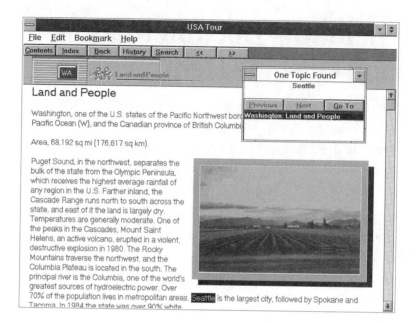

Figure 7.14:

USA DEMO: the demo application bundled with Microsoft's Viewer.

NOTE WexTech's Doc-2-Help product is a series of Word macros designed to walk you through the creation of documentation. After you finish writing with the product, you will have printed documentation and a Windows HLP file that can be distributed with your program.

If you are planning to distribute a CD-ROM product, consider the size of your documentation before you create the layout of the final text. Documentation for CD-ROM discs are usually little booklets that fit inside a CD jewel case. Other options include a booklet that substitutes for the jewel case, with a sleeve for the disc in the inner cover of the book.

Distributing the Final Product

How you plan to distribute your title depends on whether you created it for in-house use, as a marketing vehicle for your company, or as a product for general distribution. Although distribution may not impact how you create the product, it may have an effect on the type of supplemental materials you produce to accompany the product.

When you write multimedia software for the public, more time and effort is spent creating documentation and packaging than for an in-house title. Documentation for in-house use can consist of little more than some Xeroxed pages, with a suggestion to call the help desk for anyone needing more assistance. Documentation for consumer applications are designed so that the user will never need to ask for help. These booklets are usually four color, glossy, and often contain advertisements for other products available from the developer.

To create marketing materials for your software, you need to know what has already worked for your company in the development of printed or video-based marketing efforts. To design these materials, it is helpful to work closely with your in-house design or corporate communications department.

In addition to documentation, and marketing materials, you need to consider the design for the packaging of your product. The amount of effort required is dependent on the way you plan to distribute your title. If you will be distributing on floppies, you'll need to have disk labels printed up and give consideration to the type of disk mailer you plan to use. If you plan to distribute on CD-ROM, you'll need to have a graphic designed that gets used as label art on the disc itself.

If you create a video tape product, you'll need to get a label printed for the tape, and may possibly want a video box designed. Distributing On-Line is the most cost-effective solution of all, because no supplemental materials are required. The next few sections of this chapter discuss each of these distribution methods in greater detail.

Distributing on Floppy Disks

Because multimedia applications typically take up many megabytes of space, you cannot distribute most applications on floppy disks. On the other hand, your target audience may be limited if you distribute on a CD-ROM because fewer PCs have CD-ROM drives than floppy drives.

A short QuickTime or AVI movie (under 15 seconds) can take up nearly 2M of disk space. A brief (approximately 25 seconds) wave file recorded at 22KHz, 8-bit mono is more than a half a megabyte. It is easy to see that as you add more media clips to a multimedia application, it becomes difficult to think about distributing the application on floppy disk. Nevertheless, disks are a great media if you want to reach the largest possible audience (multimedia as an advertising vehicle is a good example).

If you want to distribute on disk, follow these suggestions:

➤ Make your application focused primarily around text (or hypertext), which requires less disk space compared to clip media.

The use of 16 color images (instead of 256) also will help you save file space.

➤ Do not assume your end user's machine meets the MPC specification . You may want to distribute an application that makes use of only 16-color graphics (as opposed to 256-color graphics) to ensure that your application is compatible with VGA monitors.

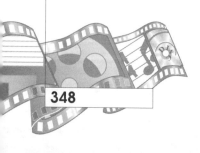

➤ Every user may not have a sound board; make sure that your application can check the available hardware or be able to run even if the sound feature is disabled.

➤ Use media elements (media clips) only for emphasis.

➤ Take advantage of media elements by using the same clips a number of times throughout the application. Use the sound of applause, for example, a number of times throughout a single application to add whimsy.

➤ Do not include any software-decompressed video files (such as QuickTime or AVI) unless they are absolutely critical. You may be able to create the same effect using a well-designed animation and a small animation runtime player.

➤ When you calculate the size of the application to be distributed, remember to include the size of the runtime files that must be distributed with the final executable file.

➤ Select authoring tools that produce smaller, tighter executable files rather than those that may seem to offer easier development.

The AutoDesk Animation Player for Windows requires 4K for the player executable and another 289K for DLLs, which need to be copied to your Windows System directory.

TIP

A number of good compression tools are available, such as PKZIP or LHarc, but if you use the Microsoft setup program for your program's installation, you should use their compression program. SETUP.EXE will handle all of the necessary decompression without requiring an additional decompression utility.

➤ Investigate a number of software-compression schemes to find out which produce the smallest files (remember that you have to include the decompression software along with the other files you distribute).

NOTE If you compress files, you need to write an installation routine that decompresses the files and installs the application on the user's hard drive.

These suggestions may help you produce an application that fits on one or two 3.5-inch high density (HD) floppies. Programs that make minimal use of media still can have impact and be effective, if they are well designed. Study advertising techniques to produce as effective a product as possible using limited amounts of time and imagery—think of the shorter commercials now prevalent in television advertising. You can make a tight, effective, floppy-based multimedia application, but it takes more time, effort, thought, and planning than a larger application.

Distributing on Compact Discs

With a large storage capacity (600M+), CD-ROM discs enable you to store and distribute large amounts of text, audio, images, animations, and some video. Not only are the discs relatively cheap to manufacture, they also are more durable than many floppy disks.

Chapter 3 lists CD-ROM disc manufacturers in the U.S.

The first step in creating a CD-ROM disc is *mastering*; in this process, microscopic pits are etched into the surface of a glass master. A blank-glass master is coated with a thin layer of photo-resistant material and then placed in a laser-burn recorder for imaging. After laser exposure, a chemical developer is applied to the photo-resistant material to etch it. What remains is a pattern of pits in the surface of the glass master, representing the bits of the data. Each pit is one micron in size. A thin coating of silver is then applied to the glass master to make the disc's surface conductive.

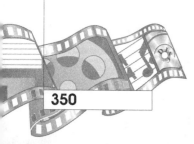

The glass master is then mounted on a holder and lowered into an electroplating bath, which plates the surface of the glass master with layers of nickel. The nickel buildup creates a *father*—a mirror image of the glass master that has a bump corresponding to each pit on the glass master. The father is separated from the glass master, trimmed, and sent to a molding machine.

From the father, a stamper disc is produced, that comes into contact with the molten polycarbonate used to press the clear discs. These clear discs have the same pattern of pits as those of the glass master. The pressed clear discs are *metal-ized* (coated with a thin layer of aluminum on the pitted side so that the laser in the CD-ROM drive can read the discs). The discs then receive a lacquer treatment (to protect the aluminum coating and prevent it from deteriorating). At this point, the CD-ROM discs are ready to be printed with label art.

The cost of mastering a disc at a professional facility starts at approximately $800 per disc and can escalate to $3,000 for one-day turnaround. Disc duplication (copies produced from the master disc) can cost $2.00 to $3.50 per disc. Many facilities require a minimum order of discs (200 or more); it may pay to shop for the best rate.

You also may want to investigate the possibility of investing in a desktop mastering system. These units cost between $8,000 and $12,000. These machines are not practical for production of a large number of discs because they can take up to two hours to produce a single compact disc. For a multimedia development shop, however, desktop mastering systems are useful for archiving data and producing test versions of a disc before sending the final master disc to the professional production facility.

Distributing on Video Tape

A number of multimedia authoring tools enable you to write your end product to video tape. The capability to write to video will spawn a desktop video revolution in the near future, similar to the desktop publishing phenomenon of the mid 1980s. Many video professionals currently use personal computers to edit video productions instead of using high-end video suites that cost thousands of dollars to rent by the hour. This trend will continue in the future as video-editing tools for the PC become increasingly sophisticated.

Many small business and home users also will become adept at the use of video editing tools designed for the lower end of the market. Home videos will develop a slicker look and incorporate special effects now seen only in the movies and on television. Video-editing shops will grow as a cottage industry, catering to specialized services such as wedding videos and small-business promotional materials.

More businesses may take advantage of these small service bureaus or develop in-house expertise to create promotional materials. Until multimedia playback devices (MPCs or hand-held CD-ROM units) become more popular, video will remain the preferred method of multimedia distribution. Instead of corporate brochures, you will see more sales-people using videos as leave-behind marketing items (this trend can already be seen in the software and hardware industries—expect to see other industries doing the same).

What sets these new videos apart from the current breed is the incorporation of special effects such as wipes, fades, text and graphic overlays, and the addition of multiple sound tracks. Some multimedia productions are created expressly for video distribution. Others are written to video tape to demonstrate the interactivity and quality of the main multi-media piece and are intended to be demo items.

Distributing Products On-Line

Although the CD-ROM disc is an important distribution mechanism, it pales beside the distribution of interactive multimedia over local and wide-area networks. With today's current compression techniques—and given the bandwidth limitations of most commercially available networks—wide-scale On-Line distribution of multimedia is not yet feasible.

This situation will change rapidly within the next year or two. Interactive cable is one of the hot new areas of multimedia; companies such as Time-Warner, IBM, and AT&T are investing heavily in the technologies to make it possible. For more information on distributing interactive entertainment over i.c. networks, see the Epilogue at the end of this book.

Distributing Multimedia Using Other Methods

As multimedia playback systems start to proliferate and change, and as our definition of what a computer is changes, the various distribution channels used for the delivery of interactive titles will change too. When personal digital assistants appear in the marketplace, flashcards will be used as a means of delivering multimedia applications. As compression and data-transmission technologies improve, more interactive titles will be delivered using radio transmissions to modems (see fig. 7.15).

For a more complete discussion of future technologies, see the Epilogue.

The distribution mechanism is less important than the quality of the application and the authoring tool used for creating it. When you select an authoring tool, be aware of cross-platform issues and make sure that the package enables you to import from a variety of file formats and can play back on a number of different platforms. Even if cross-platform availability is not currently available for a specific tool, make sure that the software vendor has cross-platform compatibility planned for a future release of the product. That way, no matter what platform dominates the industry, you and your application will be positioned to take advantage of it.

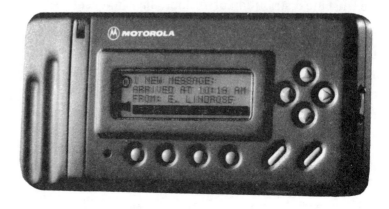

Figure 7.15:

Motorola's InfoTAC is a radio packet modem that uses the ARDIS wireless network.

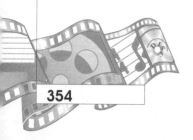

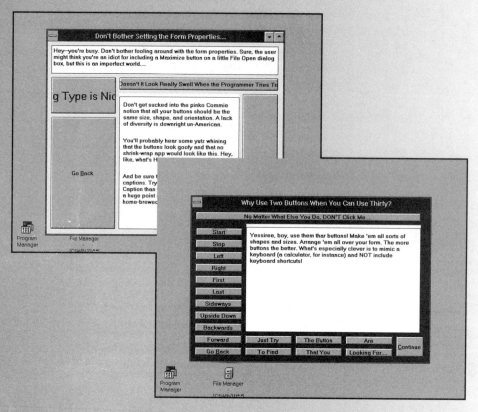

Don't Bother Setting the Form Properties....

Hey—you're busy. Don't bother fooling around with the form properties. Sure, the user might think you're an idiot for including a Maximize button on a little File Open dialog box, but this is an imperfect world....

...g Type is Nic

...oesn't It Look Really Swell When the Programmer Tries To

Don't get sucked into the pinko Commie notion that all your buttons should be the same size, shape, and orientation. A lack of diversity is downright un-American.

You'll probably hear some yutz whining that the buttons look goofy and that no shrink-wrap app would look like this. Hey, like, what's H...

And be sure t...
captions. Try...
Caption than...
a huge point...
home-brewed...

Go Back

Why Use Two Buttons When You Can Use Thirty?

No Matter What Else You Do, DON'T Click Me....

Start
Stop
Left
Right
First
Last
Sideways
Upside Down
Backwards
Forward | Just Try | The Button | Are | Continue
Go Back | To Find | That You | Looking For...

Yessiree, boy, use them thar buttons! Make 'em all sorts of shapes and sizes. Arrange 'em all over your form. The more buttons the better. What's especially clever is to mimic a keyboard (a calculator, for instance) and NOT include keyboard shortcuts!

If you've really done the job right, the poor user will be so confused that he'll start clicking on buttons he shouldn't, or just give up in frustration." —John Murdoch, in his "Lurker's Guide to Bad Design."

8

Avoiding "Muddymedia"

A clear understanding of the work and steps involved in creating multimedia software helps you take advantage of your coworkers' skills and might help create a better product. If you read Chapter 7, you are familiar with the multimedia development process and are prepared for its responsibilities. Nevertheless, you need to examine the design you plan to use. Even if the process of creating multimedia applications goes smoothly, your design might be flawed so much that the software is unusable or never sells.

NOTE

Design is more than just deciding how your software will look on the screen. Design is deciding how your software will represent its reality (its *metaphor*) and how you will lead your user to perceive that reality (its *flow*). Look, metaphor, and flow have to work congruously in an effective application.

Design also includes the software architecture—how you will make the computer do your bidding. See chapters 6 and 7 for more information on this topic.

After months of extensive research and development, probably nothing is more upsetting than receiving bad reviews because of an unknowingly poor interface or design. Critics often encounter multimedia interfaces that poorly present information to the user—the term they use for bad multimedia designs is "muddymedia." *Muddymedia* software is flawed multimedia software; the program may have one or several serious design problems. The most visible example often is the program's interface.

The interface for a multimedia application does not have to be completely intuitive, but must be easy to use. A number of problems can occur with the interface—too many buttons, crazy colors, or cryptic labels are just common mistakes. If the interface *looks* anything like John Murdoch's "Lurker's Guide to Bad Design" (described in Chapter 6), you should be able to catch it before the product ships. It is often much harder to see when an application *acts* like a Lurker's Guide. The only cure for a confused interface, a metaphor that leads away, or structure that gets in the way of a user is thinking ahead. You cannot *test* quality into a product—you can only *build* it in.

Muddymedia applications feature hyperlinks that lead nowhere in particular, cryptic help systems (or no help at all), and media elements that serve to confuse rather than clarify information. Muddymedia typifies poor Windows design and can come from different types of developers: the programmer with no understanding of design; a graphic artist who thinks he can program after spending a couple of hours with ToolBook; or the self-styled digital Fellini with a Camcorder and a copy of Video Windows.

NOTE
Nick Arnett should be credited with coining the term "Muddymedia." As a multimedia industry analyst and Sysop for the CompuServe Multimedia Forum, Nick has seen more than a few "muddymedia" applications.

As the evolution of the personal computer continues, eventually all applications will incorporate graphics, animation, video, or sound. In this sense, all Windows applications will become multimedia applications. Although it may be useful to "media annotate" certain files created in the process of doing business, this differs from creating an application that incorporates media as a part of the overall design.

As users become more sophisticated, they become less tolerant of muddymedia. You can avoid muddymedia by taking time to think thoroughly through the design of your application. This chapter helps you explore different ways to structure your application and helps you determine whether a particular application makes sense structurally as a multimedia program.

Determining the Multimedia Program You Want To Create

There are many reasons for creating a multimedia program—you might want to learn the technology or play with the toys, you could have been given the assignment to "use this equipment" or to make a splash at the next board meeting, or you could simply be trying to give your company a competitive advantage. Most reasons for creating a multimedia program are really reasons for creating a *muddymedia* program. The best reason for creating a *multimedia* program is that subject matter and the audience call for a broader bandwidth of communication that you can effectively achieve with just text and still graphics. In fact, some of the best multimedia applications start with an apology, "This didn't start out to use multimedia, but as you can see, it is just a natural." Letting the breadth of media arise from the subject, rather than the other way around, is the key to effective multimedia.

Some products just seem to make sense as multimedia programs; programs that feature volumes of information and lots of media elements are perfect candidates for this software. In these cases, creating a multimedia program can help simplify information gathering for the user. Users retain more from interacting than reading; therefore, educating and training products also can be used as successful multimedia applications. Some programs are more entertaining and fun with the interactive features that multimedia adds.

The first step in creating a multimedia application is selecting the project. The most important part of any small or large multimedia project is deciding what you want the software to communicate—to do and say. And before you can begin to design your software or the development process discussed in Chapter 7, you need to do a reality check. Is your message and your method within your means? There is no shame in starting small and building in steps to your final conception.

Finding a Good Candidate for a Multimedia Program

You might have heard the quote, "If you're not getting rich or you're not having fun, why bother?" The same thinking can be applied to a multimedia program. If a program is not full of information or if the user will not have fun using the product, why bother creating it?

NOTE Multimedia development is more costly than regular Windows application development. If you cannot add value by adding media, do not bother.

When you evaluate certain projects, ask yourself why you want to add media. If you want to add media simply to show it can be done, save yourself the trouble. If you want to add media to delete a lot of text (a picture is worth a thousand words...) or to make a complicated concept more clear, then you are on the right track.

What Works in a Multimedia Application

Each element of multimedia can help or hurt an application or document. Good multimedia applications offer text in small, easily digestible topics. You do not want to duplicate an entire book on the PC monitor because it puts too much strain on the eyes. You also do not want to force a user to scroll through screens and screens of information.

Successful multimedia applications provide in-depth topical information and information that users can access at any given time. Applications that are light on information become boring and are ineffective.

Video clips used in multimedia applications should communicate visually. A video clip of a person talking (the classic talkshow "talking heads") seldom communicates more than a still picture with the voice of the person playing in an audio track. The audio components of video must communicate. A silent animation might communicate everything that an AVI file can, and at much less cost. Always choose the minimum media to communicate.

Make sure your application takes advantage of the computer by making the program interactive. Working with an application should be different from watching TV—the program should be controlled by you. Some multimedia programs are beautiful to look at but do not offer any information or interactive elements.

A perfect case for conversion to multimedia is an instructional course that currently has a variety of printed textbooks, audio tapes, and video tapes available. A multimedia tutorial can be used to teach the course more effectively. The user can click on a button to view the video clips while reading the text. After reading and watching the video clip, the user can work on a few problem sets before going on to the next section. Multimedia development is cheaper when you are trying to incorporate a number of existing materials because you can digitize existing media by running it through a scanner. That way, you do not have to create or license media.

Marketing and advertising may be another area for multimedia development. Video and animation used in creative ways give you the opportunity to grab a user's attention and provide him or her with information about your product. You can create electronic versions of catalogs, brochures, corporate reports, and other direct mail pieces.

One big advantage to advertising through multimedia is that you stand out from the competition. Many people do not look at paper-based advertising materials that come through the mail. Most people, however, look at a demo disk because it still is a novelty. As CD-ROM drives become more widespread, you may have the opportunity to create elaborate marketing pieces on CD discs.

NOTE

One example of multimedia advertising is the MPC Sampler disc available from the MPC Marketing Council. On the disc, 30 different developers of MPC programs show demo versions of their programs. To order a copy of the disc, call (202) 331-0494.

Determining the Audience for the Document

Another factor in determining which project to create is determining the audience for whom you are creating the program. Unless the audience appreciates the end result, the effort is a waste. For a first program, a good audience is Windows and possibly multimedia aware, willing to explore, and has a need to get information quickly.

Targeting a Windows and Multimedia Aware Audience

A key definition of the audience for your first programs is that they are experienced Windows users. Experienced Windows users know about buttons, slider bars, pull down menus, and have seen and used Windows Help. You do not need to explain or simplify the interface, and you can focus on communicating your main message. It is also helpful if they have had access and exposure to MPCs (for playing software).

As more multimedia programs appear and the variety of playback devices increases and becomes more popular (handheld CD-ROM drives and devices such as the Tandy VIS, which connect to the user's television), more people will have exposure to multimedia programs. Because multimedia is in the early stages of market acceptance, you need to do some market research on your potential audience before you plan your program.

If you are creating a program for internal company use or business-to-business communication, for example, you need to make sure MPCs are available. If you create a reference product, you need to ensure that it is easily accessible (perhaps in a corporate library). Finally, if you are creating a consumer product, you must consider whether it should be developed for the MPC, an alternative playback device, or both.

At a minimum, your audience should be comfortable with the Windows operating environment. They should know how to use a mouse, how to navigate using standard Windows procedures, and how to install your application.

TIP

If you use standard installation utilities, such as Microsoft's SETUP, Sterling Group's InstallShield, or Knowledge Dynamics's Install, your users will have already experienced the use of your installer, and you will have less support load.

Targeting Those Who Are Willing To Explore

Some people are comfortable using their computers for one or two limited applications and no more. They never consider investing in new applications or using their computer for anything else. These users are often effective and efficient users of their computers, but they seldom vary their patterns of use. While these users may eventually become users of your program (and if they become users, they, by definition, become *dedicated* users), you need to invest significant effort in letting them know that they need your program. Others tend to hop about, using many different programs, finding the "latest and greatest" programs on the market. Marketing professionals identify this group as "early acceptors," and they are the ideal audience for a multimedia program. They like to play, explore, and get as much out of an application as possible.

NOTE

If your audience is computer-limited, you still can design a multimedia application to meet their needs if you are willing to put in extra time and effort. If you are creating an in-house application for inexperienced users, one strategy is to spend more time training them. A number of novice computer users do not use their computers efficiently because they do not know how and are afraid to ask for help. These people do only one or two tasks and have the necessary steps memorized. With sufficient training, these inexperienced users can be made to feel more comfortable using a multimedia application.

If you can acquaint people with on-line, context-sensitive help, they will see that they can get information when they need it—without appearing ignorant. With proper training and encouragement, these people can be shown ways to get the most out of a multimedia application.

The Broderbund Living Books series, which teaches small children to read using animated versions of children's classics, is a superb example of how multimedia can be used to entertain and educate.

Targeting Those Who Need Information Quickly

With the exception of games and entertainment-type applications, most people (in the office environment) use multimedia and hypertext applications for information they need. Hypertext excels at providing pertinent information culled from a vast collection of resources. If your audience needs easy access to information, and so much information is available it seems unmanageable, this is perfect opportunity for converting to hypermedia.

Examining Hypermedia Models

A hypermedia application is neither a book that you would read from start to finish nor a database from which you would extract one random record after another, but it combines elements of both. You can categorize most applications into one of five different models:

➤ **Linear.** From start to finish, like a novel

➤ **Freeform.** A hyperlinked "exploratorium" with navigation by concept links rather than topic

➤ **Circular.** A returning set of paths, like a programmed learning book

➤ **Database.** A series of linked records like an encyclopedia or dictionary

➤ **Compound documents.** A piece of text with excursions into media, like a memo with a doodle in the margin

The next five sections of this chapter discuss these five different models for hypermedia product development. Each section describes the model, explains the types of programs suited to that model, and mentions important elements.

Using Linear Progression

Linear progression multimedia software closely follows a book model—the skeletal structure is that of a story line (see fig. 8.1). Although the user can deviate from the story for asides or definitions, he or she is drawn back to the story. Linear progression text (in the form of hypertext) is most often used as the primary media element—other media are added to enhance the story line. Although a textual linear progression is simple to comprehend, these programs are not always desirable because users do not like to do a lot of reading on screen. Text used as the backbone for a story works when it is kept to a minimum and the media annotations are used to enhance the content.

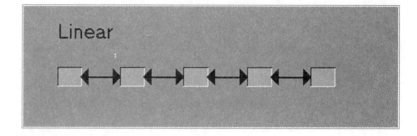

Figure 8.1:

A diagram of a linear structure.

Video or animation works well with the linear progression model. When these media are used with this model, the applications become the electronic equivalent of pop-up books. The story is told through a series of images or video clips, and the user can interact with annotations (offered in the form of text or other media).

NOTE The Broderbund Living Book, *Just Grandma and Me*, is a classic example of an electronic pop-up book for children.

Other examples of linear progression can be seen in some of the text-based electronic books being produced by the publishing industry. A hypermedia version of a story gives added value through hypertext search capabilities and the excitement of sound and moving images. Electronic stories are suited for the consumer marketplace, but linear progression also works well in the business environment in the form of multimedia presentations.

Using Freeform (Hyperjumping)

Freeform programs encourage exploration and wandering by the user, but underneath, they are tightly structured. A product that works relies on the author's expertise in constructing a model that works. Unlike linear progression, in which the user goes from screen to screen, a freeform program encourages the user to search for a specific reference and then browse the related material. The freeform structure often is used with compilations of reference materials that have been heavily indexed and cross-referenced (see fig. 8.2).

The freeform structure is ideal for general knowledge applications and educational games.

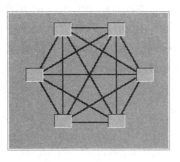

Figure 8.2:

A diagram of a hyperjumping structure.

Good navigational aids in a freeform structure guide the user to the data he or she is seeking. A poorly designed freeform program can lose the user in the information. If the user decides to explore a related link, it should be easy for him or her to go back to the previous screen. The user also should be able to save previous searches.

Design and effective use of media are important in the creation of a freeform program. As reference material, these products often have a preponderance of text, and turn into nothing more than highly-indexed, computer-resident books. If you have a reference work, study the text to find places where animation, sound, and video can clarify the text and enlighten the user. Try to keep the topics as short as possible, and use hyperlinking to extend information in layers.

TIP

Activision's *The Manhole* is a great example of a freeform program. Almost completely without text, it lets a user explore the a world reminiscent of *Alice in Wonderland*. Study it before creating any freeform programs.

Because these programs are so text-dependent, they can seem boring when compared to other types of multimedia programs. To avoid boring the user, you must use a variety of images, sound, animation, and video to liven up the data. Every effort should be made to substitute animations and videos in place of lines of text. This strategy is efficient because video clips can explain certain items more clearly than text. The application also will benefit from shorter chunks of information.

When a software developer constructs a freeform application, he or she is responsible for creating the indexes, the logical links, and any decision trees. This type of software takes more planning and effort. Decisions have to be made as to ways the user will find the first topic and what other topics should be linked to that one. After design and coding, these programs require more testing because all the decision trees must be checked.

NOTE

Reference materials and electronic magazines are documents that can be used in freeform hypermedia programs. *The Oxford English Dictionary, Microsoft's Bookshelf,* and *Nautilus* are all examples of freeform hypermedia programs that enable the user to browse through the material.

Using Circular Paths

Circular multimedia programs comprise a series of small linear progressions that return to themselves within a larger whole (see fig. 8.3). Computer-based training systems are a good example of circular path applications. For each separate training module, you follow a series of linear steps until you are finished with that particular lesson. You then are returned to the beginning of the application, where you can interact with another training module, review what you have just learned, or exit from the application.

Circular path structures frequently are used with training applications.

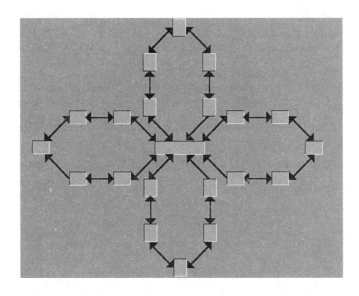

Figure 8.3:

A diagram of a circular path structure.

The construction of one of these applications is similar to building a linear application. The best circular applications are heavily indexed so that the user can browse the material if he or she wants specific knowledge. Well-designed training applications have a built-in monitoring system that tracks the user's progress while learning is taking place. If the user is too slow going through a particular module or if he or she missed too many questions during a testing module, the system can call up the pertinent material for additional study.

Using Databases

The multimedia database structure usually is adopted by corporate developers to enhance existing databases.

Databases that support multimedia include Software Publishing's Super-Base, Borland's Paradox for Windows, and Raima's Raima Data Manager/ Raima Object Manager.

In some sense, all hypermedia applications are databases because they contain indexing and search capabilities. Like databases, all hypermedia applications are made up of objects of information (in the form of text, images, sound, video, and animation) that can be manipulated by the author and accessed by the user.

This differs from an application that was designed to function primarily as a database but includes multimedia objects as fields of data. These types of databases can be used in any situation that requires database information with added media. Personnel databases that contain short video clips of employees are a good example of databases with multimedia fields (see fig. 8.4). A number of database tools are being created specifically for multimedia developers that offer a way to index, preview, and quickly retrieve media clips for incorporation into applications.

Although multimedia databases are not widely used now (because of the difficulties involved in using multimedia over networks), you can expect to see more corporate use of multimedia databases as bandwidth increases and compression algorithms improve in the next year. One of the advantages to having multimedia data in a robust database is that rule-based navigation can be applied to searching and retrieving data. In more sophisticated systems, artificial intelligence will enable the system to "learn" and apply new rules in response to a specific user's interaction with the data. This paves the way for agent technology in which the data is screened according to the user's preferences.

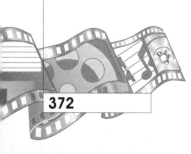

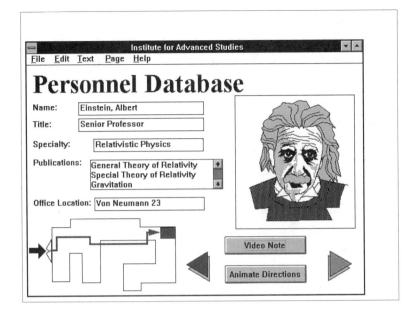

More information on agents can be found in the Epilogue, "The Future of Business Multimedia."

NOTE

Compound Documents and Memos

This type of structure applies specifically to compound documents in the workplace—primarily multimedia memos and reports. Just as all indexed multimedia programs are, in some sense, a database, all multimedia programs also are compound documents. Each program contains a mix of different media that the user can experience on demand.

Compound documents and memos have built-in expertise— they "know" how to execute their objects. They can contain media and, through the use of OLE, can contain pointers to

You can use OLE in a fixed structure document on a CD-ROM, but it probably wouldn't be efficient.

databases. A connected database enables you to incorporate interactive charts and spreadsheets into a document. One advantage of compound documents is that, in the case of a periodic report, the document you originally created can be updated quickly. Compound memos can give you more information than a standard memo and can be used as a substitute for meetings.

Like any other type of multimedia program, planning and forethought are the keys to success. Rather than write a standard memo and tack on additional media, try to make sure the media you use is a substitution for lines of text. A general rule of thumb to follow is if a media element does not enable you to cut a paragraph or more of text, it probably does not belong in the document.

Choosing the Structure of the Application

After determining the program you want to create and ensuring that your target audience will be able to use the product, you must develop product specifications. In traditional product development, a *specification* is a document that describes the product functionality from the viewpoint of the user. Making specifications for a multimedia or hypertext program is often more complicated than creating specifications for standard Windows applications. Hypertext offers numerous branching possibilities, which make flowcharts difficult and time consuming to produce. You might have to create storyboards for much of the application or write a script for it (similar to a motion picture).

Visual flowcharts such as storyboards (see fig. 8.5) and scripts are a great way to organize the structure of your program,

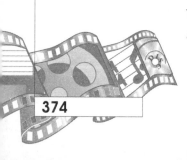

and prototypes can often be the best specifications because multimedia applications are more action-driven than text-driven. Whatever method you decide is appropriate for your application, clearly defining the application before code is created for it is absolutely critical to the success of the final product.

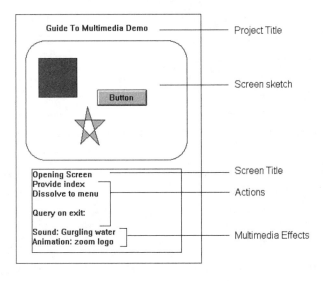

Figure 8.5:

A sketch of a storyboard.

NOTE

Developers often decide to use an authoring tool for prototyping as they think through the application. This prototype is often confused with the "real product," and production functionality is unknowingly rolled into it. This eventually leads to a longer development cycle for coding and testing and a product that is confusing to the user. Prototype, but do not confuse the prototype with the product.

Defining the Application Structure

Each hypermedia program has an *electronic skeleton* or structural model that is fleshed out with information and media. Without a skeleton, the final product has no cohesiveness; it becomes merely a pretty collection of media in the form of creative expression (multimedia poetry), but is not useful as a tool for an end user. The skeleton can follow a linear form or circular path, be freeform, function as a database, or a compound document. Before you decide on one of these models, you need to do a few things.

NOTE Linear form, circular path, freeform, database, and compound document structures are discussed in the section "Examining Hypermedia Models" earlier in this chapter.

First, you must consider why your audience will be using this tool, and you must have an understanding of your audience's needs. As Louis Henri Sullivan said "Form ever follows function." After you have a clear understanding of your program's function, the choice of which form or model to follow is relatively obvious.

Each hypermedia application needs clarity. Clarity is obtained from organizing your information into a structure and then providing your user with a clear (simple) way to navigate that structure. The structure of the program should be visible on the first screens—whether it takes the form of a table of contents, a list of available elements in the database, a map of information, or an explanation of how to navigate around the freeform structure.

In addition to showing the document structure, a well-designed program should have a list of glossary terms, different media elements (the user should able to see a list of all video clips in the program), and some sort of index listing all available topics. By scanning the first screen and the other lists, the user should have a good idea of the material contained in the program. This knowledge frees the user to choose how he or she wants to proceed next.

Have you ever called an on-line database only to become hopelessly lost in the tangle of information? If you have, chances are you used one or two strategies to re-orient yourself (other than turning off your PC). You probably went back a level or, in the worst case, went back to the beginning of the search. Good hypermedia programs offer the same options.

At a minimum, your program must enable the user to go back a screen or go to the first screen (often the table of contents). It also must tell the user when he or she has reached the end of a series of info bites and cannot go any further following a particular path. A well-designed hypermedia application gives the user at least one complete index and an on-line help system. Other important features include giving the user the ability to annotate text and leave bookmarks in the information so that he or she can return easily to a prior screen.

Using Navigational Aids

This book discusses extensively the importance of including navigational aids in your application. In addition to some of the navigation tools previously mentioned (which should be part of every multimedia application), certain navigational aids are required by specific types of media. The following lists specific types of media and the navigational tools necessary for each medium:

➤ **Text.** Text requires most of the navigational tools required by any good multimedia application. The user should be able to go forward through a thread of linked topics, go backward, go to the top (usually a table of contents), search through the text for a specific string of text, and search through an index.

➤ **Video or Animation.** If the animation or video sequence is part of the program, the user should be able to click on the animation or video object to begin playing back the sequence. If the animation or video is in a separate window, the user should be able to start playing the sequence, pause it at any point, rewind, fast forward, and mute the sound accompanying a sequence. The user also should be able to stop the sequence at any point and close the window.

➤ **Images.** An image that is embedded in a program (similar to a picture in a normal book) requires no additional navigational aids. If the image displays when the user clicks on a picture icon, the image should be displayed in a child window that can be easily resized, moved, and closed. If you offer embedded video and embedded images in your document, you need to differentiate between the two so that the user knows how to start a video sequence. One way to do this is to use a caption under each or display a movie icon near the images representing video clips.

➤ **Sound.** If a sound is embedded into the program, the user should be able to click on the sound icon to play back the sequence. If the sound is offered via a playback

Remember that you may need to license runtime players for animations or video clips as part of your application. Most of these players do not require per unit licensing fees.

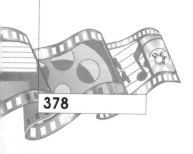

applet (audio controls that resemble the buttons found on an audio CD player), the user should be able to start playing the sequence, pause it at any point, rewind it, or fast forward it. In the case of playing Redbook audio (CD audio), the user also should be able to play any track on a disc and eject the disk.

NOTE

Redbook audio is explained in detail in Chapter 3 "Making Multimedia Work with Your Hardware."

> **Objects.** If you offer embedded or linked objects (other than media in this list) in your program, other navigational aids are possible that you may want to give your user. If you have linked another application (such as a spreadsheet), make sure the application window you invoke from within your program does not maximize upon startup. The user should be able to see the multimedia program in the window behind the spreadsheet so that he or she does not become visually confused as to what happened. As with any other media element, the user should be able to close the spreadsheet easily and return to the primary program after using the object. The user also should be able to copy the object and paste it into another Windows application.

Using Visual Tools for Navigation

Multimedia and hypermedia differ from pure hypertext in more ways than the addition of alternative media to a text-driven system. One of multimedia's biggest pleasures is a strong visual element in applications. A visually pleasing design may be one reason why many multimedia applications have been designed for the Windows interface instead of DOS. When you develop a multimedia program with a graphical user interface, include several visual aids as navigational cues for your user. Buttons with arrows indicating forward, backward, play, and stop are a few examples.

Icons are an important means of representing movie bites, graphic images, sound bites, spreadsheet objects, and other elements. These icons can be added to text to indicate other material is available and not obstruct the message of the text. Icon representations used in the Macintosh environment include picons (picture icons) and micons (movie icons). *Picons* are actual images that have been scaled down to icon size. When you click on the icon, you can see the image full size. *Micons* are previews of video clips, scaled down to icon size. A micon is similar to a picon, but it actually plays a small portion of the video. When you click on the micon, you can see the video clip played at actual size. Expect to see the inclusion of picons and micons in future MPC programs as the authoring tools for the Windows platform become more sophisticated.

Visual maps are another navigational cue you can offer in your program. A *visual map* shows all the paths available for access to information (see fig. 8.6). The map changes according to where the user has already been (useful for computer-based training systems) and shows other places he or she can go. The user can click on the map to go to another part of the program or minimize the map and continue navigating through the program.

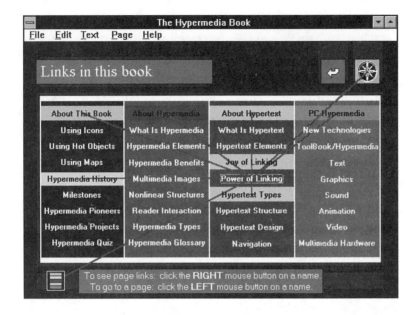

Figure 8.6:
A visual map.

Deciding Which Elements To Use in Your Program

One of the most important factors you must consider when selecting a multimedia project is the amount of available data. Although well-designed multimedia does not overwhelm the user with all the accessible information, you must make sure enough data is available to meet the user's expectations and needs. This is important no matter what type of application you design.

If your design focuses heavily on animation, interactivity, and video, you should make sure the user stays engaged when using the product so that he or she uses it more than once. All multimedia applications are a curiosity the first time around; the good ones are used several times. Make sure the application you design would not be more productive and informative in another medium. If you want to focus heavily on video, remember that even with the best compression available a CD-ROM is not capable of showing an entire feature-length film. A promotional film is better for these efforts. If you want the video to be interactive, however, multimedia makes sense. A video database with search and retrieval capabilities is a good example of this.

You also should not try to duplicate a book on screen. Books have an advantage in terms of portability (no battery problem) and readability (no resolution problem). If you need to add a great deal of hyperlinking and indexing, however, or if the sheer volume of printed material makes paper-based products less feasible, a hypertext or hypermedia document may be a better idea.

Applications that use the computer's capability to integrate tools also make good multimedia programs. If you want to offer spreadsheet capabilities in an integrated manner using object-oriented design combined with hypertext, animation, sound, and video, then a multimedia is perfect. After multimedia's curiosity wears off, users will only want programs that simplify their lives by reducing the number of sources to consult for information or the time it takes to perform a task.

Keep these suggestions in mind as you read the benefits and disadvantages of using multimedia elements in a program. In addition to the media, these elements include the navigational tools critical to the design and overall success of the application.

Adding Hypertext Jumps and Links

Any multimedia application that contains a significant amount of text also should include a hypertext engine. A *hypertext engine* helps the author cross reference a document extensively to create links between topics and related information. These links enable the user to navigate through all the words. When a user is reading the document, he or she can jump to a linked topic to view the corresponding information. If the document contains a large amount of information, hypertext makes it simple for the reader to research a topic.

From an authoring perspective, an expert with textual content needs to work with a programmer to code the document and create links. The researcher experienced with content is necessary for determining information that should be related, how the available information should be divided into easily digestible topics, and the order in which topics should be presented. Even with software that does much of the initial indexing of a document, the creation of a hypertext application involves a lot of manual data manipulation and is a time-consuming process.

Adding Heavy Indexing

One requirement for a hypertext or hypermedia document is indexing of the information. Each separate topic should be available in a master index. In addition, special indexes also should be available for large amounts of text and separate media. Similar to a table of contents in a book that contains a list of illustrations, a text-driven multimedia program should provide a list of all sounds, images, animations, and videos.

In media driven software, a different type of index is required. Each media clip should be given a keyword or series of key words describing the content of the clip. These key words should be indexed for the user. When the user clicks on a particular key word, he or she is taken to that clip.

Adding Full-Text Search

In text-driven applications, the capability to perform a full-text search is an important navigational tool. The more data your application contains, the more likely you will need to provide full-text search for your users. Many authoring tools provide the capability to index every word in a document, except for special stop words such as it, at, the, and other general words. More sophisticated indexing tools enable the user to perform Boolean searches on the text using operators such as AND, OR, NOT, and NEAR, and to search for text strings. If you want to create a text-based application, look for these capabilities in your authoring tool.

Adding Pop-up Boxes

Pop-up boxes in an application provide additional information and do not disrupt the current storyline. The user can click on the pop-up box to view the information, or continue working with the primary document (or media clip). Like jumps, pop-up boxes are created by linking two pieces of information. Unlike jumps, however, pop-up boxes display additional information in a small window that appears over the primary window (see fig. 8.7). Pop-up boxes can contain text annotations, glossary terms, images, and other media clips.

Hypertext links   Popup box

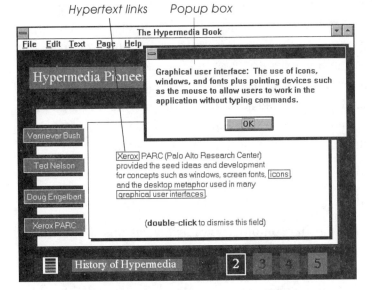

Figure 8.7:
A screen with
hyperlinks and
popups.

Adding Bookmarks

Similar to bookmarks for ordinary books, electronic bookmarks can be used by the reader to save his or her place
within an electronic document. Bookmarks can be customized with a name that can be used throughout a document.
For documents that serve as reference materials with a single
program supporting multiple users, bookmarks represent a
nonobtrusive way for individual users to mark pertinent
passages for later use. Bookmarks and user annotations (see
the next section) enable a user to customize a program to his
or her needs. This customization gives the user a sense of
ownership.

Adding User Annotations

A well-designed program gives the user the ability to copy
and paste information into other applications, and to create

notes or annotations from within the multimedia program. In the Windows environment, it is easy to take notes using the notepad application. It is more useful, however, to let the user annotate text with his or her own comments. These comments can then be stored with a pointer to the desired topic. More advanced authoring tools provide this capability. If you plan to build a text-based reference program, consider building this capability into your application.

Adding Fonts

A font that looks great when displayed at 640×480 resolution may not be readable at 600×800.

In programs that contain a lot of text, decisions about which fonts to use are a major consideration (see fig. 8.8). If you manipulate your information properly while designing the structure for the application, the data for each topic should be in small sections. Short topics are important because you will need to use large fonts for readability, and you want to avoid scrolling whenever possible. Experiment with a variety of fonts at different resolutions to find the ones that are easy to read and minimize the need to scroll.

If you use a non-standard Windows font, make sure you bundle it when you distribute your application and install it in your setup routine. If you forget to include the font you used in the design process, Windows will substitute the closest available font. This replacement usually causes the text in your program to appear in a different size or spacing on screen and can destroy the effect of a carefully designed interface.

NOTE As with any media, if you are distributing a font make sure you have obtained the necessary licensing rights from the owner of the font.

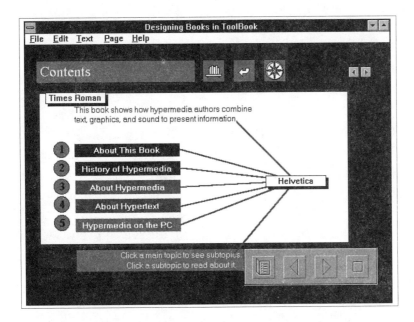

Figure 8.8:
Traditional fonts often are the most readable.

Adding Images

When you select images to include in your application, you first need to consider whether you can obtain licensing rights for the images you want to use. After you have the rights, you need to determine how the images look using a 256-color palette. Although you can use different palettes for different images in your application, you are better off using the standard Windows palette and dithering images. This prevents "flickering" as your program changes images on the screen.

You also must consider the size of your image and how the image will look displayed at different resolutions. If your image is embedded into text, it should be no larger than the primary program window so that the user does not have to scroll to view all the image displayed. If you want to use an image in a pop-up window, the image should be small enough that it does not overwhelm the text in the primary

To reduce palette "flickering" caused by changes in the palette, use Microsoft's BitEdit (included in the Multimedia Developer's Kit) to set the palette of all the images to the same palette. A good palette to use is the one in the 256COLOR.BMP wallpaper file in Windows.

window. If an image contains hot-spot links to other material, this should be indicated through captions or visual cues, such as a changing mouse pointer (the standard Windows arrow changes to a hand or a box when passing over a hot-spot).

Unless you plan to use images as part of a multimedia reference, be consistent with the images you use. Use a similar color, size, and tone for each image. If you include a visual reference, such as a company logo, on every screen of your program, try to use it in the same place on-screen. Work with a qualified graphic artist to help with the selection and creation of images and the layout of the screen.

Use consistent visual cues for images that serve as navigation aids, such as mouse pointers and sound and video icons. Test your icons on a group of users before you distribute the final application. Icons should be clear and easy to understand. If even one of your testers is confused or finds an icon cryptic, redesign it to make the meaning more clear.

Adding Sound

Make sure you include a mute button or menu selection in the design and coding of your multimedia application.

The trick to including sound in an application is ensuring the clips you select have a lot of variety. Sound clips should be included only if they add value to the information. If you include sound in your application, especially if you design a program for the business environment, you also must provide a way to mute the sound. This is critical in crowded offices—you do not want the application to become obtrusive to others.

In addition to annotating text with sound, music can be used as a cue to tell the user where he or she is in the application. If this feature is done with subtlety, this can be very effective as a backdrop.

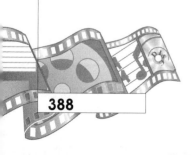

Make sure the sound clips you use in your application have been edited and the resulting clips are as clean as possible. Remove any annoying scratches, hisses, and pops from the clip. Use a sound editor to fade into a clip and fade out at the end. This gives a more professional quality to the clip and does not startle the user. Make sure all the clips in a single application play at the same volume level so that the user does not have to keep turning up or down the volume control.

Adding Animation/Video

The only consideration in choosing whether to use animation or video (or both) depends on how your application will play back the media. Each Windows animation package requires its own runtime engine for playback. If you want to include animation, you should compare the different packages and evaluate speed (some can be agonizingly slow as the animation clip is copied into memory) and cost, if any, of the runtime license. You may want to convert certain animation files to AVI format to determine if the resulting video plays more quickly.

The decision between using animation and software-decompressed video can be a tough call. If your application requires moving imagery with a fine level of detail, you probably will want to use animation because AVI movies are somewhat choppy. If you want the most cost-effective solution, use digitized video clips. The cost of creating high quality animation clips is expensive because it is so labor intensive.

NOTE

The AVI format is discussed in Chapter 3, "Making Multimedia Work with Your Hardware."

The remainder of this section discusses video, but the information can be applied to both types of media. The selection of specific video clips to use in a program differs according to whether video or other media (including text) is used most in the program. If video is the main type of media, use a consistent thematic approach to the video clips you select, particularly if you focus the program around a character or characters. If text or another medium is used most in the program, try to achieve diversity among the media clips you use.

As with any media clips, make sure you have the rights to use the clip in your program before distribution.

Although including video in a computer application is new and exciting, you still should try to limit the length and number of video clips you add. Short AVI clips can use a couple megabytes of disk space—include them judiciously and make sure that most of your program contains informational (textual) material. Limit the length of video to "video bites" so that you do not bore your user or lose the thread of information to which the video clip is linked.

Adding The Kitchen Sink

Multimedia is supposed to provide information in a more informative, more entertaining, and primarily, more efficient format. If you create a program with so many links and media elements that the user gets lost or it takes time to find information, you have failed to created a successful application. If you create a text-based application, any media you include is meant to be frosting on the cake. Too much media overwhelms and the message (the information you want to convey) is lost. If you create a media-driven application, too much text or supplemental media also interrupts the flow of information.

Restraint, structure, and careful planning are the keys to successful multimedia applications. The more media you

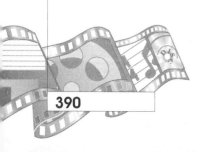

include, the more structure you need to provide the user. The more data your application provides, the more you need to make use of heavy indexing and a robust search engine.

No matter how entertaining or compelling, a media clip does not belong in your application unless it clarifies the information you are trying to provide the user. In the same way that extraneous information must be deleted from a movie script, clips that do not move your information along also must be deleted.

A final suggestion to keep in mind as you design your multimedia application: When in doubt, take it out.

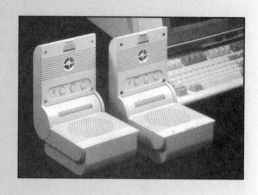

"Multimedia systems may be defined as the

'Interactive Dramatization of Information'." —

Alfred Riccomi, Multimedia PC Systems

9

Managing Different Types of Media

Previous chapters focused on multimedia from the perspective of end users and developers. But if you intend to plan and produce multimedia projects, you need to know about multimedia from the computer's point of view, as well.

That requires a look at various data types—the formats specific to different kinds of multimedia elements. This chapter presents multimedia elements from that perspective. You will get precise information on Windows-compatible file formats and conversion tools, and on various aspects of production.

These guidelines and options will help you gather and assemble multimedia elements in formats that you and your computer can work with.

Identifying Multimedia Formats

You have just been introduced to the concept of data types. This section expands that discussion and presents the tools that will help you evaluate and assemble multimedia elements: the Microsoft Windows Multimedia Development Kit and the Multimedia Viewer.

Data Types

Data type is a programmer's term. It means that each kind of multimedia data—whether pictures, sounds, or full-motion video—is viewed by the computer as a file with its own specified format, or byte structure.

It is not immediately important for you to know more about byte structures. For your purposes, you only need to know what these different formats are, and which ones are acceptable to Windows. How do you find out? The tool you need is available in the Windows environment. It is commonly called the MDK.

The Microsoft Windows Multimedia Development Kit (MDK)

Regardless of the kind of multimedia authoring tool you plan to use—even if you are a crack C programmer who can do it

from scratch—you will not want to be without an MDK. From the standpoint of a programmer, the MDK contains necessary API extensions and add-ons to the Microsoft Windows Software Development Kit (SDK). The MDK features important tools for nonprogrammers, as well. You can use the tools by themselves, or they can augment other authoring systems.

NOTE The Microsoft Multimedia Development Kit, version 1.00, is available from common retail sources. If you need further information, you can contact the Microsoft Corporation:

One Microsoft Way
Redmond, Washington 98052
800-426-9400 or 206-882-8080

The MDK contains documentation and reference material, the Multimedia Viewer, and a variety of data-conversion and editing tools. Here is a partial list of what you can expect to find:

➤ A *User Guide* and *Reference* for the Media Control Interface (MCI)

➤ A programmer's reference to approximately 135 special Windows multimedia function calls

➤ An on-line Help system

➤ Windows Multimedia Extensions (If you do not have the extensions installed on your system already, they can be installed on top of Windows versions 3.0 or 3.1.)

➤ C header files and code libraries for calling Windows' Multimedia Extensions (These files are only interesting to those who are directly programming their applications as native Windows source code.)

➤ A variety of sample components including applications, MIDI, and waveform audio files, and a Multimedia Viewer title

➤ Bitmap and palette editors, an audio waveform recorder and editors, a file-conversion utility, and a file viewer/editor for examining the binary and hexadecimal data contained in files

➤ A 3.5-inch Macintosh floppy disk with a utility for converting Macromedia Director animation sequences to a format suitable for Multimedia Windows

If you are not an experienced programmer, some of these tools may sound complicated or out of your realm of experience. You do not, however, have to be an accomplished programmer to author multimedia applications. You do not have to write a single character of C code if you want to avoid it. Editing and converting data files is as simple as using Windows Paintbrush.

Of the six manuals included in the MDK, only three will be of much interest to you if you are a nonprogrammer:

➤ *Data Preparation Tools User's Guide.* The contents of the guide will be covered in some detail in this chapter.

➤ *Multimedia Authoring Guide.* This is a small, straightforward how-to manual for creating your first Multimedia Viewer title. If you are just starting out, it is worth the effort to look it over.

➤ *Multimedia Viewer Developer's Guide.* This guide gets into the finer points of creating Viewer titles (including information about the Media Control Interface). This chapter covers some of those topics, but not in a comprehensive way. If you decide to author titles for playback under Viewer, you will be spending some time with the *Developer's Guide.*

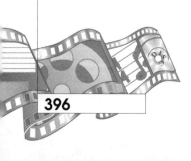

NOTE

It is important to become familiar with multimedia's technical terms and concepts. Much of the documentation assumes some familiarity, and you will get more out of your reading if you have the terminology well in hand.

To install the MDK, a system must meet the minimum requirements mentioned in the following list. Despite what ads in the trade press claim about a seemingly endless need for Windows and multimedia add-ons, the system described here is not exotic. Basic Windows-compatible multimedia machines are commonly available starting as low as $2000. This is what you need:

➤ a 286-based PC (or better)

➤ 2M RAM

➤ 30M of free hard-disk space

➤ a VGA adapter and monitor

➤ DOS 3.1 or greater

➤ Microsoft Windows 3.0 or greater

➤ MS-DOS CD-ROM Extensions 2.2

➤ a Windows-compatible mouse or pointing device

➤ an audio board

If you plan to develop multimedia applications in C, you will need the following software and hardware:

➤ Microsoft Windows Software Development Kit (SDK)

➤ any Windows-compatible C compiler

➤ a 386-based PC with 4M RAM

➤ a 256-color VGA graphics card (recommended)

Though these are the official specifications, you will do well to have a fast 386—or even a 486—with a 200M hard disk and at least 8M of RAM.

NOTE

Many people recoil from the suggestion that PCs should have so much RAM. In almost every case, however, the best way to improve your PC's performance is to add more RAM.

70-80 nanosecond, 1M×9 SIMMs—the kind of memory chips that most PCs require—run between $20 and $25. That in itself is incentive for you to follow the "More is better" rule of thumb.

Practically speaking, only a few upper limits for memory on a computer are noteworthy. A 286-based PC can only address 16M, for example. Intel 386 chips can theoretically address up to 4 gigabytes (4G) of memory, but other architectural limitations often exist, depending on the kind of PC you have.

Any PC is likely to thrive on 16M of RAM, but some may not have space on their motherboards (you would have to place a memory card in a 32-bit slot and populate it accordingly).

Make sure that you add extra memory to your system up to 8M. It is inexpensive and worth the investment.

You have already seen mention of the MDK's Multimedia Viewer. It is a rudimentary authoring tool that is suitable for nonprogrammers. The following section gives you a bit of background on it.

The Multimedia Viewer

The Multimedia Viewer is a good, simple tool for authoring multimedia titles such as electronic encyclopedias. For those with experience using other multimedia authoring and presentation software, however, the Viewer may seem less versatile. In its defense, though, it is very easy to author a simple Viewer file. Technically speaking, it is no more difficult than creating a word-processing document.

To develop a basic Viewer document, you need a word processor that can save a document in *rich-text format* (RTF). (Microsoft Word for Windows offers that as an option.) Text and bit maps, which comprise the "electronic pages," are placed in the document and saved as RTF files. Links between topics are created by attaching Viewer commands to hotspots. (*Hotspots* can be either text strings or areas of bit maps.) They trigger the jumps to different topics, to pop-up information windows, or to playback of waveform audio, MIDI files, or animations.

The Viewer also provides full text-searching and indexing capabilities.

It was implied that Viewer files are very simple to create, but how sophisticated are the applications themselves? If you are worried that developing an application in Viewer will not meet your interactivity requirements, look at some commercial Viewer applications. Microsoft's Bookshelf for Windows is a good example.

You can make calls to dynamic--link libraries from Viewer files.

Preparing Multimedia Elements

You need to consider a few options before you generate text, sound, graphic, and video elements for a multimedia document. This section sheds some light on what choices you need to make concerning your MPC and multimedia capabilities.

Choosing Fonts

Text generally represents a large percentage of any multimedia document. The choices you make are important. There are many facets to those text elements, ranging from the practical to the aesthetic. It is certainly a good idea to think about how text is going to look, but it is just as important to find out what fonts are available and how they will come across on unknown systems.

This part of the chapter provides background information on fonts and system displays, as well as practical tips on font selection. You will find out which fonts are available in the Windows environment, and what you can do to create your own. After you know what some of your options are, you will be able to make sound choices for your own projects.

A Close Look at Screen Fonts

Blocks of text are easiest to read on the printed page; a computer's system display typically pales by comparison. As much as possible, the text on your screen should attempt to emulate a clearly printed page.

On your display screen, even the smallest characters are made up of dots (pixels). To many people, the dot patterns that make up the letters are annoyingly visible. They make the characters fuzzy and generally decrease reading comfort. Comfort is also affected by the light. Reflected light, such as the light bouncing off a printed page, is much easier on your eyes than incidental light—the kind of light that shines directly into your eyes from a computer display.

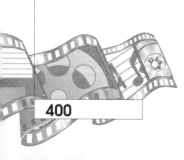

Your multimedia document will usually display text on a computer screen, so the text has to be as inviting and effective as possible. Fonts will be a primary ingredient in the content and style of your project. You must balance readability and appearance.

Windows supports a variety of fonts, some of which are very stylized. Be careful though—they are not all the same when it comes to readability. (Picture a large body of text set entirely in a brush script, or all in uppercase letters.) So how do you decide what fonts should be used for what things?

The purpose of the type is important. Does it have to be readable from a distance, as it should be for presentations to large groups? Does it need to be formal? Do you need to match the look and feel of your company's signature letterhead or logo? Does it need to draw attention?

To some extent, fonts are associated with a feel or personality that will be interpreted similarly by a wide range of people. Look at different fonts and think about what they suggest to you. If you are not confident in your own opinion, ask others. Better yet, consult with a graphic designer or typographer. People who work with various type styles on a regular basis may be able to provide information not immediately obvious to you.

Typeface Basics

Five groups of typefaces exist: Oldstyle, Traditionals, Moderns, Slab Serifs and Egyptians, and Sans Serifs. The fonts included in each group different characteristics and serve different purposes:

➤ **Oldstyle.** These fonts are based on hand-drawn humanist books from the 15th to 18th Centuries.

➤ **Traditionals.** These fonts are crisp and businesslike. They are more refined than warm in appearance. One example is the New Baskerville font.

➤ **Moderns.** These fonts have the most contrast between stroke weights (thin and thick parts of the letters). Their elegance makes them a favorite choice for ads. One example is Bodoni.

➤ **Slab Serifs and Egyptians.** These fonts have straight-shouldered serifs, low-contrast stroke weights, and a narrow, vertical pitch. They are good for fitting a lot of text in a confined space. One example is New Century Schoolbook.

➤ **Sans Serifs.** These fonts are basically 20th-century typefaces. They combine well with the others as accents and headlines. One example is Futura.

Font Basics

Fonts can vary imperceptibly or dramatically. It is important to note that they do not all complement one another. When you select fonts that will appear together on a page (say as a bold headline and a body of text) try to match general shape characteristics. Even if one is a bold sans-serif headline font, it will look good with serif fonts if they have similar forms and proportions.

NOTE

What are serif and sans serif fonts? Look at a magazine with columns of text and find a lowercase l. Chances are that the letter features more than a single vertical stroke. Serifs are the embellishments you see—the flag at the top of the l and the pedestal at the bottom. Sans-serif fonts (without serifs) have no such ornamentation. Times Roman is a common serif font; Helvetica is a common sans-serif font.

Most large blocks of text are set in a serif font because it is naturally easier to read.

Follow these suggestions when you use more than one typeface on the same page:

➤ Multiple typefaces usually look too busy or muddy—do not combine more than two typefaces on a page if you can avoid it. (Bolds and italics of the same font are not considered separate typefaces—they ought to be compatible.)

➤ Match fonts with x-heights that are relatively similar in proportion to their ascenders. If one font's lowercase x is roughly half as tall as its lowercase h, pair it with a font that has similar proportions.

➤ Look at the line-width of the letters. Is the stroke a fairly uniform width or are there extremes of thick and thin? (The letter O is a good indicator.) One aspect of complementary typefaces is a similar line-width ratio.

➤ In general, avoid matching two different serif fonts. If the two serif fonts look similar but differences are evident, they could look like slightly mismatched socks.

➤ High-contrast differences often work well if proportions are complementary (or if the typefaces look good together for some other reason). Contrasts can be large versus small, bold versus light, bold versus italic, or one color versus another color.

Monospace and Proportional Fonts

Think of what an average typewritten resume looked like before the advent of the PostScript laser printer. If that is easy for you to recall, you are visualizing the difference between monospace and proportional fonts.

The individual characters of a *fixed-pitch* or *monospace* font occupy exactly the same amount of space on a line—regardless of whether the letter is skinny (like an *l*) or wide (like an *o*). If the font is set at 10 characters per inch, each and every letter occupies 1/10 of an inch. (Courier is an example of a commonly used monospace font. It is very likely to translate consistently from one system to another.)

The characters of a proportional font allow for some individuality. The proximity from one letter to another depends entirely on the letters involved. The word "ill," for example, is made up of skinny letters which are set close together. (The same word set in a 10-pitch monospace font would take up three-tenths of an inch.) Proportional fonts will accommodate more characters per line than monospace fonts.

NOTE

Windows and other popular GUIs (graphical user interfaces) now all use proportionally-spaced fonts as their system fonts. This addition adds tremendously to the readability of words on-screen.

The sample application that accompanies this book makes wide use of the System font. It was chosen because it is simple and readable, and is likely to translate well to other systems.

It is important to remember that not all systems have the same screen fonts available. If your multimedia document is

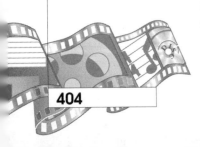

being distributed to unknown systems, some caution in this area is advisable. If the unknown system does not have a font you specified in a document, the system usually tries to substitute its closest possible fit. Unfortunately, the results can be distressing: word-wrapping can be altered, spacing can be changed, and carefully set tables can be thrown off.

With the new TrueType fonts, your display is capable of emulating the look and feel of typesetting. You have a wide variety of typefaces to choose from.

See the section "Windows-Supported Fonts" for information about TrueType fonts and other fonts supported by Windows.

Accents

Headlines and accent text should be set in a different typestyle from the body copy—even if it is only a matter of making it bolder or larger.

Headlines are much more readable set in upper- and lower-case than in all caps. In fact, all caps is generally the least readable way of setting type. This is especially true of computer displays.

Remember the earlier caution against using multiple typestyles!

Leading

Leading, or the space between lines, is an important aspect of text readability. Leading can be set in your word processor's paragraph-formatting functions, but multimedia authoring tools often have less flexibility.

In text blocks of more than one line, avoid having too little leading. Descenders (such as *p*) on an upper line can brush against ascenders (such as *k*) on an adjacent lower line. Usually, a default or automatic leading gives you only slightly more clearance between lines than you need.

ToolBook version 1.51 gives you a choice of 1-, 1.5-, or 2-line spacing .

TIP

If you have the option of fine-tuning your leading, add two points of height to the space between lines. For example, set 12-point type over 14 points of leading, 11 over 13, and so on.

Those are the most important things to look out for when setting type for the computer screen. Now take a look at the fonts you have to choose from.

Windows-Supported Fonts

Three types of fonts are supported by Windows: vector, raster, and WinOldAp. (Raster and WinOldAp are bit map fonts.) *Vector* fonts—such as TrueType and PostScript—are drawn from a font command language. This means the fonts can be scaled, skewed, and made bold just by redrawing them according to a set of rules. Postscript, Adobe's standard, is still enjoying popularity among the type foundries.

TrueType, Postscript's chief competing technology, is gaining acceptance. TrueType fonts are Microsoft's new font technology and one of the most dramatic enhancements in Windows 3.1. Like PostScript and WYSIWYG (what you see is what you get) fonts, they can be scaled on a broad range of displays.

TrueType is an open standard that font vendors do not have to pay to use. It contains a rich set of font construction parameters developed jointly for Apple's System 7 and Microsoft Windows 3.1. Before TrueType, however, Windows used mostly bit mapped fonts.

With bit map fonts, each character of each point size and typeface is an individual bit map. They are stretched, sheared, and "fattened up" to display variations such as italic

and bold. All of this stretching and twisting distorts the letters, so ultimately, the screen characters do not closely resemble the output from your laser printer! Bit mapped fonts are fast-loading, but they require a lot of disk space and are device-dependent. Windows still supports many bit mapped fonts for purposes of backward compatibility.

WinOldAp fonts only run in 386-enhanced mode. Their purpose is to support IBM's internationalization nomenclature. They are identified by the following naming convention: 40WOA.FON or 80WOA.FON. The 40 and 80 identify the font for use in 40- or 80-column mode. Font styles such as Times Roman and Helvetica must specifically identify the column width they support: TMR40WOA.FON and HEL80WOA.FON, for example.

Generally Windows stores fonts in the \WINDOWS\SYSTEM directory. Windows uses device-dependent system fonts for menus and dialog boxes. The fonts are different, depending upon the graphics standard used by your monitor: 8514, VGA, EGA, or CGA. (VGASYS.FON, for example, is a proportionally spaced system font for VGA monitors.)

These fonts follow a simple naming convention: SYS for proportionally spaced system fonts, FIX for fixed-space fonts, and OEM for the IBM character set. The raster (bit-map) fonts that you see in applications use the following naming conventions: A for CGA, B for EGA, C for 60 dots per inch, D for 120 dots per inch, E for VGA, F for 8514. For example, COURA.FON is Courier for CGA; HELVE.FON is Helvetica for VGA, and TMSRF.FON is 8514 Times Roman.

Under Windows, all compatible fonts are easy to use. You generally do not have to download them. An application's fonts are automatically available from a menu. But what if you want to add fonts to your existing set?

Adding Fonts

How are new fonts loaded into Windows? When you buy a Windows-compatible font set, it generally comes with an installation program. If no program is included, you can use the Control Panel's Fonts option to install them.

To install a set of fonts, start the Control Panel. Double-click on the Fonts icon to display the Fonts window. (Notice that a highlighted font is displayed in the box. You can view different fonts by highlighting them in the Installed Fonts list box.) To add new fonts with the Control Panel, insert a new font disk into the appropriate floppy drive and click on the Add pushbutton. Follow the instructions in the Add Fonts dialog box. (Fonts can be removed, as well.)

What is available out there? For about $100, some type foundries are selling CD-ROMs that contain complete PostScript-typeface libraries. The problem is that only a few fonts are available (unlocked) when you purchase the library. The rest are locked until you buy the access codes. You, in effect, have a large, immediately expandable font library, but do not have to pay all at once. For example, Adobe's Type On Call CD-ROM ($99) gives you 26 unlocked fonts. The rest are encrypted until you unlock them. If you were to buy Adobe's Font Folio—the entire Adobe Type Library—you would be spend $14,000. Eight vendors (Adobe, Agfa, Bitstream, The Font Company, Image Club, Monotype, NEC, and URW) have released CD-ROM fonts.

If you are planning to author multimedia applications over a long period of time, you may want fresh typefaces. Some vendors produce type-design and production tools that even include freehand, calligraphic features. (With Pen Windows, you can make realistic calligraphic strokes.) Fonts can be created from existing font masters—in fact, some products offer multiple masters. Some tools enable you to change the weighting of fonts, overlap characters, and do hint editing.

Colors

Color can be used to your advantage in a number of ways. The choices you make can contribute to organization, strategic accents, readability, and the overall appeal of your document. Here are some considerations and pointers:

➤ Choose colors carefully—avoid clashes and near-miss matches.

➤ Try to use system palette colors whenever possible. That maximizes the likelihood of your colors translating well to other systems.

➤ Keep a strong contrast between background and font colors. (Drop shadows under headline text can be effective in low-contrast situations.)

➤ Avoid displaying small text on a dithered background.

➤ Be careful with deeply saturated colors. They can shimmer on-screen.

➤ Unless there is a good reason for it, avoid stark white as a background for large amounts of text.

In spite of carefully chosen color schemes, your palette is only as good as the end-user's system. Program your application to use the system's colors whenever possible, and let users set them the way they like them.

Choosing Sound

If you plan to include audio elements in your multimedia document, you should know about a few types and formats:

waveform, Redbook, and MIDI. They are all supported by Multimedia Windows.

➤ *Waveform* audio is digital sound converted from analog wave forms. It is the most practical choice for many situations. It has potential to be high-fidelity, but the standard multimedia PC may not do it justice.

You can edit waveform files, store them in memory or on disk, and play them back through a sound card. Waveform files are identified by their WAV extension.

➤ *Redbook* audio is CD-quality, digital sound. Its quality is very high, and so is the budget required to produce it.

➤ *MIDI* audio can provide a rich audio track and give you control over the individual components of the sound. The Multimedia PC includes a MIDI (musical instrument digital interface) synthesizer to play music using MIDI command sequences.

Waveform Audio

The use of waveform audio has multimedia authoring implications far beyond just turning your PC into an expensive, digital tape recorder. Because waveforms are digital, sounds are manipulated by software components—so things that would give you fits in the analog world turn out to be simple manipulations in the digital world.

With waveform audio, it is relatively easy to play sounds backward, slow them down, speed them up, or mix two together. The biggest benefits, though, are most appreciated by anyone who has edited analog audio tape. For those people, editing sound digitally is a dream come true.

Digital audio has the reputation of being extremely high quality and somehow subject to less distortion than analog. Regardless of what happens after the audio has been digi-

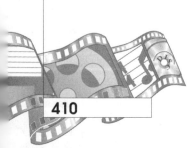

tized, however, there are sound-quality issues just as there are in the analog world.

Microphones, which are the ultimate source of all waveform audio, pick up sound vibrations from the air and translate them into analog electronic signals. The hysteresis (response lag) inherent in this process—both mechanical and electronic—introduces audible distortion.

On the output side, another type of distortion is introduced. Synthesizing musical instruments electronically, it turns out, is not quite as simple as breaking sounds down into groups of unique harmonic intensities. Relative harmonic intensities differ proportionally to frequency over the range of a musical instrument—as well as to how rapidly the amplitude rises (attack) and the duration of time a note is played (sustain).

All in all, sound reproduction is challenging. Ultimately, the quality of your audio equipment—including your PC's sound card—affects the quality of the sound.

Sound is analog, and computers only understand discrete numbers. So how is the analog waveform converted? The most common method of analog-to-digital conversion (ADC) used on all types of audio devices (compact discs, digital audio tapes, and in Multimedia Windows), is *pulse code modulation* (PCM).

Pulse code modulation has two parameters: sample rate and the number of bits contained in the sample itself. Pulse code modulation is performed by sampling a waveform at a constant rate. (Depending on the converter, the sampling rate can be tens of thousands of times per second.) Each time a sample is taken, the amplitude of the waveform is measured and stored digitally (as a number). The conversion back into an analog, electrical signal (representing waveform) uses a digital-to-analog converter (DAC).

Obviously, the process is not electronically trivial—and it is not transparent. There are filters and signal modulators needed to make the incoming and outgoing waveforms sound the same. All of this supporting electronics hardware can fit easily on one expansion board, however.

Intuition tells you that the faster the waveform is sampled and the larger the sample *word* (the set of bits), the better the reproduction. There is a point, however, where any improvements go beyond a human's ability to distinguish the differences. How much is enough?

The sampling rate must be twice the highest frequency of the sound being sampled. This is known as the Nyquist frequency. With too low a sampling rate, the resultant waveform has a much lower frequency than the original (known as an alias). In fact, to eliminate aliases, most sound digitizers filter out all frequencies greater than half the sampling rate. On the output side, digital-to-analog converters produce overtones composed of frequencies greater than half the sampling rate. They must be filtered as well.

The human ear can hear up to 20KHz, so one might expect a sampling rate of 40KHz. In fact, the sampling rate used on audio compact discs is 44.1KHz. (Low-pass filters "roll-off" slowly enough that they require about a ten percent higher sampling rate. In recording audio from VCRs, there is another slight adjustments needed to bring the sampling rate up to 44.1KHz.)

The 44.1KHz sampling rate produces much data and is overkill for recording voices only. (The fundamental frequency of speech is roughly 1KHz). Many applications, therefore, can get by with significantly lower sampling rates; in fact, Multimedia Windows APIs support sampling rates of 44.1KHz, 22.05KHz, and 11.025KHz.

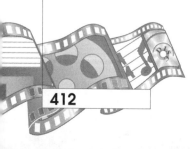

NOTE

Human ears are sensitive enough to amplitude to hear sounds as soft as the Brownian motion of molecules and as loud as a the loudest rock concert. As with frequency, human perception of sound intensity is logarithmic.

A tenfold increase in sound intensity is called a Bels (after Alexander Graham Bell). One decibel (one-tenth of a Bels) is about the lowest increase in sound intensity that the ear can perceive. The difference in intensity between sounds at the threshold of hearing and sounds at the threshold of pain is about 100 decibels.

Sample size is the second pulse-code-modulation parameter. It determines the difference between the softest sound and the loudest sound that can be recorded and played back.

With a sample size of 8 bits, the ratio of the largest amplitude to the smallest amplitude is 256. That translates to 48 decibels. A 48-decibel dynamic range is approximately the difference between a quiet room and a power lawn mower. Doubling the sample size to 16 bits yields a dynamic—nearly the difference between the threshold of hearing and the threshold of pain. A 16-bit sample size is used in compact disc recording, and is supported under Multimedia Windows.

In summary, the minimum-standard multimedia PC can sample sound at 11,025Hz with 8 bits per sample, and play back waveform audio at 11,025 and 22,050Hz with 8 bits per sample. Windows also supports other sampling rates and sample sizes up to 44.1KHz and 16 bits, respectively.

You are not going to get CD-quality sound out of the wave files sampled at the lower rates and played back on a minimum-standard multimedia PC. By the same token, however, if your goal is to save space and you only intend to play back talking voices, the lower sampling rates will fit your needs.

With waveform audio, you have the option of high fidelity or compact files. If your choice is high fidelity, you want to choose Redbook audio.

Redbook Audio

Redbook audio is CD-quality audio. It is the specification that commercial CDs are mastered and distributed under. Do not choose this format for audio if you are going to do it yourself—unless you are at home in a high-fidelity recording studio and have a healthy budget. The equipment you need for recording and processing the Redbook digital audio files must be of the highest professional quality and be under the control of a knowledgeable engineer.

If you need to examine the specifications first-hand, get a copy of the International Electrotechnical Commission's "Compact Disk Digital Audio System 908; 1987." The specification covers disk parameters such as dimensions, optical parameters of the plastic, recording and playback environment, signal measurement and fidelity, and the structure of the digital files that contain the music waveforms.

If you are planning to record high-fidelity music for distribution on a CD-ROM as part of your application, you will probably want to have a copy of these specifications. The scanning rates and filtering necessary to achieve high-fidelity, digital audio is specified in engineering terms. Recording engineers need to make sure that their digital recording equipment produces signals in compliance with these specifications. The specification also defines the tracking parameters that allow CD drives to maintain playback consistency. This includes a specification for the discs' sensitivity to a playback head's radial offset. The tolerance to optical defects, crosstalk between adjacent tracks, and random-error return rates are also specified. You also will need to consult the specification for the areas on the disc set aside for lead-in, program, and lead-out. This ensures that the heads have enough room to lock into your signal properly.

Digitally, Redbook audio is recorded as 16-bit words using a 2's compliment, least-significant-bit, CIRC error-checking scheme. The lead-in and lead-out areas are also 2's compliment, 16-bit words. The sampling frequency is 44.1KHz. Audio is recorded in a 2-channel, linear format.

As was mentioned earlier, digital-audio processing is not a trivial task. If you are interested in what is done to maximize the fidelity of the music, see Section Four of the Redbook specification. It is quite technical, however, so unless you are familiar with the electronics and techniques of digital recording, it may not be worth pursuing.

In summary, choose Redbook audio when you want the highest fidelity available. If you choose Redbook audio, plan on delivering your application on or with a CD-ROM disk. The file sizes are bigger than a simple floppy disk can handle comfortably. Committing to Redbook audio also means that you are committing to a professional recording studio with high-fidelity digital equipment. This is the expensive road, but it provides your application with fabulous-sounding audio.

MIDI Audio

Charles Petzold has written extensively on the subject of multimedia from the programmer's point of view. Here is a synopsis of what he says about the technical side of MIDI.

MIDI is the basis for creating electronic music on microcomputers. The simplest way to explain it is to look at how MIDI components are configured for multimedia operation: A (MIDI compatible) keyboard is used to generate "musical" MIDI "key-on" and "key-off" messages. These digital messages are sent to the sound card and are ultimately turned into sounds.

The keyboard, in effect, functions as the MIDI interface—though it makes no sound by itself. The PC functions both as synthesizer and sequencer. Like a synthesizer, it has software to translate MIDI messages into waveforms. The sound card makes the waveform available to headphones or to an amplifier input as an analog signal. Any sound card that has MIDI software works. (Remember that MIDI is just a special kind of bytestream.)

The various sound qualities a synthesizer produces are called *voices*. As far as multimedia is concerned, voices are little programs that run under MIDI software. If the synthesizer is polyphonic, you can play chords on the keyboard and it generates multiple "note on" messages. But MIDI does not require a keyboard to run. The keyboard, like a sequencer, is just a controller. And, like a sequencer, a PC can read or store a series of MIDI messages "in musical time."

NOTE You can monitor MIDI messages by using the MIDIMON program included with the Multimedia Development Kit.

Why would you choose to use MIDI audio? If a rich audio track is appealing to you as a multimedia author, it is worth the time to learn about it. With waveform audio, you get a whole; you cannot take it apart. MIDI offers you the control room: remix, the option of changing horns to strings, adding a drum, or even making dogs bark on pitch and in time to music.

MIDI is quite different from the Redbook and waveform audio formats described earlier. MIDI is a protocol for unidirectional transfer of digital commands—no wave forms, analog or digital, are ever on the copper. What actually travels through the cable are small digital messages, usually one, two or three bytes in length.

When you press the musical note middle C, for example, the keyboard sends three bytes expressed in hexadecimal: 90 3C 40. The first byte (90) indicates that this is a "note on" message. The second byte is the key number for middle C: 3C. The third byte is the attack, or velocity, with which the key was struck. That can range from one to 127. This three-byte message goes through a special MIDI cable into the sound card (usually a five-pin Din plug). The sound card responds by playing a tone at middle C.

You must learn a great deal more about MIDI if you intend to program with it. If you want to know more, *PC Magazine* editor Charles Petzold has written a series of articles that take you through every aspect of MIDI in technical detail. You are sure to get useful information from them, but they offer much more than you would need to know to author a multimedia title.

WARNING

PC users may fiddle with MIDI channels and board manufacturers will only default to 4 active tracks reserved for MIDI.

Choosing Images

As with audio, a number of graphics issues pit quality against processing capabilities. Image quality is dependent upon your PC's graphics-processing hardware. The minimum graphics-processing capability for a multimedia PC is VGA resolution and (preferably) a 256-color graphics card. These issues will be revisited as Multimedia Windows-compatible graphics are discussed.

Depending upon your abilities as an artist and your experience with graphics tools, you are going to have a different opinion about how well simple, inexpensive graphics software packages meet your needs. It is generally true that quality is proportional to price when it comes to graphics software. The low-end tools available for between $500 and $1,000 have come a long way in terms of their capabilities. This holds true for both bit-map- and vector-graphics editors.

Vector Versus Bit-map Graphics

There are two types of computer graphics: vector graphics (collections of points, lines, curves, and shapes) and bit-map graphics (made up of colored dots). The two graphics technologies are very different in the ways that they go about creating images, but the end result is often indistinguishable.

In this section, the distinction between vector and bit-map graphics is based on the types of pictures most easily created by each.

Vector graphics are stored as a set of graphical instructions for drawing points, lines, curves, rectangles, and so on. Unless your PC is blindingly fast, you can actually see the image being drawn as you load it. Vector-graphics software, often called *draw programs*, are most useful when you need to manipulate each piece of your image on an individual basis. Objects can be moved, scaled, rotated, and copied, and their attributes (such as line thickness or color) can be changed.

Series of images that have many of the same or similar-looking objects are best created with vector graphics. You can save small objects and parts of objects separately and import them into larger drawings. In fact, you can assemble libraries of these building-block objects, effectively speeding up graphics production.

Vector graphics is by far the method of choice for creating technical illustrations and line-art. The down side of vector graphics, however, is the problem of complexity. They can quickly become so complicated that it takes the computer a long time to execute the graphical instructions.

Many drawing programs are available—most with their own proprietary set of graphical instructions. If you want to include vector drawings from one of these programs in a Windows multimedia document, you must do any of the following:

➤ Translate the image to a Windows metafile (WMF) format

➤ Import the image into a bit-map graphics package and translate it to a Windows-compatible bit-map

➤ Provide software with your multimedia application for viewing the image

Bit-map images are stored as bits. Each pixel has an associated set of bits that specifies its color and intensity. Bit maps are used for images that have shading and lots of realistic detail. Photos, for example, are best stored as bit maps. Bit-map editors, called *paint programs*, have tools similar to those in draw programs. Images can be created from scratch with drawing and editing tools, or they can be captured with scanners or video frame-grabbers.

Some scanners are hand-held; others often look like Xerox machines; you place a photo or drawing on a glass platen and the scanner creates a bit-mapped image of it on your computer. Video frame-grabbers are usually cards that fit into the PC's bus. The card has video inputs for hooking up a camera or tape machine. The desired image is either shot with your camera or located on the tape. Once the image is available from the video source, the frame grabber makes a bit-mapped copy of it. (Paint software is then used to rectify imperfections in the scanned or grabbed image, enhance its color and brightness, and, if necessary, change its format.)

Multimedia Windows requires bit maps to be saved in the *device-independent bitmap* (DIB) format or BMP format for use in your applications. You do, however, have quite a bit of latitude in creating images. Most of the common image file formats can be translated to DIB files.

Though bit maps generally load faster than vector graphic files, they are much bigger. Two factors affect image size: *resolution* and *depth*. The greater the resolution (the greater the number of dots in the picture), the larger the image file. By the same token, the greater the depth of each dot (the larger the computer word used to specify the color and brightness of the individual pixel), the larger the image file.

NOTE

The size of an image is calculated in a straightforward manner:

height (in pixels)×width (in pixels)×color depth (in bits)/8

Resolution

Resolution is a term that means different things depending on the context. There are actually three resolutions to consider: screen resolution, image resolution, and pixel resolution.

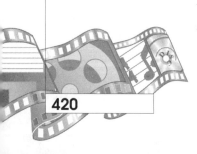

Screen resolution is the area of your monitor's display screen. Multimedia PC minimum standards specify VGA. That means your PC's screen displays 640 dots on every line and 480 lines of dots in a single raster scan. This is the target resolution for scanning your raw image.

TIP

Though some graphics cards and displays support higher resolutions, 640×480 is the maximum size you should make your images. Any other resolution or aspect ratio can potentially result in your system being unable to display a complete image on the screen at once.

The second factor you need to consider is image resolution. While screen resolution establishes the size of the "playing field," *image resolution* sets how much of the field your image will use. (For example, an image at 320×240 takes up a quarter of the screen.) An imagelarger than 640×480 cannot be seen in its entirety, though you can usually scroll around on it.

The third image-quality factor is *pixel resolution.* (Recall that a *pixel* is a single dot on the screen display.) Pixels are not necessarily the same size or shape on every screen. An image created on a screen with a 1:1 pixel aspect ratio will be badly distorted on a screen with a 1:2 pixel aspect ratio. This type of distortion is less and less common because modern display technology has been almost completely standardized on a pixel ratio of 1:1.

NOTE

Though some graphics cards can display different numbers of lines and dots per line, 640×480 is the VGA standard. SVGA (Super VGA) and other higher-

---

resolution video standards are showing up on the scene already. VGA may not be the multimedia PC standard for much longer.

VGA is not a particularly high-resolution image. People who are in the electronic graphics business often judge video-image quality against that of 35mm film (what most feature films are shot on). The effective resolution of 35mm film is estimated to be somewhere between 1024×1024 and 2048×2048, depending upon how it is shot.

Image Depth

Image depth, as you saw in the simple formula, specifies the number of bits used to describe color and brightness. VGA color-depth is not always the same from machine to machine. Standard VGA supports 4-bit, or 16 colors, at 640×480. The newer VGA graphic systems recommended for multimedia PCs can display 8-bit color—256 colors—at VGA resolution.

Even 256 colors, however, do not yield particularly high-fidelity images. These days, color graphics are emerging with 24-bit or 16 million colors. In comparison to 35mm film, which has an effective color depth of about 24 bits, VGA video lacks luster. Look for multimedia PC color-depth standards to increase to 24 or even 32 bits as a bigger bus and new graphic-chip sets become commonly available. (Though 24-bit color yields depth similar to 35mm film, 32-bit color provides an additional 8 bits of transparency to your object.)

NOTE

Color depth and resolution are not totally independent. Television has relatively low resolution (512×480)—lower resolution than VGA—but it has a realistic appearance anyway. What gives TV video that life-like appearance? Depth—the second image-quality parameter that was mentioned earlier.

TV video has analog color, which makes for extremely fine color discrimination. A very large set of colors allows a low-resolution image to be anti-aliased well. What is *anti-aliasing*?

If you have ever created a high contrast image— black and white for example—on a low-resolution monitor, you no doubt remember the jaggies. All the curves appear to have been cut as stair steps. If a system has the capability to display lots of color depth, the jaggies can be minimized by anti-aliasing the curves. The stair steps are filled in with colors that are blended between the background and the foreground. Anti-aliasing causes your eye to interpret the boundary as a smooth curve.

In summary, graphics are an integral part of multimedia, so you need to become familiar with the process of linking graphics to your applications. How the images are generated is up to you. You have a number of inexpensive tools to choose from.

Windows multimedia applications do, however, have a limited number of image formats they can accept. Vector-graphics images must be in the WMF format; bit-mapped graphics must be in the DIB format. You can convert images to these formats in a number of ways. (That information is presented later in this chapter.)

For applications with lots of images, you are faced with a dilemma: bit-mapped graphics load faster, but vector graphics are generally smaller files. As with other multimedia elements,you must consider the tradeoffs. You learn more about graphics-related issues later in the chapter.

Choosing Animation

The value of animation is clear. But it has traditionally been a cumbersome technology on a PC—that is, until recently. Animation has become a common multimedia data type due to the efforts of a few software vendors, particularly Macro-Mind (now MacroMedia).

NOTE Macromind became known as MacroMedia when it merged with Paracomp and purchased a number of Farallon sound tools.

Director, which is Macromedia's archetypal PC animation-software package, enables authors to add sound, animation, and nonlinear links to presentations easily. The resulting simultaneous, synchronized presentation of information has had tremendous impact that is defining multimedia itself.

Practically speaking, animations must be created with some third-party tool—the Windows MDK does not provide an animation development environment. Whether the tool is Mac-based (like Director), or Windows-based (like Author-ware), the animation itself comes out as a collection of data files integrated through MCI commands. (The Windows MDK actually provides a conversion utility specifically for the

Mac-based Macromedia Director.) The MDK does provide support for playing back animated sequences on the Multimedia Player.

The process of creating animation, regardless of the tool you use, involves a few steps:

➤ creating the images

➤ synchronizing the movements with sounds

➤ translating the animation file to a Windows-compatible format

➤ playing it back to verify that the animation looks and behaves the same on the Multimedia Viewer as it did in the authoring environment

Animation Authoring Packages

Different authoring packages require that you create your animations differently. All computer animations, though, are a sequence of frames.

One way to generate an animation is to create a series of still images individually—with a bit-map editor, for example—and to have your animation software flip through them like a movie. For anything but the most elementary animation, that is very hard work. You usually would have to create between 12 and 30 images per finished second of animation. You would only need to create a few animations this way before you develop an appreciation for the power of multimedia animation-authoring systems.

A more efficient way to create animation is with MacroMedia's Director. With Director, you create a *cast* of objects that are the components of your animation. Each cast member is given position, size, and color attributes with respect to *keyframes* in the sequence. A *keyframe* is a particular image in the sequence on which a significant event (an attribute change) occurs. After you have specified each cast member's attributes for every keyframe in the animation, you composite all the objects together. Your part is done.

MacroMedia Director redraws all the objects for each frame in the animation, interpolating the objects' attributes for all the frames in between the keyframes. This includes creating the sequence of frames that represents simple linear motions of objects—a comet trailing across the sky, for instance. But Director will also enables you to create a short sequence of images specifying some movement, like a cat running. It will cycle through this sequence as the object is moved across the screen. Features like these are invaluable time-savers.

All the higher-end animation-authoring environments have many features that take the labor out of animation. The smarter the program, however, the more processing power it takes to do all the drawing in a timely manner.

Drawing and painting all the images is called *rendering*. Rendering can be expensive and time-consuming. A PC may, literally, take hundreds of hours to render no more than a few seconds of full-screen, high-resolution, 24-bit graphic animation. Bear in mind that animation taxes the performance of multimedia PC machines in both authoring and playback modes. (Remember that the minimum multimedia PC machine only has 2M RAM.) If you decide to do high-quality animations, you should make arrangements (budget-wise) for rendering on a fast machine.

Here are some other tips for minimizing animation performance problems:

➤ Animation files should be kept under 500K if possible.

➤ Do not create full-screen animations. Keep things small, both in size and scope (length).

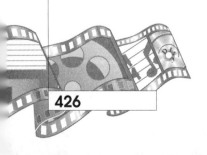

➤ Create little pieces of animation that can be combined and reused.

➤ Delete objects after they are no longer needed.

➤ Use monochrome color schemes wherever possible.

➤ Use MCI commands to play sound files and MIDI sequences directly. (In Macromedia Director, exclude these from being sound cast-members.)

➤ Test your multimedia animation extensively under Windows before you release your application.

The other important feature of authoring systems is their capability to integrate (import) images from a wide variety of sources. Many professional animators feel that this is Director's principle selling point over all the other authoring tools.

To play Director movies under Windows, you must first convert your Director file. Use the tool provided in the MDK, and then use the Multimedia Player. This requires that you have the MMP.DLL library loaded in the *libpath* of your PC.

If your animation uses MCI to control playback, you also need a special device driver: MCIMMP.DRV. You can play back Macromedia movies three ways:

➤ Write your application to call the Windows extended applications programming interface directly.

➤ Run Windows-compatible animations from the Windows Multimedia Player application.

➤ Use any authoring or playback environment that supports MCI.

Be careful, though. Movies created under different authoring systems can sometimes lose in the translation to the Multimedia Player. Transitions from one image to another may be distorted; palettesalso can be distorted, and so can the shapes of objects if there is a change in pixel resolution.

Palettes

A word about palettes is useful at this point. Recall that Windows supports 4-bit (16-color) and 8-bit (256-color) display drivers. The system provides a standard palette—either 16 or 256 colors—to choose from when you create your animations.

Palettes are animation objects. Mac-based animation pro-grams have much more sophisticated color palettes available to them than PC-based player applications. This can cause trouble. At best, you need to make sure that an animation is designed with a Mac palette that is close to your Windows target palette. You should develop the animation as 16-color. The sixteen slots in the palette should appear as similar as possible to the Windows target palette. Any changes in one palette necessitates an accommodation in the other.

The default system palettes on both the Mac and the PC are usually mappable without much distortion in display ap-pearance. If you stay with the system palette, you are usually all right. But the same 16 colors probably will not be appro-priate for all your animation needs.

At some point, you will undoubtedly need to change an object's color to one not available on the system palette. You do this by defining a new palette or by changing one of the colors on the existing palettes. When your animation reaches the point where new colors are needed, it merely loads the new palette.

When that happens, you will notice that the palettes on the source and target sides of the transfer have changed substan-tially. Whenever you are translating graphics between the

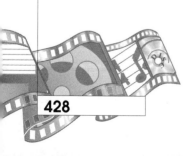

Mac and PC, you have to be sensitive to shifts in palette. Changing the palette can drastically alter a display's look because the different palettes do not contain the same colors.

Part of the process of translating Macromedia animations to the PC, then, is verifying that the palettes remain consistent across the two platforms. Even for experienced hands, this is a trial-and-error challenge. Refer to Chapter 9 of the *Multimedia Authoring Guide* for a table of how display appearance is modified by palette-mapping.

Sound Synchronization

One of the most important features of animation is synchronized sound. In Director, this is done by creating sound cast members in the Macromedia sound channel and synchronizing them on the timeline. When the Macromedia movie is translated to Windows, sound cast members are translated to wave files and synchronized automatically. The wave files, however, are embedded into the movie. That adds substantial size to the PC-based movie file. You can reduce the size by creating scripts of MCI commands that directly control multimedia devices. This makes your files smaller, but synchronization becomes more difficult. Refer to the MDK *Programmer's Reference* for more information about using **MCI WAIT** commands to perform sound synchronization.

NOTE Synchronization is easier if you minimize file opens and seeks for new files. MCI commands enables you to play back a wave file from one position in the file to another if you have audio mapped out linearly and only run the WAV file this way. Synchronization is made easier by opening a large sound file and playing it a piece at a time.

Technological Standards

One thing that has slowed the development of multimedia—particularly when it comes to animation—is a lack of widely accepted standards. Apple and Microsoft seem to be the frontrunners in developing operating-system standards that encompass the wide range of technology needed to support multimedia.

While Apple currently has the edge in image quality, Microsoft and the PC compatibles still have the lead in "bang for your buck." Apple hardware, though the Cadillac of multimedia, is still prohibitively expensive for a vast segment of the potential market. Microsoft, though it dominates the PC operating-system market, still seems to have a way to go to catch up in graphics quality.

Apple's multimedia strategy involves a joint venture (called Kaleida) with IBM. Its most salient feature appears to be a media scripting system that will evolve from QuickTime and be usable on DOS, OS/2, and Mac systems. Microsoft, on the other hand, has entered into a development venture with Silicon Graphics to develop a new graphic standard for Windows. The future of multimedia is yet to be defined, but glimpses of it are already evident.

Apple's QuickTime is both authoring software and an operating-system standard for time-based media: video, sound, and animation. It includes a compression scheme and a standard format for digital video and sound. On existing hardware, QuickTime Movies are going to be small, slow, and monophonic, but the fault is more in the current state of the hardware than a problem with QuickTime itself. QuickTime is software, so it can be installed on nearly any Mac—making the machine multimedia-ready.

Microsoft has pressed PC-compatible vendors for a standard multimedia machine in the DOS/Windows universe. As it stands today, the Multimedia PC standard is minimal, but Microsoft has begun its efforts to extend Windows into multimedia.

Microsoft, with the help of Silicon Graphics, may substantially change the nature of Windows-based multimedia through the democratic use of professional audio and video production tools. Silicon Graphics products traditionally find their way onto the expensive desktops of the creative or technical professional. Indigo, Silicon Graphics' new product, puts professional video- and audio-production capabilities into an $8,000 to $12,000 machine—which compares favorably with high-end Macs.

In the future, you will find the Silicon Graphics engine working its way toward lower-end machines while Microsoft's new operating system, Windows NT, supports multiprocessor PCs and RISC architecture. Windows NT will add significantly to the capabilities of those "low-end" machines.

To summarize, it is prudent at this point to design your multimedia applications so that animation is an accent tool, not the primary information-presentation vehicle. As for the animations themselves, keep them small and short, and if possible, create them for reuse in combination with other elements.

You definitely will want to acquire an authoring system even if you plan on doing only one complicated animation. The labor savings will be immense. If you arc crcating long, or full-screen animations, you probably will need a rendering engine—a 486 minimum, with a math coprocessor (a Weitek for example), 16M RAM, and plenty of fast storage.

While multimedia standards are not yet mature, the basics are in place. You can choose either Apple's or Microsoft's multimedia standards and not go too far wrong. Both platforms are extensible, tools for converting between the two platforms are available, and both companies have strategies for their next products already. Minimum multimedia PC machines are already on the market, starting at about $2,000, and powerful new hardware is waiting in the wings. All in all, the future of multimedia animation looks rosy, regardless of the platform you choose for development.

Choosing Video

Just as moderation is a good approach for animation, it is equally justified in the arena of multimedia video. Do not be discouraged without taking a look. By the same token, do not plan on developing your first full-length, big-screen multimedia application just yet. Full-motion, high-fidelity video with two-channel, stereo audio is currently a high-ticket item.

Aside from the pervasive problem of storage-media, video requires expensive hardware upgrades to the standard multimedia PC machine. You must add a video input card to your PC's bus. This card takes analog video from a source (camera, TV, tape player, or videodisc), digitizes it, and makes it available to Windows.

Video requires compression, which is also done in the hardware. Somehow, too, you need to acquire the video in the first place. Buying commercial video can be prohibitively expensive, though you may find reasonably priced footage if you look hard enough. Shooting video so that it has a commercial look, however, is not for amateurs. It is equipment-intensive, technical, and expensive.

That is the down side. If you are in a position to overcome these obstacles, the overhead could be well worth it. Video is the highest form of expression for multimedia. It integrates sights, sounds, words, and movement into a package with unlimited potential to entertain and teach.

Most people have a sense of the power of movies and television. Television in particular is the dominant electronic communication medium of Western society. If an application comes along that can drive the home multimedia market, it will undoubtedly incorporate video as a main ingredient. Multimedia video is the embodiment of the marriage between television and the PC.

NOTE
If multimedia achieves its potential as an educational technology, it will be through the combined effect of its emotional and direct feedback about a learner's behavior.

If you want to explore what scientists have found out about learning, you can start with the following references: *Brain, Mind, and Behavior* by Floyd E. Bloom and Arlyne Lazerson, W. H. Freeman and Company; and *Open Mind, Whole Mind*, by Bob Samples, Jalmar Press.

The ultimate multimedia title must certainly be based in interactive, full-motion video: stereo audio, photo-realistic images, and non-flickering motion. Full-motion requires playing back images at anywhere from 18 to 30 frames (images) per second. (At fewer than 18 frames per second, you can perceive flicker.)

You can eliminate head seek times by using a CD-ROM, but transfer rates are even longer.

The most serious drawback to using video is storage (in terms of both capacity and transfer rates). Non-flickering video requires a monumental data-transfer rate to maintain well for any length of time on a PC. To complicate matters, multimedia is nonlinear, so video playback is not merely streamed; there is head-seeking to contend with as well. Still, there is considerable impetus for providing a mechanism that will incorporate video into multimedia.

Multimedia Video Technology

This section contains an overview of the kind of support you can expect, and where the technology may fall short of your expectations.

Microsoft Windows with Multimedia Extensions 1.0 is now being fitted with its Audio-Video Interleave (AVI) specification that enables you to play "motion" video from a mass-storage device—most likely a CD-ROM. Because of memory and speed limitations, the best that AVI offers is a jumpy sort of animation—not full-motion video. Companies such as CompuAdd, IEV, and New Media Graphics offer video capture and digitizing on cards (composite video input or television tuner). You cannot store this video, though. Full-motion video—such as you are used to watching on television—displays 30 full-screen images (frames) per second (fps).

Incorporating video into a multimedia presentation requires some maneuvering. If the video source is an analog, NTSC (National Television Standard Committee) composite signal, it requires digitizing. Second, to maintain 30 fps, the signal has to be moved at ten times the speed of the ISA bus. Third, a single full-screen color image of digitized video can require 1.5M of disk space. Translated, that means one second of 30-

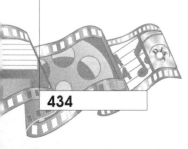

fps full-motion video would take 45M of storage. Obviously, you need additional hardware.

Two basic options are available: NTSC-to-VGA adapters that translate television signals to computer video, and compression/digitization video boards that process digital video so that it can be stored on a PC.

NTSC-to-VGA Adapters

NTSC/VGA boards offer the simplest solution. Implicit with these devices, however, is the requirement that you have an external video source (destination). Most of these add-in cards can take composite NTSC input (such as that from a regular TV, VCR, or camcorder), overlay computer-generated graphics and titles, and then output the combined signal to a television monitor or VCR—not a computer storage device. Available cards run in price from the $895 VGA-TV GE/O adapter from Willow Peripherals to Truevision's 1M $1,295 VideoVGA board.

NOTE

Most NTSC boards accomplish their task by doing genlocking. *Genlocking* means synchronizing the 31.5KHz VGA signal with the 15.735KHz NTSC signal. Some genlocking boards support VGA monitors that run at the 31.5KHz rate, though many of the older boards will display only the combined image on an RGB television monitor.

NTSC/VGA boards provide an inexpensive way of making videotaped presentations by combining computer graphics, titles, and animation with full-motion video. They are not really suitable for multimedia authoring, however. The primary problem with these boards is that they lack the MCI command control. Most also lack editing features like the ones discussed in Animation Authoring Tools (earlier in this chapter).

The most well-known exception is NewTek's $4,995 Video Toaster Workstation PC. It is an Amiga outfitted with editing hardware and software previously only available in professional editing suites—and that had a minimum price tag of $250,000.

Audio and Video Compression Boards

Despite the capabilities of NTSC-to-VGA synchronization hardware, you still cannot store enough digitized full-motion video on your PC to make it worthwhile. But there is hope in the form of a new generation of audio/visual compression boards.

These devices use a variety of mostly proprietary compression techniques to turn the analog video into a digital signal for storage, editing, and display on a PC's VGA monitor. Several compression techniques have been proposed, but only recently does there seem to be a candidate that may ultimately dominate the field: MPEG (Motion Picture Experts Group) compression.

MPEG seems to be taking the lead because it is the only compression specification to be developed by a large international committee. The specifications would be overwhelming to nonprogrammers, but suffice it to say that MPEG is a good compression scheme. It yields compression ratios equivalent to most of the other competing schemes (anywhere from 20:1 to 150:1). It can use a "lossy" type of compression algorithm, but it also can use other schemes. For example, it is possible to apply a fourier transform to the video data and remove the high-frequency components that are less visible.

It is implicit that the compression take place via some sort of chip set. There will be a translator, like a device driver, required to make the hardware device communicate with Windows. As yet, nothing has been cast in concrete, but MPEG compression hardware is being worked on now. A second version of the specification will be released soon.

At this time, the reality of the compression universe seems to be that nothing available today will become the great and all-powerful industry standard. MPEG certainly has an edge in that it has the largest core of support, but it is extremely complicated, hardware-oriented, and adds visible distortion.

NOTE

One of the first popular compression schemes was introduced by Intel. The Digital Video Interactive (DVI) compression algorithm was implemented on both its $1,895 Action-Media 750 Delivery and Capture boards (which capture and play back full-motion digital video, true-color stills, and high-quality audio).

Intel's RTV (real-time video) version of DVI, which allows for compression rates of up to 150 to 1, encodes each frame, compares it with succeeding frames, and then tosses out the redundant information.

This technique is referred to as interframe "lossy" compression. Audio is also compressed and interleaved with the video. Decompressed images can be grainy and jerky, and unsuitable for editing. Even with compression, 60 minutes of full-screen DVI video requires about 550M of disk space.

There are advantages: DVI is programmable so that it can support other standards and process video at various quality levels. It also can do real-time decoding of video from CD-ROM. And though DVI is not as high-quality as pristine, professionally created video, it is adequate for video conferencing.

JPEG (Joint Photographic Experts Group) is another popular video-compression method. Though it only offers a maximum compression ratio of 20:1 (1GB of storage would hold only 16 minutes of video!), several motion JPEG ISA products are now available. Many provide MCI support and digital signal-processing (DSP) with Motion JPEG compression.

Compression boards are available from different sources, including VideoLogic ($2,995 Media-Station MPC-compatible), New Media Graphics ($1,995 Super Motion Compression and $995 Super VideoWindows-CM board), Fluent Machines ($3,995 VSA-1000 JPEG with Fluent-Streams advanced software that allows bit-level manipulation of individual video frames), and Rapid Technology, which addresses the video-storage issue by offering 1.2GB hard disks ($2,300) in conjunction with its $1,695 Visionary Motion JPEG board and $1,295 Visionary Video 601 Framegrabber.

Microsoft takes a "software-assisted digital video" approach to compression in its new AVI (Audio Video Interleaved) standard. It is designed to quickly decompress images from any digital storage device, though the standard is tuned for a CD-ROM throughput rate of 150K per second. This loosely translates to a 160-×120-pixel, 256-color animation at a 15-frame-per-second display rate. AVI is also programmable for flexibility. You can specify a larger image at a slower frame-rate, or opt for a higher compression ratio with some loss of picture quality.

So video has not yet matured as a multimedia data type. Some standards issues must be resolved. Development and playback hardware—at this point in time—can be described only as exotic. On one hand, you can use special boards that will convert and synchronize NTSC video so it can be shown in a window; on the other hand, there are expensive compression/decompression boards that will digitize and compress analog video so that it can be manipulated directly by the PC. In the first case, you need an external video source (camera, VCR) to store the video. In the second case, you need a decompression board to play it back. And currently, not all compression schemes achieve a big enough compression ratio to make it worthwhile.

That sums up the technical drawbacks from the PC side. And you still need to acquire your video, edit it, and prepare it for distribution! Unless you are equipped to do professional-quality video production and have much experience producing tapes, this will be beyond your abilities—monetarily, if not technically. The allure of video is powerful, but the realization of a video product comes at great expense. For those who are not yet discouraged, a section on shooting videocomes later in this chapter.

Valid File Formats

The MDK provides a number of utility applets for editing and converting multimedia data types to compatible file formats. It is important to get a little practice with these tools, because hardware and software vendors are still a way from complying with an across-the-board standard set of file formats.

The problem of proprietary file formats is compounded by the potential for using almost any existing medium as a source for data. Text, sounds, and images have reasonably universal formats, but books, newspapers, compact disks, phonograph records, photographs, and video all represent valuable sources of data, too—and they all have different formats.

Before going into detail about converting multimedia data to Windows-compatible data types, it is worthwhile to examine the Windows Multimedia-compatible file formats and their uses.

Text Formats

Rich-text format (RTF) is text data with embedded paragraph, character, or graphical formatting. Basic Viewer applications are compiled from RTF files.

MS Word Format (DOC) is text data with MS Word commands built in. MS Word for Windows accepts a wide variety of word-processor document formats andcan translate them to RTF.

ASCII text (TXT) refers to raw characters with no font or other formatting data associated with it. ASCII text files are very small in comparison to RTF or to other word-processor files.

Graphic-Image Formats

MS device-independent bit maps (DIB) are the preferred way to convert bit map images created under non-Windows-based applications to a Windows-usable format.

DIB files contain information that allows Windows to interpret the pattern of bits that follows in the file. It also includes palette information, though this does not always ensure proper color-mapping.

RIFF device-independent bit maps (RDI) are tagged bit maps, similar to TIFF files. The *Microsoft Windows Multimedia Programmer's Reference* included in the MDK states that RIFF is "the preferred format for new multimedia file types. If your application requires a new file format, you should define it using the RIFF tagged file structure."

RIFF is a way of organizing information in data files. If you already have a file format, you can convert it to basic RIFF format easily.

Data in a RIFF file is tagged, which means that it is organized in chunks (blocks of various lengths), each of which is identified by an ASCII string. The string is generally four characters long, followed by the chunk's length and data. Tagged formats are useful for files that will be interchanged among different applications, such as TIFF files (tagged image file format) which store bit mapped image data.

Tagged file formats are easily extended because data is not located by tags, not offsets. Thus, the file format can be enhanced easily with additional tags.

Audio Formats: Waveform and MIDI

MS Waveform Audio (WAV) is digital waveform audio. It is encoded digitally via pulse code modulation. Wave files can be digitized at different sampling rates: 44.1KHz, 22KHz, and 11KHz.

MIDI (musical-instrument digital interface) files (MID) are a musical format that consists of commands for synthesizing sounds under Windows Multimedia Extensions.

RIFF MIDI (RMI) is a tagged sound file format.

Animation Formats

Macromedia Director movie files (MMM) are created on the Mac and ported over to the PC environment. The MDK supplies a utility for the conversion.

Image Conversion

As mentioned previously, the MDK provides a conversion utility. It is simple to use—it is like a simple bit-map editor. It converts image file formats of a variety of types to almost any of the common Windows-compatible formats, including DIB, the format of choice for multimedia authoring.

The details of file conversion are found in Chapter 3 of the MDK's *Data Preparation Tools User's Guide.* There you will find how to start the conversion program, how to select files to be converted, and how to locate target filenames and directories. It also explains how to scale (isotropic and anisotropic scaling) and colorize various image formats.

In addition to operating instructions, the chapter on "Converting a File" also goes through a number of examples specific to individual formats. There is also a chapter on editing bit maps using the MDK's BitEdit program. (This is straightforward material—bordering on trivial for anyone with experience using other bit-map editors.)

The only other image conversion that may need a little explanation is converting foreign formats to DIB files. In the Microsoft Systems Journal of July 1991 (v6 n4 p85 [12]), Albert Mirho contributed a comprehensive tutorial called "Converting foreign bit maps to Windows device-independent bit maps." If you are programming your multimedia application from scratch and need to find out how DIB files become device-independent (and what the pitfalls are), read that tutorial.

How to Create Media In-House

Much preparation goes into generating your own media elements—particularly when you are preparing your first true multimedia title. The creation end of it aside, you have tools to choose and hardware and software to acquire.

Some tools have already been mentioned in this book, but this section expands the level of detail so that you know a little more about the available products before you start shopping in earnest.

An Orientation to Authoring Systems

Finding the right authoring system is the first thing to do if you are serious about multimedia development. The Windows MDK provides a number of conversion utilities and editors—as well as the *media control interface*—but multimedia authoring systems provide two important things. They support a variety of hardware devices and file formats so that you easily can build complex productions that combine graphics, text, sound, animation, and even video data types. And they provide a framework for navigating through all that media—usually in the form of a hyperlink system.

Multimedia authoring software has been around for years, mostly in the hands of skilled professionals who were busy creating complex educational, training, and sales presentations. The programs were huge and had limited hardware support.

Today's multimedia authoring systems are still large applications, but they are considerably more manageable. Under Windows, authoring systems operate more consistently (via the graphical user interface), and they are much more device-independent. Windows also provides significant advances in memory management. In fact, the impact that Windows Multimedia Extensions has had on hardware compatibility cannot be underestimated. It works directly with CD-ROM drives, audio devices, and specialized video boards.

Device-independence really means that when companies build a new type of graphics device, they merely write a driver for Windows and the device will work with all Windows applications—including multimedia authoring tools. All Windows-compliant multimedia authoring systems are designed to access the MCI.

The MCI is a protocol layer that sits between Windows and multimedia hardware devices. Through this interface, your multimedia application can interact with any MCI-aware device through a set of straightforward commands. The MCI is an open-architecture system, which means that its details are published and there is support for new hardware manufacturers and software developers. Thisensures easy acceptance of new multimedia hardware.

A Checklist of Features

Here is a checklist of what you should expect from multimedia authoring systems:

➤ An authoring system must be capable of handling text and graphics—these make up the major portion of most multimedia titles.

➤ The system should be able to display graphics from a variety of formats.

➤ It should be able to display full-screen, cropped, or scaled images.

➤ It should offer a variety of transition effects.

➤ It should include simple paint and image-editing tools.

➤ A range of fonts (and a range of sizes) should be available for displaying text on-screen.

➤ More expensive authoring systems should be able to perform simple animations, such as moving small images across the screen.

You want to be just as certain that the authoring tool provides an adequate framework for interactive presentation of the data. Make sure that the system providesthe following key capabilities:

➤ It should easily create complex flow structures with conditional branching and logical looping.

➤ Users should be able to initiate jumps based on their input.

➤ It should provide macro capabilities: a keystroke or mouse-click should be able to spawn a chain of events.

➤ It should have a way to make corrections to complicated sequences of events.

➤ It should be easy to create and link on-screen hot buttons that trigger jumps to other parts of a presentation.

As sophisticated as most multimedia programs are, there is lots of room for improvement. Principally, they all require the completion of one task before another starts; it is difficult to synchronize events. Multimedia authoring systems *should* be capable of specifying start and end times for events based on the time elapsed since the start of the presentation. That is a feature that so far is reserved for professional video production and the time-code system (SMPTE time code) used by the Society of Motion Picture and Television Engineers.

The rest of this chapter is dedicated to reviews of Windows-based authoring systems and one QuickTime-based video-editing product.

Basic Hyperlink Authoring Tools

The authoring tools described here, Multimedia ToolBook and CorelDRAW! version 3, are relatively inexpensive and lack some of the power found in more expensive authoring systems. Both are suitable for the beginning or part-time author as well as for the experienced professional.

Multimedia ToolBook

Multimedia ToolBook's $695 price places it at the opposite end of the spectrum from Authorware. It is friendly enough for nonprogrammers and offers a visual development environment with excellent, built-in hypertext support. Version 1.5 is significantly faster than Version 1.0, which resolves the chief complaint about the previous version.

Asymetrix released ToolBook—the PC competitor to Macintosh's HyperCard—at the same time that Windows 3.0 was rolled out. It had a flaw, however. As Robert Dickinson points out in his review, ToolBook 1.0 was like a Mercedes-Benz with every conceivable option but a top speed of ten miles per hour.

ToolBook's potential was that it enabled intrepid, nonprogramming users create Windows applications quickly.

NOTE

The sample application that comes with this book was created in Multimedia ToolBook. Chapter 10, "Authoring a Multimedia Document," offers specifics about the ToolBook environment. The sample application offers a great deal of annotation about the assembly of the document, as well.

Given the more comprehensive discussion of ToolBook in Chapter 10, it seems adequate to say that ToolBook operates in a world of objects, each able to carry out a "script" written in the OpenScript programming language.

The buttons, text fields, and graphical objects can be given simple or complex tasks with a minimum of programming on the part of the author. OpenScript, ToolBook's proprietary programming language, is easy to assimilate when it comes to the most common tasks. And as easy as it is to write linking scripts, ToolBook even can automate the process when it comes to buttons and hotwords.

Multimedia ToolBook comes with some sample applications that are helpful examples and learning tools. Sample books include a multimedia tour, tutorials, a simple database, an impressive ribbon-style calculator complete with financial functions, and a tile game called Taquin. They are all impressive demonstrations of what can be done with ToolBook.

An OpenScript debugger is available from the script window. OpenScript also provides some advanced features for the more experienced Windows developer—including DDE and ways to call DLLs. It works the opposite way, too; other Windows applications can execute OpenScript statements through a DLL. ToolBook, in fact, is tightly integrated into the Windows development environment with tools for creating standard Windows dialog boxes, menus, and icons.

In short, you can create Windows applications that look and behave like Windows applications, but with ToolBook doing all the work. And best of all, Asymetrix provides a distributable runtime version of ToolBook as a standard part of the retail product.

Although ToolBook was originally positioned as a HyperCard competitor, lately it goes head to head with Visual Basic as much as any Mac product. Like Visual Basic, a number of add-on products are available, too.

ToolBook strikes a practical balance between power and ease of use for aspiring Windows-application developers. But be sure to get the most recent version.

CorelDRAW!3.0

Corel Systems' CorelDRAW! Version 3.0 ($595) and its Blockbuster CD-ROM Bundle ($1,295 with an internal drive and $1,395 with an external drive) provide a nice graphics package for professionals and intrepid amateurs. In its new release, the basic package contains both vector-graphic and bit-mapped image editors along with a valuable (if a little limited) clip-art library. The CD-ROM bundle provides more than 10,000 clip-art images, all 1,200 entries in CorelRAW! ArtShow '91, and an art book of the pictures.

CorelDRAW! is a powerful but easy to use program. Documentation is good, and two videotapes are included to help you set up and run Windows-based CorelDRAW!, with a Toshiba Information Systems CD-ROM drive, and a SCSI board. (The board comes as an option with the package.) One of the VHS-format videotapes shows how to install the

CD-ROM drive, and the other is a tutorial on using CorelDRAW!.

Though most of the drawing tools are straight forward, CorelDRAW!'s main drawback is that it works in a wire-frame environment and does not show all the fills or effects unless you preview the rendered image. (This design does speed up the graphics processing, however.)

The other impressive thing about CorelDRAW! is that it is an OLE server. This is a useful production tool. Under Windows 3.1, you can embed objects in files—like a graphic in a word-processing document. To modify the embedded object without relinking it into the document, just double-click on it; this brings up the editor used to create the object—that is, if the editor is an object-linking and embedding (OLE) server. As was just stated, CorelDRAW! *is* an OLE server, so you can use it as an immediate, efficient editor.

The Toshiba CD-ROM drive is multimedia-PC compatible. Toshiba claims that it has one of the fastest access times in the industry.

Much has been said in this chapter about animation, video, and complicated authoring systems. The truth is that a majority of multimedia titles will be simple hyperlinked references that have much text and a few static graphic images. For those authors, CorelDRAW! and CorelDRAW! Blockbuster CD-ROM Bundle are well-suited tools.

Sound-Creation Tools

This section introduces you to a variety of waveform and MIDI tools that make sound creation and editing easier. You also will discover a great resource—sound-effects libraries.

Beyond the simple waveform recorder and MIDI software available directly from the Windows MDK, here are some other tools for multimedia authors who require special audio tools:

MusicTime 1.0 and Encore 2.5 both enable users tocompose, notate, edit, and print sheet music. MusicTime, based on Encore, (for amateur musicians and hobbyists) can record music played on a MIDI-equipped instrument and display it in standard musical notation on-screen. It offers dozens of music symbols, cut-copy-paste editing, and click-and-drag techniques.

Encore, version 2.5, now includes a guitar chord feature that enables useto rs place standard guitar fret diagrams within the score. The list price for MusicTime version 1.0 is $249. Encore version 2.5, is $595. The company can be reached at the following address:

> Passport Designs Inc.
> 100 Stone Pine Road
> Half Moon Bay, CA 94019

A practical alternative to doing your own recording is purchasing libraries. Voyetra's MusiClips is a collection of songs readable by most sequencers and multimedia authoring programs. It provides multimedia authors with a rich and inexpensive source for music and effects.

Musicians can use the Type 1 Standard MIDI files to edit songs voiced for the Roland LAPC and Creative Labs Sound Blaster cards. (They are easily edited for other synthesizers, too.) All the music consists of noncopyrighted compositions, either in the public domain or created by Voyetra, so no permissions or royalties are required.

The $149 Collector's Edition of the library contains over 150 tracks:

➤ Categories include Holiday, Religious, Patriotic, and Ethnic.

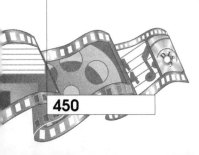

➤ The 31 Classical selections range from Bach inventions to the William Tell Overture.

➤ Original works are mood music in various pop and jazz styles—catalogued by description: "Sensitive and Emotional" or "Forceful and Steady."

If you want to edit the MIDI files but do not have a keyboard, you can do it from your computer's keyboard instead. *PC Magazine* editor Charles Petzold has written an article about creating MIDI files from your computer. You simply can download a program called KBMIDI.EXE from PC MagNet. (There is even C++ source code that Petzold says compiles under Borland C++ 3.0 and Microsoft C 7.0.)

Animation Tools

This section introduces you to three different animation authoring tools: Authorware, Gold Disk, Inc. Animation Works, and Macromedia Action.

Authorware

At $8,000, Authorware Professional for Windows (which originated on the Mac) is definitely on the high end of the most expensive authoring systems. As Alfred Poor says in his review, "If the name Authorware Professional for Windows doesn't say it, then the $8,000 list price will get the point across: This is an industrial-strength authoring tool...You probably will not want to pick this for casual use...."

Authorware projects are navigated with a visual flowchart. In fact, productions are created by dragging and dropping icons that represent media elements (11 different types) onto the flowchart. The flowchart approach to authoring forces you to work in small, manageable portions instead of displaying the entire presentation's detail all at once.

Authorware's icons are straightforward:

> *Display* places text and graphics on the screen.

> *Animation* moves an image around the screen along straight or curved paths. (You also can play canned animations from other applications.)

> *Erase* enables you to remove individual items from the screen.

> *Wait, Decision,* and *Interaction* control branches, loops, and delays.

> *Calculation* performs mathematical processes, calls special control functions (including user-defined procedures), or jumps to other files or programs.

You add an icon by dragging and dropping it into your flowchart. Icons serve a number of functions. Double-clicking on the Display icon opens a graphics editor for drawing basic shapes, adding text, or importing other graphics.

Despite a reasonably intuitive interface, its complexity is reflected in a steep learning curve. But complexity is not all bad. Authorware's main strength, in fact, is its comprehensive set of branching features.

For example, if you create a loop for the user to answer a question, you can limit the number of attempts or the length of time allowed for the response. You can offer multiple-choice answers, or you can have the user type in text; a sophisticated string-matching feature watches for the right answer. Users can drag and resize areas. You easily can create hot spots for mouse-clicks, and Authorware even willdraw attractive buttons and check boxes automatically. By using the Calculation icon, you can keep track of a user's correct answers compared to the number of attempts, and then branch to different sections based on that data.

Authorware productions execute on either Mac or DOS-based systems. It even can compile productions with the runtime module into standalone EXE files that run directly under Windows without the need for special DLLs. (The EXE files can be quite large, however.)

Authorware takes time to learn, but comes with an excellent tutorial, a number of sample applications, and a collection of source modules that you can add into your own applications. The package's $8,000 price tag is justified if you develop Windows Multimedia on a regular basis. If you do not, there a nonprofessional version of Authorware, Authorware Star, will be available soon.

Gold Disk Inc. Animation Works

In a PC Week Labs evaluation, Animation Works provided powerful, high-level authoring tools that were simpler than those found in products aimed strictly at multimedia professionals. The program also was easier to use than the low-end ToolBook, though its features compared with more advanced multimedia packages. Animation Works Interactive, in fact, aims at higher and more powerful animation tools.

Animation Works takes a cell-based approach to animation in which presentations are created a frame (screen) at a time. Frames are played back at an adjustable rate—the default rate is ten per second. Frames contain the media elements that Animation Works calls "actors."

Animation Works provides a collection of ten basic precomposed background templates. With them, you can create visuals such as bar graphs, bullet charts, and title screens. They even include built-in animations such as bullet charts that build one at a time and titles that dissolve in and out of the slide. Animation Works Interactive provides 20 background bit maps and 17 sounds. Its bit-map editor works with several common bit-map formats, which opens it up to clip-art libraries and scanned images.

Animation Works Interactive provides tools for manipulating actors in each scene, though there is nothing like the scripting language found in Macromedia Director. Each actor is manipulated using path tools for determining speed and direction.

Text elements and more complicated animations are manipulated with the same set of tools. (Animation Works includes special text tools and animations tools, including: a movie editor, a cell editor for creating or editing actors, a bit-map editor, and a runtime player. You can distribute up to 100 copies of the player before it is necessary to upgrade the license from Gold Disk.)

Animation Works Interactive and Action also can produce interactive animations that branch, loop, and gather input from buttons. This profusion of tools is confusing at first, but the application's functionality is covered entirely by commands from the menus.

Navigation under Animation Works Interactive is handled by a storyboard and a cue sheet. The storyboard shows thumbnail sketches of key frames, though they cannot be rearranged in the storyboard. The cue sheet is an event listing similar to a video editor's. A Timeline window looks like a project-management chart with bars indicating the start and stop times of different actors in the presentation. The start, duration, and exit of each object is adjusted by simply dragging bars with the mouse.

Though a bit complicated at first glance, Animation Works Interactive does have excellent on-line help and written tutorials that explain the basic concepts of animation, commands, and procedures.

Despite the documentation, Animation Works Interactive is still a complicated product to use effectively. The tricky concept of registered motion, for example, was covered well in the tutorials. (Without registered motion, a person who is walking appears to slide along the floor, and a flying bird appears to bob up and down unnaturally.)

Animation Works Interactive includes other special tools. A gravity tool enables you to automatically adjust the direction and rate of acceleration for downwardly moving objects. A magnetize tool enables users to define the relative motion between two objects. (In one example, the magnetize tool attaches a bomb to a plane, so that the bomb follows the horizontal position of the plane as it falls vertically.) Tools like these make animations appear natural and professionally produced.

Macromedia Action

Macromedia, as you will recall, is a pioneer in the field of multimedia authoring tools. Action is their Windows multimedia authoring system. This sectionreviews its use.

Action is targeted at business professionals who do not have the time or budget for serious studio production. Presented the 1991 PC/Computing Most Valuable Product award, Action is as easy to use as any Windows presentation program. The principle difference is that Action adds three types of tools to the standard presentation package: motion, sound, and links that allow branching from one part of a presentation to another. Controls resemble the controls on a

VCR. A timeline displays the synchronization of objects, whether they are text, graphics, sound, or video.

Though it is currently on the drawing board, Action does not contain a runtime module. You must "print" your presentation out to videotape and play it from a standard VCR. This requires an NTSC output card.

Some of Action's special features are as follows:

➤ You can select title-page templates from ten bundled template families. Templates make it easier to create presentations because pieces of transitional animation, as well as the graphic design, already have been done for you. Each template contains a timeline on which all its objects appear.

➤ *Compressed View* is available on the Control menu. It shows all the objects in the scene and allows editing with a click on the object. You can toggle quickly between Compressed and Scene views.

➤ You can choose from either WAV, Redbook, or MIDI audio. (This feature requires a sound card.) Templates include sound objects, and a library of sounds is available. Sounds are synchronized on the Timeline.

➤ Templates for horizontal or vertical bar charts, organization charts, and pie charts are provided. It does not include a formal charting module, so graphing data is less than easy. You also can create a chart in Excel, copy it to the Windows Clipboard, and use Paste Metafile to paste the chart into Action. You even can add motion to the chart or any of its elements.

➤ You can group objects.

➤ Scene Sorter enables you to click and drag scenes to rearrange the order in which they appear.

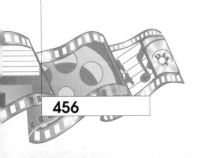

Video Tools

The video tools presented in this section are IconAuthor (an authoring system that has the best support for linking video into your title), Adobe Premiere (a Mac-based video editing and effects suite), and the Video Toaster.

IconAuthor

IconAuthor has the most powerful and flexible video support of the three packages, though its $4,995 price tag positions it in the middle of the authoring-system price range. Also flowchart-based, it is easy to use but unwieldy for large productions. IconAuthor's latest release—version 4.0—is supported by Multimedia Windows.

Like Authorware, IconAuthor provides a visual approach to multimedia authoring. You select a Display icon to tell the program to show a graphics image. An Input icon tells the program to wait for a key-press or mouse-click before advancing to the next step. Drop an icon on the workspace, and it is automatically connected into the visual flowchart of your multimedia production—precisely where you placed it.

IconAuthor also has plenty of branching tools for developing interactivity in your presentations. Toolbars organize tool icons into seven group folders. Compared with older versions of IconAuthor that displayed nonessential elements, this new interface is far easier to use. Some of Icon Author's features are as follows:

> Flow icons control routines for menus, if-then branches, and loops.

> Input icons accommodate user interaction from the keyboard or mouse.

➤ Output icons place bit-mapped images on the screen, set text with special fonts, draw graphics, and send output to printers or disk files.

➤ Data icons manage variables—for example, reading and writing stored values and working with dBASE files. They make it easy to evaluate user responses or provide cumulative, context-sensitive feedback.

➤ Multimedia icons access Multimedia Windows' components. A generic MCI icon can be used for making direct MCI calls, and video and sound icons are available, as well.

➤ Custom icons represent a set of prebuilt MCI routines designed to help you add CD-audio, MIDI, and wave-form audio elements.

➤ Extensions icons handle DDE and DLL support, controlling external devices through a serial port and managing subroutines.

Icon Author has flowchart Zoom and scroll bars. You can open more than one production flowchart at a time, which is extremely handy when you are creating a new production based on an existing one. And you can tile or cascade all open flowchart windows. Toolbars are available for frequently used commands: cut, copy, paste, and debugging, for example.

IconAuthor provides five additional programs that enables you to create images: a simple drawing program, the SmarText editor, IconAnimate (which enables you to move bit-mapped images), a Video editor that can be used for complex video effects, and RezSolution which changes the format and dimensions of a bit-mapped image. (The Video editor requires an external videodisc or videotape player in conjunction with a supported NTSC video overlay card.)

As mentioned earlier IconAuthor has excellent video support, making it the logical choice if you plan to use videodiscs or videotape in your productions. On the other hand, some weaknesses are as follows:

➤ Support of Multimedia Windows MCI is limited, and the MCI icon is difficult to use—poorly documented, except for a Windows help file.

➤ Motion can be uneven and have an unpolished look.

➤ File management is rigid, forcing you to put all files of a given type in the same subdirectory.

➤ Complex productions can become unwieldy in spite of the scrolling and zoom features.

AimTech recognizes that IconAuthor is sophisticated and not easy to learn, so the $4,995 price tag includes four days of training. Its runtime module sells for $50 per copy.

NewTek's Video Toaster

The Toaster unquestionably ushers in the era of desktop video, delivering the capabilities of a $100,000 production studio for $4,000. First available with the Amiga 2000 series, the Toaster is now available for Macintosh computers; a PC version is close to being available (if not already on the market).

The Toaster consists of a stand-alone workstation linked via serial cable to a card on the bus. The workstation condenses much of a television studio's video equipment into one easy-to-use PC companion box. It is compatible with a variety of Macintosh and PC file formats, and it comes ready to operate with a video switcher, digital effects, three-dimensional animation, broadcast paint, 35ns character generator, frame-grabber, still store, and two true-color broadcast-quality frame buffers. (The Toaster Workstation/30 provides all the functions of the standard Toaster Workstation, but adds the additional power of Motorola's 68030 processor. The processor runs at a speed of 50mHz to give the 3-D animator some punch.)

The Toaster is a product that is defining an industry. According to Christina Knighton, NewTek spokesperson, former President Bush's staff used the Toaster every night to edit and prepare the news broadcasts for his viewing. The U.S. embassy in Moscow requested one during the August coup so that videotapes could be edited to keep up with the event itself. Cable television stations MTV and VH1 have Toasters, and there is a Toaster production company called Nutopia.

Adobe Premiere

On the Mac side, Adobe Premiere ($495) is a powerful desktop video program for editing QuickTime movies. It is an impressive product. It has a streamlined user interface, sophisticated editing tools, the capability to import QuickTime movie files, PICS, PICT, and Adobe Photoshop images, and many special-effects filters. Adobe Premiere is useful in spite of the fact that some essential features are missing. (Premiere cannot generate edit-decision lists, and there is no Undo command.)

Adobe Premiere is a full-fledged QuickTime movie-editing studio in software, though you need to start with premade QuickTime movies. (Premiere lacks drivers for QuickTime video digitizers.) It offers sophisticated tools for assembling and editing QuickTime-based video, creating transitions, mixing sound, and overlaying graphics and animation.

A variety of special-effects filters are avaialbe for color balancing, brightness, tinting, posterizing, flipping, and tiling.

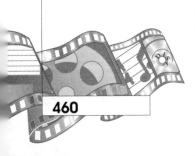

There is even a Mosaic filter, which you can animate by increasing and decreasing the effect as the clip plays. Though the list of compatible special-effect filters is long, it lacks variety and can slow things down.

To conserve disk space during the preliminary stages of movie-making, Premiere does not import the files you are working with—it creates a Project file containing pointers to those files. Similar to a professional video editor, selected clips are listed in a scrollable Project window. A thumbnail picture of each clip, and information on size, duration (in standard SMPTE format), and file type is available for each one.

Double-clicking enables you to play, hear, or see a clip. You can then indicate the in and out points for the clips you want. You can do mixing from the Construction window: by graging in clips from the Project window's edited clip list.

You have two QuickTime channels, an overlay channel, a transition channel (for wipes and dissolves), and three audio channels. After you have arranged your clips, you can pre-view selected frame ranges in a small window. When you are satisfied, Premiere compiles the completed movie as a QuickTime document—a time-consuming process. After movies have been compiled, you can play them with Premiere or with any other QuickTime-compatible application, or you can transfer them to a VCR.

Premiere's documentation is complete. The program is intuitive enough to use without the documentation, but a few tricks and techniquesare not immediately obvious. Adobe Premiere makes QuickTime movies, audio, animation, and graphics accessible to novices, but still satisfies digital-movie experts.

Video Production

All software aside, you still have to generate video. This can be the most challenging aspect of all. Video production takes planning.

Determine a reasonable budget, get some professional help, and above all, have a plan. If you are determined to do it yourself, This section gives you a brief synopsis of the basics. Video production can be broken down into seven steps: development, preproduction, shooting, audio production, graphics production and editing, and post-production. A breakdown of each step follows.

Development

Development is the first step. It can usually be handled by a couple of people who can come up with the core of the idea. Development includes instructional design, scriptwriting, and research, to name a few. The primary deliverable in the development stage is a script. Do not attempt to produce a video without a script.

Preproduction

Preproduction does not begin until after development is completed, reviewed, and approved. Script in hand, the step is to develop a budget for your project.

Many information resources are available; one of them is your state's Film Board. They often will have a guide to professionals and rental companies in the area.

After you have established a budget, make some decisions about how you will do your production. Will you shoot on location, or in a studio of some kind? What kind of equipment will you need to rent? Who will be in the video? Will you need some security? The list is very long, but it is worth it to be well-prepared.

Development and preproduction planning should take much more time to complete than shooting and the remaining steps. Take your time and plan out every detail. Videos are collections of details! Your ideas will not make it to tape if you have too many loose ends.

Shooting

Shooting is what most people think of when they think about movie-making: the lights, the camera, the crew, the actors— and dollar bills streaming out of the window.

Two kinds of shooting methods exist: single-camera film style and multi-camera TV style. Your budget will probably make the choice obvious. The multi-camera live switch is expensive, but it works for teleconferencing and other events. This is high-dollar technology, so beware. If you go the way of the single camera, you open up a variety of options.

By far, the most appealing video will be shot on film. This is nothing that you want to attempt yourself. Of lesser quality, but also professionally acceptable, is component video. This requires a professional crew as well, but a smaller, more manageable one. And finally, you can take your camcorder out and shoot all the video you want. The following is a list of tips:

➤ Eight-millimeter camcorders give the best quality.

➤ Shoot on location. A pretty spot will compensate for staging shortcomings.

➤ Use available light whenever possible. The camcorder will shade (color correct) it for you pretty well.

Hi-8mm video is the best video format available to consumers.

➤ Whenever possible, avoid synchronous sound (watching a person speaking on camera). Use voice-over narratives instead.

➤ Move the camera if you can. A wheelchair makes a great camera dolly.

Obviously shooting is too comples to fully address here, but many good books on small-format, do-it-yourself video production are available. Get one and study it if you think video is in your future.

Audio Production

Audio production has potential to be a headache—particularly if you shoot synch sound. Recording someone in a natural setting is challenging at best. Be advised that a good audio recordist can save the day.

As far as music and sound effects are concerned, record what you can on location and get the rest from a sound-effects library. Do not forget to record "silence" at every shooting location. (It is called "room tone." You and your editor will be glad you did; nothing makes an edit more jarring than jumps in the audio baseline.

Graphics Production and Editing

Graphics production and editing are grouped together here because they have been thoroughly addressed within the context of authoring systems. You will need to invest in an authoring system for sure, unless you want to rely entirely on professional help.

Post-production

Post-production is preparing your job for distribution. Do not confuse editing and post; post production happens only after you have completed your edit. In this phase, you add titles and video effects. (Again, this can be done on your authoring system.) The final deliverable from the post-production stage is the master. This is your source for duplication.

In short, creating multimedia in-house can be a fun and rewarding experience. It also can turn into a money sink. Consult with a professional before you take the plunge.

Part Four:
Authoring a
Multimedia Document

Authoring a Multimedia Document

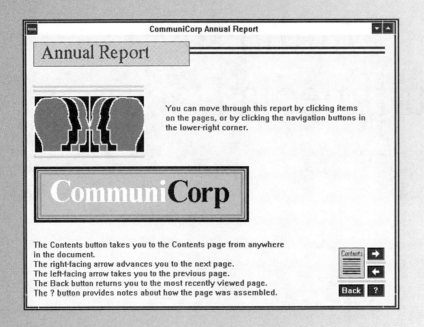

Annual Report

You can move through this report by clicking items on the pages, or by clicking the navigation buttons in the lower-right corner.

CommuniCorp

The Contents button takes you to the Contents page from anywhere in the document.
The right-facing arrow advances you to the next page.
The left-facing arrow takes you to the previous page.
The Back button returns you to the most recently viewed page.
The ? button provides notes about how the page was assembled.

"Think of Multimedia authoring as sculpture rather than writing: know your materials intimately and apply technique with style and restraint. I find it helpful to wear a floppy French beret."—Chris J. Carden, Asymetrix

CHAPTER **10**

Authoring a Multimedia Document

If you read Chapters 7 and 8, you already are familiar with many of the options and choices incorporated in the development of COMMCORP.TBK, the sample application in this chapter. This chapter revisits many of those topics and applies them to the development of the document. It discusses all the following major steps in the decision-making process:

➤ Establishing content

➤ Defining practical boundaries

> ➤ Choosing a development tool

> ➤ Laying out the structure

> ➤ Choosing design elements

The chapter then describes the way the design is turned into a multimedia document:

> ➤ Fleshing out the skeleton of the application

> ➤ Creating objects

> ➤ Establishing links

> ➤ Coding with OpenScript

This chapter is meant to be used with the Communi-Corp application on the enclosed disk. Make sure the program is running while you read the chapter.

This chapter is designed to be used in conjunction with the CommuniCorp Annual Report application on the *Guide to Multimedia Disk*. CommuniCorp is a fictitious international manufacturer of network hardware, software, and modems. You may find it helpful to load this program into Windows and run it when you reach the section "Planning the Document" in this chapter. The CommuniCorp Annual Report application on the *Guide to Multimedia Disk* is helpful in understanding hypermedia—the contents page alone contains a wealth of information about structure, design, and assembly.

When you finish reading the following introduction to CommuniCorp, install the application on your system. Complete setup instructions are provided.

Introducing the Communi-Corp Multimedia Document

The file COMMCORP.TBK on the enclosed sample disk has two purposes. At first, it seems to be a corporate report that

illustrates a multimedia document at work. Less obvious, though, is its design as a training tool. Almost every page contains hypermedia-style annotation about the assembly and design of the document.

As you may have guessed from looking at the TBK extension, the file was assembled in Multimedia ToolBook. Your sample disks include Runtime ToolBook files—the distributable version of Multimedia ToolBook. The files enable you to run the sample application in Reader mode, which is roughly comparable to the file being read-only. You cannot change the document appreciably or perform any scripting. The sample application compensates for this limitation by offering extensive pop-up notes and design tips.

CommuniCorp is a corporate report in a multimedia format. It presents a wide range of information about Communi-Corp, a fictitious company. If you ever have seen corporate reports, you know how text-heavy they can be. Communi-Corp wants to circulate information about the company in an approachable, interesting manner. The multimedia version of its report has a number of applications and will be distributed to many different types of users.

> **T**raining annotations in the CommuniCorp Annual Report are concealed in pop-up fields to avoid distractions.

Installing the Sample Application

If you are ready to install the sample application, look at the following checklists and follow the installation instructions.

Checking the Sample Disk

You should have one floppy disk that contains the following files:

➤ COMMCORP.TBK (the multimedia document)

➤ Runtime ToolBook files

➤ PC Speaker driver (a Microsoft product that enables PCs to play audio without a sound board)

➤ PREZ.WAV (an audio file)

➤ NAR.DIB (a wide-format, device-independent bit map)

Checking System Requirements

At a minimum, your system should meet these hardware and software requirements:

➤ A personal computer with a 16 MHz 80386SX or higher processor

➤ 2M RAM (4M recommended)

➤ A high-density drive (if you have only a 1.4M high-density drive, copy the sample disk to a 1.4M disk)

➤ A hard disk with 4M available disk space

➤ A monitor and graphics card for VGA or better

➤ A Windows-compatible mouse or pointing device

➤ DOS 3.1 or higher

➤ Windows 3.0 or higher

Installing the CommuniCorp Annual Report

To load and run the CommuniCorp Annual Report (the sample multimedia application), place the first installation disk in a 1.2M high-density drive.

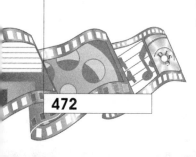

NOTE

If the A: drive is not the name of the drive you will use to install CommuniCorp, substitute another drive letter in the following steps.

1. Insert the disk in the disk drive.

2. Choose <u>R</u>un from Program Manager's <u>F</u>ile menu.

   The Run dialog box appears.

3. Type the following command in the <u>C</u>ommand Line field:

   A:SETUP

4. Press Enter or click on OK.

   The CommuniCorp Annual Report Setup dialog box appears and asks whether you want to change the default directory for the installation or any multimedia components or both.

5. The default directory for the new files is C:\COMMCORP. If you want to install CommuniCorp in a different directory, enter the new directory name in the Copy to field.

6. Below the Copy to field, you are asked to select the CommuniCorp components you want to install (the executables, the sample application, and the PC Speaker driver). Click on Continue if the default is acceptable, or deselect the files you do not want and then choose Continue.

   If the files copy properly, the following message appears:

   Installation of the Report is complete.

7. Click on OK.

Although the files are now in the COMMCORP directory, follow these steps to install the PC Speaker driver from the Control Panel:

Install all the files unless you already have TOOLBOOK.EXE on your system. If you have TOOLBOOK.EXE, you may want to exclude ToolBook Executables from the installation process.

Some AST computer systems are not compatible with the PC Speaker driver. You may get partial sound (or none) when you try to play the audio file featured in CommuniCorp.

You may want to uninstall the driver when you have heard the audio demonstration. PC Speaker can cause some surprising sounds when you press certain keys on the keyboard (Esc, for example).

1. Open Control Panel

2. From the Control Panel, double-click on the Drivers icon.

3. Choose **A**dd from the dialog box.

4. Choose **Unlisted or Updated Driver** from the list box, then click on OK.

5. The Install Driver dialog box appears and prompts you for the disk that contains the sound driver. The appropriate response is to enter the path to the installation directory you chose. If you used the default C:\COMMCORP, for example, type that name rather than accept the A:\ default offered by the dialog box.

The driver file on the installation disk is compressed. The expanded version is in the installation directory—specify the installation directory (C:\COMMCORP or whatever you indicated in the CommuniCorp Annual Report Setup dialog box).

6. Click OK or press Enter.

   The Add Unlisted or Updated Driver dialog box appears.

7. Click on OK.

   The PC-Speaker Setup dialog box appears.

8. In the <u>L</u>imit field, slide the slider bar all the way to the right. The setting **No Limit** appears.

9. Click on OK to accept the speaker settings.

   The System Setting Change dialog box appears.

10. The last step is to quit and restart Windows. Click on <u>R</u>estart Now in this dialog box to reboot the system immediately (you may hear an audio sound during the reboot), or click on <u>D</u>on't Restart Now to exit from the setup. If you choose not to restart Windows, you will not hear sound when you open the sample application.

The <u>T</u>est button in PC-Speaker Setup provides a short audio file to test your settings.

Running COMMCORP.TBK

The CommuniCorp program is launched from the Program Manager. Look for the CommuniCorp Annual Report Group and double-click on the report's icon.

NOTE   Another option for launching the CommuniCorp program is to double click on COMMCORP.TBK from the File Manager.

You should see the introductory screen of CommuniCorp's report.

NOTE CommuniCorp is a color application. If it starts in black and white on your color monitor, your computer may have fooled the installation program. Open the WIN.INI file (use Sysedit, the EDIT command in DOS 5, Notepad, or any text editor or word processor) and search for the [ToolBook] section. If the setting StartupSysColors=false appears, change it to StartupSysColors=true. Save and close WIN.INI, then start the CommuniCorp Annual Report.

Navigating CommuniCorp's Annual Report

The opening screen is the first page of a 40-page ToolBook document. Every page features a cluster of four navigation buttons (and a ? button) in the lower right corner. The functions are explained on this contents page.

The Contents button is a colorful representation of the Contents page. You press the right arrow to advance the screen one page; you press the left arrow to display the preceding page in the document. The Back button returns the most recently viewed page to the screen.

The ? button has an entirely different function. It displays information about the design and assembly of the objects on the page.

Explore the document. Look closely at the Contents page—it is a road map of the entire document. From that page, you can jump to the beginning of any section or to any subtopic.

Use the question mark button to learn more about the design and construction of CommuniCorp's Annual Report.

476

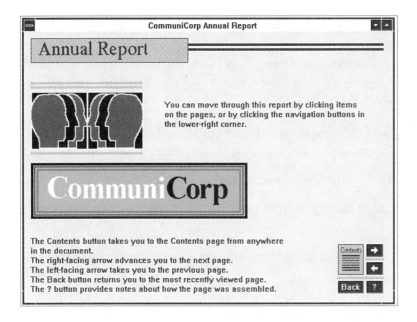

Read the instructions on the Contents page so that you can advance to distant subtopics and not have to rely exclusively on the navigation buttons. Look at the document's structure and content so that you can evaluate how well it meets some of the criteria set forth in the planning stage.

Planning Your Multimedia Document or Application

The CommuniCorp sample application included on the *Guide to Multimedia Disk* serves two purposes: it presents a corporate report in a multimedia format, and is a training tool. All the decisions made during the development stage must be made with both goals in mind.

To begin the process of developing your own multimedia application, start by establishing the content and defining the practical boundaries. In this case, a content factor (defining the audience) directly affects some of the practical considerations. It cannot be assumed, for example, that most members of the target audience own sophisticated multimedia hardware.

The following three primary considerations help establish the content of any multimedia program:

➤ Who is the intended audience?

➤ What is the audience supposed to learn from the application?

➤ What multimedia elements convey best the information?

Targeting the Audience

Consider two audiences: the audience that will view CommuniCorp's multimedia report, and the real audience—you.

For the purpose of establishing CommuniCorp's audience, suppose that the report will be distributed to a wide range of people and that it will be used in a number of ways.

CommuniCorp is a progressive company that is doing well financially, and it wants to intrigue potential investors and customers. At a time when socially responsible investing is receiving attention, CommuniCorp wants to draw as much attention to its successes as a model of corporate responsibility as it does to its financial successes.

The interactive report may be displayed in the lobbies of the company's various division headquarters. In that case, the informational piece is intended to engage random visitors.

It may be distributed to certain significant investors known to be enthusiastic computer users. It is not intended to replace the annual report—after all, that comprehensive

document must meet equally comprehensive legal requirements. For computer fans, the report is intended to be a
promotional piece that disseminates interesting information
in a more entertaining manner.

The report may be used as a presentation in a stockholders'
meeting. The report must be capable of being modified easily
so that it can be tailored for this type of meeting.

The CommuniCorp Annual Report may be distributed to
selected investment houses and bankers as an accompani-
ment to the standard print version of the annual report.

The real audience, though, is you. Most people who are
reading *A Guide to Multimedia* are learning about multimedia. It is not reasonable to expect your system to include
video overlay cards, sound boards, or media playback devices because you may not be committed to multimedia just
yet. A typical reader may be content for now with a 386
machine that runs Windows.

On the other hand, it is reasonable to expect a user to be
comfortable in the Windows environment. Virtually none of
the training must guide a user through Windows navigation
techniques. This tutorial chapter assumes a mouse is available and the CommuniCorp application does not have to
provide keyboard-only navigation.

The following ideas for the sample application are based on
an assessment of CommuniCorp's audience and you:

➤ Because the sample application must be useful to the
   widest possible range of users, it must run on a system
   not geared for multimedia. In other words, flash is
   sacrificed for the sake of usability.

➤ Assume that the user has a 386 machine running Windows 3.0 or higher.

Although the CommuniCorp Annual Report is a good template for business hyper-media, its main purpose is to help you visualize effective and entertaining multimedia.

➤ Although the report must serve two audiences, its value as a training document receives priority. Some technical credibility as a corporate report can be sacrificed in the interest of providing useful information to the primary audience: readers of this book.

Setting Goals

What is the audience supposed to get from the document? From a CommuniCorp standpoint, the audience should receive a fair amount of detail about the company's success—including such financial details as those typically seen in corporate reports. More important, the document should be a promotional piece—the user should have the impression that CommuniCorp is more than a competently run business: it has a great corporate image and a sense of responsibility to the community and its employees.

From the standpoint of the real audience—you—the document should illustrate a well-planned, well-executed multimedia application. It should use multimedia to teach multimedia.

Use the question mark button (?) to learn more about the purpose and design of each element in the annual report.

When you click on the question mark button (?) in the report to examine pop-up annotations, you see valuable notes about a variety of topics:

➤ How items are laid out and linked

➤ How design elements can be used for organization and decoration

➤ Some subjective notes about aesthetics

The information you gain from the pop-ups should help you later, when you imagine how to apply the information you learned to projects that excite you.

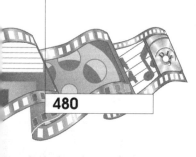

Choosing Effective Multimedia Elements

The most effective multimedia elements are not always within your grasp (see the following section, "Defining Practical Boundaries").

For the purposes of this document, all multimedia elements should be *effective* illustrations—after all, this report discusses the development and assembly of multimedia projects. You should see all the different elements in action and how they are incorporated.

Although video and MIDI files can be tremendously helpful and interesting, they are not effective if a user cannot play them back. For this reason, you need to determine whether the audience for your multimedia project will be able to use all the media you want to include. The report must contain elements that almost any user can play back.

While you read through this chapter, consider the multimedia elements used in CommuniCorp's Annual Report:

➤ Text

➤ A few bit maps

➤ A simple animation

➤ An audio file that can be played without a sound board

These media are used because they can be played on almost any machine. When you determine the media you can use and will use, you have solved the last step in establishing the project's content. The next step is to determine the scope of your document within the context of the practical world.

Defining Practical Boundaries

This section can also be called "Reality Rears Its Ugly Head." Although the preceding section concludes that flash should be sacrificed for usability, that is not the only reason flash is sacrificed. Budgets and time constraints are two of many limitations all multimedia developers must contend with.

The developers of this book's fictitious Annual Report also had constraints and limitations. One limitation the developer of this book's sample application had to accept was a ceiling on the amount of money that could be spent. The cost of the CommuniCorp application was tied to the cost of this book. Costs had to be kept under control. One challenge for controlling costs, for example, was to try to retain essential training information without incorporating high-end multimedia elements.

Time also was a factor in creating the sample application included on your *Guide to Multimedia Disk.* The Annual Report had to be produced in a few weeks so that the author could write this chapter and still meet deadlines.

A few other concerns this book's developer had to consider included:

➤ The budget for duplication and distribution of the sample application dictated that it be presented on one 1.2M floppy disk.

➤ The development tool must have distributable, affordable run-time files.

➤ Minimize the amount of programming a multimedia specialist must do.

➤ Have the author of the chapter do most of the programming. Problems and complexities can be passed on to an experienced programmer.

Although you eventually may face similar restraints, you may have more time or a larger budget if your superiors have made multimedia a priority.

Choosing Audio and Visual Elements

Now that project parameters have been defined more closely, it is easy to identify the types of audio and visual elements that can be used. The fictitious company used in this chapter has no restraints; therefore, imagine CommuniCorp has a corporate video and no budget limitations. A few guidelines do exist, though, including the following:

➤ Only existing (or easy-to-create) visual elements can be used. Clip art and original bit maps work well.

➤ Existing bitmaps can be used with no-cost permission.

➤ No video can be created for the project. Apart from the prohibitive cost, few users have the necessary playback equipment.

➤ Create one audio file that can be played back without a sound board. The size of the file must be within the space limits of the distribution disk.

➤ Minimize the number of elements that might require paid permission.

Many issues have been clarified, which may help you choose the right development tool for your project. Your choice of authoring software probably will be determined by several factors already discussed.

Choosing a Development Tool

The choice of a development tool for the CommuniCorp Annual Report was a relatively painless part of the decision-making process.

Chapter 7 "Planning Your Multimedia Project" includes a section that discusses choosing the right authoring tool for the job.

Multimedia ToolBook was chosen for the CommuniCorp project for a few reasons:

➤ Runtime ToolBook easily fits on one 1.2M disk enclosed in this book. The runtime ToolBook is small enough to leave plenty of room for the other necessary files.

➤ Asymetrix, the company that developed Multimedia ToolBook, has a liberal distribution policy. It graciously provided permission for distribution to third parties, with some stipulations.

Asymetrix also granted permission to use a large bit map that was in one of its sample applications.

➤ ToolBook is relatively easy to learn and use. It is simple—even for nonprogrammers—to script commonly used elements such as hotwords and buttons.

NOTE

Examine sample applications made on different development tools. These samples usually point out the software's capabilities and limitations. In one of Multimedia ToolBook's sample applications, for example, you can view a wide bit map in panning mode.

TIP

If you need to get permission for any part of your project, ask as early as possible. The grantor usually must do more than simply say, "Sure, go ahead." Most often, your superior must navigate legal channels, and you may have to comply with some requirements or restrictions.

Laying Out the Structure

In Chapter 8, "Avoiding 'Muddymedia,'" the most common forms of electronic structure are discussed. Two of them, freeform and linear, are best suited to the CommuniCorp document because the sample application is used in different ways.

A *freeform* design accommodates users who are likely to browse through the document in no particular order. They follow their interests and jump to distant subtopics and return to a central starting point. This method fits the description of a majority of the audience.

The default structure should be linear, however, so that document makes sense in a linear format. A *Linear* multimedia design follows closely a book model—the skeletal structure is that of a story line. Like a book, the user should be able to display the document a page at a time.

How should training notes and annotations be presented? Because the default structure is linear, the annotations also should be linear. If you study the document with the intention of seeing how it is put together, for example, you should be able to get the most effective help by advancing methodically, a page at a time. The linear method is the only way notes can be designed in a predictable order. (The notes still should be helpful, however, if you do not view them in a particular order.)

Based on these thoughts, the document should invite you to jump around but not discourage you from following a relatively linear path.

The CommuniCorp sample document is designed to be used linearly or by jumping to each topic that interests you.

Determining the Hierarchy of the Multimedia Document

See the section "Creating the Electronic Skeleton" in Chapter 8 to help you establish a hierarchy for your document or application.

The specific content for your project must be identified before you can establish its hierarchy. This process involves creating a plan for the way the most important chunks of information are presented. Is a map the best idea? A table of contents?

This process requires some research if you are not intimately familiar with the topic. For this chapter's project, refer to Elmer L. Winter's *A Complete Guide to Preparing a Corporate Annual Report*. This guide discusses the essential components of an annual report. When you need to create an annual report or any other type of financial document, always remember too much information is better than too little.

Of all the topics you can include in an annual report, seven major sections seem most important:

➤ A company profile

➤ A letter from the company president

➤ Highlights of the past year

➤ Earnings and dividend statements

➤ Balance sheets

➤ Strategies for meeting corporate goals

➤ Projections for the upcoming year

This list shows just the sections that can be included. These sections, in addition to their subtopics, cover a wide range of material about the company—enough to make the document an information-filled promotional piece, and enough to make it resemble a corporate report.

To organize this information, you need to determine its hierarchy, or the order in which the information is presented. One way to help you with this process is to think about the navigation options for the report's user. The central navigation point can be a map, but this annual report really needs a table of contents. Although a table of contents has obvious sections, it sometimes must be presented in linear form and is modeled after a corporate report, which is typically a text document.

TIP

If you have trouble choosing a hierarchy, try creating *storyboards*—that is, try to put topics to paper. If you create a page for each topic and attempt to categorize them, you soon will see whether the topics are discrete and unrelated or interconnected.

Storyboarding the Document

It is helpful to work on paper when you are in the development stage. The process of assigning each topic to a page can begin to suggest links and specific content ideas. Write notes about page content as you imagine possibilities.

The storyboarding process can be thorough and time-consuming or quick. In the early developmental stages of creating the fictitious CommuniCorp report, a piece of paper represented every topic. A heading was written on every page. (The headings are the labels that appear on every page in the final document.) Groups of topics were organized, and some individual topics were weeded out. The result was 40 pieces of paper that already had a few ideas and links drawn on them.

A project milestone for any multimedia developer occurs when a potential final outline is finished. If you are using ToolBook for your multimedia application and you have finished a rough draft of your project's final outline, you should begin to name pages according to how they are referenced in the code. You will be glad that you did when it is time to assemble the document.

In the storyboard process for CommuniCorp, a brief, descriptive name was assigned to be used during the coding phase. On the page titled Corporate Profile, for example, the storyboard also showed the name CorpProfile. In the ToolBook environment, you should assign mnemonic names—not just numbers—to objects. Object names are used in ToolBook code in the following manner:

```
to handle buttonUp
    go to page "CorpProfile"
end
```

This piece of code tells an object (probably a button) to display the page named CorpProfile when a user clicks on the object. In a 40-page document, a specific page with a name is much easier to remember than numbered page.

Although it may seem premature to assign object names to this project, names are helpful when if you intend to write linking ideas on your storyboards. Suppose, for example, that in the assembly stage a storyboard note shows a button with a link to PrezLetter. You can write the code immediately because your storyboard provides the object's name. If it said only that the link was with the president's letter, you would have to stop and find the name or number of the correct page before coding.

TIP

Pages assigned with names are easier to remember than numbered pages. Named pages also help if you have to reorganize the structure or hierarchy of your document. To avoid ruining any code written before a major reorganization, make sure you assign names to pages instead of numbers. If your code says "go to page PrezLetter," the link goes to page PrezLetter, no matter where it falls in the numeric order of pages.

After the storyboard pages for the ComuniCorp Annual Report are in a probable final order, they are numbered. This precaution has nothing to do with the coding or assembly: it preserves the progress to date in case the papers are shuffled accidentally.

If you are a "visual" person, you might benefit from spreading out all the storyboard pages. This step can help you associate and add to your notes with minimum paper-riffling. In addition, it is easier to scan for possible links if you can see all the pages at one time.

When your storyboards have enough content to provide a good foundation, you can move to the design stage.

You may find yourself developing design ideas and themes just from working with your storyboards.

Choosing Design Elements

Many design ideas for the original CommuniCorp report were conceived as the Contents page was built. The process of creating the table of contents immediately brought up issues of organization, color, and consistency. The Contents page had to display sections, subtopics, and navigation aids.

Organizing by Design

If you have not started the sample application, do so now. The material in this section is more meaningful if you have a visual aid.

Because you are working with visual media, organization is more than just having things in a logical order. You can organize and classify by color, type style, type size, positioning, and other visual elements. These kinds of enhancements to your message—whether it is obvious or understated— make your document easier to use.

The following list shows some design themes you can identify in CommuniCorp:

➤ In most cases, the background and foreground colors complement one another.

➤ The heading for each page is positioned exactly in the same spot and uses the same color scheme.

➤ Each section (first identified on the Contents page) is associated with a unique color. That color is used to display its subtopics on the Contents page, and to indicate the section number of any given page.

➤ Section numbers and other elements associated with the heading are always in a consistent location.

➤ The Contents icon, which appears on every page, is a miniature representation of the Contents page. It shows each section color in order.

➤ Instructions to users are light gray on a blue field.

➤ MS Serif font is used for heading elements. Almost all other text is in the most readable font: System. The only exceptions are those when the System font is not versatile enough for spreadsheet work.

➤ Very few colors are used overall. When consistency is not important, inconsistency makes the pages more visually appealing. Buttons, for example, might be purple on one page and blue on another.

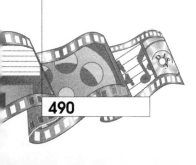

In general, an effort is made to keep pages from looking "busy" or cluttered. Pop-up fields and annotations are a perfect alternative to cluttered pages of information.

During CommuniCorp's development, two additional design decisions had to be made because of concerns about disk space. These concerns also may surface during your project's development:

> ➤ A tip in the ToolBook documentation warns that speed and file size are affected by the use of multiple backgrounds.

The solution to this problem is to use a single background for the entire document. Although it is nice to use different background colors to differentiate different sections, this certainly is not crucial. Different colored screens might even be distracting if a user "hops around" much.

> ➤ How should the training annotations be displayed? One way to show information about the CommuniCorp's design elements is when the user clicks on an object on the page, he or she receives pop-up information or commentary about the object. This approach is not practical, however, unless a second version of the document is created. (The objects on the pages had to be functional for real jumping, not just for training.)

The best way to include training information in the CommuniCorp report was to follow the same suggestions you should use if you want to include additional information in your own document or application: provide users with a single small button they can click on for page notes. Group it with the navigation aids so that it is out of the way. You do not need to create a second version of the document, and you certainly should avoid cluttering the page with extra training buttons such as Text, Graphics, and Buttons.

The CommuniCorp navigation groups appears on the first page of the annual report, with explanations nearby.

The decisions made in this section helped develop the navigation group for CommuniCorp; they also should help you finalize your own application's interface.

The first page of CommuniCorp's Annual Report is not the Contents page because the report is a promotional presentation. For public relations reasons, a title page with the corporate logo is more useful. Navigation aids still are introduced on the title page.

Designing Navigation Aids

Most multimedia documents have four basic navigation options. In most cases, a user should be able to:

➤ Jump to the central page (Contents)

➤ Move forward one page in the sequence

➤ Move backward one page in the sequence

➤ Return to the most recently viewed pages to retrace steps

Look at the navigation group on the first page of CommuniCorp (disregard the ? button for now). Each button appears on that page. The buttons were created on a single background to be used throughout the document.

The Contents button is the most complex. It is a transparent text field with a group of colored lines laid over a button. Because the text field is transparent, the button below it can detect a click. The button's code is simple to write:

```
to handle buttonUp
    go to page "Contents"
end
```

The other buttons and their code in the CommuniCorp Annual Report were cut and pasted from ToolBook sample applications. The only alterations were in their sizes and in

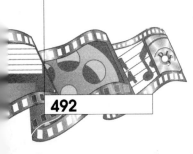

the label for the "Back" button. (Buttons are easy to size and reposition.) The appropriate code came with the buttons.

After the navigation buttons were pasted into CommuniCorp's report, a question mark (?) button was planned to provide annotation for users. This button was not created on the background with the others, but was placed temporarily in the group while sizing and detailing were taking place. The purple lines in the group are nonfunctional, but they tie the group in visually with the color scheme of the page.

After all the navigation buttons were finalized, the ? button was deleted from the background—it is a foreground element. This distinction is explained on the first page of CommuniCorp—if you click on the ? button.

Dialog-Box Options

In some parts of your multimedia document, you may want to offer users a choice. A user, for example, may want to jump to another page or stay where they are, based on the context of a situation. These crossroads are handled easily with a dialog box. The dialog box might ask "Do you want to go to the Transportation page?" You can specify as many as three choices in the ToolBook environment, and coding each choice is easy.

Looking at the ? Button: Pop-up Training

Probably the most important part of the CommuniCorp design for you is the inclusion of pop-up training. The CommuniCorp report resembles a real business document, but it actually is a tutorial. By hiding information in pop-up boxes, this multimedia document can teach you methods of good design and show you the results. Pop-up boxes that you

Disk-space limitations and clutter were eliminated during the design of the Communi-Corp Annual Report by using a button that provides pop-up annotation.

access provide details about CommuniCorp's design and assembly.

TIP

Early in the design process, find out whether your development tool enables you to disable buttons. It might make a difference in how you lay out your navigation group.

During the design of CommuniCorp, unfamiliarity with ToolBook led to an erroneous assumption: the ? button can be programmed to appear disabled on pages with no training annotation. Programming was well under way when it was discovered that the ? button had to be concealed, which made the navigation group look off-balance.

At this point in your application, some basic design elements have been decided. The Contents page is the central navigating point and the document is organized into sections. When possible, consistent use of color and positioning underscore the presentation of particular types of information.

Some of these elements were chosen as the Contents page was being created. ToolBook has enough versatility as a drawing and design tool that it is easy to create objects and move them around. Coding should be done when the design is stabilized, however.

TIP

Resist the temptation to produce repetitive design elements on every page until you are certain that they will stay. If your document is 40 pages long and you change your mind about something that exists on every page, you may resist changing the design.

Gathering Multimedia Elements

The production of multimedia elements for CommuniCorp is not an overwhelming job. Remember that CommuniCorp should not take months to develop. This sample document is supposed to provide training on how to assemble a report, and it must accomplish this task on a relatively simple computer system. For this reason (and for obvious practical reasons), the following assumptions affect the media you can include in the report:

➤ The report cannot have videodisc or CD-ROM elements

➤ The audio cannot be in a format that requires a sound card

➤ The report cannot use photos of nonexistent buildings, products, or people

Multimedia elements you can add to the CommuniCorp report include:

➤ Clip art and graphics that can be imported from sample applications (if you obtain permission)

➤ Bitmaps created in Windows Paintbrush

➤ Animations created with ToolBook draw objects

➤ An audio file that can be played using Microsoft's PC Speaker (or files that do not require a sound board for playback)

➤ Multimedia playback-control buttons taken from ToolBook's widget collection (and stripped of their code if the buttons are to be nonfunctional)

The developers of your *Guide to Multimedia Disks* obtained permission to use figures from Asymetrix Corporation.

Clip Art and Graphics

Clip art does not require permission of any kind as long as you are an authorized user of the source. ToolBook, for example, has a clip-art file. A piece of clip art—a rectangle with three silhouettes—was used to make the CommuniCorp company logo.

The word "CommuniCorp" was created in Paintbrush and imported into ToolBook. The use of Paintbrush to create it offered three advantages:

➤ A slightly better font quality and selection

➤ The kerning (spacing between letters) could be adjusted by cutting and moving the letters

➤ ToolBook text strings within a single field cannot be more than one color. The same is true of Paintbrush, but you can join two separate strings and fine-tune them.

Another graphics element is a wide-screen device-independent bitmap. ToolBook's sample application has a fascinating feature that immediately suggested a use in the CommuniCorp document. The sample displayed a viewing window with two panning buttons for panning left or right. The wide bitmap plays behind the window as you hold down one of the buttons.

Go to the Headquarters page to see an example of a panning photo.

The panning trick is used on the Headquarters page. This feature can be used to pan a wide shot of the interior or exterior of the new CommuniCorp headquarters. Because no wide photograph of CommuniCorp headquarters exists, obviously, the technique is illustrated with the wide bit map in ToolBook's sample application.

NOTE

The panning code is contained in the buttons so that they can be pasted easily into CommuniCorp. The wide bitmap, NAR.DIB, is a large bitmap file. To see the file, look at the contents of your sample application disk.

The NAR.DIB bitmap does not exist as part of the COMMCORP.TBK document; it is accessed when a user enters the Headquarters page. When you installed CommuniCorp, you installed NAR.DIB in the same directory.

Animation

ToolBook makes it possible to create animations in a few ways. The CommuniCorp document features a simple animation that hides and shows a series of *draw objects*—ToolBook vernacular for objects created with the ToolBook drawing tools. The technique is discussed briefly near the end of this chapter.

The Audio File

The only audio element in the annual report included on the *Guide to Multimedia Disk* is part of a letter from CommuniCorp's president, Mr. Kindly. A button on the Text Version page plays audio of a portion of the letter to simulate a CD-ROM. The text is an alternative for those who do not have a CD-ROM drive.

PC Speaker, a Microsoft driver, enables any Windows-based system to play back audio without a sound board. The audio file, PREZ.WAV, was obtained by having someone speak into

Go to the Text Version page in CommuniCorp to hear the President speak.

a microphone hooked into a sound board. The file was edited to clean up the starting and ending points, and then it was saved.

NOTE

To preview the file using Windows' Media Player, you must have a sound board.

Playback Control Buttons

Control buttons are included in this document only as an illustration of ToolBook widgets and as a reminder that users of any multimedia document should be offered some kind of control over playback devices. Because users' systems may not have the MCI driver they need to play back audio and video elements, the media-playback control buttons are disabled (one exception is the panning controls on the Headquarters page). The code for the buttons was included when they were pasted on the page, but subsequently was removed.

Now that CommuniCorp's multimedia elements are identified, the preliminary steps are behind you. It is time to start assembly.

Assembling the Document

The CommuniCorp report is about to take shape. The remaining steps to turn the report into an integrated, easy-to-use multimedia document include:

➤ Fleshing out the skeleton

➤ Creating objects

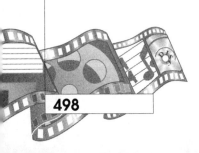

➤ Establishing links

➤ Coding with OpenScript

If you have useful storyboards you can refer to, place them within easy reach.

Multimedia ToolBook (version 1.51) was used as the development tool for CommuniCorp. The document you see as a user differs greatly from what a developer sees. You are viewing Runtime ToolBook, which operates only in Reader mode. In this mode, you cannot:

➤ View the full range of menus

➤ Display or use tools or color palettes

➤ Edit objects or write scripts

➤ Access Help or sample applications

Author mode, on the other hand, has a full complement of drawing tools and menu items that enable you to create and script objects such as buttons, fields, hotwords, and draw objects.

The content and design elements are stable enough for you to begin creating pages. This stability provides a framework for the inclusion of objects.

Fleshing Out the Skeleton

To begin creating the document, you need to decide the priority of the elements on the pages. What do users need to see right away? What information is optional? Answers to these questions help you decide which objects are presented at the first layer. Optional items should be presented with links and hidden pop-ups.

Your approach to creating the document may differ, depending on the development tool you use and your familiarity with it. If you are confident that a particular object has a particular behavior, for example, you may want to write its code right away. It is not realistic to expect that every object in the document will be created before the coding starts.

In an effort to delineate between creating objects and linking them with code, the two processes are described as though they had happened in separate stages.

Creating Objects

In the ToolBook environment, virtually everything is an object. Buttons, fields, draw objects, pages—and even entire books—are programmable objects.

This section introduces the most commonly used ToolBook objects. Again, you are encouraged to look at Communi-Corp's report. The examples shown here are intended to direct you to the document—CommuniCorp is a better illustration.

ToolBook's programming language is called OpenScript. ToolBook is a good authoring package for nonprogrammers because it is easy to link objects and perform elementary moves.

Run CommuniCorp now to help you see and understand the following sections.

If you are interested in the particulars of how objects are created in ToolBook, click on the ? button of CommuniCorp's title page or Contents page. The first two pages are heavily annotated with information.

Background Elements

You cannot differentiate between the background and the foreground in Reader mode. (The background elements are detailed in the annotation for the title page.) An author, however, can display the background separately.

Briefly, the background objects are items that will be carried throughout this document. Because every page has the double gray lines at the top and the navigation group in the lower right corner, those objects are a part of the background.

The section titled "Designing the Navigation Aids," earlier in this chapter, discusses the creation of navigation objects.

Pages and Headings

If you still have the Contents page displayed, you can see the heading in the upper left corner. Every page has a heading and a color scheme similar to this one. The headings were created with text fields, which is the only way to generate text in ToolBook. These particular text fields are objects, but because they do not perform any kind of action, no coding is associated with them.

Because each page receives a heading in the annual report, it makes sense to name the page at the same time. Do you remember the coding names on the storyboards? They now come into play and help you start creating buttons that display other pages for the user.

Buttons

You can create an elementary ToolBook document with just a little knowledge of buttons and scripts. Buttons are a primary navigation tool. You can use buttons to jump to other places to display other objects or to hide objects. The buttons in this document (with the exception of the widget control buttons) perform only those three tasks. With few exceptions, the coding for any one of these tasks consists of three short lines.

Buttons contribute to the organization of the CommuniCorp Annual Report in several ways. Click on a topic button on the Contents page. The resulting display of subtopics is another set of buttons. If you click on one of those buttons, you jump to another page. Leave the subtopics of the Contents page displayed for a moment to examine a few details.

The gray topic buttons are pushbutton-style buttons. This is the default type of button created when you use the button-drawing tool. To change the attributes of the button, such as its style or color, you set Button Properties.

The Button Properties dialog box enables you to make several choices about button styles and provides access to the Script window. A button's appearance or label often makes a suggestion about its action. The script carries out the action.

As an example of how button color can be used for organization and consistency, look at the section numbers (text fields) and the subtopic buttons you displayed. The subtopics are the same color as the section to which they pertain. The colored lines that branch to the subtopics are the same color too. When you get to pages of that section, they have a color-coordinated section number in the upper right corner.

In the following sections, you can see how button links are created with OpenScript code. The links, after all, are more important than are design elements. They control what the user gets to see at any particular time.

Text Fields

Text fields are objects that also can be scripted to perform tasks. They often are used to initiate jumps and to display other objects, but they are more versatile than buttons. You may be able to label a button, but it is limited in the number of characters it can display. Text fields can display large amounts of text, and the text can be formatted.

Text fields commonly are used to display pop-up information. If you have explored CommuniCorp, you have seen text fields in a number of different roles and with a number of different styles.

Hotwords

Hotwords are strings of text specified as objects; therefore, they become programmable. The hotwords you select and create are displayed in a way that sets them off from surrounding text. That is a visual cue to users that something will happen if they click on the hotword.

Words and phrases that require definitions or annotation are often turned into hotwords; a mouse click causes a pop-up text field to show itself. A click on a hotword can also send you to another page.

These are just some of the uses for hotwords. They appear intermittently in CommuniCorp. To see a hotword in action, go to the Operating Objectives page of CommuniCorp and click on the hotword in the green field.

Draw Objects

Draw objects are graphical elements created with drawing tools from ToolBook's tool palette. They can be created with a number of line widths, and can be colorized or filled with a number of patterns. The television animation on the Video Profile page is an example of draw objects being displayed quickly and hidden with OpenScript coding.

Like buttons and fields, draw objects can be programmed to respond to button clicks.

Video Windows

No true video windows exist in CommuniCorp, only graphics elements that represent video windows. (You can find them by looking for Contents lists that refer to videos.) If you plan to program in ToolBook and want to display videodisc (or CD) elements, you should know about a special tool.

Interactive Generation, a multimedia specialist in Seattle, developed "Clipmakers" for IBM's Advanced Academic Systems. CD Audio and Video Clipmakers enable users to edit audio and video elements and to paste the edited material into a ToolBook document. Video Clipmakers enable you to draw a shape and turn it immediately into a live video window. In either case, whether you are adding clips to a document or creating video windows, no coding is required. All necessary code is generated for you.

As you can see, although only a few types of objects exist, they can take a number of different forms. They also have a variety of purposes, which are defined when you start writing the code that connects the objects.

Establishing Links

The discussion of links in this section emphasizes their purpose; much less weight is given to specific examples. If you take an extended trip through CommuniCorp, numerous

links are demonstrated for you. Every time one action leads to another, you are experiencing a link.

In the ToolBook world, links are created between objects. In the CommuniCorp document, buttons can connect you to pages or cause other objects to display or hide. In general, though, their actions are not limited to those functions. You are encouraged to browse through the CommuniCorp document so that you can experience links firsthand. The ? button often provides annotation about linking choices.

Links are easy to create in ToolBook. Three simple lines of code link objects:

1. The user action to which the object should respond, usually a mouse-button click or double-click.

2. The action that should take place when the click happens; often, a click results in the user going to another page or in another object being shown or hidden

3. The end of the instructions for that action

The code might look like this:

```
to handle buttonUp
show field "p1info"
end
```

Button Links

Button links are the most common tool for steering users in a certain direction or for offering possible side trips.

Buttons do not usually display information other than to offer options or transportation. When they are linked to pop-up text fields or to other pages, however, they can become a wealth of information.

Two objects should be linked if one object can enhance the other or move the user toward a goal.

Buttons that offer side trips are often linked to another page. In some circumstances, you will want to create a button on the destination page that returns the user to the departure point, especially if the user does not have a backtracking button among the navigation aids.

NOTE Refer to the section titled "Special Destinations," later in this chapter for more information about enhanced button navigation.

Text Field Links

Text fields were used in a number of different ways in this document—most often as a static chunk of information. They usually are linked to another object only if a pop-up field is necessary.

NOTE The Contents page is the only text field that is linked extensively. The section numbers are text fields, and are linked to the first page of their corresponding sections. When users click on a section number, they go directly to the beginning of that section.

Go to the Operating Objectives page in Communi-Corp to see a visible text field.

In most cases, a text field pops up when a user clicks on a button associated with the field. The script for that action is contained in the button or hotword (or whichever object) initiates the action. Most of the time, the only scripts written for text-field scripts are hidden instructions.

If you have the Operating Objectives page on-screen, click on the button labeled "Fields of Interest;" it is linked to a text field that appears. Most of the other pop-up text fields on this page are dismissed with a click, such as this one. Try dismissing the text field.

The script for this text field contains a much more interesting script—it is linked to a dialog box that offers a side trip.

To anticipate what the user might need or want is one of the most important parts of linking. In this case, the developer thought that if users were interested in CommuniCorp's business pursuits, they might be interested in looking at CommuniCorp's acquisitions.

Links to Dialog Boxes

If you chose to examine CommuniCorp's acquisitions, you now should be looking at a dialog box created with code in the text field's script.

Make sure the Acquisitions page is on-screen when you read through this section (click on Yes on the Operating Objectives page).

NOTE

The dialog box is not a named object. You do not create it on the page and display it by saying "show dialog Acq." The ToolBook program creates dialog boxes on the fly when it encounters "ask" or "request" code in an object's script.

Click on Yes to go to the Acquisitions page. To return to the Operating Objectives page, just click on the Back button. To forego the side trip, click on No.

Hotword Links

A number of hotword links are in CommuniCorp. They are used in three ways:

➤ To display a paint object (a bitmap of a script window)

> ➤ To annotate captions in graphs and tables (examples are shown in the Divisions and Earnings Statement pages in CommuniCorp)

> ➤ To expand on a comment in a text field

> ➤ To send the reader to another page of possible interest

Hotword links can help organize and divide text into smaller more direct points.

Special-Destination Links

In certain circumstances, the standard navigation aids do not offer a route that is quick enough for a user. Suppose, for example, that on page 5 of a document you offer users a side trip to a section that begins on page 10. The section is made up of seven pages. What do users do when they reach the end of the long section and want to return to page 5? The back-tracking button retraces their steps only one page at a time. The use of a contents page might be quicker, but it probably still would involve a couple of detours.

A well-designed document offers a special button on the last page (or even on strategic pages) of the long section. That special button is linked back to the point of departure: page 5.

You will see some special destination buttons in Communi-Corp. Because CommuniCorp has no long sections, special destination buttons are included primarily for illustration purposes.

Coding with OpenScript

The OpenScript programming language is mentioned briefly here to give you an idea of creating code for the sample CommuniCorp document.

It is not assumed that ToolBook is your chosen development tool; if you are curious enough to want more complete information, look for OpenScript books or documentation.

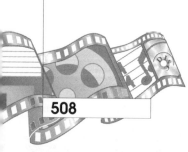

Not all coding tasks are as simple as the ones presented here; for the most part, however, an application as simple as CommuniCorp can be written by a nonprogrammer.

In the ToolBook environment, coding can be applied to any object: buttons, fields, hotwords—even entire pages and books. The application of this code is done with OpenScript, a programming language specific to ToolBook.

Most nonprogrammers find OpenScript easy to use. The most common (and simple) tasks often are scripted with only these three lines:

```
to handle buttonUp
    go to page "OpObjectives"
end
```

The first line usually is the same unless you want to specify a different mouse action as the trigger. You can, for example, connect the action of the second line to a double-click, a right-button click, or the button being held down.

The second line is the one that changes most often. It has a verb and an object. In the preceding example, the action is specified (go to), and the destination is a page object that has been named "OpObjectives". Other commonly used verbs are show and hide.

The third line is a simple end statement.

NOTE
You are not limited to a single action item. By inserting additional lines, you can tell an object to show itself, hide itself, and then do something else.

The television screen animation on the Video Profile page has a lengthy script. The script dictates a series of hide and show activities that take place when the "VidProfile" page is entered.

The coding is created and displayed in an object's script window. The run-time version of ToolBook does not display property-setting dialog boxes and script windows for the objects in CommuniCorp.

TIP

To see an example of a script window, go to the Corporate Profile page. Find the hotword on the page and click on it.

Incidentally, the script window (which is a paint object) has its own script:

```
to handle buttonUp
    hide self
end
```

The script tells it to hide when the user clicks on it.

Determining Who Gets the Code

The object a user clicks on gets the code. This statement oversimplifies matters because exceptions exist. In general, however, it is a good rule of thumb.

The following list illustrates this rule:

➤ If a user clicks on a button and the action is supposed to display a text field, the "show" code is assigned to the button. The resulting text field stays on-screen forever unless it is told to do something else.

➤ If a user clicks on the text field and the action is supposed to dismiss it, the "hide self" code is assigned to the text field.

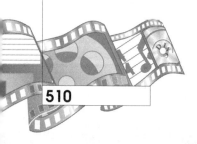

➤ If the text field is supposed to be dismissed by clicking on a second button, the "hide field" code is associated with the second button.

OpenScript is a relatively approachable language. It is popular because people with good ideas can assemble a document (CommuniCorp, for example) and not need to know programming languages.

Now you have seen the project from start to finish, at a level of detail that is practical for orientation purposes. Whether you use ToolBook or another authoring package, you should be able to apply some of these principles to your own projects.

"The entertainment and information industries will no longer be monolithic, impersonal, synchronous, colloquial or prepackaged. They will be redefined as distributed, responsive to consumers' personal needs and interests, timely, international and dynamically presented." - Walter Bender, Principal Research Scientist, MIT's Media Laboratory

The Future of Multimedia

Multimedia technology changes so rapidly that predicting the future is a tricky proposition. Despite this difficulty, certain trends have emerged and will continue to gain importance. These trends will shape multimedia's evolution and dramatically affect the way you live and work.

As this technology evolves it will change everything, from entertainment, to education, to the manner in which you hold business meetings. Three forces are driving this evolution:

➤ Dramatic improvements in microprocessor power

➤ Software improvements

➤ The convergence of the technology, communications, entertainment, and consumer-electronics industries

Increasing Computer Power

The first and most important reason for the changes in multimedia technology is the ever-increasing power of microprocessors. A new generation of chip is developed every 18 months. The new Intel Pentium chip, the successor to the 80486, is capable of more than 100 million instructions per second (MIPS). This type of processing power for a desktop machine was inconceivable five or six years ago.

Not only has the desktop computer become more powerful, but specialized chips are being developed to handle the specific demands of multimedia applications. Digital signal processing (DSP) chips, for example, are currently being designed to handle the compression and decompression of audio, imaging, and video.

A compression standard will enable the same file to be used on different platforms.

DSP chips already are being built into motherboards in the next generation of multimedia machines. DSP chips are beginning to support compression standards—most notably, MPEG. With a single compression standard in place, any type of multimedia machine (Mac, MPC, UNIX, or a new breed of hand-held device) will be capable of playing back the same video, image, or audio file. The inclusion of DSP chips on the motherboard enables real-motion video to be included in multimedia applications.

Software Improvements

The second force behind the evolution of multimedia is the on-going improvements being made to microcomputer

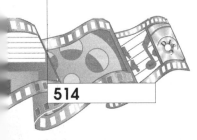

software. Each month brings a new set of tools designed to take advantage of the new processing power. These tools enable developers to create special effects that used to be available only at television production or recording studios. The tools give multimedia producers the power to create titles that have a professional look and feel. Consumers, who are accustomed to the slick presentations shown on television, require this professionalism.

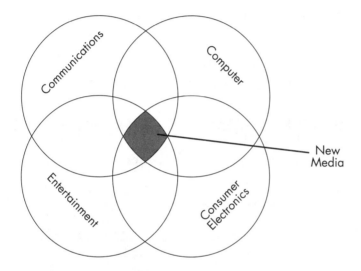

New Media

Figure E.1:

New media products result from the convergence of mature industries.

Convergent Technology

The third factor is the convergence of the computer, communications, entertainment, and consumer-electronics industries (see fig. E.1). These four mature industries now are experiencing less growth than in the past and are looking for a way to create new markets. Multimedia and interactive consumer electronics offer a rich opportunity.

Although these industries can enjoy huge potential rewards for being technically innovative, the risks also are great as companies struggle to establish successful hardware and software standards. Because no single company is large enough to take on this challenge alone, industry giants are forming alliances. Here are just a few examples of such alliances:

➤ Software companies and media companies. For example, Microsoft has purchased more than 20 percent of the British book publishing firm Dorling Kindersley (see fig. E.2).

➤ Hardware leaders, such as IBM and Apple's joint venture, Kaleida.

➤ Cable companies and telephone companies, such as Tele-Communications Inc., AT&T, and US West.

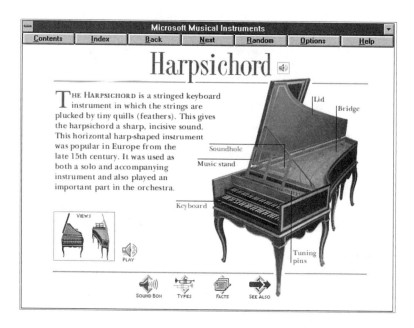

Figure E.2:

Microsoft's Musical Instruments is the first product to result from the Microsoft-Dorling Kindersley alliance.

The computer industry is in a confusing period as it struggles to emerge with a logical set of standards and distribution mechanisms that will win the marketplace. In late 1992, 11 major computer and communications companies formed

First Cities, an alliance created to investigate the interactive-TV market. Some major players include Apple, Kodak, Tandem Computers, Philips, Bellcore, Southwestern Bell, and US West. These companies have contributed more than $5,000,000 to this venture. In 1994, after studying the marketplace, the group plans to conduct a joint field test by wiring more than 10,000 homes for interactive TV.

NOTE

As companies push today's technology forward in an effort to create marketable products, research is moving forward at organizations such as MIT's Media Lab. These research projects provide a peek at the products you will see near the end of this decade.

The remainder of this chapter examines the future of multimedia. Although these products may seem like something from a science fiction movie, they will seem commonplace by the end of the century. The end of this decade starts the Digital Age; let's look at what it might hold.

Information at Your Fingertips

In his keynote address at 1990 Fall COMDEX, Microsoft Chairman Bill Gates described his vision for the future, summed up by the phrase "information at your fingertips"— or IAYF. Although this phrase has joined "downsizing" as one of the most overused expressions in the technology industry, it conveys a powerful image. IAYF means that information from multiple databases (on multiple servers around the world) are easily accessible. End users have access at any time to updated information, and gaining this access will be a simple matter. This information can take any of the following formats:

- ➤ Numerical data
- ➤ Charts
- ➤ Graphs
- ➤ Text
- ➤ Images
- ➤ Sound
- ➤ Animation
- ➤ Video

In this best of all possible computing worlds, users have access to whatever information they need. The operating environment, networking protocol, and application work together to provide the information in a manner that seems transparent to the end user.

In the past few years, Microsoft and other companies have done much to make IAYF a reality.

As a concept, IAYF does not assume that a specific computing environment exists; that is, not every node on a network is a workstation on someone's desk. The machine we tend to think of as a computer will change. Sometimes it will be a workstation, and other times it will look more like a home television or a new hand-held hybrid that works as a combination cellular telephone, fax machine, personal-information manager, and electronic-mail retrieval system.

The end user's ability to access information from multiple locations will forever change the way business is done. Software tools will become increasingly sophisticated and will provide a simpler means for end users to determine the information they want and how they want it reported to them. The role of MIS departments will change from pro-

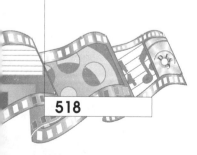

grammers who write code to create reports, to information facilitators responsible for maintaining and updating information, serving as system administrators, and providing more flexible front ends to the information. These front ends will be designed to let users control the ways in which they receive information.

Accessing Multimedia across Networks

In the future, most of the information you receive may be stored at a remote location. You will download it on an "as-needed" basis and pay for just the information you use. To a certain extent, you can take advantage of this type of capability today for some text-based information, by using such services as America On-Line and CompuServe.

Although you can download multiple media in the form of files, to try to access sound or video in real time is impractical. Because you must download a file in a compressed format to a PC, decompress the file, and then view it or play it, you can spend more than 20 minutes downloading a single image or video file.

Before multimedia can be provided in a practical way over local or wide area networks, the following two problems must be addressed:

1. Media must be compressed so that transmission is practical.

2. Networks must be improved so that simultaneous access of large files does not bring the network "to its knees."

A number of companies are working on products that will bring video capability to digital networks. Starlight Networks,

Inc., offers a good example of the evolution of this type of technology.

The StarWorks Video Networking System

Starlight Networks, Inc. has developed the StarWorks Video Networking System, which is designed to be compatible with any desktop video system and any network operating system.

The problem with the use of video on today's networks is that the typical network is designed to handle short bursts of data. The network usually cannot handle the simultaneous, continuous, large-block data transfers needed for streaming video. To overcome this problem, the StarWorks system incorporates software that is designed to be used on a dedicated video (media) server and desktop-based video network interface software.

This software is a Media Transport Protocol (MTP) that is compatible with other standard network protocols, such as IPX and TCP (see fig. E.3). Compatibility with existing network protocols and operating systems ensures that users' existing desktop applications (or those located on other file servers) can be used without problems.

StarWorks' Capabilities

The StarWorks video server software provides video storage management and video-session and stream-management functions. Even video that is compressed by Intel's DVI requires 1/2 to 1 gigabyte of storage for a single hour. StarWorks uses a streaming RAID algorithm to store video across an array of Winchester disk drives.

Emerging technologies will allow users to access huge media files across a network without disrupting the network for other users.

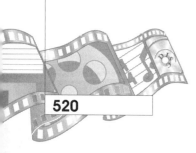

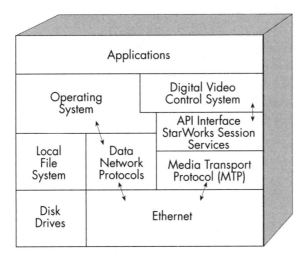

Reprinted with permission from Starlight Networks, Inc. © 1992.

Figure E.3:

The StarWorks Media Transport Protocol (MTP) allows video to co-exist with other network traffic.

 NOTE Compressed video requires a continuous transmission speed of 1 to 2 Mbps (megabits per second).

On a 486-based server, StarWorks software provides a bandwidth of up to 25 Mbps; therefore, it allows 20 simultaneous sessions using Intel's DVI video at 1.2 Mbps, or 12 simultaneous sessions using JPEG video at 2 Mbps. The software works independently of the video source. Multiple sources using DVI, JPEG, or other compression technologies can be used, up to a total transfer rate of 25 Mbps.

StarWorks is compatible with all major compression standards, including the following:

➤ DVI

➤ JPEG

➤ MPEG

> ➤ P*64
>
> ➤ QuickTime
>
> ➤ AVI

The StarWorks architecture is compatible with the following networking systems:

> ➤ NetWare
>
> ➤ NFS
>
> ➤ LAN Manager
>
> ➤ AppleShare

Video Teleconferencing

While companies such as Starlight Networks work on the technical issues of efficiently providing video across local area networks, other companies are working on the applications that will use that video in the corporate environment. In the coming years, a primary use of video in business will be *video teleconferencing.*

NOTE

A number of companies have designed or are designing products specifically for video teleconferencing. One company, Northern Telecom, has designed VISIT—a family of personal-computer-based multimedia communications applications. The system incorporates a small video camera, video board, and software that enable you to conduct video teleconferencing, share workscreen space, conduct high-speed file transfers, and manage voice-messaging services from your computer. VISIT requires a Switched 56 or ISDN line, or it can work with the PBX system in your office.

What is Video Teleconferencing?

In a video teleconferencing system, instead of calling a co-worker on the phone, you point and click to a phone book with that person's number listed. When your co-worker answers, you see his or her live video image in a small window on your screen. (Your image is transported by a small camera on top of your computer monitor.) You and your co-worker can "meet," view the same document on your respective screens, annotate the document to express ideas, transfer files, and log incoming calls.

Video teleconferencing not only can save a great deal of money in travel costs, but it can be a more efficient way to conduct meetings. All your PC's resources are readily available on your desktop; you will not forget to bring a critical document or have to check a fact and call someone back later.

Video teleconferencing will enable end users to communicate visually and aurally across their network.

Other Uses for Networked Video

Although video teleconferencing will be one of the primary applications for networked multimedia, video will be useful in a variety of business situations. Manufacturing companies can use video for training applications, making just-in-time and on-demand training prevalent. Owners of the contents of video (such as film and movie studios and advertising agencies) can archive video clips and re-use the material, and the use of digital editing will become more common. Video clips will be used in all types of corporate communications and marketing materials.

Video and other media annotation of spreadsheets, electronic mail, and documents will become another standard business practice in the near future. You will be able to access multimedia materials from remote databases and not worry about where the original files are stored on the wide area network. You will make greater use of OLE, which will maintain pointers to information that is updated elsewhere; as the information changes, associated graphs and charts will be updated dynamically.

Interactive Television

Most companies focusing on new media agree that the current media-delivery standards (such as CD-ROM, CD-ROM XA, and CDI) are interim steps. The lion's share of the marketplace will not be realized until interactive television is a reality. Interactive TV is big business; although experts disagree on the numbers, the consensus is that it will create billions of dollars in revenue before the end of the century.

Interactive TV is likely to be the biggest future media-delivery standard.

The first step in moving toward interactive TV is the transition from analog television signals to a new delivery standard: digital advanced television (DATV). DATV will make much more efficient use of the available cable bandwidth. (With the use of digital compression, four or six programs can fit in a channel that now can provide only one analog program.)

NOTE

The International Standards Organization is close to adopting MPEG2 as the international compression standard. If MPEG2 is adopted worldwide, interactive TV will be able to feature programming from around the world. You should be able to see television and receive information from other countries.

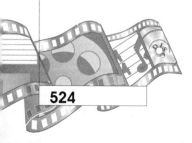

As with other media conversion from an analog to digital format, DATV will allow for greater flexibility of information. DATV will enable easier transcoding among different display formats, such as PAL, NTSC, HDTV, and VHDTV. When television transmission is supplied in DATV format, you will be able to use televised video in conjunction with other types of data.

Networking Interactive TV

If the handling of multimedia over a local area network is difficult, the problem is multiplied a million times when you think about providing interactive entertainment through television networks. The biggest problem is that no networked backbone exists with the bandwidth required for true interactivity.

Cable and telephone companies are competing to see who can provide this interactive capability to the United States first. The cable companies have an advantage because they already have in place a wide-bandwidth transmission system that can service as much as 90 percent of all U.S. homes. Unfortunately, however, the cable companies do not have in place the switching technology to handle user communications back to the cable operator.

Telephone companies, on the other hand, do have the switching technology, but they are faced with the expensive prospect of replacing the copper twisted-pair wire (which serves most U.S. homes) with fiber-optic cable. Twisted-pair wire does not have the bandwidth to handle the multiple parallel channels required for interactive data transmission. AT&T, however, has announced compression algorithms that might make delivery over twisted-pair wire feasible.

Regardless of which industry wins the race, the future of television will bring more than 500 channels of programming into every home. With so many available channels, the role of television will expand beyond canned entertainment provided at specified times. By using ISDN or another multimedia channel-switching technology, users will be able to interact instantaneously with the television.

The Effects of Interactive TV on Users

With interactive TV, users will be able to use an infrared remote in conjunction with a box on top of the television to specify movies on demand directly from cable companies. Viewers also will be able to pause or rewind the action, as if watching a videotape. They will be able to use their TV for continuing education, in the form of *distance learning*: the teacher can be at another location and respond to questions as though all students were in the same room.

With interactive TV, viewers will be able to manipulate images in much the same way they can with videotape.

By using virtual reality technology, students will have the opportunity to experience and learn in a new way: they will be able to "visit" a historical event or learn about physics by experiencing what it might be like to be the size of an atom. Sports fans will be able to use the remote device to pan from side to side or to zoom in on the action in a game.

No paper-based publication can serve as a practical television guide for 500 channels. TV watchers will use guides incorporated into the interactive TV service. You will be able to specify the type of entertainment and information you want to see (news, sports, movies, and music videos, for example) and refine selections until you indicate the exact items you want to view. You also will be able to set up a series of selections (in much the same way you can program a CD player to play songs in a specified order).

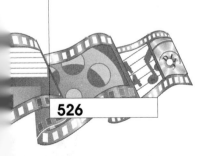

Interactive TV will be used for more at-home services. Home shopping will increase dramatically, as will home banking, and interactive video dating services will become prevalent. Interactive TV may well replace many items you are familiar with today, including audio-only telephones and text-only computer networks.

The possibilities of interactive TV are limited only by imagination. Although the description may sound fantastic, companies are working on the technology. Market analysts at Boston's Bain & Company, Inc., estimate that more than 40 million households will have some type of interactive television by the year 2002.

Modular Windows and Cross-Platform Compatibility

Microsoft is positioning itself for the future by developing Modular Windows, a scaled-down version of the Windows 3.1 operating environment. Rather than the 8 megabytes required for total installation of Windows 3.1, Modular Windows requires only 1 megabyte of storage, which makes it more practical for use with a variety of developing technologies.

Because Modular Windows maintains 75 percent of the standard Windows APIs, it is an easy platform to develop for, for anyone who already is working with Windows. The concept is that a developer can write a program for the standard Windows interface and then easily port the application to all the different devices that run with Modular Windows. Microsoft released a Modular Windows SDK (Software Development Kit) at the end of 1992.

Modular Windows will bring Window's capabilities to a variety of new platforms.

Modular Windows is incorporated in ROM on the Tandy VIS Player. This CD-ROM unit looks like a standard audio CD player and hooks up to a television set. Users with a wireless remote can interact with CD-based programs that are created for use with the device. Microsoft has plans to use Modular Windows on other devices, including CDI players, "smart" phones and other computerized consumer devices, and personal digital assistants.

NOTE

With the release of Modular Windows, Microsoft's charter seems to have changed from "a computer on every desk and in every home, running Microsoft software" to "an appliance on every desk, on every person, and in every home, running Microsoft software." After all, why limit themselves?

Portable Multimedia

The future of multimedia is in portable computers.

Multimedia has been described as "technology in search of a need." It is easy to see why when you look at the confusing variety of available platforms. In the business environment, multimedia will be integrated with PC desktop applications, but the long-term future of business multimedia may be in portable multimedia players. You can look at the products available today and easily make guesses about the ways in which they might evolve.

MMCD

The MMCD is Sony Corporation's answer to portable multimedia. Because the player already has been described in this book, the description won't be repeated here. This chapter is

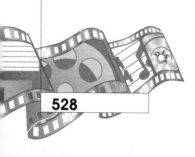

primarily concerned with the implications of the device, which is designed to serve the needs of traveling business professionals.

The concept behind the development of the MMCD was to provide a means of storing large amounts of information and allowing access to the information "on the road." Discs created for the MMCD player can hold the following types of information:

> Travel reference material and directions.

> Dictionary and encyclopedic reference material.

> Sales and marketing presentations. (The unit can be connected to a television monitor by way of an RCA jack, for viewing the information on the disc in 256 colors.)

A number of video-content owners offer MMCD titles. If the machine is successful in the marketplace, the number of titles will grow as will the number of companies who create corporate reference material, for distribution to personnel in field locations.

Other Emerging Portable Technologies

A disadvantage to the MMCD is that the first version of the product does not allow color viewing without an external monitor. Philips saw Sony's oversight as a marketing opportunity and has developed a portable color CDI player. This hand-held device has functionality similar to the MMCD's. If Modular Windows is adapted for CDI, developers will be able to develop CDI titles quickly (a lack of titles has been one reason the product has not achieved critical mass in the marketplace).

Some people believe that it is just a matter of time until the technology to make portable multimedia a practical business reality can be offered at a price that can create a thriving market. They foresee a world in which paperback books and Walkman-type radios are replaced by portable players that offer the best of both worlds.

Cynics who disagree with this theory point out that many people prefer more processing power, in the form of a personal digital assistant or notebook computer. They claim that, because people do not want to do much reading on a PC screen, the use of portable multimedia devices will be limited to searches of reference material. The critics believe that people prefer the ease and portability of a paperback book.

The debate continues over whether people prefer to use paper or computers while traveling. The debate extends to multimedia technology.

To some extent, both sides are correct. You can make the most accurate assumptions by looking at some developing trends. The increasing sales of flash cards for portable information managers (such as the Wizard) imply that people will want to access reference information while they travel. Business professionals, however, will want to store their own information, write memos, and access their electronic mail (as indicated by the popularity of laptop and notebook computers). People prefer color to monochromatic images, as indicated by the increasing popularity of color notebooks. They will want cellular communications capability while traveling, as indicated by the sale of more than 10 million cellular phones in the past few years.

NOTE More than anything else, business people do not want to lug around any more items than they already carry. Today's true business "road warrior" needs one carry-on bag devoted exclusively to technology. That bulging bag may contain a

notebook computer with cables and rechargeable battery pack, a cellular phone, a Wizard with a flash card or two, and at least one box of PC diskettes.

Seeking Solutions to Portability Problems

The ideal solution, therefore, seems to be a color notebook with a cellular modem, CD-ROM drive, and a PCMIA slot— right? Not necessarily. The cost and weight of a machine that tries to be all things to all users is impractical for most people. You can expect to see a whole range of hybrid solutions, with varying functionality and price points.

A number of machines will be designed to meet the specific needs of vertical marketplaces. The current crop of portable multimedia devices are not functional enough; as they are enhanced to allow communications and user storage capability, they will gain more acceptance in the marketplace. Machines will be sold in modular units that can be linked together as users' needs evolve.

Paying for Shared Information

As the internetworking infrastructure improves, along with improvements in compression technologies, you can expect to access more information (of all media types) by downloading it from a variety of sources. Although the information may be stored somewhere in optical format, you will be able to access the information you need, and only what you need, and not worry about where it is stored. You will have to pay for only the information you access.

Before this scenario can take place, a number of changes must occur not only at the technology level, but also in considering information ownership and the ways we pay for information. Under the current model, numerous owners may hold rights to a single factoid of information.

> **A**s we share more information, we must find creative ways of paying for it.

Consider the example of a small film clip. The movie studio responsible for distributing that clip holds certain rights. The studio may have to pay royalties to many people for use of that clip—the director, the writer, and the actors in the clip. The studio may share electronic distribution rights with other companies. If a soundtrack has been included in the clip, a new set of rights must be addressed before the clip is used. In a newsclip, the people filmed in the clip may own the rights to the use of their image.

NOTE

If a clip is offered in a digitized, compressed format on an on-line system and you want to download it, how should you be charged? In today's digital environment, you download the clip, pay access time while you are on the system, and possibly pay for a long-distance phone call. Chances are that the primary holders of rights to that clip never receive payment while you use or view it.

In the future, the on-line service will track your use of the clip. Your on-line charges will reflect the clip charge, which will be used to pay royalties to all appropriate parties. This scenario is similar to the way in which pay-per-view TV operates now.

How Today's Research Will Be Reflected In Tomorrow's Technology

To see what will happen in the next two or three years, you have to look only at the products that are beginning to enter the marketplace. To envision the end of the decade (and the end of the millennium), look at the research being conducted at such places as MIT's Media Lab or the University of Washington's Virtual Reality Lab.

Research is very extensive in the following areas:

- ➤ Virtual reality
- ➤ Interface design
- ➤ Holography
- ➤ HDTV
- ➤ Other "blue sky" technologies

University research facilities are underwritten in large part by major international corporations who hope to capitalize on new technologies that result from the labs' research and development efforts. MIT's Media Lab, for example, allows corporate sponsors to access the Lab's intellectual property rights six months after the rights have been filed. Some corporations have directed research contracts with the Lab. A corporation funding directed research has immediate access to the property rights, with an opportunity to develop the product six months before other Lab sponsors.

The remainder of this chapter describes some of the research being conducted and speculates about the use of this research in the business and consumer marketplace.

Media Lab's Electronic Newspapers

Media Lab's Electronic Publishing Group, led by Walter Bender, conducts research that will influence the way the world receives information. The process that news publishers now use to collect and disseminate information is good for gathering and organizing vast amounts of time-critical information. In a world connected by telephone and television networks, however, you have nearly instantaneous access to data from around the world. Forget "information at your fingertips"—we are up to our ears in data and are drowning rapidly. We need a way to redefine and reorganize all the information and tailor it in a way that is responsive to individual needs.

Newspapers of the future will not be paper, but smart electronic devices.

The "newspaper" of the future will not be a paper-based product. Each day, your personal communications device (which may be a smart TV that occupies an entire wall of a room or a multimedia workstation or a personal digital assistant) will download the day's news. Interface agent technology (described later in this section) will be used to tailor the news to your specific interests. Because the agent will know your preferences, you may see the sports news first, followed by world events and the science section. You may watch film clips of the news; when a clip piques your interest or you need more background information, you double-click the video frame and a text-based news item will appear on a screen. After you read it (which is not hard on the eyes, thanks to HDTV), you return to viewing the video sequence. The system will be smart enough to consider your personalized needs, based on your personal schedule: you can see, for example, the weather report for Chicago on the day you are scheduled to take a trip. Your charges will be based on transactions and will appear on a monthly "information bill."

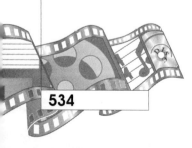

A key to making this vision a reality is the development of *interface agent technology*. Agents are computational entities that emulate the function of an editor or personal assistant. The agent filters through the terabytes (trillions of bytes) of available information and creates a subset tailored to your needs and interests. Agent programming involves artificial intelligence. Agents can "learn" your preferences by collecting information over time about what you choose to view.

MIT hosts an annual symposium on interface agent technology (see fig. E.4).

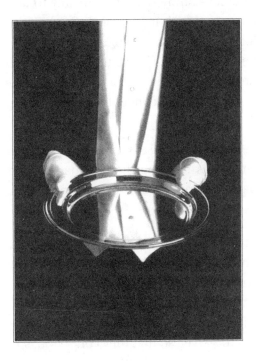

Figure E.4:
The invitation to MIT Media Lab's 1992 Interface Agents Symposium.

The process of creating agents starts with *user modeling*, or determining a user's interests and needs with respect to data collection. Census data is the starting point for creating a user model. Each user is part of a "community" defined by geographic location, and is refined further through demographic information. The user profile is refined and updated through user activity. Users have access to a number of different profiles or models. If you want to "see the world through your boss's eyes," for example, you can download information for a week or two based on that person's profile.

WARNING

The management of agent information brings up complicated legal and moral issues concerning privacy. Should advertisers be able to purchase agent information and therefore have the ability to tailor commercials specifically to target audiences and their interests? Is the ability to use different profiles a valuable educational tool? Students in school, for example, could get a sense of perspective about someone in another culture. To some, the agent concept may sound suspiciously like Big Brother.

Regardless of these issues, agent technology may enable us to bring the overload of information back into manageable proportions.

Future technology will bring the "talking head" to life.

The "talking head" was another Media Lab project, which focused on how to deliver "the transmission of human presence" through technology. In the original experiment, video transmissions of faces talking were projected onto video screens sculpted like human faces. The screens had the capability to swivel, so that they could nod, shake their heads, and turn towards each other. Television tubes, molded like human faces, gave an uncanny resemblance to a real head talking to you in the same room.

Although the primary purpose of agents is to filter data, the agent "interface" will enable you to have a humanesque interaction with your computer. The interface will use video and audio to present a human presence on the PC screen. You will be able to select how your agent appears to you and the personality characteristics he or she displays. Your agent

will be able to "talk" to you, reminding you of appointments and offering suggestions.

The Changing World of Video

This chapter already has discussed the vision of interactive TV. This section addresses some of the research being conducted that will enhance the future of television. Today the line between television and movies is blurred because of cable TV and VCRs; this distinction will continue. The quality of video and audio and the size of the screen you associate with movie theaters will begin to move into the home.

You will go to "movie" theaters for experiences you cannot access through your home network. These "experiences" may be 3-D holographic movies, large virtual-reality game rooms, or audience participatory interactive theater (the interactive part of the experience, however, will come from video rather than from live actors).

NOTE

The "movie" experience will focus primarily on entertainment as it does today, and "television" will provide a variety of services, including entertainment, education, information, and communications.

The electronic newspaper described in the preceding section of this chapter will be a hybrid between the publishing industry you know today and the world of cable television. Walter Bender says that the future of cable television will offer from 600 to 6,000 channels. One of these channels will be designated as the "designer" (user-programmable) channel for the interface agent. Video news clips and text-based news stories will be linked, and tailored to a user's specific interests. Users will be able to "fast forward" video clips by clip content rather than by frame, as they do now.

HDTV and VHDTV will become the new standard for television monitor resolution. This capability is necessary if television is to metamorphose from a passive entertainment device to an information and communications tool. HDTV is required, at minimum, to enable people to read large amounts of information on screen without ruining their eyes. To shoot HDTV is an expensive proposition; Media Lab has been working on algorithms that can increase the resolution of standard videotape to HDTV levels. In addition to providing better-quality video, this technology can be used to enhance individual frames from current television clips to create high-quality graphics images.

These algorithms can be used to visually enhance certain sections of an image or video sequence. Higher-quality resolution can be in certain spots on a video sequence, to provide focus and draw users' attention to that section of the frame. This capability is the equivalent of highlighting something on-screen, but it adds subtlety to the process and does not detract from the rest of the picture.

Numerous text-based multi-user simulation environments (MUSE) are in use today on Internet, in which players log in and create characters. A character can enter and move around in virtual environments representing rooms or city sections. Users can interact with numerous objects in each environment (and other characters). Each object is governed by a set of characteristics and rules. Each MUSE is an object-oriented database, which continually evolves as users create new characters, objects, environments, and rules.

The television of the future will incorporate MUSE capabilities with virtual reality technology. Television will cease to be

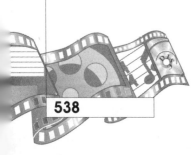

a flat, two-dimensional medium and will become a virtual environment. Virtual reality devices such as data gloves and goggles will enable users to enter virtual environments for education and entertainment. Because the virtual experience is provided through a cable network, users will be able to interact with each other in multiuser virtual simulations. The combination of object-oriented, rule-based systems and virtual reality will bring about the cyberspace described in science-fiction novels.

The Changing World of Audio

Research that will be reflected in the next generation of multimedia computers is coming from Archer Communications Inc./QSound, Ltd. This company's QSound product is a multidimensional sound localization technology that requires nothing more than standard stereo equipment for playback. Using reverberation algorithms, PC speakers can produce a 3D sound effect: When you stand or sit in front of a PC, you seem to hear sound around you and in back of you.

This virtual audio effect adds another dimension of reality to multimedia applications, especially games and simulations. QSound is licensing the technology to DSP chip and custom hardware manufacturers so that tomorrow's multimedia PCs will feature 3D sound.

The QSound effect is so real—and startling—that you may turn around to look for hidden speakers.

Media Lab's Music and Cognition Group is working on audio parsers with harmonically sensitive filters that enable the computer to "listen" to music or speech recordings. In compressing the audio information, rather than compress the sound, the computer captures the gestural information that caused the sound. (Compression involves capturing information about the way the fingers move on the keyboard to produce the music rather than the waveform of the

539

sound.) Computerized renderers will play back the performance at the time of decompression, by mimicking the keystrokes that created the music in the first place.

Although this technology is years away from commercialization, the long-range implications are exciting. By capturing the gesture information compression ratios of 10,000 to 1 are possible. (An average audio CD will be capable of holding about two years' worth of music.) Years from now, computers will have the capability to "listen" to streams of audio information and recognize acoustic events, which will give you an entirely new way to index audio information. You will be able to search a vast database for all interviews given by a particular celebrity, for example, by matching the sound of the voice instead of using a text-based index.

The Future "Notebook"

In the future, you will only need one portable device, not several.

As mobile professionals begin to expect more communications capabilities and processing power on the road, they face a heavy burden. Different machines meet their various digital needs. Each machine, although lightweight by itself, becomes part of a group that users must lug from place to place. A new group of digital devices are being developed to help replace the group of devices required for similar functionality today.

These machines go by many names: personal digital assistants (PDAs), personal communicators, and personal information appliances (PIAs). No matter which name is used, they share common functionality—fax, electronic mail, cellular communications, and personal-computing data management (address and phone files, notes, and calendar management, for example). A PDA is differentiated from a notebook by the following qualities:

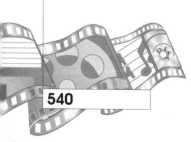

540

➤ Smaller size (between 2 and 5 pounds)

➤ Sleek design (it has no keyboard)

➤ A pen input device

PDAs use a graphical user interface, and the software designed for use with a PDA is supposed to be intuitive for end users.

The first of the PDA machines to hit the market is AT&T's EO, with these two models:

➤ EO Personal Communicator 440 (2.2 pounds)

➤ Personal Communicator 880 (4 pounds)

The machines, built around the new Hobbit processor chip, use the PenPoint Operating System from GO Corporation. The operating system, plus nine personal-management applications, are supplied in each machine's ROM. Every EO has the following features:

➤ Built-in high-speed data modem (14,400bps, V.32bis)

➤ On-board fax

➤ Built-in microphone and speaker (for voice annotation)

➤ Free subscription to AT&T EasyLink Mail Service

EO Personal Communicators include a high-speed serial port and cable (for exchanging data with IBM-compatible computers), a parallel port (for connecting to printers or an optional 1.44M floppy drive), and a PCMCIA slot (two slots in the 880). Other options include a cellular phone connection (see fig. E.5), internal hard disk, and RAM (expandable to as much as 12M). The 880 also offers a VGA port for connecting the EO to standard VGA monitors and a SCSI port for connecting external hard drives.

Figure E.5:

The EO Personal Communicator 880.

You will be able to choose from a number of other PDAs in addition to the EO. Apple is preparing to launch Newton, its first PDA product. Newton is the first in a family of personal digital products from Apple. Other hardware manufacturers plan to produce personal digital devices. Although Microsoft has not announced a specific product, it clearly intends to have a PDA running Modular Windows, which may emerge as a market leader.

Some people argue that PDAs are trying to fill a niche that does not exist. The argument is that notebook and subnotebook PCs are becoming so light and are offering full compatibility with the software on desktop machines that to spend the same amount of money on a machine powered by a different chip and (possibly) a different operating environment is unnecessary. The winner in the battle between notebooks and PDAs will be determined primarily by weight and ergonomics.

The PDA prototypes have created a stir because of their light weight (2 to 5 pounds) and sexy design. The pen interface lets users input information by enabling them to sketch out ideas and store the sketches as image files. Although compatibility

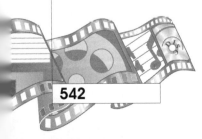

with current software is an issue, if enough people adopt a particular PDA, it will create a demand for PDA-compatible desktop software.

If PDA-type devices are part of the immediate future, what does the far future hold? A look at computing trends during the past decade shows that the size of the units will continue to shrink, and that the microprocessors' power will continue to grow. Chips will be designed for more special purposes: certain chips (such as the Intel line) will continue to support the data needs of business; other chips will be used for portable machines or home entertainment units. Standards among operating environments and communications protocols will enable these different machines to communicate and share data.

If technological trends continue as they have in the past few years, all our appliances will contain microprocessors (this trend already has begun with VCRs, digital alarm clocks, and microwave ovens). The production of powerful computers the size of "sticky notes" will not be a problem; a problem may occur, however, in manufacturing batteries that are small and powerful enough to run this new breed of machine.

The Battery Problem: Is Smaller Better?

The processing power of the ever-shrinking portable computer is equal to or competitive with desktop machines—this has not been a difficult technical feat. Nevertheless, technology has not made comparable improvements in one area: the size and durability of batteries. This problem soon will become more obvious if batteries remain the same size and weight and the units for which they provide power continue to shrink. With today's notebook batteries, you do not have enough power to last an airline flight from New York to San Francisco, unless you recharge the power system.

The battery life issue will increase the competitiveness and popularity of PDAs (with their lower-power-consumption chips). The PDA chips not only require less power, but the smaller, efficient design also is an advantage in trying to make the battery last as long as possible.

The demand for color has created a catch-22 for battery makers.

Manufacturers of notebook computers have devised methods to try to make batteries last longer, including making lower-resolution screens that do not use as much energy. As the graphical user interface becomes standard on handheld computers, however, the need for higher-resolution screens increases, as does the demand for color monitors. These high-resolution monitors make it easier to work, but they drain the battery more quickly. It makes work easier, but you cannot work nearly as long.

Saving system resources is another method that manufacturers use to save energy. Although it seems efficient to have your computer "sleep" after a specified period of not touching the keyboard or mouse, this solution is short-term. With the integration of RISC-based processors in desktop workstations, true multitasking operating environments are becoming the norm. This multitasking capability will trickle down to portables some time in the future. If you use a machine capable of running tasks in the background, you do not want it to "sleep" when you are not interacting with it.

Two scenarios exist in which the battery problem may be overcome. In the first, battery manufacturers begin to create more powerful, longer-lasting batteries capable of recharging more quickly. In the second scenario, PDAs or subnotebooks have widespread market acceptance, and vending machines at which you can recharge your batteries are available everywhere. Recharging would be as easy as getting gas for your

car: you go to a recharging station, use your credit card, and recharge. (This scenario assumes that recharge times are much quicker than today's standard.)

Batteries are not the only issue as palmtop-size computers or PDAs reach critical mass. Information input becomes another issue. Keyboards scaled down for notebooks still can be used by anyone except people with very large hands. As the computer shrinks, however, keyboard input becomes impractical. The use of mice (or trackballs) with portables also is cumbersome. If the trackball is not built into the unit, it sticks out awkwardly and may be cumbersome to use.

Pen-input devices seem to solve keyboard and trackball difficulties, but the algorithms have not been perfected for handwriting recognition. These algorithms will improve, but pen-based systems still require a learning period, in which users teach the pen how to read their handwriting. (Critics of pen devices claim that, during the learning period, the pen teaches the user how to write.) Even as the algorithms improve, pen-input devices will require users to learn an entirely new system of editing marks.

Someday, you may be able to recharge your computer at a battery filling station in a few minutes.

WARNING Miniaturization is a great trend, but, in the long run it will cause a new set of problems, because of theft or loss of equipment.

Theft can be deterred with the use of password-protection schemes (which will entertain a new generation of hackers). Theft can be overcome with the use of machine-specific passwords as a part of the handshake process, when a user attempts to log in to a network. The network will know the code for your specific unit and may be able to determine location (a process that is not easy on Internet, but will be possible with future networks). If you report the loss or theft of your machine, the police department can be notified when someone tries to log on with your equipment. Your equipment can then be recovered. (The recovery of your data is another matter.) New business opportunities will be created in the form of machine password-protection services and services that automatically back up incremental data whenever you log on to a network.

The New Wallpaper: Is Bigger Better?

One of Windows 3.1's fun features is wallpaper (see fig. E.6). The Windows wallpaper option enables you to change the background of your desktop to any bit map in your Windows directory. Wallpaper is an enjoyable way to customize your workspace.

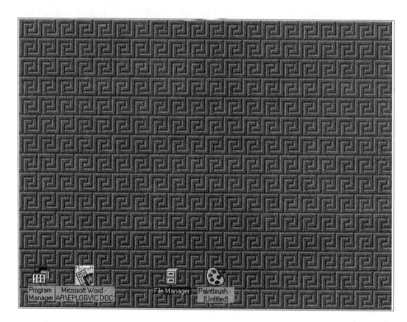

Figure E.6:

Windows Wallpaper, as we know it today.

Bill Gates is changing the way we think about digital "wallpaper". In 1989, he founded Interactive Home Systems (now called Continuum Product Corporation, or CPC) to develop digital libraries and the technology for displaying high-resolution images. Steve Arnold, president of CPC, says that the company's charter is "A redefinition of digital publishing for the next decade." Another important CPC goal is the development of software to enhance the electronic image, in an effort to reproduce quality that is as close as possible to the original image.

CPC's first project is ViewPoint, an interactive tour of the Seattle Art Museum, which uses touch screens to let visitors view the museum's collection and receive additional information about the image, the artist, and the artist's culture.

NOTE

Although ViewPoint is the first product produced by CPC, Gates plans to use the company's technology in his new home, on the shores of Lake Washington. High-definition, wall-size video displays will be installed as a test; Gates hopes to market the screens commercially by the end of this decade. These screens will be programmed to display alternating sets of images.

Gates is acquiring these images through CPC. The company is trying to obtain digital rights to great works of art. Rumor has it that CPC has contacted the Art Institute of Chicago, the National Gallery in London, and the Smithsonian in Washington, D.C. In March 1991, Gates purchased non-exclusive rights to more than 1,000 of the Seattle Art Museum's collection of 18,000 works.

These works certainly can be used as "wallpaper" in conjunction with large-scale video screens. Depending on how the rights are negotiated, however, the digital images may be used also in multimedia titles being published through Microsoft.

Other companies have begun to acquire digital rights to images. Eastman Kodak has acquired a stock photo company—the images will be used in conjunction with the company's developing line of products for the photo CD. Optical Technology Resource, Inc., has acquired rights to the collections in the Frick Museum and the Brooklyn Museum.

Conclusion

Based on the movement of today's products and the areas being researched, we can guess at the products of tomorrow. Some of these predictions are identical to predictions made more than 20 years ago. Advances in technology coupled with widespread adoption of computers make it more likely that these ideas will reach fruition before the end of this decade. Certain trends that have developed in the past five to ten years will continue: increased processing power, miniaturization of the computer, integration of chips into home-consumer devices, and an increased emphasis on the capability to network with others and draw on vast resources of information.

The types of applications that will be developed for the new breed of machines are more difficult to predict. Because of the convergence of the computer, communications, consumer-electronics, and entertainment industries, sophisticated products will be introduced to the home market. Everything will become available, from virtual-reality simulations to interactive television, from computers that use voice and images to communicate with users to the use of the Mona Lisa as your wallpaper. The types of products being developed are based on the traditional media or software paradigms—a new model for new media development has yet to emerge. In some sense, this new model will evolve naturally from the needs of the marketplace.

Certain needs that emerge will demand new media solutions. The management of vast amounts of available information is one area that is ripe for development. Another area that will see much activity is games, as new media provides gaming companies with the capability to create more realistic simulations. Entertainment and education will develop their own models for delivering products in a new media format.

This chapter has given you a glimpse of the future. I hope that it has sparked your imagination and started you thinking about the types of new media products you might want to create.

Glossary

Although the world of multimedia uses media you are familiar with—text, video, sound, animation, and images—this industry uses new technologies that have produced new standards and terms. Like the rest of the computer industry, multimedia also has its share of unfamiliar acronyms: ANSI, SGML, MSCDEX, MPEG and others define standards, software, or new technologies that affect multimedia. If you are familiar with these terms and abbreviations, it helps you understand the business and ask the right questions when shopping for multimedia hardware or software.

Applet A small application with a limited set of capabilities. An example is the Sound Recorder bundled with Windows 3.1.

Bitmaps Images composed of sets of bits in the computer's memory that define the color and intensity of each pixel.

CD-DA The digital sound format used by standard audio CDs; also known as the Redbook standard.

CD-ROM Compact Disc Read Only Memory; a disc containing a variety of data types, such as text, audio, video, and images. CD-ROM drives connect to a computer enabling users to access data.

CD XA CD-ROM Extended Architecture. An extension of the CD-ROM specification that interleaves audio data with other data types (such as text or video).

Clip A file of sound, video, or animation that you can link or embed into other documents.

Compact Disc Digital Audio Standard (see CD-DA)

Compound documents Contain data objects produced by more than one application. A spreadsheet with an embedded sound clip is a "compound document."

Custom Control A special Dynamic Link Library (DLL) that acts as an extension to the Microsoft Visual Basic Toolbox. When you add a custom control to the program, it becomes a part of the VB development environment and provides added functionality to your programs.

Direct Memory Access (DMA) channel A dedicated microprocessor that transfers data from memory to memory without using the CPU, enabling data to be transferred at a much faster rate than if the CPU was used.

Embed A copy of a data object, which is stored within a client document by using OLE.

Enterprise-Wide Computing The sharing of resources and files, and communication using email; enterprise-wide computing is accomplished by networking an entire corporation.

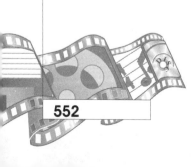

Father The mirror image of a glass master, which is produced during the duplication of CD-ROMs. A father has a bump corresponding to each pit on the master. CD-ROM discs are pressed from the father disc.

Hypermedia A term coined to describe applications that contain hypertext and multimedia elements.

Hypertext Text that has been formatted with a variety of *hot links* and is heavily indexed. The hot links enable a reader to jump between related conceptual topics; the index enables users to search for topics by using keywords.

Hypertext engine A runtime program that enables an end-user to work with a hypertext document after it has been written, indexed, and compiled by the author of the hypertext document. Each hypertext authoring program comes with its own hypertext engine or reader.

Info bites Chunks of easily digestible data of any type—text, sound, video, and other media.

ISO-9660 First known as the High Sierra format, this standard describes how data should be written to a CD-ROM disc.

JPEG Joint Photographic Experts Group; a compression standard that compresses all redundant data within a frame.

Link A pointer to a data object, which is stored within a client document using OLE. If the linked object is modified, the modifications will appear when the object is called from the client document.

Local bus A motherboard that allows a computer display card to have direct access to the microprocessor and permits the transfer at the same speed as the system clock.

Mastering: The first step in duplicating CD-ROM discs. A master is created by the developer (using a WORM drive) or at the duplication facility (which creates a master using data delivered from the developer on tape or some other media).

Media Control Interface (MCI) Media Control Interface, Microsoft's programming interface for controlling multimedia devices.

Micons Moving Icons. In the Macintosh world, micons are previews of video clips, scaled down to icon size.

MIDI Musical Instrument Digital Interface. A standard protocol for the interchange of musical information between musical instruments, synthesizers, and computers.

MPEG Motion Picture Experts Group standard; a compression standard that compresses all redundant data between frames.

Multimedia An adjective that describes applications and documents that have been enhanced by the addition of sound, animation, or video or all of these media. Multimedia is also used to describe hardware that enables users to access these capabilities. Finally, multimedia is a term used to define those applications in which media is a primary focus.

Object An encapsulated module that features a combination of information and instructions that work on that information

OLE Object Linking and Embedding; A way to transfer and share information between applications. OLE enables you to embed or link objects from one application into a compound document created by another application.

554

Picons Picture icons. In the Macintosh world, picons are actual images that have been scaled down to icon size.

QuickTime Extensions originally designed for Macintosh's System 7, a technology that compresses and decompresses video and synchronizes audio with video sequences.

Raster format Another name for bit-mapped images. Raster images are made up of dots.

RIFF Resource Interchange File Format; a tagged file structure developed for multimedia resource files, based on an Electronic Arts IFF file.

Sampling The translation of an analog waveform into a digital format by taking tiny (discrete) samples of the waveform at fixed intervals as the sound is captured.

Scalable Performance Part of Intel's codec (compression/decompression) technology, which allows the video image to adapt to the performance of the hardware available in the computer. The better the system performance, the better the quality of the image.

SCSI Small Computer System Interface; a single interface card in a single PC slot onto which you can connect (daisy chain) together a number of external SCSI devices. SCSI is faster than a serial connection.

SGML Standard General Markup Language, an ASCII text-coding scheme. Many authoring tools and compilers enable you to use data in SGML format.

Tagging The process of using special codes to "tag" certain parts of the raw text, indicating sectional divisions (such as chapter headings and topical headings) and links between the sections specified.

Vector format Images stored as a series of geometric instructions.

Waveform file A digital representation of an analog waveform, taken by sampling the waveform during the digitizing process. Waveform files used with Windows have a WAV extension.

Widgets In Asymetrix Multimedia ToolBook; objects that come with scripts to access the Windows MCI. Users who are not skilled programmers can merely cut and paste widgets into a book to control CD-ROM drives, sound boards, and other media devices.

Installing the *Guide to Multimedia Disk*

A ttached to the inside back cover of this book should be a 1.2M floppy disk. This *Guide to Multimedia Disk* contains a sample multimedia document that you use in conjunction with Chapter 10, "Authoring a Multimedia Document." This document—a fictitious annual report for the CommuniCorp Corporation—includes a number of elements common to the multimedia environment, including hyperlinks, voice, and pop-up boxes. The Annual Report was created using Multimedia ToolBook from Asymetrix Corporation.

Although this sample application is multimedia-related, you do not need a multimedia PC to use it. The application runs on a PC that meets or exceeds these requirements:

- A personal computer with a 16MHz 80386SX or higher processor

- 2M RAM (4M recommended)

- A high-density drive (if you have only a 1.4M high-density drive, copy the sample disk to 1.4M disk)

- A hard disk with 4M available disk space

- A monitor and graphics card for VGA or better

- A Windows-compatible mouse or pointing device

- DOS 3.1 or higher

- Windows 3.0 or higher

The *Guide to Multimedia Disk* contains a number of files that make up the CommuniCorp Annual Report. These files include:

- COMMCORP.TBK (the multimedia document)

- Runtime ToolBook files

- PC Speaker driver (a Microsoft product that enables PCs to play audio without a sound board)

- PREZ.WAV (an audio file)

- NAR.DIB (a wide-format, device-independent bit map)

The purpose of each of these files is described in Chapter 10.

Installing the CommuniCorp Annual Report

To load and run the CommuniCorp Annual Report, place the installation disk in a 1.2M high-density drive.

NOTE If the A drive is not the name of the drive you will use to install CommuniCorp, substitute the correct drive letter in the following steps.

1. Insert the *Guide to Multimedia Disk* in the disk drive.

2. Choose <u>R</u>un from Program Manager's <u>F</u>ile menu.

   The Run dialog box appears.

3. Type the following command in the <u>C</u>ommand Line field:

   `A:SETUP`

4. Press Enter or click on OK.

   The CommuniCorp Annual Report Setup dialog box appears and asks whether you want to change the default directory for the installation or any multimedia components or both.

5. The default directory for the new files is C:\COMMCORP. If you want to install CommuniCorp in a different directory, enter the new directory name in the Copy to field.

6. Below the Copy to field, you are asked to select the CommuniCorp components you want to install (the executables, the sample application, and the PC Speaker driver). Click on Continue if the default is acceptable, or

Install all the files unless you already have TOOLBOOK.EXE on your system. If you have TOOLBOOK.EXE , you may want to exclude ToolBook Executables from the installation process.

deselect the files you do not want and then choose Continue.

If the files copy properly, the following message appears:

`Installation of the Report is complete.`

7. Click on OK.

Installing the PC Speaker driver

The *Guide to Multimedia Disk* includes Microsoft's PC Speaker driver, which enables your PC's speaker to play sounds and voice. The speaker driver is used in the sample CommuniCorp report to play a segment of the President's letter. If you followed the preceding steps, all the files for the sample multimedia document should be in the COMMCORP directory. You now need to follow these steps to install the PC Speaker driver from the Control Panel:

Do not use the driver file on the installation disk because it is compressed. Use the driver installed in C:\COMMCORP or the directory in which you installed the CommuniCorp report.

 NOTE Some AST computer systems are not compatible with the PC Speaker driver. You may get partial sound (or none) when you try to play the audio file featured in CommuniCorp.

1. From the Control Panel, double-click on the Drivers icon.

2. Choose <u>A</u>dd from the dialog box.

3. Choose Unlisted or Updated Driver from the list box, then click on OK.

4. The Install Driver dialog box appears and prompts you for the disk that contains the sound driver. The appropriate response is to enter the path to the installation directory you chose. If you used the default C:\COMMCORP, for example, type **C:\COMMCORP**

rather than accept the A:\ default offered by the dialog box.

5. Click on OK or press Enter.

   The Add Unlisted or Updated Driver dialog box appears.

6. Click on OK.

   The PC-Speaker Setup dialog box appears.

7. In the Limit field, slide the slider bar all the way to the right. The setting **No Limit** appears.

8. Click on OK to accept the speaker settings.

   The System Setting Change dialog box appears.

9. The last step is to quit and restart Windows. Click on Restart Now in this dialog box to reboot the system immediately (you may hear an audio sound during the reboot), or click on Don't Restart Now to exit from the setup.

The Test button in PC-Speaker Setup provides a short audio file to test your settings.

NOTE

You may want to uninstall the driver when you have heard the audio version of the president's letter. PC Speaker can cause some surprising sounds when you press certain keys on the keyboard (Esc, for example).

To remove the PC Speaker driver, follow these steps:

1. Click on the Drivers icon in Control Panel.

2. Highlight Sound Driver for PC-Speaker.

3. Click on Remove.

4. A Warning Box appears asking you to verify your decision. Click on Yes to proceed.

5. Restart Windows.

Running COMMCORP.TBK

Another option for launching the CommuniCorp program is to double click on COMMCORP.TBK from File Manager.

The CommuniCorp program is launched from the Program Manager. Look for the CommuniCorp Annual Report Group and double-click on the report's icon.

The opening screen, shown in figure B.1, is the first page of a 40-page ToolBook document. Every page features a cluster of four navigation buttons (and a ? button) in the lower right corner. The functions are explained on this contents page.

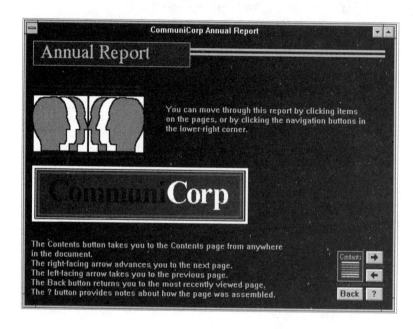

Figure B.1:

The opening screen of CommuniCorp's Annual Report.

See Chapter 10 for information on the design of the Annual Report and for information about the elements that make up each screen.

NOTE

CommuniCorp is a color application. If it starts in black and white on your color monitor, your computer may have fooled the installation program. Open the WIN.INI file (use Sysedit, the EDIT command in DOS 5, Notepad, or any text editor or word processor) and search for the [ToolBook] section. If the setting StartupSysColors=false appears, change it to StartupSysColors=true. Save and close WIN.INI, then start the CommuniCorp Annual Report.

Index

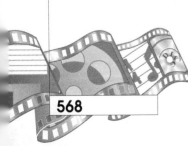

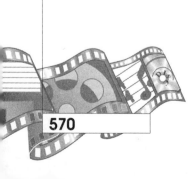

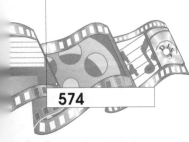

I

P

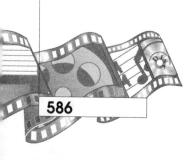

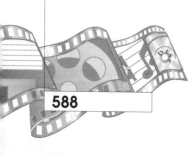

U

Update command, 73
Updated Driver dialog box, 475
user annotations, 385
user modeling, 535
user's MPC, 121–12
    audio board, 122
    upgrade kits, 122

V

vector fonts, 406–407
vector format, 556
vector graphics, 40–41
    Computer-Aided Design
    (CAD) software, 41
    rendering, 40
    vs bitmap graphics, 418–420
    Windows metafile format, 40
VGA, 422
VHDTV, 538
video
    adding, 44–47, 389
    AVI (Audio Video Inter-
    leave), 167
    changing face, 537–539
    choosing, 432–439
    Codec (compression/
    decompression), 166
    compression, 170–173
    compression boards, 436–
    439
    developer's MPC, 119
    DVI (Digital Video Interac-
    tive), 167
    file compression, 45
    frame grabbers, 168–170
    genlocking, 169, 435

hardware compression, 172–
    173
HDTV, 538
Indeo technology, 167
JPEG (Joint Photographic
    Experts Group), 167, 438
lossy compression, 437
MPEG (Motion Picture
    Experts Group), 167
multi-user simulation
    environments (MUSE), 538
Multimedia Encyclopedia,
    171
multimedia technology,
    434–435
network uses, 523–524
NTSC (National Television
    Standards Committee), 166
NTSC-to-VGA adapters, 169,
    435–436
PAL, 166
playback boards, 170–173
QuickTime, 167
software-only decompres-
    sion, 171
standards, 166–167
technology, 165–174
teleconferencing, 45
tools, 457–461
video discs, 173–174
Windows 3.1, 59
Video Blaster, 81
video clips, 80–83, 93, 370
    multimedia applications
    development, 362
video database, 382
video discs, 173–174
video files and Object Linking
  and Embedding (OLE), 80–83

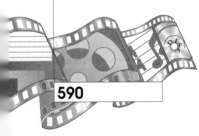